WEST 40
Memphis
EAST 40
Nashville

BUDDY HOLLY HALL

J.T. HUTCHINSON

BUDDY HOLLEY
SEPTEMBER 7, 1936
FEBRUARY 3, 1959

Lubbock
Littlefield

WHAT CAN WASH
AWAY MY SIN?
NOTHING BUT THE
BLOOD OF JESUS

MADE
IN LBK

BUDDY HOLLY PL
ONLY

'Where would we all be without Buddy Holly?'

JEFF BECK 1944–2023

PRESENTED BY THE BUDDY HOLLY EDUCATIONAL FOUNDATION

BUDDY HOLLY

WORDS OF LOVE

Buddy Holly

GENESIS PUBLICATIONS FINE LIMITED EDITIONS SINCE 1974

This book first appeared as a limited edition of 559 numbered copies, signed by Roger Daltrey and Pete Townshend, with the TBHEF proceeds going to Teenage Cancer Trust and Teen Cancer America.

ISBN: 978-1-905662-98-2

Printed and bound in Turkey

10 9 8 7 6 5 4 3 2 1

Genesis Publications Ltd
Genesis House
2 Jenner Road, Guildford
Surrey, England, GU1 3PL

www.genesis-publications.com

THE BUDDY HOLLY NOTEBOOK
These pages are from a loose-leaf notebook which belonged to Buddy Holly and the Crickets.

The majority of items in the notebook appear to have been written by Buddy and Jerry Allison. It is unknown who created these sketches.

PRESENTED BY THE BUDDY HOLLY EDUCATIONAL FOUNDATION

BUDDY HOLLY

WORDS OF LOVE

Buddy Holly

GENESIS PUBLICATIONS FINE LIMITED EDITIONS SINCE 1974

CORAL

THIS WEEK'S NEW RELEASES

RELEASES for sale from 21st OCT. 1960

NO NEW RELEASES THIS WEEK

Every Buddy Holly Fan Will Want This!

BUDDY HOLLY

learning the game

45-Q 72411

ALL SINGLE RECORDS SHOWN ON THIS SHEET ARE AVAILABLE ON 45 r.p.m. ONLY, EXCEPT WHERE OTHERWISE STATED

WARNING: Copyright subsists in all Decca Group recordings. Any unauthorised broadcasting, public performance, copying or re-recording of Decca Group records constitutes an infringement of copyright and will render the infringer liable to action at law. Licences for public performance or broadcasting may be obtained from Phonographic Performance Ltd, Avon House, 356/366 Oxford Street, London, W.1.
DECCA GROUP RECORDS MUST NOT BE SOLD BELOW FIXED PRICES

...ment, London, S.E.11 PHONE : RELIANCE 8111

...al Recordings by Coral Records Inc. N.Y. U.S.A.

R.S.

Songs by BUDDY HOLLY

Released by DECCA • BRUNSWICK • CORAL

A FOOL'S PARADISE *
AN EMPTY CUP
BABY WON'T YOU COME OUT TONIGHT
BLUE DAYS - BLACK NIGHTS
BO DIDLEY
BROWN-EYED HANDSOME MAN
CRYING, WAITING, HOPING
DON'T COME BACK KNOCKING
EARLY IN THE MORNING
EVERY DAY
GIRL ON MY MIND
HEARTBEAT
I'M CHANGING ALL THOSE CHANGES
I'M GONNA LOVE YOU TOO
I'M GONNA SET MY FOOT DOWN
I'M LOOKING FOR SOMEONE TO LOVE
IT DOESN'T MATTER ANYMORE
IT'S NOT MY FAULT
IT'S RAINING IN MY HEART
IT'S SO EASY
IT'S TOO LATE
LAST NIGHT
LEARNING THE GAME
LISTEN TO ME
LITTLE BABY - BABY ME
LONESOME TEARS *
LOOK AT ME
LOVE ME
MAILMAN, BRING ME NO MORE BLUES
MAYBE BABY
MIDNIGHT SHIFT
MODERN DON JUAN
MOONDREAMS
NOT FADE AWAY
NOW WE'RE ONE
OH BOY
PEGGY SUE
PEGGY SUE GOT MARRIED
RAVE ON
REMINISCING
ROCK-A-BYE-ROCK
ROCK AROUND WITH OLLIE VEE
ROCK ME MY BABY
READY TEDDY
SEND ME SOME LOVIN'
SLIPPIN' AND SLIDIN'
TAKE YOUR TIME
TELL ME HOW
THAT MAKES IT TOUGH
THAT'LL BE THE DAY
THAT'S WHAT THEY SAY
THINK IT OVER
TING-A-LING
TRUE LOVE WAYS
VALLEY OF TEARS
WAIT TILL THE SUN SHINES NELLIE
WELL, ALL RIGHT
WHAT TO DO
WISHING *
WORDS OF LOVE
YOU ARE MY ONE DESIRE
YOU'RE SO SQUARE (BABY I DON'T CARE)
YOU'VE GOT LOVE

* Not on any L.P.

August 1963

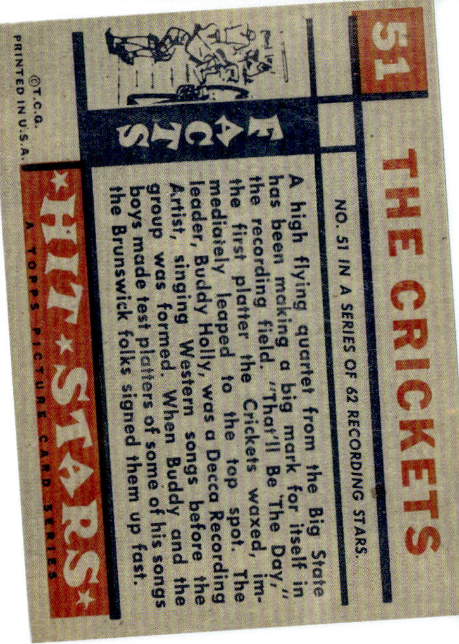

The BUDDY HOLLY *Legend*

MR. AND MRS. L. O. HOLLEY
(PARENTS)
3208 56TH ST. • LUBBOCK, TEXAS 79413

A list of the songs by BUDDY HOLLY, *and* BUDDY HOLLY AND THE CRICKETS *that have been released on Decca, Brunswick and Coral labels.*

THAT'LL BE THE DAY - BUDDY HOLLY

Decca L.P. No. DL 8707

Side one — You Are My One Desire
Blue Days - Black Nights
Modern Don Juan
Rock Around With Ollie Vee
Ting-A-Ling
Girl On My Mind

Side two — That'll Be the Day
Love Me
I'm Changing All Those Changes
Don't Come Back Knocking
Midnight Shift

THE CHIRPING CRICKETS

Brunswick L. P. No. BL 54038: also re-released as BUDDY HOLLY and THE CRICKETS on Coral L.P. No. CRL 57405 (Mono.) and Coral L.P. No. CRL 757405 (Stereo.)

Side one — Oh Boy
Not Fade Away
You've Got Love
Maybe Baby
It's Too Late
Tell Me How

Side two — That'll Be the Day
I'm Looking for Someone to Love
An Empty Cup
Send Me Some Lovin'
Last Night
Rock Me My Baby

BUDDY HOLLY

Coral L.P. No. CRL 57210

Side one — I'm Gonna Love You Too
Peggy Sue
Look at Me
Listen to Me
Valley of Tears
Ready Teddy

Side two — Every Day
Mailman, Bring Me No More Blues
Words of Love
You're So Square (Baby I Don't Care)
Rave On
Little Baby

THE BUDDY HOLLY STORY

Coral L.P. No. CRL 57279

Side one — It's Raining in My Heart
Early in the Morning
Peggy Sue
Maybe Baby
Every Day
Rave On

Side two — That'll Be the Day
Heart-Beat
Think It Over
Oh Boy
It's So Easy
It Doesn't Matter Any More

THE BUDDY HOLLY STORY - Vol. II

Coral L.P. No. CRL 57326

Side one — Peggy Sue Got Married
Well . . . All Right
That Makes It Tough
Now We're One
Take Your Time
What To Do

Side two — Crying, Waiting, Hoping
True Love Ways
Learning the Game
Little Baby
That's What They Say
Moondreams

REMINISCING

Coral L.P. No. CRL 57426 (Mono.) and CRL 757426 (Stereo.)

Side one — Reminiscing
Slippin' and Slidin'
Bo Didley
Wait Till the Sun Shines Nellie
Baby, Won't You Come Out Tonight

Side two — Brown-Eyed Handsome Man
Because I Love You
It's Not My Fault
I'm Gonna Set My Foot Down
I'm Changing All Those Changes
Rock-A-Bye-Rock

THE CRICKETS with BUDDY HOLLY

Two singles on the Brunswick label, that are not on any L.P.:

Fools Paradise (*backed with* Think It Over)
No. 9-55072 (104,994)

Lonesome Tears (*backed with* It's So Easy)
No. 9-55094 (105,562)

One single on the Coral label that is not on any L.P.:

Wishing (*backed with* Brown-Eyed Handsome Man)
No. (62369) (113,149) released July, 1963

Buddy Holly

FAN CLUB

THIS CERTIFIES THAT ____________________
IS A MEMBER IN GOOD STANDING

DISTRICT ____________ PRES. ____________

Above: 'Hit Stars' trading card, issued in 1957 by Topps as part of a series of cards featuring recording stars. The Crickets are No. 51 in the collection.

Bottom left: Buddy Holly Fan Club membership card

Top, middle: Coral new releases leaflet, October 1960

Top right, centre and bottom right: An info leaflet on Buddy's song releases created by the Holley family

Opposite, top left: Collectors card from Holland, circa 1960s

Opposite, top right: Booklet from the Dutch Buddy Holly Appreciation Society

Opposite, centre left: Publicity photo of Buddy taken in late 1958 or early 1959

Opposite, centre right: Kane Disc Stars trading card number 16, 1959

Opposite, bottom: Excerpt from a Buddy info sheet by Larry Holley

BUDDY HOLLY

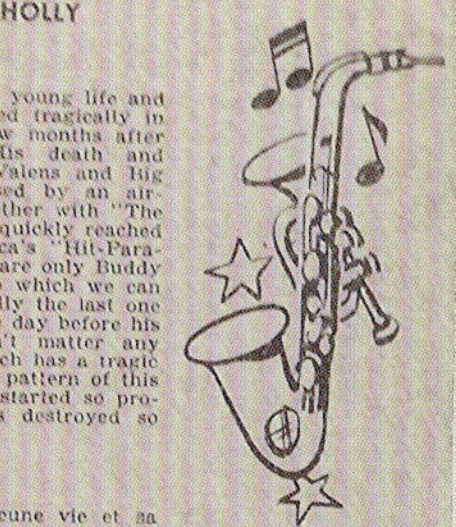

Born in 1938. His young life and quick career ended tragically in March 1959, a few months after his marriage. His death and that of Ritchie Valens and Big Bopper was caused by an airplane crash. Together with "The Crickets" he had quickly reached the top of America's "Hit-Parade". Today there are only Buddy Holly's records to which we can listen and especially the last one that was made the day before his death: "It doesn't matter any more", a title which has a tragic sound against the pattern of this young life which started so promisingly and was destroyed so cruelly.

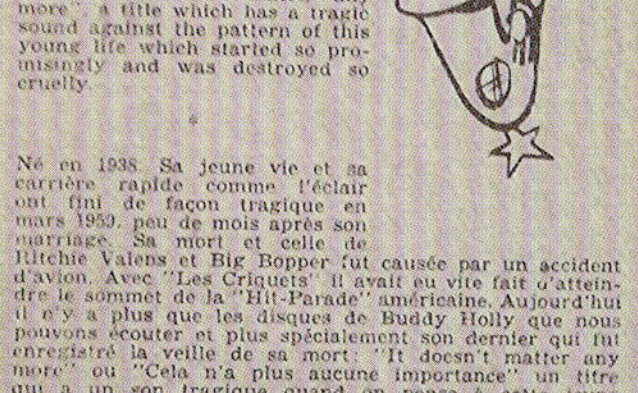

Né en 1938. Sa jeune vie et sa carrière rapide comme l'éclair ont fini de façon tragique en mars 1959, peu de mois après son marriage. Sa mort et celle de Ritchie Valens et Big Bopper fut causée par un accident d'avion. Avec "Les Criquets" il avait eu vite fait d'atteindre le sommet de la "Hit-Parade" américaine. Aujourd'hui il n'y a plus que les disques de Buddy Holly que nous pouvons écouter et plus spécialement son dernier qui fut enregistré la veille de sa mort: "It doesn't matter any more" ou "Cela n'a plus aucune importance" un titre qui a un son tragique quand on pense à cette jeune existence qui avait débuté avec tant de promesses et qui fut si cruellement détruite.

PRINTED IN HOLLAND

A Series of 50
No. 16
BUDDY HOLLY AND THE CRICKETS

Buddy Holly was the founder of this sparkling group who have had a considerable number of recordings in the top ten since their first record "That'll be the day" became No. 1 in England. Buddy took violin lessons at the age of eight but a few years later changed to the guitar and when he was fifteen started to tour clubs singing and accompanying himself. In only a few years The Crickets and Buddy Holly have become top names. Their records include: "It's so easy/Lonesome tears," Q 72343; "The Crickets," FEP 2003; "Buddy Holly," LVA 9085. Killed in air crash.

* * *

Issued by
KANE PRODUCTS LTD.
East Grinstead, Sussex, England

He got his recording contract soon after he had graduated from high school. Needless to say he was very happy.. his dream had come true at last... his next thought was, 'will I make a hit'? Next he picked out a group to play with him... all boys from Lubbock whom he knew..., and he decided to call them The Crickets. As we all know, he did make a hit, several of them, his first one being, "That'll Be The Day". After that things moved fast for Buddy ... and we all know the tragic end of his short but happy life ... We, his family and you, his faithful fans still have his wonderful voice in song ... and we also have you to to cheer us up with your letters about him - I really do not know what we would have done with out his fans who love his songs and have kept his name alive. We thank you and love you for it.

BUDDY'S AUTOBIOGRAPHY

Buddy wrote his autobiography near the end of his sophomore year at Lubbock High School, using a pad from the Morrow-Thomas Hardware Company, Amarillo, Texas

Left to right: Pages one to five

Opposite: Pages six and seven

MORROW-THOMAS HARDWARE COMPANY
AMARILLO, TEXAS
316 Polk Street
Phone 3-4358

My Autobiography

I was born one fall day, a certain particular one, because it was Sept. 7, 1936 and school for that year was starting. It was also the first Monday of the month and Dollar day, and also Labor Day, so you see, It was very eventful in more ways than one. Mr. and Mrs. L. O. Holley were the happy parents of this bouncing, baby boy, or so I'm told, because I was a little young then to be remembering

MORROW-THOMAS HARDWARE COMPANY
AMARILLO, TEXAS
316 Polk Street
Phone 3-4358

it now.

My life has been what you might call an uneventful one, and it seems there is not much of interest to tell. I was born here in Lubbock and except for a year and a half when I moved to the Roosevelt School District, I have lived here all my life so far. I don't remember too much of this period of my life up until the time I started to school at Roscoe Wilson when I was seven. Since then I remember most of the more important events of my school days.

MORROW-THOMAS HARDWARE COMPANY
AMARILLO, TEXAS
316 Polk Street
Phone 3-4358

Plane Geometry class in the last week of school; I am behind with my Biology work and will probably fail every course I'm taking. at least that's the way I feel. But why quit there? I may as well go ahead and tell all. My father's out of town on a fishing trip, and he is really going to be proud of my latest accomplishments when he gets back. as of now, I have these on the list. When I was driving our pickup Sunday afternoon against a hard wind, the hood came unfastened

MORROW-THOMAS HARDWARE COMPANY
AMARILLO, TEXAS
316 Polk Street
Phone 3-4358

and blew up and now it's bent so that it won't fasten down good. Before I got home, I stopped at a boy's house and he knocked a baseball into the front glass, shattering it all over me. as if that wasn't enough, I had an appointment to apply for a job with a drafting firm yesterday afternoon and when my mother came after me, she let me drive on towards town. I had brought a picture of the choir and she was looking at it. She asked where I was, and I pointed to my picture. Just as I looked back up we hit

MORROW-THOMAS HARDWARE COMPANY
AMARILLO, TEXAS
316 Polk Street
Phone 3-4358

It was during the 4th grade that I moved to Roosevelt and continued to school there until I finished the 6th grade. I then moved back to the Lubbock School Dist. and started to Junior High School at J. T. HUTCHINSON. It was great to be back among my old grade school friends and everything clicked right off. It was really a joy to me to become a westerner of Lubbock Senior High School. Little did I know what the last nine weeks of my sophomore year held in store for me. This will make the second time I have given my English theme for my test; I got kicked out of

MORROW-THOMAS
HARDWARE COMPANY
AMARILLO, TEXAS
316 Polk Street
Phone 3-4358

the back of a Chrysler and tore the front end of our car up. So you see I hope my father gets to catching so many fish that he will forget to come back for a little while.

Well, that's enough of bad things for a while. I have many hobbies. Some of these are hunting, fishing, leatherwork, reading, painting and playing western music. I have thought about making a career out of western music if I am good enough but I will just have to

MORROW-THOMAS
HARDWARE COMPANY
AMARILLO, TEXAS
316 Polk Street
Phone 3-4358

wait to see how that turns out. I like drafting and have thought a lot about making it my life's work, but I guess everything will just have to wait and turn out for the best.

Well, that's my life to the present date, and even though it may seem awful and full of calamities, I'd sure be in a bad shape without it.

FINIS
FINALE
In other words,
THE END

Contents

FOREWORD	*Maria Elena Holly*	8
FOREWORD	*Paul McCartney*	9
INTRODUCTION	*Greil Marcus*	10
CHAPTER ONE	*1953–1955*	14
	The Buddy Holly Educational Foundation Ambassadors	34
CHAPTER TWO	*1956*	48
	The Buddy Holly Educational Foundation Ambassadors	60
CHAPTER THREE	*1957*	94
	The Buddy Holly Educational Foundation Ambassadors	132
CHAPTER FOUR	*1958*	176
	The Buddy Holly Educational Foundation Ambassadors	258
CHAPTER FIVE	*1959*	311
	The Buddy Holly Educational Foundation Ambassadors	338
CHAPTER SIX	*Legacy*	362
HONOURED FRIENDS & ACKNOWLEDGEMENTS		385
AFTERWORD	*Roger Daltrey & Pete Townshend*	408

Words of Love

BY MARIA ELENA HOLLY

My heartfelt thanks go out to everyone who has graciously contributed their personal handwritten quotes and reminiscences about Buddy Holly and the Crickets in this amazing book. To read how their music has influenced and inspired so many incredible international artists, musicians and entertainment industry personalities has been a truly moving experience for me.

Without the dedication, time and effort afforded by my dear friend and co-founder of The Buddy Holly Educational Foundation (TBHEF), Peter Bradley Snr., and his son Peter Jnr., in meeting those individuals to kindly provide these incredible 'Words of Love', this book would not have come to fruition.

The purpose of this publication is twofold. Firstly, and for the first time ever, to set down for posterity personal handwritten homages from major artists, musicians and songwriters, encompassing different genres and eras, showing how much the music of Buddy Holly and the Crickets impacted them, and continues to do so for following generations of aspiring artists and musicians. Secondly, to give Buddy Holly and the Crickets fans everywhere the joy of seeing so many fascinating artifacts, memorabilia and original photographs to tell their story and celebrate their legacy.

Buddy would be overwhelmed and humbled that so many of the world's finest artists and musicians, covering eight decades, have dedicated such warm words about him and the music he and his close friends created. I hope you enjoy reading this book as much as I have. Take care.

Sincerely and with love, **MARIA ELENA HOLLY**

Foreword BY SIR PAUL McCARTNEY

The first time I ever heard Buddy Holly was when the record 'That'll Be the Day' came out. It sounded energetic. I thought it was a black band and we couldn't figure out how they did it. It was Buddy Holly and the Crickets. He was playing the lead guitar, which we loved, but he was also singing it, which we loved, and he'd written it, which we loved. So on a number of levels he was very inspirational. He became a hero for us and gave us the idea to go and do it ourselves.

There were other people – the Everly Brothers provided the harmony, Jerry Lee Lewis and Little Richard provided the energetic rock and roll – but it was Buddy Holly and the Crickets who were the major inspiration to us in The Beatles. We wanted to be a group like that. We even made our name The Beatles because we thought it was very clever of them to name themselves the Crickets with the double meaning of the English game of cricket and the little grasshoppers but it turned out that they didn't know about the English game of cricket. Meanwhile, we've gone and named ourselves something to do with an insect, but it had that double meaning.

Buddy was a great hero to all of us and because he wore glasses this even allowed John Lennon to wear his in public and not have to whip them off if there was a girl passing by!

We love you Buddy. **PAUL McCARTNEY**

Introduction BY GREIL MARCUS

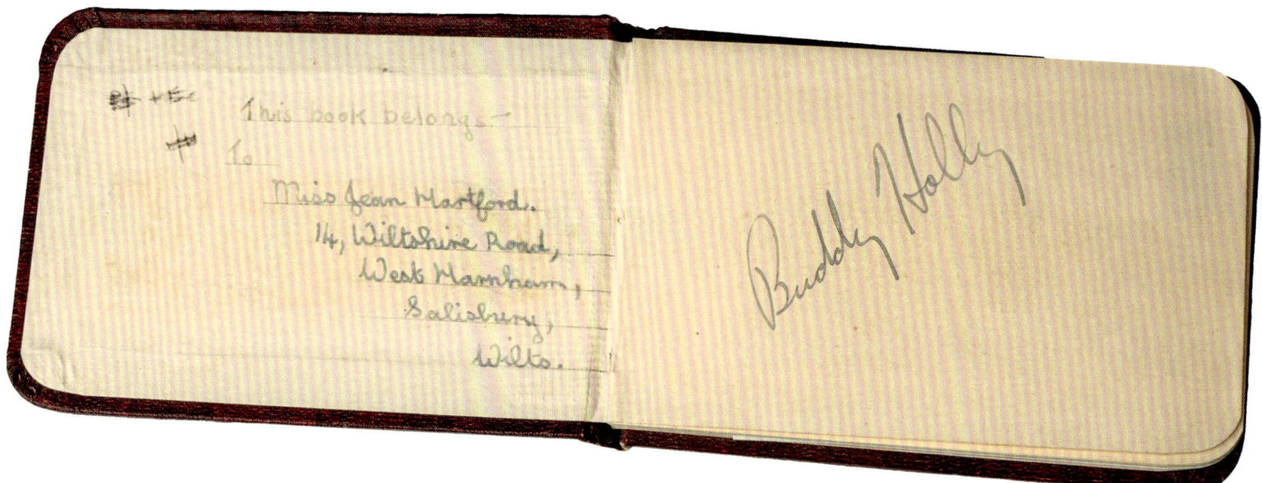

Like every rock and roll pioneer, Buddy Holly made the music as he found it, on his own terms, proving that someone who looked like anybody else, someone unassuming and bespectacled, could make records as tough and passionate as any by the most glamorous and dangerous stars.

The sound that Buddy Holly achieved was sharp, lucid, bright and comfortable; the violence in his rhythms and his words – the guitar solo in 'Peggy Sue', the vehemence in 'That'll Be the Day' – was disguised by melody and lilt. From 'I'm Looking for Someone to Love' to 'Maybe Baby' to 'Crying, Waiting, Hoping', he offered wit, lightning emotional shifts and constant musical invention – an incessant curiosity over which way a melody or a phrase or a beat wanted to go. As a singer he was most recognisable for his abrupt shifts from low tenor to near falsetto – sometimes he seemed to be lapsing into baby talk. In the context of his complete recordings – an enormous body of work for a rock and roll singer professionally recording for barely more than three years – these seemingly helpless mannerisms come across as moments of absolute exuberance and emotional freedom. Unlike Elvis Presley, whose music dramatised deeply buried American obsessions with race and sex, or Chuck Berry, who not only described America but from song to song reinvented it, or Fats Domino, who crystallised a form, Buddy Holly created a music that felt personal, intimate – though it was never in any sense confessional or autobiographical. He made a world in which his listeners felt that they knew him; they could imagine that he sang for them, that their own feelings had called forth his songs. Unlike the rest of the founders, he remained ordinary.

But his achievement, the result of talent and ambition that concealed themselves, was not ordinary. His music was never stylised. The radical primitivism of 'Not Fade Away' sounds as much like a lost blues 78 from the 1920s as, if it first appeared a lifetime from now, it would feel new, a radical cutting back of everything that gets in the way of saying what you really want to say. The determination and maturity of the late, living room demo of 'Well ... All Right' suggests what Bob Dylan was trying to live up to with 'I Threw It All Away'.

So long after his death, Buddy Holly remains a part of the common imagination because he consciously used the oppositions in his music and his persona – soothing melody against unpredictably leaping rhythm, lyrical playfulness against the most direct statements, the anonymous everyman against the explosive individual – as a way of being in the world. He thus provided a whole world of possibility, in which almost any response to any situation could be put across without bombast or sentimentality. The only spectacular aspect of his career was the plane crash that ended it.

Page from an autograph book which belonged to Jean Hartford

LARRY HOLLEY In the summer of 1936, I was playing on our front porch at 1911 6th in Lubbock, Texas, when a friend of mine made the remark that our family was soon to have an addition. I denied the fact, because nobody had checked with me and I was the oldest child, even though I was only ten at the time. I had noticed that mother had been losing her figure. September 7th rolled around and my brother, Travis, and sister, Pat, and I were sent over to a cousin's house to spend the day. When we returned home that night they told us that we had a little brother. It caught me by such surprise that I cried a little.

And what a brother he was! Mother named him Charles Hardin Holley, after both grandfathers, but we would call him Buddy. Well, he made his presence known right from the start and we all sorta spoiled him, because he was so much younger than the rest of us. We moved way out in the country right after that, and I can still remember pulling Buddy around in a box like a sled many times. He really liked that.

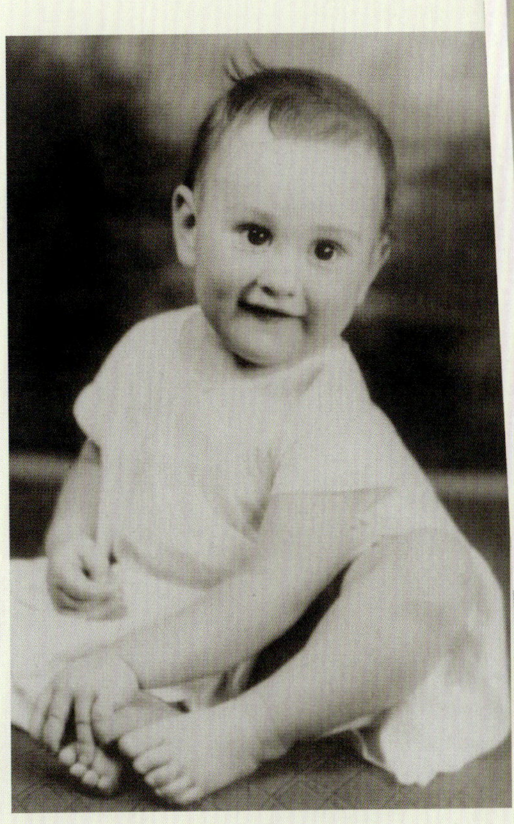

CHILDHOOD PHOTOGRAPHS
Born Charles Hardin Holley on 7 September 1936, Buddy was the youngest of four children to Lawrence Odell 'L.O.' Holley and Ella Pauline Drake Holley. From early childhood, he was nicknamed 'Buddy'.

Buddy at one year old (above, left), at four years old (above, centre) and five years old (above, right)

Top right: Buddy's childhood home, 1911 6th Street, Lubbock, Texas

My name is Buddy Holley. I want to tell you about myself so that you will know me better. I was born in Lubbock, Texas, 7 September 1936. I am 13 years old and have two brothers and one sister. There are six in my family. I have two pets. One is a dog and the other is a rabbit. (8 September 1949. Buddy for one of his first assignments in English class at Hutchinson Junior High School)

CHILDHOOD PHOTOGRAPHS
Opposite: Buddy holding a toy gun at eight years old (top left), Buddy at 10 or 11 years old (top right), Buddy at 13 years old (bottom left and right)

This page: Buddy with his cousin, Sam Modrall (top left), Buddy with his father Lawrence (top right), Buddy with his arm in a sling and hair dyed blond at 14 years old (above, left and right)

Buddy at 17, a photo taken for his 1954 high school yearbook

CHAPTER ONE
1953-1955

3 Holly's accoustic guitar with the leather cover he made himself

Holley, Buddy

Books for the First Year

The books checked below have been read this year:

Pre-primers
- Now We Read ✓
- We Look and See ✓
- We Work and Play ✓
- We Come and Go ✓
- Elson-Gray
- More Dick and Jane Stories
- Bob and Baby Pony ✓
- Tom and Jip
- Spot ✓
- Happy Days
- My Dog Laddie ✓
- Rides and Slides ✓
- Who Knows
- Little White Rabbit ✓

- Off We Go ✓
- Jack + Nell ✓
- Before Winky ✓
- Winky
- Fun for you ✓
- Nip + Tuck ✓
- Nip + Tuck at Play ✓
- Now We Go Again ✓
- Here + There ✓
- Good Morning + Good Night ✓
- Ted + Sue ✓

Primers
- Tom Jip and Jane ✓
- Jo-boy ✓
- At the Farm
- Good Companions ✓
- At Home and Away ✓
- Pet Pony
- We Three ✓
- At Work and Play ✓
- Fun with Dick and Jane ✓
- We Grow ✓
- Bob and Judy ✓
- Good Times with Our Friends ✓

- Fun in Story ✓
- Peter's Family ✓
- Real Life Reader ✓
- The Fun Book ✓
- We Three + Scottie ✓
- Everyday Classic ✓
- Story Hour Reader Primer ✓
- Child Library Primer ✓
- Surprise Stories ✓

Reader.
- Our New Friends ✓

Life-lines of BUDDY HOLLY

1. Buddy Holly was born September 7, 1936, in Lubbock, Texas.
2. His full name was, Charles Hardin Buddy Holly. He was always called Buddy, even through school.
3. He was the youngest of four children. There are two brothers and one sister, Larry, Travis and Patricia (Pat).
4. His brothers sing and play the guitar also, though only as a pass-time.
5. Buddy's talent for singing began to show at an early age. He won a first prize singing on a talent show when he was five years old.
6. He entered public school at the age of six and his singing was more-or-less forgotten for a few years
7. He made above average grades and was active in junior baseball, Cub scouting, soap-box derby racing and other school activities.
8. He was elected king of the grade school while in the sixth grade, which meant he was well liked with his school mates.
9. Buddy took up his singing again when he was 12 years old. Contrary to rumor, he did not play the violin, but he studied the piano for awhile. His Dad bought him a guitar which proved to be a natural for him and soon he was entertaining his school mates with his singing and playing.
10. His favorite sports were fishing and water skiing and riding his motorcycle.
11. His favorite hobby was leather tooling, making bill-folds, belts, leather cowboy chaps and guitar covers.
12. It was'nt all play with Buddy as he was a good worker too. He helped his Dad and brothers in the construction business, learning the carpentry and masonry trade very well.
13. Buddy kept on with his singing through junior and senior high school and was a popular entertainer on all of the school programs. During his junior year he and another boy teamed up as a singing duo and started their own radio show. This was known as, "The Buddy and Bob Show", over KDAV in Lubbock. This became a popular request program for the teenagers and was heard throughout the surrounding states.
14. Buddy graduated from high school in 1955.

-194 SESSION

Holley, Buddy — Name of Pupil — 1st Yr. Pri. Grade — Roscoe Wilson School

Holley, L. O. — Name of Parent — 2711 No. House — 28th Street

Lubbock, Tex. — Town — Lubbock County

List of Books—Title		Book No.	List of Books—Title		Book No.
Agriculture			History	Year	
Arithmetic	Year			Year	
	Year		Language	Year	
Basal Reader	Year			Year	
	Year		Phys.-Hygiene	Year	
Civics				Year	
Drawing	Year		Spanish	Year	
	Year			Year	
Geography	Year		Spelling	Year	
	Year			Year	
Handwriting	Year				
	Year				

I certify that the pupil's record on the books listed on this card is clear.

Mrs. E. F. Pilley Teacher Mrs. Ivy Savage Principal

Original and duplicate cards should be kept on file by the teacher. When all books have been returned the pupil should be given this original card, fully receipted. Without it he will not be granted free textbooks for the next session.

Over

READING LIST

Buddy's reading list (top left and above) for his first year of school at Roscoe Wilson Elementary in Lubbock, TX. In 1949 at Hutchinson Junior High he met Bob Montgomery. Together, they performed at school assemblies and local radio shows, in which typically Bob would sing lead and Buddy would harmonise. Bob went on to co-write some of Buddy's songs, such as 'Heartbeat', 'Wishing' and 'Love's Made a Fool of You'.

Top right: Buddy at 17, around the time he made his first recordings, 1954

Left: Buddy at 13 years old for the Roosevelt Elementary 1949 yearbook

SONNY CURTIS Lubbock is a big country town. It's flat in Lubbock and it's flat outside of Lubbock. If a tree grows, they cut it down quickly, so it won't spoil the view. The tallest building has always been 20 storeys high.

MARIA ELENA The first time I went to Lubbock, the plane landed without an airport. Coming from New York, I was so surprised. It was completely flat, and very dusty.

EDNA GUNDERSEN Lubbock played an enormous role in Buddy's development. It's such an isolated and desolate area, a flat little town in the panhandle of Texas, not a sophisticated area where he was exposed to musical trends or influential musicians. He was left to his own devices with a very creative mind, which let him flower outside of what was going on in New York, Los Angeles and Nashville. It let him draw from regional influences, which made him sound unique because he was less confined by the categories that music fell into at that time.

SONNY WEST Buddy and I were listening to the same music. Before we had a chance to listen to rock and roll, Hank Williams appealed to a lot of the young people I knew.

LARRY HOLLEY With Buddy, everything had to be right now. If he wanted to write a song, he'd just pick up his guitar and get right on with it. If he felt like doing some leatherwork, even if the family wasn't through with Thanksgiving dinner, he'd go get all his tools and materials and spread them out on the floor. It was almost like he knew he didn't have much time to do all the things he wanted.

PAINTING
Buddy developed a keen interest in art from an early age. Pictured above is his art box, and, left, one of his paintings, an unfinished canvas featuring a cowboy hat and pair of boots, done in gouache and graphite. According to his brother Larry, this was created when Buddy was between the ages of 12 and 14. This passion for art was accompanied by an interest in music, as well as leatherwork.

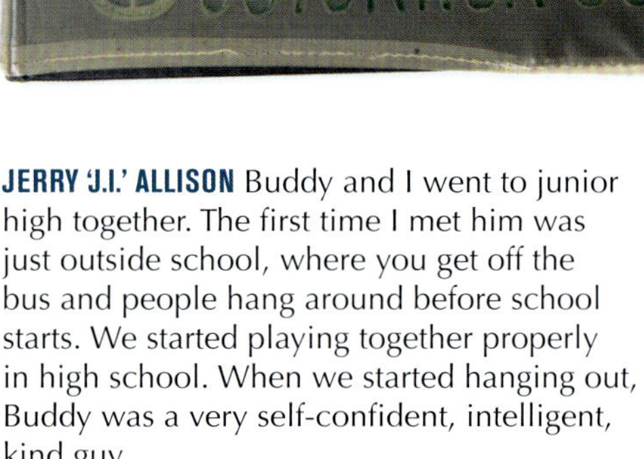

JERRY 'J.I.' ALLISON Buddy and I went to junior high together. The first time I met him was just outside school, where you get off the bus and people hang around before school starts. We started playing together properly in high school. When we started hanging out, Buddy was a very self-confident, intelligent, kind guy.

. . . . . Class of '55

ROSE MARY HOLDER
NORA HOLLAND
JOHN HOLLARS

J. M. HOLLERS
BUDDY HOLLEY
STELLA HOLTON

JERRY DON HOPKINS
VAN HORN
JACK HOUSE
JAMES ROY HOWARD

JOYCE HOWARD
PAT HOWARD
STUART HUDNALL
SUE HUFSTEDLER

Ringing up two of the cash registers every day in the Lubbock Senior High cafeteria are senior checkers Morris Seales and Tommy Price, right. Harrington is having her tray checked.

HIGH SCHOOL
Buddy's 1953 and 1954 'Westerner' yearbooks from Lubbock High School during his sophomore and senior years. On 19 February 1954, Buddy, Bob Montgomery and Larry Welborn performed during a contest at the Lubbock High School Westerner Roundup. Admission was 25 cents. Bob Montgomery had written a song, 'Flower of My Heart', for this event and the trio won the contest. They each received a 'Westerner' belt for their efforts. The song was also chosen as the official song for the Class of 1954. Buddy graduated from Lubbock High School, the first from his family to do so, on 27 May 1955. The graduation ceremony took place at Fair Park Coliseum. Throughout high school, Buddy dated Echo McGuire, a local girl who attended the same school (opposite).

Top right: The Lubbock High School Class of '55; Buddy is in row three, sixth from the left

October 25, 1955

Hi honey!

I'm very unhappy, cause I didn't get a letter from you today. Why don't you write to me? I didn't have my book report ready this morning because I wrote to you!

I just got out of tennis. I just can't hit the ball! When I do, it goes the opposite direction than it is supposed to.

I've got you a chapel seat by me for Saturday morning. We are assigned seats and the boy next to me said that you could use his.

About those clothes, another boy brought some of them back, but there are still some skirts that she didn't send. Ask her to have them pressed and bring them, if you don't mind.

Sugar, have you quit smoking? We were talking about the bad effects of this terrible habit in psychology today. Please do, for me? I can hardly wait until Friday night. Til then → I love you.

Echo

A Volland Card
MADE IN U.S.A.
25MC327

I love you even if you are nineteen!

Happy Birthday

Echo

Buddy
Love, Echo

ECHO McGUIRE I came from a very conservative church background, and I didn't even dance. So when Buddy would play for dances, I did not go. He accepted that as the way I was, but it was a separation between us.

Deep down inside, I probably knew it was the type of life I couldn't be a part of. When he started to make records and become known as a musician, I shared in his excitement, but I think I realised that this was going to come between us. I could see the direction that he was going in, and it just wasn't what I wanted for myself. It wasn't that I loved him less or fell out of love with him; I think I still loved him, but I couldn't see myself in that position.

DEAR SIR,
WE ARE A GROUP OF HIGH-SCHOOL BOYS THAT HAS ORGANIZED ONE OF THE LEADING HILL-BILLY & WESTERN BANDS IN LUBBOCK. WE ARE INTERESTED IN HELPING NEIGHBORING HIGH SCHOOLS TO RAISE FUNDS AND AT THE SAME TIME RAISE MONEY FOR US TO HELP PAY OUR WAY THROUGH HIGH SCHOOL.
I KNOW THAT YOU WOULDN'T WANT TO LET JUST ANYONE PLAY AT YOUR SCHOOL, SO IF YOU HAVE NOT HEARD OF US, WE ARE THE 580 RANCH HANDS & BUDDY AND JACK, AND WE HAVE TWO RADIO PROGRAMS EVERY SUNDAY AFTERNOON AT 3:15 O'CLOCK AND 3:30 O'CLOCK RESPECTIVELY. THE RADIO STATION WE ARE ON, IS KDAV (580 ON YOUR RADIO DIAL). IF IT WOULD NOT BE ASKING TOO MUCH, WE WOULD LIKE TO REQUEST YOUR LISTENING TO OUR PROGRAMS AND SEE IF YOU LIKE US. IF YOU NEED ANY REFERENCES, YOU MAY WRITE TO HI-POCKETS, OR DAVE STONE % RADIO STATION KDAV HERE IN LUBBOCK, AND ASK THEM ABOUT US. NOW, HERE IS WHAT

·(NEXT PAGE)·

WE WOULD LIKE TO ASK YOU ABOUT. WE WOULD LIKE TO COME TO YOUR SCHOOL AND PLAY A STAGE SHOW FOR THE ENTERTAINMENT OF THE CITIZENS, SCHOOL-CHILDREN, AND NEIGHBORING FARMSPEOPLE OF YOUR TOWN. WE COULD ADVERTISE OVER THE RADIO WHEN WE WERE GOING TO BE THERE AND GET A GOOD AUDIENCE BUILT UP. I KNOW THAT IF YOUR SCHOOL IS LIKE OUR SCHOOL, IT CAN ALWAYS USE SOME EXTRA MONEY. WE HAVE HELPED QUITE A FEW SCHOOLS AROUND AUSTIN, TEXAS, TO GATHER MONEY IN THIS WAY AND THEY WERE QUITE SATISFIED WITH THE RESULTS. IF YOU ARE AT ALL INTERESTED IN THIS, WE WOULD APPRECIATE IT VERY MUCH IF YOU WOULD WRITE TO ME, BUDDY HOLLEY
2304 - 1ST STREET
LUBBOCK, TEXAS

LARRY HOLLEY As Buddy grew older and started school, we noticed that he was exceptionally smart and was the first one of us that made good grades. Daddy always wanted us to be able to do something special, so he had us take music lessons. My dad had a sister who was good on the piano and Mother was very talented as a singer. She could harmonise on any song she heard. Even though our family were just living from hand to mouth, we still took music lessons.

MARIA ELENA Buddy had loved music since he was a boy. His mother said when he was five years old, he would sing and play a small, cheap guitar.

LARRY HOLLEY Eventually I started letting Buddy set some tile on the easier jobs. He really surprised me how well he did this work. Tile setting and fingering guitar strings do not work together, so I didn't want Buddy to do much of it. Buddy was spending most all his free time playing with local musicians, several of them were with him for a while.

MARIA ELENA He'd often play the radio while working – he'd take that radio everywhere. Larry would get upset and say, 'You're not fast enough, you're just listening to the radio,' and eventually he took it away, which was the last time Buddy worked with Larry.

DON McLEAN Buddy was happy not to be laying tile in the family business; he wanted to make a living with his guitar, have the exhilaration of a hit record. His love of music opened doors for him and that took him around America and other countries, and that probably made him the happiest guy in the world. He saw that if he hadn't had a career in music, he'd be putting down linoleum. I don't think that thrilled him too much.

KDAV RADIO

On 19 September 1953 Dave Pinkston started a new Lubbock radio station called KDAV. The station was the first in the country to feature 100 per cent country music, no block programming, and featured many local artists performing live. Shortly after KDAV first went on the air, two youngsters performed live and were then asked to play regularly on a programme called The Sunday Party. *Those two youngsters, Buddy Holley and Jack Neal, soon began performing live each weekend on their own* Buddy and Jack Show. *During their first broadcast on 4 November 1953, they sang 'Your Cheatin' Heart', 'Got You on My Mind', 'I Couldn't Keep from Crying' and 'I Hear the Lord Callin' for Me'. When Jack Neal got married and left the duo, Bob Montgomery and Larry Welborn joined Buddy as Buddy, Bob and Larry (opposite, top left, pictured at KDAV in 1955). Sonny Curtis sometimes sat in too. Buddy Holley's hand-printed letter (above) was created to send to local schools to seek dance jobs. The KDAV building (opposite, top right) remains today as KRFE.*

LARRY WELBORN We didn't have much to do in Lubbock, so we played music. At the time, I was 15 and playing a little club called Tommy's Dance Land, and Buddy and Bob were a couple years older than me. They'd heard of me, as there weren't many musicians around back then. They came to the club and asked if I wanted to do a radio show with them. I was playing guitar at the time, and they wanted me to play bass, which I'd played earlier in my life. I told them I'd love to. I borrowed the school bass, as I didn't have one at the time, and every Sunday afternoon I took it down to the radio station, KDAV, and we played a show.

KEVIN MONTGOMERY My dad and Buddy were in a duo called Buddy and Bob. They met when they were about 13 years old and learned how to play guitar together, then wrote some songs together. My dad told me they used to pick cotton, roof houses and do anything they could just to pay for the first demos they did, and so they were working just to make music.

The first show they did together, they played a song called 'Too Old to Cut the Mustard' at the school talent show and dedicated it to the oldest teacher in the school. They were just a couple of best friends learning how to make music together, and the rest is history.

SONNY CURTIS I met Buddy and Bob Montgomery one afternoon in Lubbock when we were all about 14. Buddy and I shook hands, got our guitars out and started playing. There was no small talk. Soon enough, I joined Buddy and Bob and started playing with them. Buddy loved to pick and sing. He was tall, thin, wore glasses, and he was shy, in a way, but also a smart aleck.

JACK NEAL His hair bothered him more than anything else. It was always real curly, and he didn't care for that. He wanted it to be straight so he would comb it right back like the smart guys. He used to say he'd never have had curly hair like that if his folks hadn't made him wear a toboggan hat when he was a little kid.

LARRY HOLLEY Bob Montgomery and Buddy were good friends and played any place they could. Jack Neal was another fine singer that Buddy teamed up with and they played on Sunday afternoons on KDAV radio station. Don Guess played with Buddy some as well, as did Tinker Carlen and Larry Welborn, who has gone on to be a great guitar player. Sonny Curtis was very helpful to Buddy.

SONNY CURTIS Buddy and Bob were close friends. They had a steel guitar player who played upright bass, Don Guess, and another bass player, Larry Welborn. I played the fiddle when I joined, a time before rock and roll had settled in. We were mostly playing country, and when we'd do gigs, we'd play trio songs. It was a free-for-all, we just loved music.

JACK NEAL The 16th and J booked us a lot of times. It was a big barn of a place at Avenue J and 16th Street – I think it may have been a church some time before. Trouble there used to come just like a twister out on the plain. One minute it'd be quiet, the next there'd be bottles flying. We'd carry on playing and try to calm things down with our music. If we were playing a real jumpy number, we'd cut it to something more mellow and two-step.

March 18, 1964
Copy of infor
sent to
Peter Skrypcak

L. O. HOLLEY
SWIFT 9-4254 5001 42ND STREET
LUBBOCK, TEXAS

1.
Buddy's full name is 'Charles Hardin Buddy Holly'. He was always called Buddy.

2.
He was the youngest of our four children. He has two brothers and one sister, Larry, Travis and Patricia (Pat).

3.
His brothers sing and play the guitar also, but have just about given it up.

4.
Buddy started singing when he was five years old and made his first public appearance while five on a talent show. He won first prize.

5.
He started to school when he was six years old and his singing was more or less forgotten then, except for class singing in the school room, and an occaisional school program, when they would ask him to sing.

6.
He was an average student in school. He played base ball some, Cub Scouting, Soap box derby racing along with the usual activities.

7.
He was elected King of the grade school while in the 6th. grade, which meant he was well liked.

8.
It was at this time also that he took up singing again, when he was 12 years old. His Dad bought him a guitar and he would entertain the kids on the school bus, riding to and from school, as he sang. His favorite song was Hank Williams, "Love Sick Blues", which he could do quiet well, yodeling and all.

9.
He did not take up singing as a profession till much later.. while in his finishing year of high school.

10.
Because he could sing quiet well he usually had a spot on most of the school programs while going to school. He and one of his friends teamed up together and made their own radio show over one of the local radio stations, KDAV, and called it "The Buddy and Bob Show". This was while he was still in school. They did this for about a year.

11.
Later, he organized a small combo and they played for the Youth Center, a place where the young people would gather for entertainment. Needless to say he was doing quiet well by this time and was pretty much in demand as an entertainer, singing and playing over the country

Top: Buddy performing with local band, Borger, TX, 1955

Above: Buddy and Bob Montgomery at the grand opening of a local store. This is the only known photo of Buddy playing a banjo, which his brother Larry loaned him ten dollars to buy, 1955.

BUDDY HOLLEY LARRY WELBORN BOB MONTGOMERY

Buddy and Bob

"WESTERN AND BOP"

BUS. MANAGER
HI POCKETS DUNCAN

KDAV BOX 1319
LUBBOCK, TEXAS

BUDDY AND BOB BUSINESS CARD
A business card for Buddy, Bob Montgomery and Larry Welborn, who briefly played bass for the duo. Together they sang harmony duets at local clubs and high school talent shows. This act was Buddy's first as a professional musician. They were managed by Hi-Pockets Duncan, whose name is seen in the bottom left corner. Hi-Pockets was a pioneer of Texas radio and a champion of rock and roll.

THE RHYTHM PLAYBOYS BUSINESS CARD
During the time between duo Buddy and Bob and the legendary Buddy Holly and the Crickets, Buddy performed very briefly with Bob Montgomery and Don Guess as the Rhythm Playboys, making this business card very rare. Together, they made jingles and such for local radio stations in Lubbock. On 4 May 1954, the Rhythm Playboys performed at the Brownfield High School for the Distributive Education Class. The group was to receive 50 per cent of the net receipts for the 8 PM show.

JERRY 'J.I.' ALLISON Buddy played the banjo, Bob played the guitar and they sang old hillbilly music. In high school I used to play in Cal Wayne and the Riverside Ranch Hands, which was a true country band, at a pretty funky club called the 16th and J. Buddy used to come by and join in. That's what got my career started. Before that I was stocking groceries at a store called Furr Food, which paid 40 cents an hour.

We'd play stuff like Bill Haley and '40 Cups of Coffee' when rock and roll began, and then we started hanging out: Buddy, Bob, Sonny Curtis, who played the fiddle, and Don Guess, who played the steel guitar, and me. Then I began playing with his group and Buddy got to sing some rock and roll songs with them. Some of the guys didn't like that. Don Guess quit and Sonny went on the road with Slim Whitman.

SONNY CURTIS Mr and Mrs Holley not only supported Buddy, Bob and me, they were behind us. If we didn't have their car to drive, we wouldn't have made it to gigs. They were terribly supportive. We were raised with a religious background. Mine and Bob Montgomery's families were Church of Christ, which is a pretty strict Protestant religion, and Buddy was a Baptist. We used to have spirited discussions about religion and the Bible as we were riding down the road to play those sinful rock and roll songs.

JERRY 'J.I.' ALLISON Sonny was famous around town. Waylon Jennings once said he got his stench from Sonny, like Buddy got his stench from Carl Perkins and Elvis. He was born about 30 miles down the road and his family were farmers, but Sonny didn't fit that groove.

MARIA ELENA When Buddy lived in Lubbock, he would get up early every Sunday to go to one of the local shanty towns where they had small black churches, so he could listen to them sing. Not only because they were at a church, but they had great music. That's where he got the idea of doing an album with gospel singer Mahalia Jackson, but we later found out she liked her music to be solely hers and didn't like to collaborate. Buddy thought he could convince her otherwise, but he didn't get a chance to. We later went to California looking for Ray Charles, but when we got there, he was on tour. I later met Ray, who told me he would've collaborated with Buddy.

LARRY HOLLEY The boys all had lots of fun playing and learning together. They practised anywhere they could and it must have been in many different places around town, because I still run into people that tell me they used to lose some sleep over the noise they made. They did not realise then that people would ever pay to hear them later.

LARRY WELBORN Buddy bought a gold-top Les Paul when we were doing the Sunday show. He played that until Fender came out with the Stratocaster, and his brother ordered one for him.

JOHN THOMAS It's 23 April 1955. The bell above the door to Adair Music Company in Lubbock, Texas, clangs as a young, bespectacled man strains to prop the door open so he can squeeze a guitar case and amplifier into the store. The proprietor, B.E. Adair, looks up, pauses tallying cash register receipts at the counter along the store's back wall and says, 'Oh, hello, Buddy. What can I do for you today?' The young man puts down the guitar and amplifier, pushes up the glasses that have slipped down a nose shiny with perspiration and says, 'Well, Mr Adair, I was in here a couple of days ago and I had a lesson with Mr Hankins. He was playing one of those new Fender guitars, it's called a Strato-something, I think. It sure looked slick. And, well, I got to thinking …'

The guitar that Buddy lugged into the shop that fateful day was the Les Paul gold-top he had purchased there only months earlier. Some accounts have him expressing dissatisfaction with the instrument's weight and craving the lighter Fender instrument. Buddy's Les Paul, according to Walter Carter of Nashville's Carter Vintage, is 'pretty typical' of most 1952 models. The amalgam of features on this guitar – no serial number, early logo, a bound fingerboard, no treble/rhythm indicator and tall knobs – places it, Carter said, 'Probably mid- or even late 1952, probably before 1953.'

The amplifier, which Buddy bought at the same time he bought the guitar, for a combined sum of $305, is also a 1952 Les Paul model, of the 'G' variant, in Gibson parlance. Buddy scratched his name into the end of the Gibson's speaker cone, employing the 'Holley' spelling, and he is depicted in a couple of photos playing the guitar and amp with his early Buddy and Bob duo, though no recordings in which the Les Paul is used are documented to exist. The warm sound of a Gibson amplifier, though, seems as incongruous to Buddy's music as the matching Les Paul guitar. In 1958, while living in New York City, Buddy did purchase a Magnatone amp for home use, but he typically gigged with Fender amplifiers that suited his Stratocaster.

Top: Bob Montgomery, unknown guitarist and Buddy performing at Lubbock High School, circa 1955

SONNY CURTIS I sold guitars at Adair Music Company and taught guitar lessons. Clyde Hankins worked in the shop too; he was a great guitar player. He was what we called a jazz berry. He knew Buddy very well and I think he might have sold Buddy his first guitar.

Buddy purchased a Gibson Les Paul gold-top model guitar from Adair Music Company in Lubbock. Buddy's name can be seen scratched into the back of the speaker cone of the 1952 Gibson Les Paul amp (opposite). Buddy was dissatisfied with the Les Paul, and no recordings of Buddy using the Les Paul are known to exist.

MARIA ELENA Buddy was in the audience for Elvis's show in Lubbock. From then on, they became good friends and went to the movies together from time to time. When Buddy died, Elvis called from Germany.

JERRY 'J.I.' ALLISON Back then, Sonny played like Scotty Moore, Don Guess played like Bill Black and Buddy sang like Elvis.

LARRY WELBORN Buddy would try and imitate Elvis. Elvis was a great guy, as nice as you could be, and we opened for him at the Fair Park Coliseum in Lubbock. We went over to the motel where he was staying and heard him singing in the shower as he was getting ready to go out. He only got paid $75 for that show. Back then, rock and roll was the devil's music, but watching Elvis made everybody want to play the devil's music. The girls were screaming and everybody loved him. It was his whole attitude; he was like Buddy. He knew where he was going.

SONNY CURTIS Seeing Elvis was like a motorcycle headlight in a hurricane. It was the first week in January of 1955 and Elvis was wearing white buck shoes, red pants, and an orange jacket – talk about loud. We'd never seen anything like it, and that's when it first dawned on me that it was about a lot more than music. There's sex involved in music – the girls were going nuts that day.

A local disc jockey, Dave Stone, brought Elvis out. We did freebies for him all the time, so Buddy, Bob, Jerry Allison and I got to hang backstage with Elvis. We were all blown away and the next day, we started playing rock and roll. I played lead guitar, Buddy's guitar, and he played my Martin D-28, and Don Guess played an upright bass. It wasn't hard for us to get gigs as a rock and roll group, because we started playing those songs immediately.

GARRY TALLENT Like many performers, Buddy was excited and influenced by Elvis, but he had his own slant on it. Even when he tried to be Elvis, it was very Buddy. His uniqueness was inherent within him. He had something different to offer; he wasn't a matinee idol, which made him more popular with the boys because they didn't see him as a threat to their girlfriends.

KEVIN MONTGOMERY Buddy and my father, Bob, wanted to play bluegrass when they first started out. That's who they were trying to be and then when Elvis came through town, which had a big influence on them, they started going in a different direction. Elvis was a couple years older than them, and my dad once said he, Elvis and Buddy went to a movie together. Imagine if a bomb had gone off in that movie theatre in Lubbock, how the world would have changed …

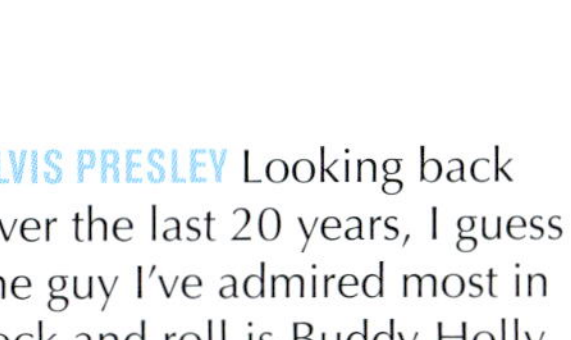

ELVIS PRESLEY Looking back over the last 20 years, I guess the guy I've admired most in rock and roll is Buddy Holly.

FRANK SINATRA If Elvis was the King, Buddy was the Crown Prince.

ELVIS IN LUBBOCK
Buddy saw Elvis Presley for the first time when he went to Fair Park Coliseum (opposite). On the same bill were Jimmy & Johnny and Billy Walker. Although no advertisements can be found for this appearance, Sonny Curtis believes the date to be Sunday 2 January 1955, as he opened this show with Billy Walker. Buddy and Bob Montgomery can be seen in the far right. An ad for Elvis's appearance in Lubbock on 13 February also stated that Elvis 'returns to Lubbock'. Buddy supported Elvis at his 13 February show, and also later that year. Elvis is pictured on this date opposite, bottom right.

HAND-TOOLED LEATHER GUITAR COVER
Elvis performing with his leather-covered guitar at the Cleveland Arena, Cleveland, OH, 23 November 1956 (above). This was the likely inspiration for Buddy's hand-tooled leather guitar cover (left and overleaf).

J-45 GUITAR
Buddy Holly bought this 1942 Gibson J-45 from a pawn shop in Lubbock. This would have been one of the guitars made during the war by the women who kept the Gibson factory going. For a while it was owned by Gary Busey, who played Buddy Holly in The Buddy Holly Story *in 1978.*

The serial number on the guitar has faded. It features a sunburst finish, spruce top with round sound hole, mahogany back, sides and neck, rosewood fingerboard; 24¾ in. scale; five-ply white and black binding; set neck with mother-of-pearl dot inlays; headstock with gold script Gibson logo and 'Only a Gibson Is Good Enough' banner decals; metal tuners with plastic heads; rosewood bridge; celluloid tortoiseshell pickguard; no truss rod due to metal restrictions in wartime manufacturing; and a hand-tooled leather cover designed and made by Buddy in tan, black, white and grey leather. Buddy's personalised design (left and overleaf) incorporates his name, his home state of Texas, as well as the A- and B-sides of his first record release, 'Blue Days, Black Nights' and 'Love Me', on the front, sides and base edge. He had wanted people to know he had made a record, even if they hadn't heard it.

BLUE
DAYS
BLACK
NIGHTS

TEXAS

"LOVE
ME"

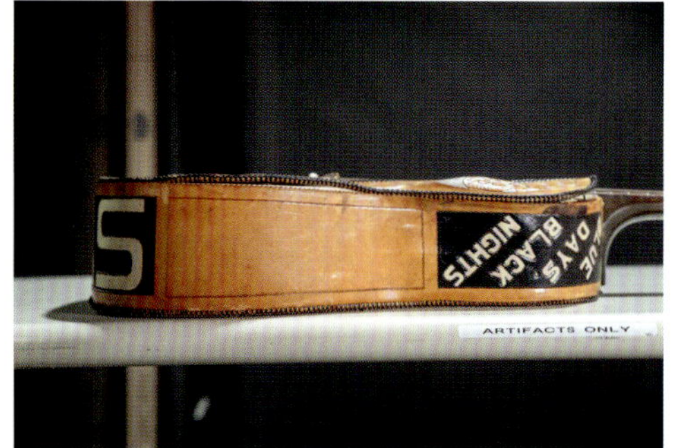
ARTIFACTS ONLY

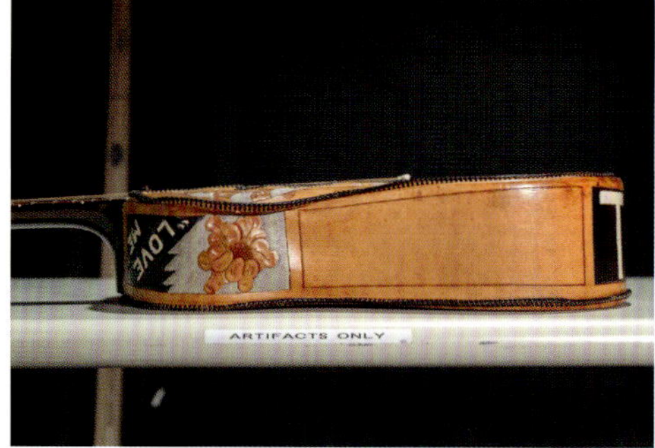
ARTIFACTS ONLY

"LOVE
ME"

BLUE
DAYS
BLACK
NIGHTS

BUDDY
HOLLY

BLUE
DAYS
"LOVE
ME"

"LOVE
ME"

BUDDY
HOLLY

GIBSON J-45
Though Buddy Holly was famous for performing with a Fender Stratocaster, he composed many of his hits on this Gibson J-45. It is probably the acoustic guitar used to record 'Everyday', 'Send Me Some Lovin'', and 'It's Too Late'.

Below: Buddy out shopping for leatherwork materials in downtown Lubbock, age 13

EDNA GUNDERSEN This was the dawn of rock and roll, the beginning of a revolution, and there was so little happening. Not many people were aware or partaking in it. Buddy didn't have many models to pull from, but once he saw Elvis, that inspired him. But everything that came from Buddy after that was from his own imagination. It was quite a repressive era, and as geeky as Buddy appeared, he was breaking all the rules. In many ways, he was far more radical and unconventional than most of the people that he influenced.

JERRY 'J.I.' ALLISON When Buddy, Bob, Don and Larry had a country band, Buddy and I were into rock and roll, so that was when he invited me to join them.

SONNY CURTIS Buddy liked leatherwork. He made the leather case for his guitar, and he made Elvis a wallet. Pink and black were the big colours then, so the wallet was black with 'Elvis' written in pink, with pink flowers on it. We were on our way to Nashville and stopped at Sun Studios in Memphis. Nobody was there other than secretaries, and he left the wallet with them. Glen D. Hardin, who later played piano for Elvis, told Elvis about that wallet and he was disappointed that he never received it. That wallet is still out there somewhere.

GRAHAM NASH He hand-tooled the whole cover. I'm convinced he must have seen the picture of Elvis where his guitar is covered in leather; he had it on in Nashville. I think he did his own version. I've seen the guitar before, when Gary Busey owned it. Somebody put it in my arms and the first thing I did was turn it around, strum it and break a string. Of course my wife, devilish as she is, said, 'That's the last of the original strings.'

Part of the process of this whole thing is to get as close to the flame as you can get without being burned. And I was very close to the flame. It's Buddy Holly's guitar, on which he wrote most of his famous songs.

SONGS

LET THE GOOD TIMES ROLL
I FEEL GOOD
MONEY HONEY
SHAKE RATTLE & ROLL
ROLL OVER BEETHOVEN
HONKY TONK
FORTY CUPS OF COFFEE
LOST DREAMS
HEY DOLL BABY
THAT'LL BE THE DAY
LOVE ME
BLUE DAYS BLACK NITES
MODERN DON JUAN
MY ONE DESIRE
BROWN-EYED HANDSOME MAN
RAZZLE DAZZLE
BLUE SUEDE SHOES
TING-A-LING
OOBY-DOOBY
I'LL NEVER LET YOU GO
HARBOR LITES
SMOKY JOE'S CAFE
ANNIE HAD A BABY
SEXY WAYS
BABY LETS PLAY HOUSE
GOOD ROCKIN' TONITE

TUTTI-FRUTTI
IM LEFT YOU'RE RITE SHES GONE
RIP IT UP
LONG TALL SALLY
READY TEDDY
SLIPIN' & SLIDIN'
BO DIDDLEY
CINDY LOU
MAKIN ME A USED TO BE
I GOT A WOMAN
WHY DID YOU LEAVE
HOUND DOG
DON'T BE CRUEL
BE BOP A LULU
THAT'S ALL RIGHT
ROCK AROUND WITH OLIVEE
I FORGOT TO REMEMBER
THE GREAT PRETENDER
TRYING TO GET TO YOU
LAWDY MISS CLAWDY

SONGS TO LEARN

ROCK HOUSE
ALL AROUND THE WORLD
THE GIRL CAINT HEP IT
DROWN IN MY OWN TEARS
AINT THAT LOVE
JEM DANDEE
TICK TOCK
ROCK AROUND THE CLOCK
MAY BELLENE
TOO MUCH MONKEY BUSINESS
GOING HOME
LOVE IS STRANGE
WHY OH WHY
AINT GOT NO HOME
BLUE MONDAY
YOUNG LOVE
YOURE THE REASON I'M IN LOVE
BUTTERFLY

ALBERT LEE There was a West Texas influence from his upbringing, which had a lot to do with the construction of his songs. They were like Spanish songs linked with country music, which was a unique blend. He started out wanting to be Elvis, but quickly he found his own niche where he felt comfortable. In that short space of time, he churned out so many great songs, all very simple, yet classics.

JERRY 'J.I.' ALLISON Black music was a massive influence; it was 95 per cent of our music. We just loved Fats Domino, Chuck Berry, Little Richard, blues, rock, rhythm and blues. In Texas, they'd only play Pat Boone's version of 'Tutti Frutti', but we had a station in Louisiana that had a show called Stan's Record Revue. For about an hour every night they'd play the real music, so we'd sit and listen to that.

Above and left: Joe B. Mauldin, Buddy Holly, Jerry Allison and Niki Sullivan rehearsing at the Cotton Club, Lubbock, TX, May/June 1957. No pictures are known to exist of Buddy playing his leather-covered J-45. In this image Niki is playing Buddy's J-45 prior to their tour starting in August 1957. Niki was initially recruited to fill in the sound as the band began touring.

These images were acquired by Bill Griggs in 1981 as damaged photographs. Bill captured them with a yellow filter over a camera lens to improve the quality.

Opposite, top: Larry Welborn, Buddy and Bob Montgomery
Fort Hood, TX, summer 1955

Opposite, bottom: Song lists written out by Buddy in his notebook

THE BUDDY HOLLY EDUCATIONAL FOUNDATION *Ambassadors*

NILE RODGERS *'Sexy Ways'*
RICHARD THOMPSON *'Baby, Won't You Come Out Tonight'*
PAUL CARRACK *'Work with Me Annie'*
JOE ELY *'Down the Line'*
RICHARD HAWLEY *'Baby Let's Play House'*
T BONE BURNETT *'I Wanna Play House with You'*
KEVIN MONTGOMERY *'Flower of My Heart'*
PETER NOONE *'Baby Let's Play House'*
JOHN SEBASTIAN *'I Guess I Was Just a Fool'*
BETH NIELSEN CHAPMAN *'Door to My Heart'*

THE SONGS: *1953–1955*
This section features TBHEF ambassadors who have song titles for their guitars that were either released by other artists and inspired Buddy's songwriting and early musical endeavours, or were written, recorded, performed or demoed by Buddy between 1953 and 1955.

THE BUDDY HOLLY EDUCATIONAL FOUNDATION AMBASSADORS

Lifetime custodians of Buddy Holly-inspired guitars

From his time writing, performing and recording, right up to the present day, the most iconic musicians of each era have always acknowledged how Buddy Holly influenced them. Some have been vocal, repeatedly telling interviewers on film and in the press about Buddy's impact on their careers, others have released hit cover versions, and sometimes whole albums, of Buddy Holly and the Crickets music. Some began their careers in bands which only performed Buddy Holly and the Crickets songs, or modelled their appearance, their sound or even their band's name after them. With others it's more subtle: a pilgrimage and a performance at the Surf Ballroom, formative childhood memories of the Crickets on a Dansette record player, bonding with parents or grandparents as they grew up to his music.

The Buddy Holly Educational Foundation honours these icons in music who accompanied or followed Buddy, presenting them with a custom-built replica of his iconic Gibson J-45, the instrument on which he wrote so many of his much-loved songs. The guitars are hand-built by master luthiers, Dan Roberts and Tony Klassen in the US, Alister Atkin and Mick Johnson in the UK, with hand-tooled leather covers in homage to the one Buddy made himself. We were especially honoured when Judy Edwards, the wife of the late Nokie Edwards, who was one of our earliest ambassadors, made some of our original hand-tooled leather covers. More recently they have been tooled by Pete Allen, himself a veteran leather worker.

The original 19 guitars were each built with one of the frets from Buddy's own Gibson J-45 fitted inside the body, visible through the sound hole. We were fortunate to come into possession of these when the original guitar was refretted, and so our first 19 recipients truly have part of Buddy's soul installed in their instruments. From Peter Frampton to Mick Jagger, those artists literally write with Buddy Holly's influence at their fingertips.

Our ambassadors, every one referencing the creative musical genius of Buddy Holly and the Crickets, are also presented with a certificate from Maria Elena Holly, with copies of many of them displayed in the Buddy Holly Center in Lubbock.

Whenever appropriate, ambassadors assist in promoting the Foundation's aspirations and goals, including helping raise funds for our associated charities, Teenage Cancer Trust and Teen Cancer America, or attending our regular songwriting retreats in the UK and USA.

The ambassadors keep their guitars for their lifetime, after which their families bequeath them to another artist or musician so they may keep the singer-songwriter tradition moving forward, inspired by Buddy. Surf-rock pioneer Nokie Edwards's guitar was presented to Brian Wilson, while innovative Duane Eddy's was passed to the Edge. It was a particular privilege to present Ringo Starr with the guitar that had belonged to his close friend Keith Allison.

Ambassadors featured in this book span eight decades in entertainment, from iconic legends to new generations of artists and musicians, all with one common bond: a love and appreciation of the incomparable music legacy created by Buddy Holly and the Crickets.

We thank them all.

PETER BRADLEY SNR
Co-founder TBHEF

NILE RODGERS *'Sexy Ways'*

THERE CAN BE LITTLE ARGUMENT THAT FEW MUSICIANS HAVE COLLABORATED AS DIVERSELY AS NILE RODGERS, from jamming with Jimi Hendrix as a teenager, through his disco days with Chic and Sister Sledge, to producing David Bowie, Madonna, Eric Clapton and Jeff Beck, right through to Nile's huge hit 'Get Lucky' in the 21st century with electronica stars Daft Punk. Nile is the ultimate cross-genre guitarist.

With Buddy's boundless enthusiasm to work in new musical styles, it is easy to imagine him meeting and collaborating with Nile. As the Chairman of the Songwriters' Hall of Fame, Nile knows what it takes to be a great songwriter, mixing a writer's early inspirations with new ideas to produce something original, creative and everlasting.

Nile's Foundation guitar is called 'Sexy Ways', after a Hank Ballard and the Midnighters song that has a special place in Buddy's story. Before his career took off, Buddy was working with his brother Larry in the family tiling business, and they stopped at a juke joint late one night returning from a job. The juke joint's band were playing Hank Ballard songs, and when Buddy joined in with the band on guitar, the appreciative audience spread the word until the place was packed and rocking. Larry always said that he knew that night Buddy would be a success in music, and resolved then to do all that he could to support Buddy in his dream to be a musician. – *Mike Read*

To Buddy,
You are Rock n Roll!
N. Rodgers

SEXY WAYS
'Sexy Ways' was released by Hank Ballard and the Midnighters in 1954.

NILE RODGERS Man, I loved Buddy. I've worked with so many people in music and I just know we'd have collaborated if things had been different.

'You can hear Buddy's musical ideas across the whole spectrum of music. Everybody is inspired by something he did!'

RICHARD THOMPSON My older sister had just about everything by Buddy Holly released in the UK, and that pumped through the wall from her bedroom to mine, just at the point where I was starting on the guitar.

As the years went by, I never lost my deep admiration for Buddy, and also realised the quality of his singing and songwriting. He had a knack for the simple, which is actually one of the hardest things to achieve – to find new ways of saying the same thing with the same chords is immensely difficult.

'Buddy Holly was my original guitar inspiration … He has been a beacon for so many musicians down the generations.'

INSPIRED BY GUITARISTS LIKE BUDDY HOLLY, Richard Thompson co-founded the legendary folk group Fairport Convention in 1967, at the age of 18. He left the group in 1971 to pursue diverse songwriting and session-playing interests.

As a virtuoso guitarist, Richard has been honoured in myriad ways, from a Mojo Les Paul Award for 'Guitar Legend' to an OBE from Her Majesty Queen Elizabeth II, and an Honorary Degree from the University of Aberdeen. It's a remarkable career when your plaudits come from such varied places.

Bless you Buddy! My first musical experience, trying to master the solo on "Peggy Sue".

A real thrill,

R[illegible]

BABY, WON'T YOU COME OUT TONIGHT

'Baby, Won't You Come Out Tonight' was first released on Coral on 18 February 1963. Written by Buddy Holly and Sue Parrish, it was recorded by Buddy on 7 December 1955 at Nesman Studio, Wichita Falls, TX.

When Nashville agent Eddie Crandall (see page 52) sent Buddy a telegram on 3 December 1955 to request some demos, this was one of the songs that he received. Crandall used these demos to help secure Buddy a recording contract with Decca Records.

'The first record I ever bought was "It Doesn't Matter Anymore" with "Raining in My Heart" on the flipside.'

PAUL CARRACK'S ICONIC VOICE CAN BE HEARD on such global hits as 'How Long' by Ace, 'Tempted' by Squeeze and 'The Living Years' and 'Over My Shoulder' by Mike and the Mechanics. Since 2000, Paul has released over a dozen solo albums on his independent Carrack-UK label.

In 2012 Paul was the subject of an hour-long BBC Four documentary *Paul Carrack: The Man with the Golden Voice*. That same year, he was one of the recipients of the BASCA Gold Badge Award in recognition of his unique contribution to music.

Paul's songs have been recorded by many artists, including Tom Jones, Eagles, Diana Ross, Linda Ronstadt, Michael McDonald and Jools Holland, and he has toured with or played sessions for many others, such as Elton John, Eric Clapton, B.B. King, Ringo Starr, the Smiths, Madness, Simply Red and the Pretenders.

It was during his solo UK tour in 2018 that Paul was presented with his J-45 replica at Sheffield City Hall, where Buddy Holly and the Crickets appeared in March 1958 during their only UK tour. The 'Work with Me Annie' guitar is named after a 1954 Hank Ballard and the Midnighters song covered by Buddy. Paul talked about his new guitar and TBHEF on stage before playing a great version of 'Raining in My Heart'.

The first record I ever bought
was 'Raining in My Heart' with
'Guess it doesn't matter any more'
on the B side.
My brother John & I went halves
He had 5 shillings & I had 1s/4p.
Best money I ever spent.
I am so honoured I can't tell
you. I'm surely not worthy.
thank you.

PAUL CARRACK I was absolutely blown away to be presented with the Buddy Holly guitar. My brother John, who had turned me on to Buddy, was in the audience and it made for a very special night. To be in such esteemed company is a real feather in my cap. I am truly honoured.

WORK WITH ME ANNIE

Written and recorded by Hank Ballard and the Midnighters, 'Work with Me Annie' was released on Federal Records on 14 January 1954.

This was one of Buddy's favourite songs to perform with Bob Montgomery and Larry Welborn on The Sunday Party *on KDAV. The song was banned by most white pop stations because of its suggestive lyrics.*

JOE ELY *'Down the Line'*

My family moved to Lubbock in 1959 & discovered Buddys' music the same year. He changed my life and filled it full of Song... He filled my heart and inspired my soul

Eternally Grateful

Joe Ely

DOWN THE LINE
'Down the Line' was first released on a 1965 compilation of Buddy and Bob rarities called Holly in the Hills. *It was written by Buddy Holly and Bob Montgomery and recorded on 7 June 1955 at Nesman Studio, Wichita Falls, TX.*

JOE ELY SPENT HIS TEENAGE YEARS IN LUBBOCK, and his wife, Sharon, talks of a 'mystical link' between her husband and Buddy Holly. Growing up in West Texas, the wind was an unseen force. It moved all that was in its way. Buddy Holly used that force to fill the sky with music and song, influencing many musicians who came after him. His lyrical imagination and unforgettable melodies will linger as long as the wind continues to blow. One of the musicians lucky enough to be captured by this force was Joe Ely.

Joe's eponymous debut solo album was released in 1977 and the following year he met the Clash in London, with a mutual musical respect emerging between the group and Ely. They toured together, Joe sang backing vocals on the Clash's 'Should I Stay or Should I Go' and the band name-checked him in their song 'If Music Could Talk'. Sadly, the death of the Clash's front man, Joe Strummer, meant that a planned collaboration never happened.

Joe's song 'Brainlock' was featured in the 1980 film *Roadie* and in 1998 he contributed a song to the soundtrack of the Robert Redford film *The Horse Whisperer*. Joe was made Texas State Musician in 2016, a designation held for a year, and in 2022 he was inducted into the Austin City Limits Hall of Fame. – *Mike Read*

JOE ELY Having spent much of my life travelling all over the world, I have met countless musicians who have shared a mystical connection with Buddy Holly's music and his way of touching our hearts with song.

'I will forever be grateful for Buddy's inspiration and will carry it wherever I go … Rave On!'

RICHARD HAWLEY My first memory of Buddy's music is clear as day, it was my Aunt Jeannie and my mum smoking cigarettes flicking their ash in an empty glass of some kind … in a room filled with my sleeping cousins … they were singing us to sleep … looking out the door … raining in my heart … some stuff, old songs … I'll never forget the closeness and the distance all at the same time … I drifted some after … never came back …

BABY LET'S PLAY HOUSE

Written by Arthur Gunter, 'Baby Let's Play House' was a demo recorded by Buddy in 1954 or 1955. The song (under the alternative title 'I Wanna Play House with You') is another that was first released on the 1965 Holly in the Hills *compilation. It is a good example of how Buddy and his fellow musicians moved from country and western to rockabilly, inspired by Elvis.*

'Thank you Buddy xx'

IN THE YEARS THAT HAVE ELAPSED SINCE RICHARD HAWLEY abandoned band life full-time – first with the Longpigs and then as Pulp's guitarist – he has forged one of the most singular and diverse careers in modern music. Richard's affinity with 1950s rock and roll is clear through his look and music, and it is easy to draw parallels between some of his most thoughtful ballads, such as 'Open Up Your Door', and some of Buddy's later works.

As well as releasing a string of solo albums that have managed the rare feat of being both critically acclaimed and commercially successful, Hawley has worked with a host of impressive collaborators – friends such as Arctic Monkeys, Manic Street Preachers, Elbow and Paul Weller, alongside personal heroes that include US guitarist Duane Eddy (his 2011 album *Road Trip* was co-produced by Richard), Shirley Bassey (for whom he wrote the smouldering ballad 'After the Rain' in 2009), Nancy Sinatra, the late Lisa Marie Presley, and British folk royalty Martin Carthy and the late Norma Waterson (he was an integral part of 2013's Bright Phoebus Revisited tour). There are also bona fide pop stars such as Robbie Williams, All Saints and Texas, all of whom Hawley has played with in differing capacities through the years. His song 'Tonight the Streets Are Ours' was featured in *The Simpsons* and *Exit Through the Gift Shop: A Banksy Film*.

In recent times his songs have appeared in television dramas *Peaky Blinders*, *The Full Monty* and *Hijack*, as well as the hugely acclaimed musical named after his 2012 album *Standing at the Sky's Edge*. 'Dear Alien (Who Art in Heaven)', co-written with Jarvis Cocker and Wes Anderson for Anderson's film *Asteroid City*, made the 15-song shortlist for 'Best Original Song' at the 2024 Oscars.

The award-winning *Standing at the Sky's Edge* musical features 20 Richard Hawley songs and won Best New Musical and Best Original Score at the 2023 Olivier Awards. Following its sell-out runs at Sheffield's Crucible Theatre and London's National Theatre, in February 2024 it began a six-month run at London's West End Gillian Lynne Theatre.

Also in 2023, Richard played five acclaimed shows with John Grant, performing the songs of Patsy Cline, as well as releasinga 'best of' compilation called *Now Then*, which became his fourth Top Ten album. 2024 saw Richard release his tenth studio album, *In This City They Call You Love*, which debuted at number five in the UK charts.

DEAR
BUDDY
THAT WAS
A HECK OF A
WAY TO TREAT
A GUY THERE
WAS NEVER
ANYBODY
BETTER
T B

T Bone's message (above) refers to a 1957 phone call between Buddy and Paul Cohen of Decca Records regarding his contract *(see page 104)*

'Often when I'm in New York, I eat at Table 53 at P.J. Clarke's, where Buddy proposed to Maria Elena.'

(JOSEPH HENRY) T BONE BURNETT IS ONE OF THE MOST IMPORTANT and influential people in music today. He is a 12-time Grammy-winning record producer with a magic touch, who has achieved that rare and elusive combination of artistic integrity and massive commercial success.

He has been a creative force in music for more than 50 years, putting his name to a whole catalogue of classic and lasting albums as diverse as *Raising Sand* with Robert Plant and Alison Krauss, *August and Everything After* by Counting Crows and *Spike* by Elvis Costello.

Immersed in the vibrant radio waves of The Beatles and Buddy Holly, he went on to cut his teeth in psychedelic bands in the 1960s and with Bob Dylan on the massive and extraordinary Rolling Thunder Revue tour in the mid-1970s.

On screen, he helped stage the magnificent *Black & White Night* Roy Orbison television tribute in 1988, was the founding executive music producer for the globally successful *Nashville* television series and has become the go-to producer of movie soundtracks, following his mega-success with *Crazy Heart*, *Walk the Line*, *Hunger Games* and – the biggest of all – the blockbuster film *O Brother Where Art Thou*, which sold more than nine million copies and took American roots music to a whole new generation of young fans and musicians.

He is a respected activist on behalf of artists' rights and, perhaps most important of all, T Bone has become a vital and dedicated musical archivist, capturing unvarnished recordings by some of America's greatest-ever musicians. Willie Nelson, John Mellencamp, Greg Allman, Alison Krauss, Ryan Bingham, B.B. King, the Secret Sisters and Gillian Welch, alongside the Chieftains, Diana Krall, Elton John and Leon Russell are among those who have worked with T Bone since the turn of the century.

Without doubt, T Bone is special. His meticulous attention to detail and unique sensitivity to the creative process underpin his peerless ability to infuse his work with the deepest emotion and authenticity. He truly believes that all the elements and dynamic range of sound that characterise the best recorded music were most in tune together at exactly the time when Buddy was making his classic floor-to-tape recordings in the 1950s.

T Bone Burnett is a great friend of the Buddy Holly community and a huge hero of mine. – *Bob Harris*

KEVIN MONTGOMERY *'Flower of My Heart'*

KEVIN MONTGOMERY Dad was a boyhood friend of Buddy Holly's. They learned to play guitar together and had a duo called Buddy and Bob. They wrote songs like 'Heartbeat', 'Wishing', 'Down the Line' and 'Love's Made a Fool of You'.

KEVIN'S FATHER, BOB MONTGOMERY, was one of Buddy's earliest songwriting partners, as the pair met in junior high school in 1949 and performed together both on stage and for local radio shows for almost a decade.

When Buddy decided to pursue a career as a solo performer, Bob decided to concentrate on songwriting, penning many of Buddy's much-loved songs, often co-writing with Buddy and Buddy's producer Norman Petty. *Holly in the Hills*, a compilation of Buddy and Bob recordings, was released in 1965 and featured 'Wishing', 'Flower of My Heart' and 'Got to Get You Near Me Blues'.

Kevin Montgomery grew up in Nashville with Bob, surrounded by music, and then learned his trade busking in New York. Kevin made his album debut in 1993 with *Fear Nothing*, opening shows for such artists as Sheryl Crow and David Crosby, and was featured on many compilations, including duetting with Mary Chapin Carpenter on the Buddy tribute album *Not Fade Away*. Sir Paul McCartney was so impressed with Kevin's songwriting that he invited Kevin to perform with his band at the Buddy Holly Week in 2000 at London's Mermaid Theatre. – *Mike Read*

When I was 11 years old Dad
brought home the Buddy Holly
Collection put out by MCA.
I delved into it and found
"Flower of My Heart". I spent
many days after school
singing along with "True Love
Ways"... "Flower of My Heart"
is still in my set list.
Music has taken me around
the world. Buddy's life and
music were magic.
The music is timeless.
Here's to Buddy and Bob!

FLOWER OF MY HEART

'Flower of My Heart' was one of the tracks on the 1965 Holly in the Hills *compilation. It was written by Bob Montgomery and recorded by Buddy and Bob in 1954 or 1955 at Nesman Studio, Wichita Falls, TX. Bob wrote this as the class song for the Lubbock High School 'Westerners'.*

BY THE AGE OF 14, PETER NOONE HAD APPEARED IN TWO ROLES in the new TV soap *Coronation Street*, the second role being Len Fairclough's son Stanley.

Two years later, Peter joined Manchester group the Heartbeats and then three of the group, including Peter, merged with members of another local band to form Herman's Hermits. Before their rise to fame, the band was still nameless. As teenagers rehearsing in a local pub in England, Peter Noone, a fan of Buddy Holly, would wear thick, black-rimmed glasses and mimic Holly's voice. One day, the pub owner bluntly asked, 'What are you doing? You don't look like Buddy Holly – you look like Sherman from the Bullwinkle show.' This offhand remark became the inspiration for the band's name.

Herman's Hermits' UK hit singles included the number one 'I'm into Something Good', as well as 'Can't You Hear My Heartbeat', 'Silhouettes', 'Wonderful World', 'A Must to Avoid', 'No Milk Today', 'There's a Kind of Hush' and 'My Sentimental Friend'. They also notched up numerous hits in the US, including two number ones in 1965: 'Mrs Brown, You've Got a Lovely Daughter' and 'I'm Henry VIII, I Am'. That year, they ran out as Top Singles Act of the Year in the *Billboard* chart, with The Beatles at number two. In 1966, they were nominated for three Grammy Awards, and between 1964 and early 1968, no Herman's Hermits single failed to make the US Top 40. John Lennon promised Peter that he and Paul McCartney would write a song for him, so imagine his delight when in the office at EMI Manchester Square, he saw a tape box with 'For Noone' written on it. It was actually The Beatles song 'For No One'! He never got the song.

The band also appeared in films, including *When the Boys Meet the Girls*, *Hold On!* and *Pop Gear*. Their final single, as Peter Noone & Herman's Hermits, was 'Lady Barbara' in 1970. The following year, Peter left to pursue a solo career, recording, touring, and having a hit with David Bowie's 'Oh! You Pretty Things' (retitled as 'Oh You Pretty Thing'). As busy as an actor as he is as a singer, Peter has made appearances in such TV series as *Married . . . with Children*, *Dave's World*, *My Two Dads*, *Too Close for Comfort*, *Quantum Leap*, *Laverne & Shirley* and the soap *As the World Turns*. He also toured the US in the lead role in *The Pirates of Penzance* and won the 2019 Las Vegas casinos Entertainer of the Year award.

A big Buddy Holly fan, Peter admits, 'Buddy and the Crickets were my inspiration. As a lad I had the old Dansette Major record player and a really nice lady who owned a record shop in Woodsend Circle in Flixton would alert me to any findings of 78s, 45s or 33 1/3rds and I sat and dreamed and sang along, never imagining that one day I'd be allowed to sing the great stuff for others. I still remember the moment I heard the incredible and impossible descending string part on "Raining in My Heart" and thinking: *That's it . . . Kismet, Hardy!*' – *Mike Read*

BUDDY,
I NEVER MET YOU BUT I HAVE LIVED MY LIFE WITH YOUR MUSIC IN MY HEART! "HEARTBEAT" WAS MY FIRST LIVE SONG WITH MY GROUP CALLED THE HEARTBEATS!
THANKYOU FOR ALL THE GREAT SONGS – THE SONGS OF MY LIFE!

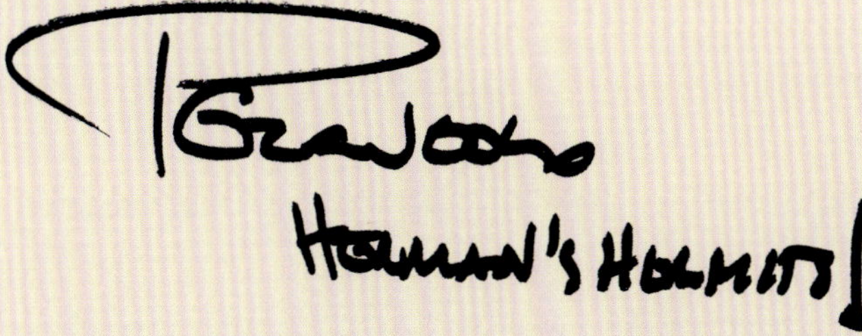

I GUESS I WAS JUST A FOOL
'I Guess I Was Just a Fool' was recorded by Buddy at Nesman Studio, Wichita Falls, TX in December 1955. It was one of the demos sent to Eddie Crandall in response to his telegram *(see page 52)* *to Buddy. It was re-recorded by Buddy in 1956 at Norman Petty Studio and was not released by Coral until 18 May 1964 on the* Showcase *compilation album.*

Thanks, Buddy...
You taught me about
Texan music...
and Lightnin' Hopkins!
John Sebastian

IN MID-1960S AMERICA, JOHN SEBASTIAN OWNED THE AIRWAVES. Without doubt, the songs he wrote for his band the Lovin' Spoonful are among the best we've ever heard.

Think of 'Nashville Cats', surely the sharpest and most observant song written about Music City, TN. Or the timeless 'Daydream', perfectly capturing the euphoric feeling of a beautiful, tranquil day. And 'Summer in the City', which always reminds me of New York on a hot, humid summer afternoon, sun blazing down. 'Walking on the sidewalk, hotter than a match head' has got to be one of the great lyric lines.

John co-founded the Lovin' Spoonful with Zal Yanovsky in Greenwich Village in 1964, and they somehow exactly captured and embodied the bohemian vibe of the time. Their sound was amazing – an alchemic blend of jug band, Beatles, folk, pop and psychedelia. They called it 'good time music' and the energy of rock and roll played a huge part in driving the rhythm of this glorious hybrid.

Both John and Zal loved the music of the 1950s. They were big fans of Duane Eddy and Roy Orbison and John would later endlessly talk about the influence of Fred Neil on his writing style. He met Fred when working on a Judy Collins album for the Elektra label in the mid-1960s and was massively impressed. 'I was bowled over by Fred,' he said. 'He'd written "Candy Man" for Roy Orbison and was involved in a lot of that Tex-Mex stuff. Buddy Holly and him and Buddy Knox and those guys. They were all friends.'

The first Lovin' Spoonful single, 'Do You Believe in Magic?', stormed into the *Billboard* charts in October 1965, beginning a run of seven consecutive Top Ten hits, propelling them to third in the top sellers list the following year, beaten only by The Beatles and the Rolling Stones! Heady days indeed.

Their music captured a beautiful moment in time ... love and a feeling of optimism, and that hazy, crazy moment still feels inspiring today. The band created a sometimes-underrated legacy that was finally acknowledged by their induction into the Rock and Roll Hall of Fame in 2000.

The Lovin' Spoonful broke up in 1968, but John continued to release beautiful music. His first solo single, the sweet and gentle 'She's a Lady', remains a personal favourite and his last-minute appearance on the stage of the legendary Woodstock Festival in 1969 was an absolute triumph. But his biggest chart success was still to come.

Commissioned to write the theme for a massively successful American TV series, he took the resulting song 'Welcome Back' to the top of the *Billboard* singles chart in May 1976. And in 2024, as an honoured ambassador for The Buddy Holly Educational Foundation, he was presented with a Buddy Holly guitar named after the song 'I Guess I Was Just a Fool', to acknowledge his enormous contribution to American music. – *Bob Harris*

BETH NIELSEN CHAPMAN *'Door to My Heart'*

Dear Buddy ~
Your brilliance as a songwriter lives on in the DNA of songwriters every where and those to come... You burned so bright and I have aspired to emulate your simplicity and strength. ♡

Beth Nielsen Chapman

GROWING UP THE DAUGHTER OF AN AIR FORCE MAJOR, twice Grammy-nominated Nashville-based recording artist and songwriter Beth Nielsen Chapman had already lived in Texas, New Hampshire, Massachusetts, California and Germany by the time she turned 13 in 1969, before settling in Montgomery, Alabama, the middle child in a family of five kids. She was the one clinging to her guitar like a life raft, navigating her path of chaos by turning to songwriting at the age of 11.

Influenced by the hits that flowed from the musical melting pot of military radio stations playing Frank Sinatra, The Beatles, Motown, singer-songwriters, blues, rock and roll and country classics, Beth was always drawn to what made a song stand out. In that regard nothing could ever top the brilliance of Buddy Holly. In 1957, when 'That'll Be the Day' and 'Peggy Sue' were smashing the charts, Beth was a one-year-old, but those songs were still blazing across the airwaves when she reached the age of writing her own songs.

Beth's music has been remarkably diverse, from *Prism* (2007), on which she sings in nine different languages, to *The Mighty Sky* (2012), a Grammy-nominated astronomy CD for kids, to other works featuring legendary guests such as Vince Gill, John Prine and Duane Eddy. Her song 'Sand and Water' (1997), written in the wake of her husband's death, was performed by Elton John on tour to honour the memory of his friends Princess Diana and Gianni Versace. In 2016, Beth collaborated with Olivia Newton-John and Amy Sky to create *Liv On*, an album about coming through grief.

In addition to releasing her own albums, Beth has written other songs, including seven number one hits, for artists such as Bonnie Raitt, Willie Nelson, Bette Midler, Elton John, Neil Diamond, Michael McDonald, Mary Chapin Carpenter, Keb' Mo', Roberta Flack, Waylon Jennings and Indigo Girls. 'This Kiss', her mega-hit for Faith Hill, was ASCAP's 1999 Song of the Year.

Inducted into the Songwriters Hall of Fame in 2016, Beth, a breast cancer survivor, inspires others to fully blossom into their creative life. She has been a keynote speaker and teacher of workshops on creativity, songwriting, grief, and healing through art at universities internationally, including the Royal Scottish Academy of Music and Drama, the Liverpool Institute of Performing Arts and the Berklee School of Music. Beth considers it the highest honour to be an ambassador for The Buddy Holly Educational Foundation.

'Every Buddy Holly song is airtight. He raised simplicity and depth to an art form.'

DOOR TO MY HEART

Written by Bob Montgomery, 'Door to My Heart' was recorded by Buddy and Bob between 1954 and 1955. The song was not released until 18 January 1965, when it appeared on the Holly in the Hills compilation.

PUBLICITY IMAGE
This hastily arranged portrait was commissioned after Buddy received his contract from Decca and was taken in either late 1955 or early 1956. Buddy signed the contract on 25 January 1956. When he received his copy of the finalised document on 8 February 1956, he saw that his last name, Holley, had been misspelled as Holly. It has stayed that way ever since, as Buddy was worried that if he sent the corrected contract to Decca, they might not send it back.

I am 19 years old – was born here in Lubbock, Sept. 7, 1936 and been living here ever since that time. I finished high school at "Tom S. High" last June.

CHAPTER TWO

1956

I have been picking the guitar and singing since I was 12 but it was in Jr. High & High school that I began singing & playing for programs, winning several contests. When Radio Station KDAV of Lubbock first went on the air I took my guitar and went out to get on the "Sunday Party", a Sunday afternoon program which still operates from KDAV. Dave Stone who is manager of KDAV was very kind and tolerant and gave me a spot on the program. Taking advantage of Dave's kindness I continued playing from KDAV for several months. One day Dave said to me "Would you really like to have a recording contract" Soon after that he went to Nashville, Tenn. and took some dubs (unofficial records) that I had made – A contract with Decca was the result So here I am, Wondering just what happened – So you see the credit really belongs to Dave Stone who has ~~done~~ and still is doing a lot for me. At present he has made arrangements for me and my band to join a group from the Grand Ole Opera, touring for A.V. Bamford. We will join them at Oklahoma City

SONNY CURTIS Elvis got a drummer and Buddy said we needed one too. He'd heard about a kid called Jerry Allison, so Buddy and I drove down to see him at school. He hadn't had his growth spurt yet; he was just a little guy. He came running up to the car after he was done with practice, and I thought surely this isn't the guy that you want to play drums with us? But Jerry was a great drummer, even in the beginning.

JERRY 'J.I.' ALLISON I remember that day. At the time, I was a little beady guy playing in the Lubbock High band. We used to march up and down the street around the high school. Right after marching practice, I saw Sonny and Buddy parked up in Buddy's '55 Oldsmobile waiting, and I went over to hang out for a while.

This page and opposite, bottom left: A series of early publicity pictures taken at the end of 1955. Buddy was 19 years old.

CPCo. Phone 42-1416

Cedarwood Publishing Co., Inc.
146 SEVENTH AVENUE, NORTH • NASHVILLE 3, TENNESSEE

February 8, 1956

Mr. Buddy Holly
c/o T. V. Holly
Route #5
Lubbock, Texas

Dear Buddy:

Enclosed is your Decca recording contract ready to be signed and returned to Decca Records, 50 W. 57th Street, New York, New York.

Also, send at least 4 pictures, 2 different poses of yourself along with the contract. They will use the pictures in promotion of your first release.

Be sure that this is done immediately as it will hold up getting your record out.

Sincerely,

Jim

Jim Denny

JD:r

Encl.

JERRY 'J.I.' ALLISON When Buddy got a record contract with Decca in 1956 it was a big deal. I was still in high school at the time, but when the summertime came around and I got out of school, I went down to Nashville and we recorded some tunes, but it didn't feel serious. I played drums, and it was all fun. I thought if a record comes out maybe I'd get a Cadillac.

SONNY CURTIS The first Nashville session was 26 January 1956. They wanted to get rock and roll started there, so Buddy signed a contract with Decca, and it was Buddy, Don Guess and me on the sessions. They didn't let Buddy play guitar in the studio; he just stood at a microphone in the corner and sang. I've always been mystified about that; he could've played rhythm just as good as Grady Martin. By this point we'd recorded demos with Norman Petty, but Nashville is where it happens, so we loved being there. That session was a delight. We were all young and thought we'd made it, that all we had to do was go back home, start acting like Elvis and wait for the money to come in. When we got back to Lubbock, it was back to the same routine, but we couldn't wait until 'Blue Days, Black Nights' came out. It got a good review in *Billboard*.

Dear Mother and Daddy,
We decided to stay in the motel for a while so you can write us here. Be sure to mail it Air mail so it will get here before we leave if we come back right after the session. I don't know anything for sure yet, except we will have a session.
Our address is 819 MURFEESBORO RD.
NASHVILLE TENN.
Love, Buddy

BUDDY's first recording contract was with DECCA RECORDS, dated Jan.25,1956, just a few months after his nineteenth birthday, (9/7/1936). BUDDY also signed a writers agreement with CEDAR WOOD PUBLISHING CO. on Jan.25,1956, which was for a three year period, in which agreement, Buddy agreed to record only songs furnished or approved by Cedarwood Publishing Co. and agreed that all songs written in their entirety or as co-writer should be published by Cedarwood Publishing Co. for a period of three years, but this agreement was terminated on Jan.7,1958 with certain conditions being agreed to by all parties concerned and duly signed by the three parties and with a notary acknowledgement, 7th- day of January, 1958.

continued, next page

FIRST DECCA RECORDING SESSION
On 26 January 1956 Buddy had his first recording session for Decca, at Bradley's Barn in Nashville, TN, produced by Owen Bradley. It ran from 7.15 PM to 10.15 PM. Four songs were recorded, 'Love Me', 'Don't Come Back Knocking', 'Midnight Shift' and 'Blue Days, Black Nights'. Bradley didn't want Buddy to play guitar and sing, so session musician Grady Martin played guitar along with Sonny Curtis. Decca charged Buddy $385.97, which would be deducted from any royalties that accrued. He had two further sessions for Decca, one in July and one in November.

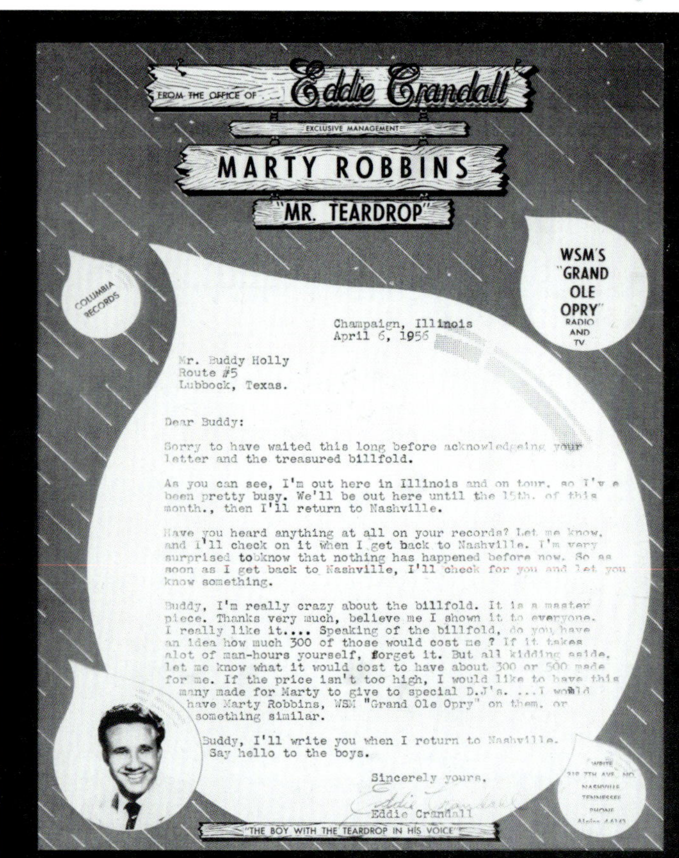

FROM THE OFFICE OF Eddie Crandall

EXCLUSIVE MANAGEMENT

MARTY ROBBINS

"MR. TEARDROP"

COLUMBIA RECORDS

WSM'S "GRAND OLE OPRY" RADIO AND TV

Champaign, Illinois
April 6, 1956

Mr. Buddy Holly
Route #5
Lubbock, Texas.

Dear Buddy:

Sorry to have waited this long before acknowledgeing your letter and the treasured billfold.

As you can see, I'm out here in Illinois and on tour, so I'v e been pretty busy. We'll be out here until the 15th. of this month., then I'll return to Nashville.

Have you heard anything at all on your records? Let me know, and I'll check on it when I get back to Nashville. I'm very surprised tobknow that nothing has happened before now. So as soon as I get back to Nashville, I'll check for you and let you know something.

Buddy, I'm really crazy about the billfold. It is a master piece. Thanks very much, believe me I shown it to everyone. I really like it.... Speaking of the billfold, do you have an idea how much 300 of those would cost me ? If it takes alot of man-hours yourself, forget it. But all kidding aside, let me know what it would cost to have about 300 or 500 made for me. If the price isn't too high, I would like to have this many made for Marty to give to special D.J's. ...I would have Marty Robbins, WSM "Grand Ole Opry" on them, or something similar.

Buddy, I'll write you when I return to Nashville. Say hello to the boys.

Sincerely yours,

Eddie Crandall

"THE BOY WITH THE TEARDROP IN HIS VOICE"

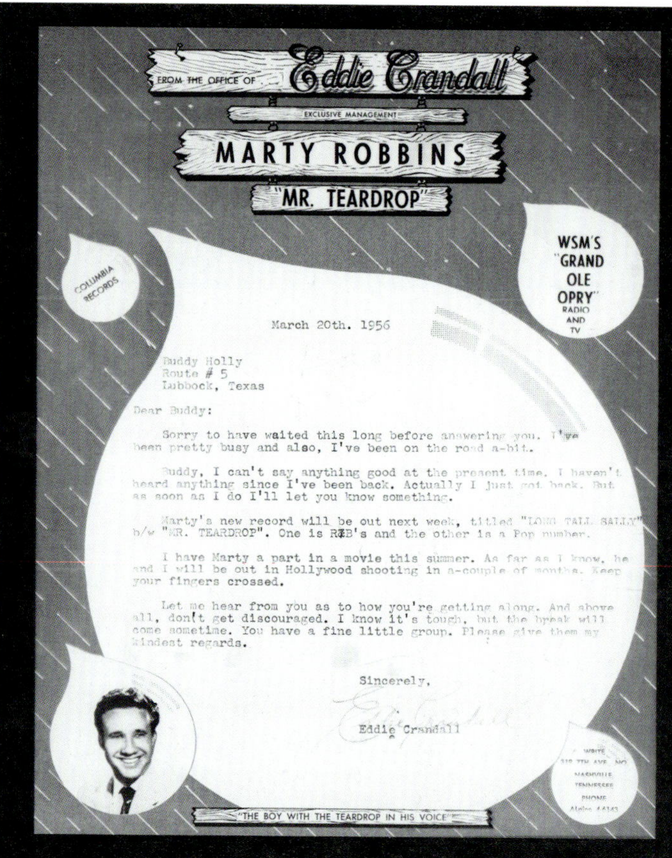

FROM THE OFFICE OF Eddie Crandall

EXCLUSIVE MANAGEMENT

MARTY ROBBINS

"MR. TEARDROP"

COLUMBIA RECORDS

WSM'S "GRAND OLE OPRY" RADIO AND TV

March 20th. 1956

Buddy Holly
Route # 5
Lubbock, Texas

Dear Buddy:

Sorry to have waited this long before answering you. I've been pretty busy and also, I've been on the road a-bit.

Buddy, I can't say anything good at the present time. I haven't heard anything since I've been back. Actually I just got back. But as soon as I do I'll let you know something.

Marty's new record will be out next week, titled "LONG TALL SALLY" b/w "MR. TEARDROP". One is R&B's and the other is a Pop number.

I have Marty a part in a movie this summer. As far as I know, he and I will be out in Hollywood shooting in a-couple of months. Keep your fingers crossed.

Let me hear from you as to how you're getting along. And above all, don't get discouraged. I know it's tough, but the break will come sometime. You have a fine little group. Please give them my kindest regards.

Sincerely,

Eddie Crandall

"THE BOY WITH THE TEARDROP IN HIS VOICE"

My junior year, my singing partner and I started singing on radio station KDAV on Sunday evenings. Soon after this I started singing semi-professionally. Eddie Crandall heard me sing on a show with Bill Haley in October 1955. He asked me to send him some dubs in Nashville. Soon after I was notified that I would have a session. (2 March 1956, Buddy in reply to a letter from Paul Cohen of Decca Records requesting a 'biography' of his life)

JERRY 'J.I.' ALLISON Earlier on we did a fair tour, where you play local shows like the Lubbock County Fair. Buddy got pulled over by the cops for speeding and he said, 'Hey, we're out promoting the fair for Lubbock and you're cutting into our time.' And they let him go! I think if I'd have said that they'd have slapped me, put me in handcuffs, took me out behind the barn and beat the hell out of me. But that was Buddy.

On 14 October 1955 Eddie Crandall, a Nashville agent who represented Marty Robbins (a fan of Buddy's music and leatherwork), watched Buddy perform at Fair Park Coliseum in Lubbock as he supported Bill Haley and the Comets along with Bob and Larry. Crandall was so impressed by Buddy that he wrote to Pappy Dave Stone of KDAV radio: 'Dave, I'm very confident I can do something as far as getting Buddy Holly a recording contract. It may not be a major but even a small one would be beneficial to someone who is trying to get a break . . . Col. Parker suggested I try and help Buddy as he's pretty well tied up, and with your friendship I'll try my darndest to help him. Marty Robbins also thinks Buddy has what it takes. So all we can do is try, OK?'

In January 1956, Crandall rang with the exciting news that he had taken Buddy's demo to Nashville talent agent Jim Denny, who owned a publishing company called Cedarwood. Denny would offer Buddy a songwriter's contract with Cedarwood and also try to get him a recording deal with Decca.

Left: Jerry Allison, Buddy and Sonny Curtis on stage at Fair Park Coliseum, Lubbock, TX, early 1956

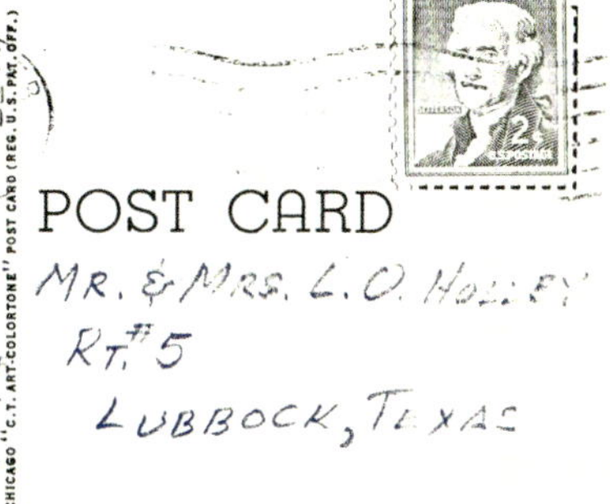

The fabulous new Turner Turnpike was completed at a cost of over $38,000,000. It has reduced the driving distance between Tulsa and Oklahoma City to 88 unimpeded miles.

HI,
WE'RE HERE ON THE TURNPIKE NOW. THE SHOWS YESTERDAY WENT OFF REAL GOOD. WE DID BETTER LAST NITE. ALL THE GUYS ON THE SHOW GOT A KICK OUT YOUR CALL LAST NITE. WE HAVE TWO SHOWS TONITE, [illegible] 7 & 9
SEE YOU FRIDAY,
LOVE Buddy

OKLAHOMA NEWS CO., TULSA, OKLA.

GENUINE CURTEICH-CHICAGO "C.T. ART-COLORTONE" POST CARD (REG. U.S. PAT. OFF.)

MAY 10 1956

POST CARD

MR. & MRS. L. O. HOLLEY
RT. #5
LUBBOCK, TEXAS

Dear Mr Denny,

Here are some tapes with original songs on them. I wrote some of them and other people wrote some. We have more songs, but the night we cut the tapes we didn't have them completed. I especially like the first song on the larger tape. I think it's the best of the bunch.

It seems to me we should have another record soon so that people won't tire of this one. I haven't had any reports from Decca but I do know it's doing fair here in Lubbock. 'Blue Days, Black Nights' is No. 6 and 'Love Me' is No. 11 on the bestsellers here.

We went on a short tour for Mr Bamford and the people really seemed to like the two songs, although they had never heard the record before.

We will be looking to hear from you as to when we will have another session. Sincerely, Buddy Holley

(10 May 1956, letter from Buddy to Jim Denny at Cedarwood Publishing)

LETTERS AND POSTCARDS

Sent Thursday 10 May 1956, the picture postcard depicts the Turner Turnpike, which runs between Tulsa and Oklahoma City. Although Buddy stated that he would be doing two shows that night, only one show was advertised in the local newspaper.

LARRY HOLLEY Buddy seemed to think that I hung the moon, because I was an older brother and had been around a little. He would ask my advice on many things, some private, and I always tried to steer him right or help in any way I could. Going back a few months, he had told me he would go to Nashville if he had a thousand dollars. I said, 'Why don't you just ask for the moon?' However, I got the money for him and he blew six hundred of it on a Fender guitar, then bought a red sport coat and took off there. He made some recordings down in Nashville, but they didn't sound right or something and they sat on them and never released them, until a year or so later after Buddy was already getting famous. By this time, Buddy had made his mind up to pursue a musical career or bust a gut. He was playing around town for everything that came along. He sang a lot with Bob Montgomery, who was almost like a brother.

SONNY CURTIS We'd gone on the road pretty unprepared, without any stage uniform like the other bands had, or even a name to call ourselves. When we stopped off in Oklahoma City, we went to a haberdasher's and bought some white pants and two shirts each, a blue one and an orange one. So when we went on stage that night, we told them to announce us as the Two-Tones.

Right: Sonny Curtis, Buddy Holly and Don Guess, Odessa, TX, 10 May 1956

As a new Decca recording artist, Buddy had been offered his first professional tour: a week on the road with Faron Young's Grand Ole Opry Show, visiting spots such as Tulsa, OK. With him he took his sidemen Sonny Curtis and Don Guess, but not Jerry Allison, who was still in high school.

ALBERT LEE Buddy was into country to begin with, before Elvis was discovered. Then when Buddy recorded for Decca, he did some rockabilly sounds that were in that pocket. After 'That'll Be the Day', he found his own style very quickly, which came from the influence of the Mexican area that he was living in and the rock and country music he was listening to.

A V Bamford
[illegible] Dilling
N Hollywood

Dear Mr Bamford,

I would like to thank you for the tour you put my band and myself on last spring. We enjoyed it very much. It was our first tour of that sort and we were just a little "green" at it, but I believe it helped us in every respect. Ray Odom is a fine person to work with and he helped us a lot.

I have talked to some friends that were traveling around the north-eastern part of the country this summer and they said my record ("Blue Days - Black Nights", Love Me") was very popular around Washington D.C. and through Missouri. I thought I might offer the suggestion that if you could put us on a tour it might help you as well as us if you could book us a few places where our record is most popular. We have a better act made up now and we will certainly appreciate anything you can do for us. Thanks again for the help you've given us.

Sincerely, Buddy Holly

JERRY 'J.I.' ALLISON We'd seen *The Searchers* and John Wayne had said 'That'll be the day' about five times in that movie. When we got back, Buddy and I were practising, and he said we ought to write a song. I'd never written a song before, and so I said, 'That'll be the day!' We ended up writing those heavy lyrics. After about 30 minutes we said, 'Well, we've got a song, something else to play at dance gigs.' We recorded it in Nashville and Owen Bradley said it was the worst song he'd ever heard. Buddy was singing in a higher key, and we were playing it the way we would at dances. It felt like we played it two million times. But when that record came out, all our friends were amazed. When we re-recorded it, we didn't make any big changes. The first version was too high and since the first recording we'd been performing all over the place, so it evolved into the way we did it at shows.

The John Wayne movie The Searchers *opened at the State Theater in Lubbock, and ran through 20 June 1956. Buddy and Jerry went to see it. During the movie, John Wayne would mutter 'That'll be the day' each time he was disgruntled about something.*

Opposite: Buddy's letters to his friend Mrs E.R. Bragg, which express his frustration at how he is being treated by Decca, 1956

Lubbock, Texas
Route #5
July 17, 1957

Mrs. E. R. Bragg

Dear Friend -

I'm sorry I've been so long about answering your letter, but I have been working every day and playing a few programs at night so I have really been short on time, and now I'm getting ready to go back to Nashville for another recording session. I will leave today - I'm taking the boys in my band with me - I talked with Jim Denny and he's arranging for us to have a spot on the Grand Ole Opera but I dont know what date that will be, so keep your fingers crossed for us.

I am taking about a dozen songs with me to Nashville - some of them are very good, I think, but of course they will have to approve what I put on record and I hope they will let me put out about 4 Songs this time - a lot depends on my next songs. I have thought about changing my style some, but they say they want the same for the present.

I sure do appreciate what you are doing for me and if you still want to start a fan club for me, that would really be great and I will certainly be willing to cooperate in any way, but you would have to let me know what you would want me to do and I'll be glad to do any thing to help. I'll be back to Lubbock in a few weeks and I will write you then. Heres hoping my next songs will prove to be worth your time and effort.

Best Regards and thanks for everything

Buddy Holly.

Mrs. E. R. Bragg

Dear Friend

I was out of town on a fishing trip last friday so I didnt get to see you. I didnt catch any fish either!

No, I am not giving up and I would still like to have your help as soon as I can get things to going again. There's no reason why my next releases should be delayed much longer. But until some-thing is out I hate for any one to have to stick their neck out for me. I really do appreciate your attitude about it and as soon as I know something definite I'll let you know - shouldnt be long now.

There are sure a lot of new ones coming out now. It almost makes me frantic because mine have been delayed. - I keep feeling like I'll hear some-one else singing mine just any time. ha ha

Oh well, they told me before I went into this it was "dog eat dog" - now I know what they meant.

Well so long for now and if you get discouraged waiting on me, dont mind letting me know:

As Ever

Buddy Holly

NASHVILLE JUL 19 1 PM 1956 TENN.

THIS SIDE OF CARD IS FOR ADDRESS

POSTAL CARD

Mr. & Mrs. L. O. Holley
Route #5
Lubbock, Texas

WED.

Dear Mom & Dad,
We got here to Nashville at 11:30 tonite and checked into the Bel Aire Tourist Court. Everythings gone just fine, but we haven't talked to anyone yet. We will in the Morning.
I guess that's just about all for now so I'll turn in and get some sleep. I'll write again and tell you more when I know more.
Love, Buddy

SONNY WEST I met Buddy Holly in 1956. KDAV had an open mic show on a Sunday afternoon, and he was there to do his show with Bob Montgomery. I'd known of Buddy because we were both trying to get records out, but he had already gone to Nashville and got a contract with Decca. I was waiting for them so I could sing, and when they came out, Buddy and I were introduced and we said a few niceties. He seemed more serious about music than most of the young guys I knew. I could see him playing through the glass in the studio – he was concerned about the pronunciation and how he played.

By the time I knew Buddy and Bob, they were playing all the rock and roll they could. Elvis had already been through West Texas by that time, so they were picking up on that.

NASHVILLE JUL 21 12 PM 1956 TENN.

THIS SIDE OF CARD IS FOR ADDRESS

POSTAL CARD

MR. & MRS. L. O. HOLLEY
ROUTE #5
LUBBOCK, TEXAS

Dear Mother and Dad,
We are going to record Sunday afternoon. They like our songs. We're going to do one slow one, I think. I guess we'll probably be home Tues.
Love,
Buddy

BOB HARRIS Unlike a lot of other rock and rollers at the time, Buddy was self-contained. He was writing his own songs, he was active in the production, he knew how he wanted the songs to sound, and he was incredibly prolific. Like The Beatles, when John and Paul wrote 180 songs in the period of their first few years. Buddy's output was comparable to that. He was an artist with a lot of conviction about what he did and the way he did it. He wasn't a puppet on a string.

In July 1956, while in Nashville, Buddy wrote a short letter to his parents that read: 'Dear Mother and Dad, We are going to record Sunday afternoon. They like our songs. We're going to do one slow one, I think. I guess we'll probably be home Tues. Love, Buddy.'

A typewritten account by L.O. Holley, Buddy's father, about his son's songwriting process (opposite, bottom)

SECOND DECCA RECORDING SESSION
Buddy had his second recording session for Decca in Nashville on 22 July 1956. It was produced again by Owen Bradley and ran from 10.30 PM to 1.30 AM. Five songs were recorded: 'Rock Around with Ollie Vee', 'I'm Changing All Those Changes', 'That'll Be the Day', 'Girl on My Mind' and 'Ting-A-Ling'. Buddy's group – Sonny Curtis on guitar, Don Guess on bass, Jerry Allison on drums – were referred to as the Three Tunes at this session.

The version of 'That'll Be the Day' that Buddy recorded in Nashville is different from the one that finally became his first hit. Decca didn't release the Nashville version. Buddy's first release, in April 1956, had been the Ben Hall song 'Blue Days, Black Nights'. The record didn't sell well. His second release, in December 1956, 'Modern Don Juan', didn't sell well either and Decca, after six months, did not renew Buddy's option.

Right: Buddy, Jerry Allison and Bob Montgomery as they get ready to leave for Nashville for Buddy's second Decca recording session, 19 July 1956

In writing his songs, it would have been hard to tell which he wrote first, the words or the tune, as he seemed to come out with both about the same time ... he never spent a lot of time sitting down to do either .. for instance, he might stop eating just long enough to jot down a few words and say 'I think I have a new song.' Then perhaps, when we had finished our meal he would pick up his guitar and run through a few bars .. and usually that was it. I really do not know how he learned so much in such a short time ... he never spent a lot of time practicing the guitar as most boys do around the house. Occaisionally he would say, 'I heard something the other day that I'd like to try',then he woulcd pick up his guitar and you would think that he had been playing that particular part for years. In short he could do, with his guitar, just as he did with his voice, most any thing he tried.

SONNY CURTIS After a session in Nashville where we recorded 'That'll Be the Day', we went outside to the back alley of Bradley's Barn. There was a kid that worked in the studio there and he said that his favourite song of the session was 'That'll Be the Day'. We always remembered that because that kid had it down. Of course, it wasn't the same version that made it big.

KEVIN MONTGOMERY It became apparent that they were more interested in Buddy as a solo artist, not Buddy and Bob. I heard that my dad said to Buddy, 'Look, just go for it. This is your chance.' He was a little hurt, but he got over it. Near the end, Buddy asked him to move to New York and run the publishing company he was starting. They were in talks about that when Buddy passed.

EDNA GUNDERSEN When recordings don't sound the way they want them to, many artists give up. In the case of Buddy, he came back home, found Norman Petty, travelled to a tiny studio in Clovis, and made these fabulous-sounding records. At that time, it was unheard of.

KEVIN MONTGOMERY They would've been very scared and hopeful because this was their big shot. Owen Bradley was the biggest producer in Nashville for many years, and one of the fathers of country music, so they would have been trying to impress. My dad told me that on the 15-hour drive back from Nashville, he, Jerry and Buddy had one hamburger to share between the three of them.

Hi-chee-o-do,

Well we finally got here about 2:00 o'clock in the afternoon yesterday. (Monday) We are staying in the Bel-Air Motel (same one as last time) right now but we are going to look for an apartment that we can rent by the week today.

We saw Mr. Denny yesterday and talked to him for 10 or 15 minutes. He's glad we came and he said as soon as Mr. Cohen gets here we will start working on material and things.

We took in a movie yesterday evening and then we came back and went to bed about 8:30 and slept till just now (12:15). We were pretty tired. We left York, Nebraska, Sunday about 2:00 P.M. and drove straight through. Echo was sure glad to see me. We just rode around Sat. nite and looked at the town and the college. Sun. morning I went to church with her. Then we went out to eat and then Don & I left for Nashville.

We don't know anything for sure yet about when the session will be except that it will be after the 11th. I'll write our new address as soon as I know it so Bye for now.

Love, Buddy

P.S. Did Daddy find a car of some kind?

Dear Mother and Daddy,

Well here it is, Monday night and there's not much to do. We're just sitting "at home" reading. That's what we did last night, too. The convention was going strong all week-end and it seems awfully quiet now. Nearly every singer in the country was here and we met nearly all of them. Elvis wasn't here but Scotty and Bill were and we talked to them a lot. Gene Vincent was here. We met him and he was tickled about it. He said he had one of my records. We met the Governor of Tennessee (Clements) Thursday night. He came over to us and introduced himself.

I talked to Mr. Denny today and he talked to Paul Cohen on the phone. (He's in town but I haven't got to meet him yet)

He said he would set up our session just as soon as he could. It may be about 3 or 4 days though, and if it is I'll have to call home for some more money. I wouldn't have but I had to buy a battery for the car. I'll call tomorrow and let you know, although it will probably be yesterday to you. (By the time this gets there)

Well that's about all there is to say except that we're doing just fine. A little homesick, though. I guess we'll come home right after the session. See you soon.

Love, Buddy

This page: A letter Buddy wrote to his parents about his third and final Decca session

This page and opposite: Buddy had his third and final recording session with Decca Records in Nashville on 15 November 1956. Three songs were recorded: 'Rock Around with Ollie Vee', 'Modern Don Juan', 'You Are My One Desire'.

THE BUDDY HOLLY EDUCATIONAL FOUNDATION
Ambassadors

BUZZ CASON *'You Are My One Desire'*
VAN MORRISON *'Brown Eyed Handsome Man'*
JOAN JETT *'Love Me'*
DAVE GROHL *'I'm Gonna Set My Foot Right Down'*
RONNIE WOOD *'Rock-A-Bye-Rock'*
JAMES BURTON *'Blue Days, Black Nights'*
JEFF BECK *'Be-Bop-A-Lula'*
TOMMY STEELE *'Good Rockin' Tonight'*
JOOLS HOLLAND *'Honky Tonk'*
YUNGBLUD *'Blue Suede Shoes'*
SHARLEEN SPITERI *'I Forgot to Remember to Forget'*
DUANE EDDY *'Holly Hop'*
THE EDGE *'Holly Hop'*
CHRIS ISAAK *'Blue Monday'*
TONY IOMMI *'Shake, Rattle and Roll'*
ROBERT PLANT *'Modern Don Juan'*
BRUCE SPRINGSTEEN *'Because I Love You'*
JOE LOUIS WALKER *'Bo Diddley'*
VINCE GILL *'Because I Love You'*
BUDDY GUY *'It's Not My Fault'*

THE SONGS: 1956
This section presents TBHEF ambassadors with guitars named after songs that were written, recorded, performed or demoed by Buddy in 1956.

WHEN IT COMES TO A MUSICAL CAREER, BUZZ CASON DID IT ALL. He was a singer, songwriter, musician, sideman, recording artist, record producer, song publisher and author.

In the late 1950s James E. 'Buzz' Cason was a member of the Casuals, Nashville's first young rock and roll combo. They subsequently became Brenda Lee's backing band and toured with her around the world. In the 1960s, after relocating to California, Buzz had a brief recording career under the name of Garry Miles and recorded a cover version of 'Look for a Star', theme song from the British film *Circus of Horrors*.

In Los Angeles he became the assistant to Liberty Records producer Snuff Garrett, producing acts including Bobby Vee, Gary Lewis, and the Crickets and playing alongside budding session musicians like David Gates, Leon Russell and J.J. Cale. The Crickets at the time were enjoying a career revival, and Buzz toured the UK with the group in 1964, playing guitar and drums and providing lead vocals. They performed at the Royal Albert Hall and appeared live on *Ready, Steady, Go!*

It was as a songwriter that Buzz had probably his biggest successes. He co-wrote the song 'Everlasting Love' with Mac Gayden and this became a big US hit for soul star Robert Knight and a number one hit in the UK for Love Affair and in recent times a hit for Jamie Cullum. Another big success was 'Soldier of Love', co-written with Tony Moon, a major cross-over hit for R&B star Arthur Alexander and also a massive US hit when revived by rock superstars Pearl Jam. However, the song had already gone global with The Beatles' version, included in their *Live at the BBC* collection.

Buzz joined forces as a co-publisher with fellow songwriter Bobby Russell and the partnership scored big with Russell's compositions 'Honey', a signature hit for Bobby Goldsboro, and 'Little Green Apples', a biggie for Roger Miller. Other songs in Buzz's hit list include numerous Stateside hits like 'Sandy' (Ronny and the Daytonas), 'Popsicle' (Jan and Dean), 'Emmylou' (Oak Ridge Boys), 'Another Woman' (T.G. Sheppard), 'To Love' (Placido Domingo) and 'Love's the Only House' (Martina McBride).

In 2012 Buzz was reunited with the Crickets when he participated in the band's induction into the Rock and Roll Hall of Fame. In 2018 he got together with fellow singer-songwriter Billy Swan to record the album *Billy & Buzz Sing Buddy*, which features their own arrangements of Buddy's classic songs recorded as their tribute to the man.

Living up to his name, Buzz maintained an industrious career in music as a performer and recording artist right up until his death in June 2024 aged 84. – *John Firminger*

My time with the CRICKETS was a highlight for me and GREAT FUN! Especially "La Bamba" on '64 tour of England ROCK ONWARD BOYS! Buzz Cason

YOU ARE MY ONE DESIRE
'You Are My One Desire' was originally released on Decca on 24 December 1956. It was written by Don Guess and recorded on 15 November 1956 at Bradley's Barn, Nashville, TN with Buddy Holly on vocals, Don Guess on bass, Harold Bradley and Grady Martin on guitars, Floyd Cramer on piano, Farris Coursey on drums, and E.R. 'Dutch' McMillin on alto sax, and was produced by Owen Bradley.

VAN MORRISON *'Brown Eyed Handsome Man'*

Buddy
was an enormous influence
on the whole music scene
to follow. Van Morrison.

VAN MORRISON WAS 13 WHEN BUDDY HOLLY DIED and Coral Records swiftly released his number one hit 'It Doesn't Matter Anymore' – and 14 when that record finally dropped out of the charts. Van and his friends were playing skiffle, then Shadows-style tunes, and then performing in showbands, a particularly Irish institution that required considerable versatility and a precise familiarity with the current hit parade. Then came his band Them, from which point on our knowledge of his career becomes easier to access.

I mention the earlier times because it would have been pretty much impossible for Van never to have played any Buddy Holly songs in those showbands. In 1963 alone, Buddy posthumously had a string of Top Ten hits, one of which, 'Bo Diddley', inspired the Rolling Stones' cover of Buddy's 'Not Fade Away' in February 1964 – when Van's career proper was about to begin.

And what a career! Forty-something solo albums, and a list of awards and accolades which would easily fill this entire page. We'll settle for two Grammys, a handful of Hall of Fame inductions, a pair of doctorates, the OBE and the knighthood. Oh, and the gold-plated Antony Dannecker harmonica that I was able to present to him when we took part in Lead Belly Fest at the Royal Albert Hall in 2015.

I've had the honour of working with Van over the years: from interviewing him on the BBC World Service in 1982 (and several times since) through being booked on harmonica when he played with his band on Radio 2 in 2008, to singing his song 'Fame' with him on his album *Roll with the Punches* in 2017. I am also immensely grateful for Van's generosity in appearing numerous times at my fundraising charity concerts. It's a delight to see that this massively influential singer-songwriter is now a Buddy Holly Educational Foundation ambassador.

On Van's 1983 album *Inarticulate Speech of the Heart* there is a song called 'Rave On, John Donne'. In addition to Donne, the song names other poets such as Walt Whitman, Omar Khayyam and W.B. Yeats – with the title of one of Buddy Holly's most-loved songs before each name.

Rave on, Buddy Holly! – *Paul Jones*

BROWN EYED HANDSOME MAN

Written and recorded by Chuck Berry in 1956, this song has been covered by many artists, including Buddy Holly. Buddy's recording was a posthumous hit in the UK in 1963, where it peaked at number three, and was released on the album Reminiscing, *which reached number two on the UK albums chart. Buddy's version also peaked at number three in Ireland. Buddy closed his set with this song at his last performance, at the Surf Ballroom, Clear Lake, IA, on 2 February 1959.*

Keep up the
work you do
memorializing his
Spirit!

Rock on Forever
Buddy!

Joan Jett

THROUGH TALENT, ENERGY AND DRIVE, JOAN JETT HAS CREATED A FULLY UNCOMPROMISING ROCK AND ROLL LIFE. She has been a performer, songwriter, guitarist, producer and record label owner, and in 2015 she was recognised for her incredible impact and influence with induction into the Rock and Roll Hall of Fame.

Her career began as a teenager in the mid-1970s as a founding member of the legendary all-female band the Runaways. From the start, Joan made loud, hook-laden records that conveyed both toughness and joy. Sporting a low-slung guitar, shag haircut and black leather, she took over a role dominated by male rockers and excelled at it.

Joan's authentic attitude and her powerful musical lyricism were rooted in the sound and style of rock and roll – carrying on the spirit that Buddy Holly helped create. Generations of artists and fans have been captivated by Buddy Holly's lyrics, rhythms and vocal style. Along with his great melodies, every guitar player raves on about Buddy's iconic Fender sound, driven by a confident right hand delivering powerful downstrokes and well-timed upstrokes. This distinct delivery was taken even further when Buddy delivered rhythmic chord-based solos in lieu of single-note lines. This mixture made pop songs sound like rockers and set the stage for power pop, punk and garage – three of the hallmarks of Joan Jett's incredible career.

She formed the Blackhearts in 1982, and their classic four-piece sound carried the flag for straight-ahead, take-no-prisoners rock and roll. The Blackhearts' potent mix of hard rock, glam, punk, metal and garage rock blasted through the airwaves and sounded fresh and relevant in any era. Their biggest hit, 'I Love Rock 'n' Roll', which went to number one in the US in 1982, is timeless – as pure and simple a statement about the music's power as Chuck Berry's 'Roll Over Beethoven'. Three of their albums – *I Love Rock 'n' Roll*, *Album* and *Up Your Alley* – reached the US Top 20, powered by songs written by Joan and bandmate Kenny Laguna. By covering songs from all corners of the rock catalogue – from Sonny Curtis to Tommy James to Sly and the Family Stone – the band effortlessly broke down barriers between genres and eras.

The honesty and power of Joan's records makes you believe that rock and roll could change the world. This no-nonsense attitude and Joan's style has been a major influence on countless artists, including Nirvana, Green Day and a host of Riot Grrrl bands. In addition to writing and performing, Joan has produced a wide range of artists including the Germs, Bikini Kill and L7. When American record labels rejected her debut solo album in 1980, Joan and Kenny Laguna launched Blackheart Records and for the last four decades the label has championed cutting-edge artists. – *Greg Harris (President, Rock and Roll Hall of Fame and Museum)*

LOVE ME

'Love Me' was originally released on Decca on 16 April 1956. It was written by Buddy Holly and Sue Parrish and a demo was first recorded by Buddy on 7 December 1955 at Nesman Studio, Wichita Falls, TX. 'Love Me' was on the flipside of Buddy's first release, 'Blue Days, Black Nights'.

Buddy —
Rock and Roll
will
NEVER DIE
Thanx to you.......

DAVE GROHL *'I'm Gonna Set My Foot Right Down'*

I'M GONNA SET MY FOOT RIGHT DOWN
'I'm Gonna Set My Foot Right Down' was first released on the 1965 Coral compilation Holly in the Hills. *Written by Buddy Holly, it was first recorded between February and April 1956 at Norman Petty Studios in Clovis, NM. The song features Sonny Curtis on guitar, Don Guess on stand-up bass and Jerry Allison on drums.*

THE WORLD KNOWS DAVE GROHL AS THE MAGNETIC FRONT MAN, RIPPING GUITARIST, AND PASSIONATE VOCALIST of the legendary Foo Fighters, and he is all that and more. After bringing us unforgettable rock anthems and epic live shows for nearly three decades, it's almost possible to forget for a moment that he was also the mighty drummer for one of the most ground-breaking bands in rock history – Nirvana. And yet there's even more to his story. Dave has produced award-winning records and music videos, directed major documentary films, and collaborated with countless legendary musicians, from Sir Paul McCartney to David Bowie to Norah Jones. His passion and endless curiosity are deeply embedded in every project he undertakes. Like Buddy Holly, Dave is most at ease when he's in the studio, creating and refining new sounds.

Similarly, Dave's professional music career began in his teens. Dave joined a band in Washington, D.C., dropping out of high school to play drums on their nationwide tour. From that auspicious start, he connected with artists across the country, which eventually led to him joining Nirvana. Dave's intense and powerful drumming propelled the band forward and served as the heartbeat to Kurt Cobain's brilliant lyrics, and their work inspired an entire generation of fans and opened the door to numerous artists.

After Nirvana, Dave quickly became a sought-after collaborator, receiving an attractive offer from Tom Petty to join the Heartbreakers. He auditioned by playing drums for the band on their nationally televised appearance on *Saturday Night Live*. After being offered the job, Dave declined so he could focus on his own solo material, resulting in the Foo Fighters' celebrated debut album. Dave played nearly every instrument on the record, and after releasing it, he assembled a first-class band to bring his vision to life and take the songs on the road. This kick-started decades of wildly successful Foo Fighters tours, and massive songs like 'Everlong', 'Learn to Fly' and 'Times Like These'. Outside the band, Grohl has produced other artists, collaborated on numerous recordings, founded the supergroup Them Crooked Vultures with John Paul Jones, and produced, directed and starred in award-winning music documentaries, including *Sound City* and *Sonic Highways*.

Along the way, Dave has collected many accolades, including music's highest honour – induction into the Rock and Roll Hall of Fame – first with Nirvana in 2014 and later with the Foo Fighters in 2021. With this rare achievement, he joins an elite group of artists who have been inducted more than once, including icons Tina Turner, Neil Young, Stevie Nicks and Paul McCartney. As one of the most important and influential musicians of his generation, Dave Grohl fits right in with this distinguished group.
– Greg Harris (President, Rock and Roll Hall of Fame and Museum)

BUDDY
HOLLY

ROCK-A-BYE-ROCK

'Rock-A-Bye-Rock' was originally released by Coral on 18 February 1963. It was written by Buddy Holly and first recorded by him circa 1956 at Norman Petty Studio.

Rock-a-bye-rock
Displays all of Buddy's
rock n'roll prowess on the strat!
I'm honoured to carry the
tradition on.....
Ronnie

RONNIE WOOD IS MANY THINGS TO MANY PEOPLE, from rock hero with the Faces and the Stones to revered visual artist to loving father and grandfather. But he is also a lifelong music nut who retains his boyhood passion for the artists that helped shape him. Buddy Holly was an immovable part of that education, as now reflected in Ronnie's cherished status as an ambassador of The Buddy Holly Educational Foundation.

In 2019, Ronnie took delivery of a guitar named after Buddy's composition 'Rock-A-Bye-Rock', and took to social media to tell the world how much he was enjoying it.

As a 1991 addition to his bespoke portfolio of paintings of fellow stars, Ronnie had unveiled a new portrait of Buddy, John Lennon and Elvis Presley, using light and shadow and working in sepia tones to capture the personality of three stone-cold legends. Ronnie's portrait of Buddy features on the front cover of this book.

Much later, the vast TV audience for his *Ronnie Wood Show* would see him chatting and playing along with his friend Paul McCartney as they marvelled at Buddy's song craft on 1957's 'Peggy Sue', a song that launched and inspired countless careers. Ronnie himself was just ten years old when it became part of the first rock and roll explosion.

Ronnie is much associated with the influence of such giants as Chuck Berry, whose riffs he spent endless hours perfecting in his bedroom, and great blues players such as Buddy Guy. Many may be surprised to know that jazz was also part of his background, from 'trad' musicians like Jelly Roll Morton to later notables such as Kenny Burrell.

But Ronnie was also much moved by that two-year purple patch of seminal singles that Buddy delivered before his desperately early departure. It all contributed to the 'tasty inventiveness' that prompted Penny Valentine, in *Sounds* way back in 1973, to describe Ronnie as 'a man who understands his instrument and its place in the music he's playing. It's the kind of work that brings a smile to your face – and half the time you're not even aware that you're grinning.' – *Paul Sexton*

BUDDY HOLLY
ROCK
BUDDY HOLLY

JAMES BURTON *'Blue Days, Black Nights'*

A GUITARIST LOVED BY ALL THE GREATS, LOUISIANA NATIVE JAMES BURTON began teaching himself the instrument during childhood and was good enough to be considered a pro by the age of 14 years old. One of the first melodies that he wrote was Dale Hawkins's 'Susie Q', which James also played on. While still a teenager, he left for Los Angeles, where he joined Ricky Nelson's band and began playing in the studio as a session musician. In 1964 he got a call from Johnny Cash to play dobro on a TV pilot for a new musical show called *Shindig!*, which turned out to be incredibly popular.

It was at this point he became one of the most in-demand session guitarists and a member of the legendary Wrecking Crew – the name given to the top studio musicians in Los Angeles. During this time, James worked with Phil Spector, Johnny Cash, the Byrds, the Beach Boys, Glen Campbell, Joni Mitchell, the Monkees and Buffalo Springfield, among countless others.

In 1968 James was invited by Elvis Presley – who had watched the *Ozzie and Harriet* show just to see him play guitar – to back him on his comeback television special. At the time he was working with Frank Sinatra and declined, but the following year Elvis called back and asked him to put up a band for his Las Vegas residency. James would remain with Elvis until his death in 1977. After that, James went on to work with John Denver – with whom he remained for 16 years – Roy Orbison, Emmylou Harris and Elvis Costello. James also created the James Burton Foundation, which raises money to give guitars to children.

Not only did James invent and popularise 'chicken pickin'' – which became his trademark – the impact of his signature guitar sound, a blend of Louisiana twang and fast-paced blues, was instrumental in defining the evolutional guitar sound of the 1960s, which can be heard on many of the biggest records of the period.
– *Mike Read*

It was a Blue Day + Black Nite in Los Angeles when Rick Nelson + I heard on Radio That Buddy Holly, Big Bopper + Richie Valens Plane Crashed. Was a very sad day for Rick Nelson + I. Buddy Music + Lyrics will live forever. I Loved his music + songs. God Bless Buddy + all his wonderful friends + fans. A Great Legacy. JB.

BLUE DAYS, BLACK NIGHTS
'Blue Days, Black Nights' was recorded by Buddy on 26 January 1956 at Bradley's Barn, Nashville, TN. After Buddy's first recording session with Decca and many weeks of waiting for his songs to be released, he was informed his debut single would be 'Blue Days, Black Nights' with 'Love Me' and would come out on 16 April. In anticipation of imminent success, Buddy spent hours tooling his famous leather overjacket for his Gibson J-45. His actions were somewhat premature, as the single did not do well, but his breakthrough was little more than a year away.

JAMES BURTON Buddy was an amazing rhythm guitar player; everything stood out with his guitar playing because his arrangement of the songs was fantastic. He was a great songwriter too.

I liked that he would play the instrumental part of the song in chord progressions and change his patterns back and forth. A lot of guitar players would have a hard time doing what Buddy was doing because his thing was keyed off his songs. All entertainers today took a little something from Buddy, his career, his music and his songs. Buddy lives forever, like Elvis.

'His music was so unique, and his songs were so great.'

Opposite: James Burton underneath an Elvis Presley statue outside the Shreveport Municipal Memorial Auditorium, from where Louisiana Hayride*, a TV and radio country music show, was broadcast. It helped launch the careers of some of the greatest names in American country and western music – including Elvis, who performed his debut release, 'That's All Right', in October 1954 on the show.*

This page: James outside the James Burton Foundation Studio. The foundation supports music education for those in need through guitar donations and music instruction to schools, hospitals and community service organisations.

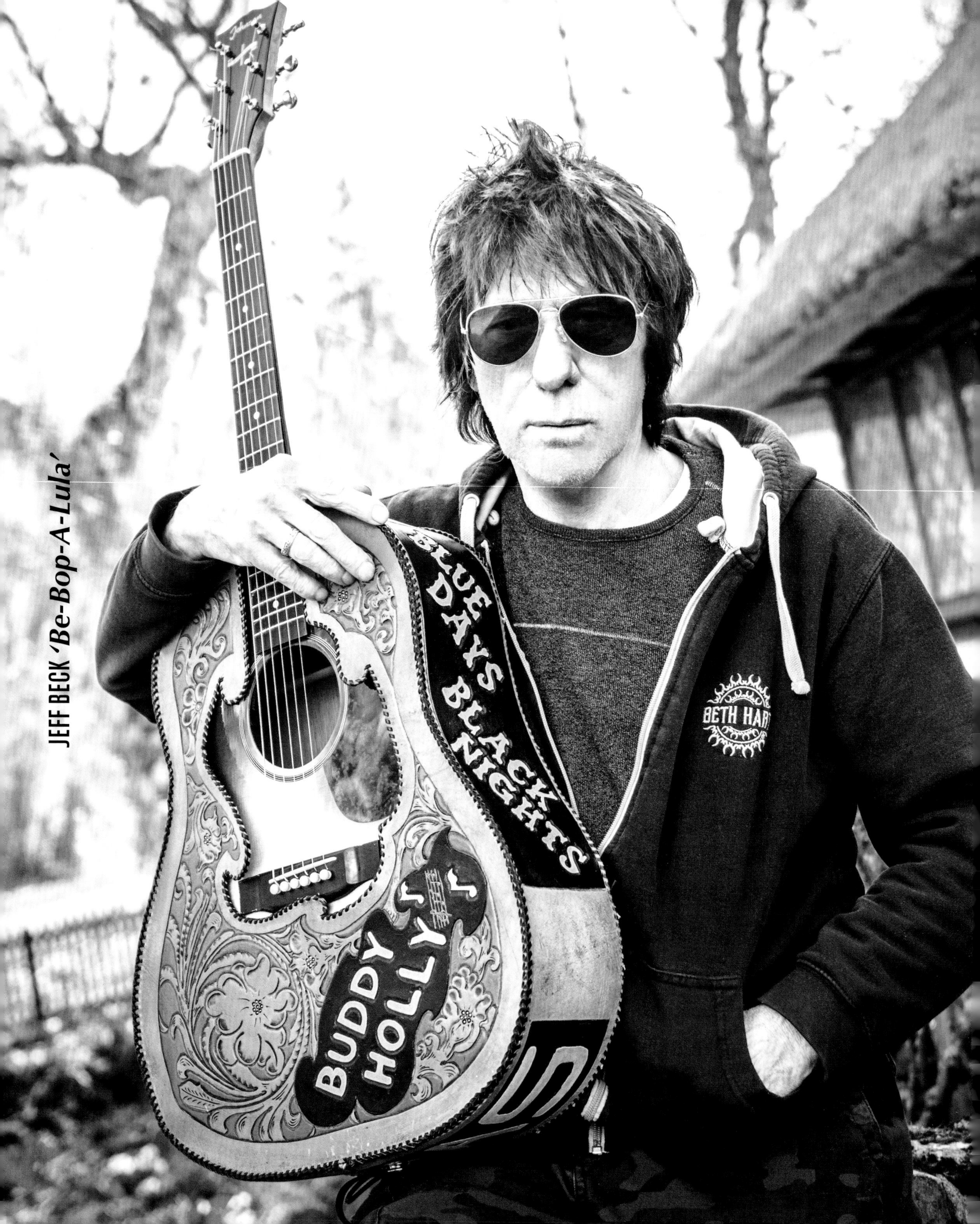

JEFF BECK *'Be-Bop-A-Lula'*

Where would we all be without Buddy Holly?

Jeff Beck x

IN THE FERTILE 1960S BREEDING GROUND FOR ENGLISH MUSICIANS, it was astonishing that one group, the Yardbirds, would feature Jimmy Page, Eric Clapton and Jeff Beck in their line-up.

With the Yardbirds, Jeff Beck transformed the sound of the guitar in pop music, experimenting with the fuzz box, feedback and distortion. He produced classic guitar riffs for the band on records like 'Heart Full of Soul' and 'Over Under Sideways Down' and, way ahead of its time, helped to shape psychedelic pop.

In 1967, following his departure from the Yardbirds, Jeff recorded 'Hi Ho Silver Lining' with Rod Stewart on backing vocals and Rak Records boss Micky Most as producer. It was a huge hit and made the charts again in 1972 and 1982 after being reissued. It earned Jeff just £40 in royalties and he famously hated the song, describing it as 'like having a pink toilet seat around your neck for the rest of your life'.

That same year the Jeff Beck Group was formed with Ronnie Wood and Rod Stewart. By 1968, the band were flat broke and ready to pack it all in, but legendary manager Peter Grant persuaded them to go to America for a short tour. They were booked to support the Grateful Dead at the Fillmore East in New York and, by all accounts, they blew the Dead off the stage. By the end of the tour in San Francisco, Grant had secured the band a new album contract with Epic Records. They returned to England and recorded *Truth*, credited to just Jeff Beck. After their fifth tour of America, on the eve of the Woodstock Festival, the band broke up. Jeff said he had a love–hate relationship with Rod Stewart: 'He loved me, and I hated him.'

In subsequent decades Jeff played with Eric Clapton, Brian Wilson, Roger Waters, Jon Bon Jovi, Kate Bush, and, with his old bandmate Rod Stewart, hit the charts with a cover of Curtis Mayfield's 'People Get Ready'. On 4 July 2009, Jeff finally got the 'pink toilet seat' off his neck with a triumphant performance of 'Hi Ho Silver Lining' with David Gilmour and Imelda May.

Following Jeff's death in January 2023, I asked Mark Knopfler what he thought of him; he gave a simple four-word answer: 'He was the best.'
– Johnnie Walker

BE-BOP-A-LULA
'Be-Bop-A-Lula' was first released by Gene Vincent and His Blue Caps on Capitol on 22 May 1956. The song went on to become a foundation of rockabilly music. Upon hearing it for the first time, Buddy Holly wanted to sing like Vincent.

TOMMY STEELE *'Good Rockin' Tonight'*

Dear Buddy -
still remember when I
saw you 'live' in
Nashville. -
It's an honour to be
in 'The Book'
Keep strummin' man!!

TOMMY STEELE I saw Buddy Holly play, but I don't remember the songs. What stays in my memory of that night to this day was the presence of the man – a gentle performance but a strong beat … and that lilting voice. Before I saw Buddy and I was playing my guitar and singing on board ship, it would be numbers like 'There's a Hole in My Bucket' and 'A Pub with No Beer'.

I never recorded any Buddy Holly songs, but if asked I'd have picked the one I sang at concerts, 'Everyday'.

GOOD ROCKIN' TONIGHT
'Good Rockin' Tonight' was first released on Coral on 20 January 1969. It was recorded by Buddy late 1956 at Venture Studio, Lubbock, TX.

Although this song was written and recorded by Roy Brown in 1947, and another version from 1948 by Wynonie Harris also exists, it is believed that Buddy Holly first heard Elvis Presley performing the song and then decided to do it himself.

MANY ARTISTS, INCLUDING THE BEATLES, REGRETTED NOT SEEING Buddy Holly and the Crickets on their one UK tour, but young Thomas Hicks, a merchant seaman, got to see Buddy Holly in the States. When he began singing professionally, that merchant seaman would take a new name, Tommy Steele, which was based on the first part of his full family name, Still-Hicks.

Back in England on shore leave, Tommy met Lionel Bart and Mike Pratt at a party in Soho, after which the three of them began writing songs together.

Like several major singers from the mid- to late 1950s, Bermondsey's Tommy Steele was discovered at the 2i's Coffee Bar on Old Compton Street, considered to be the nursery of British rock and roll. He had a string of hits and was considered the country's first rock and roller, topping the UK chart with 'Singing the Blues'. Such was his meteoric rise to fame that the film *The Tommy Steele Story* hit the cinemas before Tommy was 21. 'A Handful of Songs', which he co-wrote, won an Ivor Novello Award for 'Outstanding Song of the Year' in 1958, as another film, *The Duke Wore Jeans*, hit the silver screen. In 1959 his third film, *Tommy the Toreador*, featured his big hit 'Little White Bull'.

When asked, as many musicians have been, which direction they think Buddy would have taken musically, Tommy simply answers, 'The same … why mess with perfection?'

In the 1960s he developed into what became known as an 'all-round entertainer', as the music industry then didn't believe in the sustainability of rock and roll. He starred in stage shows in the West End and on Broadway, including *Half a Sixpence*, *Singin' in the Rain*, *She Stoops to Conquer*, *Hans Christian Andersen* and *Meet Me in London*, as well as appearing in more films, such as *The Happiest Millionaire* and *Finian's Rainbow*. In 1981 he had two books published: *The Final Run*, a Second World War novel dealing with the Dunkirk evacuation, and *Quincy*, a children's book based on Tommy's TV film *Quincy's Quest*.

Rock and roll pioneer, songwriter, film star, stage actor, novelist, sculptor and artist, Tommy has even been exhibited at the Royal Academy. He was awarded the OBE in 1979 and the Freedom of the City of London in 2019 and was knighted in 2020 for services to entertainment and charity. I presented Tommy with his Buddy Holly guitar at the London Palladium where he has headlined more productions than any other artist. A plaque to that effect is prominently displayed in the theatre's Cinderella Bar. – *Mike Read*

JOOLS HOLLAND *'Honky Tonk'*

THERE ARE MANY JOOLS HOLLANDS. There's the radio host, the TV host, the author, the model railway enthusiast, the Deputy Lieutenant of Kent, the *bon vivant* and the raconteur. Then there's the pianist, the singer, the songwriter, the band leader, the sideman, the session player and occasionally even the guitarist.

His TV series *Later...* – conceived by Jools and the BBC producer Mark Cooper – is the nearest thing we have to *The Old Grey Whistle Test* in modern times and, like *Whistle Test*, the show has featured many of the greatest musicians in the world in its 30-year archive-building history. Jools is also a touring musician – playing concerts all over Europe with his splendid big band, the Rhythm and Blues Orchestra. At heart, though, Jools has always been a rocker, or a 'boogie-ist', as he puts it. Look to faded teenage greaser photographs and his recent work with pan-global rockabilly band the Barnestormers for confirmation of a love that spans a lifetime.

As a member of the Barnestormers, Jools plays alongside American drummer Slim Jim Phantom from the Stray Cats and powerhouse Scottish-Australian vocalist Jimmy Barnes. In summer 2023, they released a wonderful album that drew inspiration from their favourite music of the 1950s, and nestling at track ten on the record is a song called 'Real Wild Child'.

It's been covered many times over the years, by Iggy Pop and Joan Jett among others, but the original version was written and recorded by Australian rocker Johnny O'Keefe, inspired by a mass brawl at a wedding Down Under. It was first released, under its original title, 'Wild One', in 1958, the year Buddy and the Crickets made their only visit to the antipodes, playing concerts from 30 January to 5 February on a package tour that also featured Paul Anka and Jerry Lee Lewis.

Although they played only a few dates together, the opening act on the bill made a huge impression on these visiting Americans. The band was called the Dee Jays and the front man was Johnny O'Keefe. Buddy and Jerry Lee were massively impressed by the song and when they got back to the US, they went straight into the studio to cut it themselves.

Sadly for the Killer, his recording languished in the Sun Records vaults for over a decade, but Buddy's version, with Crickets drummer Jerry Allison on lead vocals, was renamed 'Real Wild Child' and became a one-off US hit in the summer of 1958, released under Jerry's middle name of Ivan. Now, 65 years later, Jools and the Barnestormers have breathed new life into the fire of a classic song.

Throughout all his roles at the heart of music, Jools has always treasured Buddy's music and now the broadcaster, bandleader and boogie-ist has gone back to his roots.

HONKY TONK
When I first got into music I danced with joy to the music of Buddy Holly – So now I'm grown up (almost) it's a great honour to be part of this wonderful book & project

HONKY TONK
'Honky Tonk' was first released on Coral on 18 May 1964. It was written by Bill Doggett, Berisford Shepherd, Clifford Scott and Billy Butler and recorded by Buddy in late 1956 at Venture Studio, Lubbock, TX. Bill Doggett first entered the charts with this song on 8 August 1956, reaching number two.

Right: Jools with former Squeeze bandmate Chris Difford

YUNGBLUD *'Blue Suede Shoes'*

*'Buddy stood for innovation; doing things his own way and leading with his gut … and that downstroke guitar was just punk as f**k.'*

SOME PEOPLE DISCOVER ROCK AND ROLL, others have it thrust upon them. Dominic Harrison – aka Doncaster pop-punk tearaway Yungblud – grew up in his father's guitar shop and, as he puts it, 'didn't have a choice'. His calling was set.

Since he burst onto the scene in 2017, Dominic has carved out a world of his own across his three genre-smashing studio albums with a neon intensity and hardcore dedication to his fanbase, known affectionately as the Black Hearts Club. They come together in search of community; a place to be for those who stand out. That same spirit is what Yungblud loves about Buddy Holly.

'Buddy stood for innovation; doing things his own way and leading with his gut,' he says. 'He was the first to do it. He is the inventor of the two-minute masterpiece. He wrote simple songs that would shape people's lives and that downstroke guitar was just punk as f**k.'

Now with his Buddy Holly Atkin hand-painted parlour guitar, which Dominic calls 'a songwriter's guitar with one of the greatest names on it', he continues to play the icon's music and pen new material. Inspired, Yungblud has now launched his own guitar – creating an SG Junior signature with Epiphone. Hoping to have the same impact as Buddy did on him, he wants his instrument to inspire 'unfiltered expression and a chance to express what you feel – what you have to and can only say through music'. – *Andrew Trendall (News Editor*, NME*)*

BLUE SUEDE SHOES

Buddy Holly's version of 'Blue Suede Shoes' was first released on Coral on 18 May 1964. It was written by Carl Perkins and recorded by Buddy in late 1956 at Venture Studio or at his home in Lubbock, TX.

Carl Perkins first charted with this song on 22 February 1956, reaching number two in the Billboard *chart. Elvis Presley's better-known cover version, released in September of that year, only just made the Top 20.*

Above: Yungblud performing at Glastonbury with Chris Difford, 25 June 2022

As an undiscovered artist, Dominic attended The Buddy Holly Educational Foundation's first songwriting retreat in 2014, hosted by Chris Difford. The Foundation helped to guide him to success in his early career and welcomed him back to subsequent retreats.

He was presented with his Buddy Holly guitar by Mick Jagger at Anfield Stadium, Liverpool, 9 June 2022, when the Stones played there.

SHARLEEN SPITERI *'I Forgot to Remember to Forget'*

Buddy
The original, I will
always love you & be
inspired by your
timeless music
Texas

SHARLEEN SPITERI I love Buddy's songs as I've always been a big believer in melody and lyrics. I feel that his songs relate to people's lives and emotions across different generations. I think people feel like they are a part of his songs … he seemed to make them inclusive, and I learned so many harmonies listening to Buddy's music.

I was presented with the guitar 'I Forgot to Remember to Forget', which was named after a song first performed and recorded by Elvis. I'm a big fan of Elvis, as well as Buddy Holly, so it was perfect for me. I'm very fussy about my guitars, but the body on my copy of Buddy's J-45 is wonderful, and the neck is really slim. When I played it, it just fitted into my body. I thought, 'Oh yes, this feels right.'

'I often listen to one of Buddy's songs and think, "Ooh, I wish I'd written that …"'

SHARLEEN SPITERI CO-FOUNDED THE ROCK BAND TEXAS, who released their first album, *Southside*, in 1989. Their debut single, 'I Don't Want a Lover', made the UK Top Ten and the US Top 100. Since then, the band have sold over 40 million records. Their tenth studio album, *Hi*, was released in May 2021 and became their highest-charting album in the UK since 1999's *The Hush*, reaching number three on the UK albums chart. Sharleen has also released two solo records, *Melody* and *The Movie Songbook*.

Born and raised in Scotland, Sharleen discovered music partly through her parents' record collection, which included Buddy Holly, the Everly Brothers and Elvis Presley. Though she wasn't alive at the same time as Buddy Holly, his songs have always resonated with her.
– *Mike Read*

I FORGOT TO REMEMBER TO FORGET

When Elvis Presley came to the Cotton Club in Lubbock in October 1955, high school student Buddy Holly was the warm-up act featured on the bill. Buddy sang his favourite Elvis song, 'I Forgot to Remember to Forget', which was a hit at the time, imitating Elvis's voice and moves. Coincidentally, three years later, Buddy returned to the Cotton Club, where he would play his final hometown show. Though by then his songs had attracted a lot of attention, fewer than 50 people came to see him on his return.

DUANE EDDY *'Holly Hop'*

DUANE EDDY WILL BE FOREVER REVERED as an original guitar hero, who put a deep and resounding twang into rock and roll. On a string of late 1950s and early 1960s instrumental hits, he used dramatic single note melodies on the lower strings of his guitar, pronounced tremolo and vibrato, and liberal doses of echo. He became the most successful instrumentalist in rock history, charting 15 Top 40 singles in a five-year span and selling more than 100 million records worldwide. Duane died in April 2024, a few days after his 86th birthday.

Appropriately, Duane's Buddy Holly guitar is named after an instrumental demo Buddy recorded, 'Holly Hop'. – *Mike Read*

On a Show of Stars Bus Tour in Late 1958, Buddy and I stood backstage and swapped guitars. He played my Gretsch and I strapped on his Stratocaster.

We stood there checking out the guitars and Buddy commented on how great the neck on my Gretsch was.

Suddenly he looked at me and burst out laughing. He said, "You look funny in my guitar!"

I realized he looked a bit odd with the Gretsch. We stood and laughed ourselves silly while exchanging our guitars back where they belonged. Wish he was here today.

Duane Eddy

DUANE EDDY I knew Buddy Holly's music before I ever met him. We used to play his songs in the country band I worked with in Arizona; the singer loved the songs, and I loved playing those great guitar solos. That was in 1957. His guitar licks were indelible, every guitar player that heard them never forgot them. I wish he were still with us; I'd love to hear the music he'd be creating today.

> ***'Buddy Holly was a rock and roll pioneer, with his distinctive singing style.'***

HOLLY HOP

'Holly Hop' was first released on Coral on 20 January 1969. It was written by Buddy's mother, Ella, and recorded in late 1956 at Venture Studio, Lubbock, TX. Lubbockite Jack Davis has stated that this song was being performed by Buddy and Bob on their KDAV Sunday Party *radio show two or three years earlier than this recording.*

Buddy –
You kept all the
rockers rolling!
Go Buddy
Go Buddy
Go Go Go …

THE EDGE *'Holly Hop'*

FROM ONE GUITAR HERO TO ANOTHER, the chain of music stretches ever onwards as pioneering guitar legend Duane Eddy's personal Buddy 'Holly Hop' guitar crosses the Atlantic Ocean to reach the hands of U2's the Edge, Ireland's greatest living guitar hero, and one of the most inventively brilliant guitarists in rock history.

David Evans has been known as the Edge since he was a teenager in Dublin in the 1970s. He is a founding member of U2, a world-conquering rock group who have improbably retained the exact same line-up since their debut performance in a school gymnasium in 1976. The Crickets pioneered the essential four-piece band line-up and U2 have taken it to a whole other level of lifelong loyalty, commitment and spiritual, political and musical quest. In 48 years together, singer Bono, guitarist the Edge, bassist Adam Clayton and drummer Larry Mullen Jr have sold over 150 million albums, conducted record-breaking and technologically innovative stadium tours, won 22 Grammy Awards, and spearheaded world-changing campaigns for human rights and social justice. And they have done it whilst making some of the most ambitious, progressive and inventive rock music ever heard.

You might wonder what the connection could be between an original 1950s rock and roll star and a guitarist born in 1961, two years after Buddy Holly's untimely death? Celebrated for his pioneering use of effects to distort, expand and utterly transform the sounds of his guitars, the Edge is renowned as one of the most futuristic exponents of his instrument, a kind of guitar scientist. Indeed, the Edge built his first Flying V electric guitar with his older brother Dick Evans in their garden shed, following instructions from an electronics magazine. As U2 progressed, the Edge's use of a Memory Man delay pedal transformed their sound, allowing him to play simple notes, riffs and harmonics that built up into an astonishing wall of echoes. By the time of their emergence as post-punk heroes with debut album *Boy* in 1980, U2 already sounded like the future, and they have never stopped expanding and exploring. Nevertheless, the Edge's playing is aligned with the same principles as Buddy Holly's: playing the instrument in service of songwriting.

Buddy was not a flashy player, and neither is the Edge. There is no shredding, none of the frantic excess of notes that became so prominent in rock guitar playing from the 1980s on. For the Edge, as for Buddy, it is always about the song, even though the guitar is central to framing those songs with beautifully clear lines and riffs that thread sections together. Simplicity, melody, imagination and rhythm: it is the guitar as a means to an end – and not just an end in itself.

Duane Eddy would have understood this. A contemporary of Buddy's, Eddy was really the first guitar hero of rock and roll. He was only 19 when he started scoring instrumental hits in 1957 showcasing his clean, resonant guitar sound and carefully articulated motifs. Eddy's distinctive style focused on touch, tone, melody and the spaces between notes. That his Buddy Holly guitar has been passed along by his widow Deed to another guitarist who understands the importance of space, restraint and atmosphere is a wonderful thing. When the Edge first removed the guitar from its case, he immediately launched into playing U2's classic 1988 single 'Desire'. 'There it is,' he noted. 'The Bo Diddley rhythm, just like "Not Fade Away".'

Back in the earliest days of U2, when the teenage band went under the name the Hype, attempting to learn their chops playing ropey cover versions, they would sometimes launch into the Stranglers, pub rock charger 'Go Buddy Go'. It's a rambunctious belter about a night on the tiles that traces an implicit line from rock and roll to punk. Talking to the Edge about the influence of Buddy Holly on his playing (and, let's face it, Buddy influenced every rock guitarist's playing), we realised there was something more that connects them: a revolutionary spirit of change for the better. U2 were not a punk band, but their political idealism was shaped by that musical moment in time. As an original rock and roller, Buddy played the most revolutionary music of his own times, working at the cutting edge by bringing black sounds and culture to white audiences to expand musical and social horizons. There is a continuity of that spirit in the dazzlingly modern sounds of U2. We're still all rocking at the Holly Hop. Go Buddy Go. – *Neil McCormick (Chief Music Critic for the* Daily Telegraph*)*

BUDDY
HOLLY

BLUE MONDAY
Buddy's version of 'Blue Monday' was first released on Coral on 20 January 1969. It was written by Fats Domino and Dave Bartholomew and recorded by Buddy in late 1956 at Venture Studio, Lubbock, TX. Fats Domino first charted with this song on 26 December 1956, reaching number nine.

'I love Buddy's music. I love Buddy. He should have been around a lot longer.'

CHRIS ISAAK Some years ago I travelled to Clovis, New Mexico to play a music festival. I met up with Vi Petty. She invited me over to her studio, a church, and I remember seeing cats walking all over and keyboards everywhere. Vi played on some of my favourite Buddy Holly tracks. 'Valley of Tears' has Vi on piano and Norman Petty on organ. (My favourite Buddy Holly songs were usually the oddball tracks, 'Love Is Strange', 'Blue Days, Black Nights'.) And as we walked through the church/studio piled high with instruments and boxes, I remember looking down at my feet and seeing a photograph of Buddy Holly lying on the floor. I was surprised because it was a photo of Buddy I had never seen, and I thought I'd seen them all. Vi was very nonchalant, 'Oh, that's Buddy. The cats knock things over.' Vi also had me moving equipment for the show we were playing. She had me put a little keyboard into a van for the show. I plinked one of the keys. It was the celeste off 'Everyday' by Buddy Holly. I remember saying, 'Shouldn't this be in a museum or Paul McCartney's living room?'

Buddy's music has always been an influence to me. I could figure it out and it worked in the three-piece band I started out in. I must have played 'Blue Days, Black Nights' a million times on stage. And when I saw the leather guitar cover Buddy made for himself, I started making cover designs for my guitar. I made guitar straps with my name and flowers (Buddy's work was better).

I read everything I could about Buddy. The more I knew about him the more I liked him. Two examples: I read that he and his band had a pocketful of money and decided to go in and buy motorcycles. I think they went into the Harley Davidson dealer who looked at these young pups and said, 'I got no time for this and you got no money.' So Buddy went across the street and he and the boys bought Triumphs, I believe. Then they all rode across the street for a grand 'screw you!' and waved at the salesmen who turned them down. I love that story. Maybe because more than once I've been told, 'You can't afford it!' The other story that I love about Buddy Holly is one from his school days. I think he was supposed to write a report for school, one of those 'my vacation' kind of essays. He is only a kid, maybe 12, 13. He writes of all the trouble he got in breaking his dad's headlight by accident. But I love the way he sums it all up at the end of his report. 'My life is a terrible wreck, but I'd be in worse shape without it.' I like those words so much, and so many times when I had two wheels in the ditch that quote would give me a smile.

CHRIS ISAAK IS A TRUE, AUTHENTIC TALENT, across music, the movies and TV. In front of the camera, his acting credits include pivotal roles in *That Thing You Do!* and *The Silence of the Lambs*. He even appears in an episode of *Friends*.

Behind the cameras he has created soundtrack music for multiple films, including *Eyes Wide Shut*, *True Romance* and *Wild at Heart*, from which he released his signature global hit 'Wicked Game' in 1989. But his true love is the music of the 1950s.

He has evolved a fabulous retro-rockabilly vocal style, which he took to Memphis to record the album *Beyond the Sun* at the legendary Sun Studios, the home of the rock and roll music that so much inspired Buddy Holly and his buddies in the Crickets.

'It all starts there,' said Chris, 'and those guys all went on and just kind of took off like rocket ships.' – *Bob Harris*

MY FAVORITE MUSIC, AND B.H. GAVE ME ONE OF MY FAVORITE QUOTES.

"MY LIFES A TERRIBLE WRECK
BUT ID BE IN WORSE SHAPE
WITHOUT IT"

YA GOTTA LOVE
THAT GUY!

Chris Isaak

TONY IOMMI *'Shake, Rattle and Roll'*

TONY IOMMI IS ONE OF THE MOST ICONIC OF ALL UK GUITARISTS. His work with Birmingham-based band Black Sabbath helped create a whole new genre of music – heavy metal. Their songs were infused with themes born from Iommi's love of horror movies, delivered with menacing, molten, guitar-driven ferocity and head-splitting levels of recorded volume. Since the release of their breakthrough album *Black Sabbath* in February 1970, they have sold more than 75 million records worldwide and have been a hugely influential force in the careers of many guitar-driven groups that have followed – a legacy that saw them inducted into the Rock and Roll Hall of Fame in 2006.

Nowadays rock fans associate Iommi with his Gibson SG, a dark-red guitar with a fearsomely heavy tone. In reality, he down-tuned his strings to ease the pain on his fingertips which were damaged in a work accident before the band was even formed. Just playing was initially really difficult but he invented an amazing DIY prosthetic and from his misfortune came a unique playing style that defined the Black Sabbath sound and propelled them to superstardom.

Tony first got interested in the guitar in the late 1950s. It's hard to imagine now, but in post-war ravaged Britain, there was an embargo on certain American goods coming into the country. The only readily available electric guitars in the UK were usually second-hand and battered – discovered in pawn shops or brought in by merchant seamen and the like, and even those were hugely expensive. But there was one instrument that the new 1950s rock and roll generation dreamed of owning more than any other – the Fender Stratocaster, the iconic instrument of the day. Imagine then the impact of seeing one of these beautiful guitars on British TV for the first time in the hands of Hank Marvin, the first true UK guitar hero. Tony Iommi cites him as a massive influence, as did pretty much every other young guitar player in the country at that time. – *Bob Harris*

SHAKE, RATTLE AND ROLL

Buddy Holly's version of 'Shake, Rattle and Roll' was first released on Coral on 18 May 1964. The song was written by Charles Calhoun and recorded by Buddy in late 1956 at either Venture Studio or at his home in Lubbock, TX.

There were previous versions of the song by 'Big' Joe Turner, Bill Haley and Elvis Presley, each with various lyric changes. It is clear that Buddy was familiar with the different recordings, because he borrowed lyrics from each of them for his own interpretation.

Buddy Holly
the icon .....
who influenced
a lot of the greats
of today.
We are all forever
grateful !!!

ROBERT PLANT *'Modern Don Juan'*

Will —

I finally woke up

about 1959 aged eleven

and BANG!

Never looked back

"looking for someone to love"

'He sang my teen life, just for me.'

ROBERT PLANT REMAINS ONE OF THE MOST COMPELLING front men that rock music has ever witnessed. Growing up in Halesowen, a small town in central England, he had a passion for singing as a young boy and, at ten years old, began impersonating Elvis and listening to rock and roll. By his mid-teens, Robert had discovered the blues. Alongside various odd jobs, including laying tarmac and working at Woolworths, he became involved in the Birmingham music scene, met drummer John Bonham, and joined a succession of bands.

In 1968, Robert was invited by guitarist Jimmy Page to become the lead singer of Led Zeppelin. Throughout the band's 12-year existence, he brought a mythical quality to the studio and a larger-than-life presence to the stage that had much to do with their many successes.

Robert first began contributing lyrics during the making of *Led Zeppelin II*, and from there he went on to write lyrics to most of the band's songs, including 'Immigrant Song', 'Stairway to Heaven' – which he wrote spontaneously while the music was being recorded – and 'Since I've Been Loving You'.

He has gone on to have a fascinating solo career, which has included collaborations with a range of different artists, notably Alison Krauss, a bluegrass-infused singer and fiddler, with whom Robert has been recording and performing since 2007. Their first record together, *Raising Sand*, won a Grammy for Album of the Year. He also teamed up with Jimmy Page and Jeff Beck in supergroup the Honeydrippers, and worked again with his former bandmate in Page and Plant from 1994 to 1998. Robert's more recent projects include Sensational Space Shifters and Saving Grace.

MODERN DON JUAN

Released in December 1956, 'Modern Don Juan' was the second (and last) of Buddy's Decca singles. Written by Don Guess and Jack Neal and backed with 'You Are My One Desire', the song was recorded at Owen Bradley's studio in Nashville, TN, in November 1956, during Buddy's final Decca session. Country session musician Farris Coursey, who had previously appeared on three number one hits on Billboard's *country singles chart, played drums on the recording. The song was later included on Buddy's 1958 album* That'll Be the Day.

ROBERT PLANT The sweet orchestral backdrop to 'It Doesn't Matter Anymore' was my introduction. A massive posthumous hit. Little did I know what he was really about, but was I going to find out – and quickly too. The older kids down the street had it all down, and BANG! That voice gliding and spiralling – one minute he was a tough guy, the next minute forlorn and broken hearted, hung out to dry. That sweet baby voice gets ominous and rock and roll bad.

Rockabilly, rock and roll, ballad and schmooze – all of his stories and characters over and gone in a little over two minutes. Genius …

BRUCE SPRINGSTEEN *'Because I Love You'*

BECAUSE I LOVE YOU

'Because I Love You' came out in 1963 as a flipside to 'Wishing' on Coral Records. Buddy thought up this heartfelt song, tinged with Texan blues, in his garage in Lubbock with the Crickets, as the band honed their sound. He recorded it in 1956 at Norman Petty's studio in Clovis, NM, with Sonny Curtis, Don Guess and Jerry Allison.

Buddy!
the pure
stuff...
beautiful writer
beautiful singer
just the best
Bruce

'I play Buddy Holly every night before I go on. It keeps me honest.'

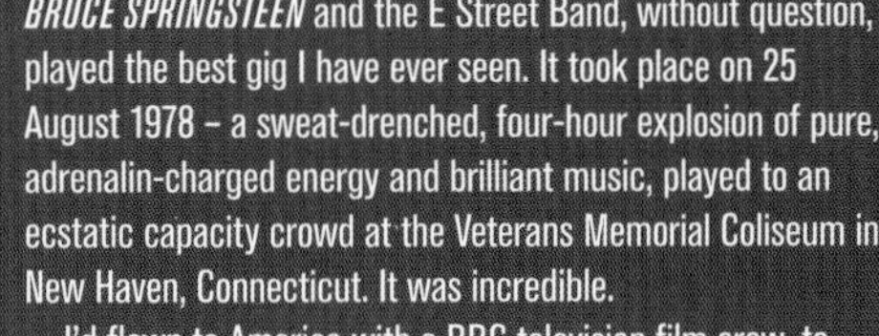

BRUCE SPRINGSTEEN and the E Street Band, without question, played the best gig I have ever seen. It took place on 25 August 1978 – a sweat-drenched, four-hour explosion of pure, adrenalin-charged energy and brilliant music, played to an ecstatic capacity crowd at the Veterans Memorial Coliseum in New Haven, Connecticut. It was incredible.

I'd flown to America with a BBC television film crew, to interview Bruce and to capture the excitement of this once-in-a-lifetime moment for *The Old Grey Whistle Test*, the legendary TV music show I was presenting at the time.

It felt like Bruce was unleashed from the management restrictions that had prevented him from playing live for far too long and, as an intro to his own 'She's the One', he and the E Street Band tore into an inspired version of Buddy Holly's 'Not Fade Away', originally released as the B-side to 'Oh Boy!' back in 1957. Their version was authentic and fantastic, and they included rock and roll songs in the set for the rest of that huge, sweeping Darkness on the Edge of Town tour, still widely regarded as Bruce's best tour ever.

The set was peppered with a selection of rock and roll classics – 'Summertime Blues', 'Around and Around', 'Lucille', 'Good Rockin' Tonight' and other great Bruce favourites.

Buddy Holly was across American culture in the summer of 1978. The hit movie *The Buddy Holly Story* opened in May, and Bruce and his little sister Pam caught it at a screening in Los Angeles on 2 July. It made a big impression, and three days later, on stage at the Los Angeles Forum, he delivered his review: 'It's funny,' he said, 'because I could never really picture Buddy Holly moving. To me, he was always just that guy with the bow tie on the album cover. I liked the picture because it made him a lot more real for me.'

Then, the following night, if you'd been passing the Sundance Saloon in Calabasas and fancied a country-rock night out, you would have caught Oklahoma's Old Dog Band doing Chuck Berry's 'Carol', with two very special guests joining them on stage – Bruce and actor Gary Busey, who played the part of Buddy Holly in that self-same film.

The very next night Springsteen played 'Rave On' for the first time on the tour. 'Not Fade Away' popped up two days later and 'Oh Boy!' was a regular in the set by the end of the month.

And then, in August, came the double-whammy. Bruce played two shows in Philadelphia on the 18 and 19, and who should turn up as a special guest on stage for both of those iconic gigs? Gary Busey, who joined in on the Gary U.S. Bonds classic 'Quarter to Three' on the first night and performed fabulous versions of 'Rave On' on both nights.

It was a moment that was destined to happen, and for a very good reason: 1950s rock and roll was still a very big thing in 1978 and Bruce had evolved an important pre-stage ritual that included Buddy's music. – *Bob Harris*

JOE LOUIS WALKER *'Bo Diddley'*

Buddy Holly
= Rock + Roll
Soul
Ballads + Blues
which comes to
American music -
Buddy left us a high bar
which we'll never be able
to scale or surpass,
but we try Buddy,
Thanks Buddy,
Joe Louis Walker

'If you say the name Buddy Holly, you're saying rock and roll!'

JOE LOUIS WALKER Buddy Holly has an influence on all electric guitar players who came after him, including me. A rite of passage when any young guitar player wants to 'Rock Out' is to play any Buddy Holly song. Like Chuck Berry, if you play rock and roll, there are signature Buddy Holly guitar licks that are part of the electric guitar vocabulary.

KNOWN AS JLW, CALIFORNIAN BLUES guitarist, singer, songwriter and producer Joe Louis Walker's early influences include T-Bone Walker, B.B. King, Amos Milburn and Meade Lux Lewis. He began playing guitar at the age of eight and had built quite a reputation by the time he was 16. He played with such artists as John Lee Hooker, Buddy Miles, Otis Rush, Willie Dixon, Steve Miller, Muddy Waters, Jimi Hendrix and many more. After the death of his close friend Mike Bloomfield in 1981, JLW forsook the world of blues to enrol at university. However, he returned to his blues roots after graduating, and in 1988 and 1991 won Contemporary Blues Male Artist of the Year Awards. Steve Cropper produced three of his albums during the late 1990s, including Grammy-winning *Deep in the Blues*. His 2015 album, *Everybody Wants a Piece*, was also nominated for a Grammy. JLW was inducted into the Blues Hall of Fame in 2013. – *Mike Read*

BO DIDDLEY
'Bo Diddley' was written by Ellas McDaniel (aka Bo Diddley), who had a number four hit with the song in 1955. Buddy Holly's version was recorded in late 1956 at Venture Studio, Lubbock, TX, and first released on Coral in January 1963.

FEW PEOPLE ARE MORE DESERVING OF A BUDDY HOLLY GUITAR THAN VINCE GILL. He is the kindest of men – a country music superstar whose magnificent career has earned him the respect of musicians and fans from all genres and all generations.

His career began as lead singer with the glorious country rock band Pure Prairie League in the 1970s. He then joined Rodney Crowell's backing group for a while before launching his own phenomenal solo career in 1984, scoring no fewer than 20 top five singles in the American charts, five of which reached number one. He has won multiple Grammy Awards and 18 major Country Music Association Awards and in 2007 was inducted into the Country Music Hall of Fame, a supreme acknowledgement of his huge contribution to the country music community. As I write, he is the president of the Country Music Hall of Fame.

For 12 years, Vince was also the gently respectful host of the CMA Music Awards, bringing warmth, wit and charm to country music's biggest night. I was there on behalf of the BBC Radio 2 *Country Show* for the first time in 1999 and I vividly remember being on the red carpet at the end of the evening, watching in awe as the rhinestone stars swished out of the Grand Ole Opry and into the fleet of limousines waiting to take them away. It was a moment to see and be seen . . . except for the compere of the show.

As I looked on, Vince appeared from the stage door. Changed out of his onstage finery into a plaid shirt, a pair of blue jeans and boots, he had a smile on his face and a guitar across his shoulders as he wandered unrecognised across the parking lot. He then climbed into his pick-up truck, switched on the lights and drove unnoticed into the night. The biggest star of the show was also the most humble. The man is an absolute legend!

He has always talked about how much he loves Buddy's music and, at various times, 'Maybe Baby', 'Peggy Sue' and 'Rave On' have all made it onto the Vince Gill set list.

He is successful and kind in equal measure, but I believe that it is his guitar playing that most eloquently demonstrates his unique super-power. Vince's wonderful, natural style has levels of interpretive brilliance and emotional expression that literally make him one of the best guitar players on the planet.

Vince has become a full-time touring member of the Eagles since 2017, and now he and his wife Amy are the proud owners of Buddy Holly guitars (called 'Because I Love You' and 'Door to My Heart'), presented to them by The Buddy Holly Educational Foundation. These are genuinely lovely things and no one deserves them more. – *Bob Harris*

WHAT A GIFT BUDDY WAS FOR ALL OF US TO BE INSPIRED BY

Vince Gill

VINCE GILL *'Because I Love You'*

BECAUSE I LOVE YOU
First released on the Coral compilation Reminiscing *in February 1963, 'Because I Love You' was written by Buddy Holly and recorded with Sonny Curtis, Don Guess and Jerry Allison in 1956 at Norman Petty's studio in Clovis, NM.*

Buddy,

Without you I probably couldn't play (smile)

Buddy Guy

IT'S NOT MY FAULT

Buddy recorded this Ben Hall and Weldon Myrick song in early 1956 at Norman Petty's studio in Clovis, NM, but his version was not released until it was included on the Coral compilation Reminiscing, *which came out on 18 February 1963.*

BUDDY GUY AND BUDDY HOLLY BOTH PLAYED FENDER STRATOCASTER GUITARS. They were both born in 1936, 39 days and one very long day's journey – from Lettsworth, Louisiana to Lubbock, Texas – apart.

They were also musically closer together than one might initially imagine. In the mid-1950s, Buddy Holly was influenced by, and indeed recorded songs by, some of the very same artists that Buddy Guy would have been listening to – people like Chuck Berry, the Clovers and Bo Diddley. Buddy and the Crickets clocked up four Top 20 rhythm and blues hits in 1957 and 1958, including 'That'll Be the Day' and 'Peggy Sue', which both reached number two (in the case of 'Peggy Sue', that was one place higher than its position in the pop chart). The first of those hits earned them a week-long gig at the famous Apollo Theater in Harlem in August 1957, where an initially sceptical audience was won over by their performance of 'Bo Diddley'.

It's unlikely that all of this could have escaped the attention of Buddy Guy, who has always given credit where it's due; he is quite a modest person, in spite of his illustrious position in the pantheon of blues greats of the last six or seven decades. It is fair to say that he also takes inspiration from outside the usual list of blues elders – from jazz, rock, soul and even, more recently, electronica. Having absorbed into his music such a broad range of influences may well have helped put him in the vanguard of younger bluesmen who created the new 'West Side' version of Chicago blues in the late 1950s.

I had the honour and pleasure of interviewing Buddy Guy more than once on my various radio shows. On one of those occasions he talked to me in his private apartment at his blues club in Chicago; he greatly enjoyed being the proprietor of a place where blues was played week in, week out.

Whenever I think of Buddy Guy now, I'm seeing him with the polka dot guitar which has become a sort of trademark. I've witnessed his extraordinary, and widely influential, intensity, both vocally and instrumentally, in many different locations and been bowled over by it – and also by his ability to relax totally and enjoy an intimate relationship with an audience. Enthralling music and supreme showmanship. I find it irresistible.
– Paul Jones

THE HANK THOMPSON TOUR
Buddy pictured backstage
Fort Homer W. Hesterly Armoury,
Tampa, FL
13 January 1957

CHAPTER THREE

1957

FEB. 22
CLOVER CLUB
AMARILLO, TEXAS

JOHN MACDONALD
711 SOUTH 2nd.
ARTESIA, NEW MEXICO

HI POCKETS DUNCAN (W.J.)
" " DRIVE IN
AMARILLO, TEXAS
DRAKE 2-0756

In the spring of 1955 Buddy's manager from KDAV, Hi-Pockets Duncan, took over a Western swing hotspot just outside Amarillo, TX called the Clover Club. Buddy was a regular visitor at the club when he wasn't making much money, as Hi-Pockets would feed him and give him advice. In return, Buddy would perform at the club. On 22 February 1957, Buddy and Jerry Allison travelled to Amarillo and performed at the Clover Club.

Bamford Sets C&W Pkg. on 15-Day Swing

CINCINNATI—A. V. Bamford, c.&w. promoter, with headquarters in North Hollywood, Calif., has inked Hank Thompson and His Brazos Valley Boys to head up a country and western package on a 15-day tour opening January 9 at Little Rock, Ark.

Featured with the Thompson combo on the tour will be Wanda Jackson, Mitchell Torok, Hank Locklin, Cowboy Copas, George Jones and Justin Tubb.

Following Little Rock, route is as follows: New Orleans, January 10; Birmingham, 11; Jacksonville, Fla., 12; Tampa, 13; Savannah, Ga., 15; Charleston, S. C., 16; Ocala, Fla., 17; Miami 18; Macon, Ga., 19; Atlanta, 20; Montgomery, Ala., 21; Pensacola, Fla., 22, and Memphis 23.

DESMOND CHILD For any songwriter, it's always a struggle to be recognised. As time goes on, new generations discover Buddy Holly and become fans, and it takes that rebirth from generation to generation to make up a long-lasting legacy. That's what Buddy Holly has.

GARRY TALLENT When the big bang of rock and roll happened, Buddy was ready. He had the Decca Records machine behind him for a brief time, which he had a lack of control over, but when he went to Clovis, Norman Petty let him work on his own time and use his instincts. It wasn't until he arrived in Clovis that Buddy Holly and the Crickets worked as a band. They were able to hone their sound and figure out what worked best for them, not the producer.

THE HANK THOMPSON TOUR
Fort Homer W. Hesterly Armoury
Tampa, FL
13 January 1957

Top: Don Guess and Buddy Holly on stage

Left: Jerry Allison, Buddy and Don Guess

Below and opposite, bottom: Buddy with fans

Fort Homer W. Hesterly Armoury, Tampa, FL 13 January 1957

BUDDY HOLLY
AND THE
CRICKETS

BUDDY HOLLY
AND THE
CRICKETS

THAT'LL BE
THE DAY

CHORUS

THAT'LL BE THE DAY M-MM
" " " " " " "
" " " " " " "
M-MM
WHEN I DIE

HUM ON VERSES

CHORUS
VERSE
CHORUS

GUITAR

CHORUS
VERSE
CHORUS

HUM ON ENDING

I'M LOOKIN

HUM ON VERSES

CHORUS

I'M A LOOKIN - 1
" " - 2
" " - 3
" " - 4
" " - 5
" " - 6
AHHH -

VERSE - 1
CHORUS

VERSE - 2
CHORUS

GUITAR

VERSE - 3
CHORUS

GUITAR VERSE - 4
CHORUS

DRUNK MAN
STREET CAR
FOOT SLIP AND
THERE YOU ARE

Top right, above and opposite: Rehearsing 'That'll Be the Day' in June Clark's living room, Lubbock, TX, 23 February 1957. This was to test the backing vocals of Gary and Ramona Tollett and June Clark. The 'Buddy Holly and the Crickets' sign on the drum kit was possibly made by Jerry Allison's brother, James Allison.

PAGES FROM THE BUDDY HOLLY NOTEBOOK
Buddy has handwritten the song structure of 'That'll Be the Day' and 'I'm Lookin' for Someone to Love', as well as noting down one of his mother's favourite phrases, which found its way into 'I'm Lookin''. Buddy wrote this song as he was driving with his brother Larry, Niki Sullivan, Larry Welborn and Jerry Allison to Norman Petty's studio in Clovis, NM, to record 'That'll Be the Day' on 25 February 1957.

18 Norman Petty's studios, Clovis, New Mexico

SONNY WEST Norman Petty's studio is at 1313 West Seventh Street in Clovis, New Mexico, about 90 miles northwest of Lubbock. It was one of the best studios in the country because Norman knew how to record; he'd worked at it for a long time.

JERRY 'J.I.' ALLISON Norman was known for having a good studio. He grew up in Clovis and his dad owned a garage, which remained in the front part, and the upstairs was turned into an echo chamber. Norman lived there and the studio was next door. It's a railroad town in the middle of the desert. We hung out there a lot because the studio had an apartment in the back and some roll-out beds, so we'd sleep until we were ready to record again.

LARRY HOLLEY When I first went to Clovis with Buddy, Jerry Allison and Niki Sullivan, there were several other people along to help out. Buddy was going to cut two songs at Norman Petty's studio: 'That'll Be the Day' and 'I'm Lookin' for Someone to Love'. I thought I could help as a critic, but not so with Buddy. He had all his stuff together and knew how he wanted to do it. It didn't take this big brother long to know that he had already passed me long ago.

LARRY WELBORN 'That'll Be the Day' wasn't any good when they recorded it in Nashville, so Buddy went over to Clovis and tried it there. He called and asked if I wanted to play bass on the record. I thought it took about 12 hours to cut the record, but Jerry Allison said it took 30 minutes. I don't know which one of us is right, but I remember playing for a long time, because back then you couldn't fix anything. You had to play it right.

KEVIN MONTGOMERY Norman was monumentally important and ahead of his time. He put in the effort to study how to make the studio get the sounds he wanted out of it and the sounds Buddy could get out of it. He also gave those guys some place to come and record in New Mexico and use a studio that was state of the art at that time.

THAT'LL BE THE DAY
A Buddy Holly and the as-yet-unnamed Crickets recording session took place at Norman Petty's studio in Clovis, NM on 25 February 1957. This session produced the hit version of 'That'll Be the Day' and 'I'm Lookin' for Someone to Love'. Each band member received an acetate of the two songs, as did Norman Petty. Jerry Allison remembered that the session cost $60, which also included the four acetates given to the band. Buddy picked up his acetate of 'Brown Eyed Handsome Man' and 'Bo Diddley', which had been recorded at an earlier date.

KEVIN MONTGOMERY The gear Norman had developed in the studio was ground-breaking. He built an echo chamber next door with tiles; even the way they recorded the drums in different places was before its time. Clovis is quite hard to get to, and they didn't have Amazon to come in and drop off the equipment the next day. You had to seek out the equipment Norman had, and really want it.

ALBERT LEE Norman Petty didn't write the songs, but he gave them a unique sound through the recordings. Vi Petty, his wife, added touches to the music. It was a combination of that studio, the Pettys, the Crickets and the great songs that they put together. It wasn't just Buddy, they were all contributing to the songs.

JERRY 'J.I.' ALLISON Norman Petty and Vi were nice people. When we were recording, Vi would bring out some cookies or sandwiches and make tea for us, so on top of being very talented at the piano, she was also a nice person. If it wasn't for that studio, I'd probably be selling shoes.

GARRY TALLENT The music from Norman's studio didn't sound manufactured. Their recording process felt very organic; they would go in, try songs and remake them, and they succeeded. The sound of those records still stands up musically today.

JERRY 'J.I.' ALLISON There wasn't anybody telling us what to do, because we were paying for the time. We were doing exactly what we wanted to, with some friends backing us up. It was total freedom.

PETER ASHER Buddy was fascinated by the making of records and very innovative in the studio. The records, especially the self-produced ones, feature quite abnormal drum parts. They're so cool. A typical producer's instinct would have been to put regular old rock and roll drums on any of those songs, but he persisted in an original aesthetic for his whole career.

'OK ... let's do it!'

(This was a common phrase from Buddy before a session. From early on Buddy had an authority and maturity about him in the recording studio.)

Above: A selection of recent images taken at Norman Petty Studios in Clovis, NM

Left: A limited edition reproduction of Buddy's J-45 acoustic, signed by Maria Elena Holly and Peggy Sue Gerron, and two Altec 601 speakers used by Norman Petty in the control room of his studio

JERRY 'J.I.' ALLISON At the time, Joe B. Mauldin was playing in a group in Lubbock called the Four Teens. I knew him from school, when he and I would smoke in the car during our study hall period. We hired him for a three-hour dance show in Clovis, and on the way back to Lubbock, we asked him if he wanted to be in the Crickets. There wasn't a nicer guy in the world, which means so much when you're travelling together. He told us he'd join, if it didn't interfere with his job, school, or the Four Teens – he ended up quitting his job, school and the group.

BOB HARRIS Buddy wasn't well treated by the industry. There are some fascinating recordings that were made at the time of him on the telephone to a guy at Decca, just trying to find out what was happening with his next recording, and he's just bashing his head against a brick wall. Looking back now, you wonder how that happens, and how they couldn't see his value.

Paul Cohen

April 25, 1957

Dear Buddy---

Mr. Cohen asked me to write you for the lyrics to your song, "That'll Be the Day", which we need as quickly as possible for copywriting purposes.

Please send same directly to our office at 130 West 57th St.

Thanks much.
Sincerely,
Rusite Wireston
Copar Music Inc.

Buddy Holly
RT. #5
Lubbock, Texas

Buddy: Well, uhh, you remember those songs that we cut back in the summertime that never was released?
Cohen: Yeah.
Buddy: I wondered if I could get you to send me a release on them so we might try do something with them.
Cohen: Oh no, you can't have those, you can't release them for five years.
Buddy: They wouldn't do that no way whatsoever, would they? I mean, Decca didn't seem to be doing too much for me and I thought I might try somewhere else.
Cohen: No, anything that you made for Decca, even if they never released it for five years, you can't make it, any of those songs.
Buddy: Uhh huh. Well, it's, it makes me feel sorta bad. I just thought maybe seeing they weren't doing anything with them that –
Cohen: Don't feel bad about it.
Buddy: I can't hardly keep from it, Paul. It seems sorta a heck of a way to do a guy.
Cohen: You haven't made any of these yet, have you? I mean cut 'em for anybody?
Buddy: No, sir.
Cohen: Well, before you do, let me know. Maybe we can work out something.
Buddy: We was wanting to cut a master like you said on our own, pay for it ourselves and see if we could sell it to somebody.
Cohen: Let me hear it first …

(28 February 1957, a recorded phone call between Buddy Holly and Paul Cohen of Decca Records in which Buddy discovers that his previous contract with Decca prevents him from recording and releasing 'That'll Be the Day' and other songs he recorded with Decca on any other label.)

PAUL COHEN
50 WEST 57TH ST.
NEW YORK, 19, NEW YORK
COLUMBUS 5-2300
NIGHT 5-2364

NORMAN PETTY STUDIO

CLOVIS, NEW MEXICO
7565 RES. 6931
PRIVATE PHONE
UPSTAIRS
5944

Handwritten letter to Buddy from publishers Copar Music Inc. of New York City, 25 April 1957

A page from the Buddy Holly Notebook in Buddy's handwriting with contact details for Paul Cohen at Decca Records and for the Norman Petty Studio

WORDS OF LOVE
Buddy recorded 'Words of Love' on 8 April 1957, harmonising with himself by combining tape recordings of each part. The song was not a notable hit, although it is regarded as one of his most important recordings and is available in most standard Buddy Holly collections.

'Words of Love' contract (opposite, top left), original acetate from 'Mailman Bring Me No More Blues' and 'Words of Love' recording session at Norman Petty's studio (opposite, top right) and first pressing (opposite, bottom left)

AGREEMENT made this 12th day of April 19 57 between NOR VA JAK MUSIC CO. , hereinafter designated as PUBLISHER and

BUDDY HOLLY .... of ....

.... of ....

.... of ....

jointly and/or severally designated as WRITER.

WITNESSETH:

(1) The Writer hereby sells, assigns, transfers and delivers to the Publisher, its successors and assigns, all of his rights, title and interest in and to a certain heretofore unpublished original work, as annexed hereto, written and/or composed by the Writer, now entitled,

WORDS OF LOVE

including the title, words and/or music thereof, as well as the entire exclusive right to publicly perform and televise, together with the right to secure copyrights and renewals therein throughout the world, as proprietor in its own name, or otherwise, and to have and to hold the said work, copyrights and renewals thereof and all rights of whatsoever nature thereunder existing.

(2) The Writer hereby warrants that the said work is his sole, exclusive and original work, that he has full right and power to make the within agreement, and that there exists no adverse claim to or in the said work, which is free from all liens and encumbrances whatsoever.

(3) In consideration of this Agreement, the Publisher agrees to pay the Writer, jointly, only the following royalties:

(a) ..3..¢ per copy, in respect of regular piano copies and/or orchestrations, sold in the United States and for which the Publisher received payment.

(b) ..50.% of the net amount received by the Publisher, in respect of regular piano copies and/or orchestrations sold and paid for in any foreign country.

(c) ..50.% of the net amount received by the Publisher, in respect of any licenses issued authorizing the manufacture of parts of instruments serving to mechanically reproduce said work, electrical transcriptions, or to use said work in synchronization with sound motion pictures.

(d) ..50.% of the net amount of performing fees received by the Publisher in the United States, only provided said fees include both Writer and Publisher shares and are payable on a fixed and determinable basis.

(4) The Publisher agrees to render to the Writer on or about February 15th, and August 15th, of each year, so long as it shall continue publishing or licensing said work, covering the six months ending December 31st, and June 30th, of each year respectively, royalty statements accompanied by remittance of the amount due.

(5) All sums hereunder payable jointly to the Writer shall be divided and paid in the following manner:

.100.% to...BUDDY HOLLY..................of ....

......% to..................................of ....

......% to..................................of ....

(6) The Publisher shall have the right to alter, change, edit or translate the work or any part thereof, in any way it may be necessary. In the event it be necessary for the Publisher to cause lyrics to be written in other languages for and as part of the work, the publisher shall in such event have the right to deduct from the heretofore agreed royalties payable to the Writer, the cost or obligation thereof, but in no event more than a sum equal to one-half.

(7) The Writer hereby grants and conveys an irrevocable power of attorney authorizing and empowering the Publisher, its nominees, successors and assigns, to administer any and all rights in and to the said work, and collect and receive any and all the fees therefrom; also to file application and renew the copyrights in the name of the Writer, and upon such renewals, to execute proper and formal assignments thereof so as to secure to the Publisher, its successors and assigns, the renewal terms of, in and to said copyrights and/or works.

(8) The Writer hereby agrees to indemnify and save harmless the Publisher against any loss, expense or damage by reason of any adverse claims made by others with respect to the work, and agrees that all expenses incurred in defense of any such claims, including counsel fees, as well as any and all sums paid by the Publisher, pursuant to a judgment, arbitration or any settlement or adjustment which may be made in the discretion of the Publisher, or otherwise, shall at all times be borne by the Writer, and may be deducted by the Publisher from any money accruing to the Writer under this agreement or otherwise.

(9) The Writer agrees that he will not assign this Agreement nor any sums that may become due hereunder, without the written consent of the Publisher first endorsed hereon.

(10) Except as otherwise herein provided, this Agreement is binding upon the parties hereto and their respective successors in interest.

WITNESS: .... Writer

NOR VA JAK MUSIC CO.

Buddy Holley .... ~~Writer~~

L. O. Holley .... ~~Writer~~
PARENT

WITNESS: NOR VA JAK MUSIC CO.

By ....

EDNA GUNDERSEN He recorded the vocal and doubled up the tape for 'Words of Love' so it thickened the vocal, a studio technique that made the sound richer. It made the recording match the sound he had in his head; it was like what he did with reverb and echo in the studio. This was primitive equipment too, so he was very smart in making the most out of the simplest of recording tools.

DESMOND CHILD As a producer I come from the Phil Spector school of the Wall of Sound, so my records sound enormous. I find it difficult to make a record that has few elements but feels complete. That's what Buddy Holly was an expert in; every part was perfect. He mastered the art of reduction to the simplest elements and that's one of the things that makes his music so extraordinary.

VILLAGE THEATER, LUBBOCK
On 11 May 1957, from 12 AM until 2 AM, Buddy Holly and the Crickets performed at the Village Theater in Lubbock along with the Four Teens, Tinker Carlen and the Cats, and Pat and Shirley Richardson. Although Buddy Holly and the Crickets appeared at the top of the bill, the Four Teens were listed in the largest print. The ad stated 'Come and see the biggest "rock and roll" stage programme presented by Lubbock's rock and rollers. Man! What a Show!' All seats were $1 for the two-hour show and went on sale at 11.30 PM after the scheduled motion picture had ended. With the money from the gig, the next morning Buddy went to Furr's Auto Exchange and purchased a red 1955 Cadillac. Buddy is shown playing with Tinker Carlen with his jacket off (this page) and with the Crickets with his jacket on (opposite).

STUFF TO DO
Change Oil
Dentist
Talk To June
WRITE ARR.
~~Contact Larry~~
~~Get #69 Check Cashed~~
~~(SEE KEITH)~~
— I GIVE PLUM UP —

See Niki About Car
IN CASE

DON McLEAN Buddy wrote around 60 songs in a short time, and every one is a hit. 'That'll Be the Day', 'Peggy Sue' and 'Rave On' are great records, and then there are the beautiful string arrangements in his last sessions that followed. 'It Doesn't Matter Anymore', 'Moon Dreams' and 'True Love Ways' take your breath away. This was a very talented man who had tremendous breadth, who set the standard for The Beatles in his diversity of songs and styles. He had a tremendous influence on me.

EVELYN THEATRE, DUMAS *Buddy Holly and the Crickets performed at the Evelyn Theatre, in Dumas, TX with the Rhythm Orchids. Gary Tollett (pictured left) also performed with Buddy Holly and the Crickets backing him up. Jerry Allison wrote in his notebook that he 'did swell'. 14 June 1957*

Opposite, top left to bottom left: 'I'm Gonna Love You Too' / 'Listen to Me' 45 rpm single signed by Maria Elena Holly and 'It Doesn't Matter Anymore' / 'Raining in My Heart' 45 rpm single, signed by Buddy, Ritchie Valens and Dion DiMucci

Opposite, top right: A promotional image of Buddy and the Crickets taken at Norman Petty Studios

JERRY 'J.I.' ALLISON Sonny West had recorded a demo called 'Oh Boy!' which Glen D. Hardin played on. We got it from Norman, learned it, and recorded it. Sonny's version was good, a little faster than ours, but I was sure glad we found it.

SONNY WEST The first of the songs I wrote after my initial session at Norman's studio was 'Oh Boy!' and I came to the studio soon after to record it. I brought one or two musicians with me, and we did a demo recording called 'All My Love'. I wasn't thinking about a title, I just came up with a song that happened to be very catchy – like a nursery rhyme. Instead of rock and rolling, there were cute lyrics about being in love. Around the same time, Buddy had recorded 'That'll Be the Day' in Clovis, and it started getting a lot of attention. Norman could see that it was going to be a big song.

Buddy was coming in and out of the studio to record, and Norman played the demo I had made of 'Oh Boy!' and he liked it. Norman told me they were looking for a follow-up record to 'That'll Be the Day'. When I heard his version, I loved it. It sounded so much better than mine, for a lot of reasons, but he had an excitement in his voice that I didn't have. It was a big deal for me.

CLIFF RICHARD When I heard 'Oh Boy!' it was instant. After listening to it for the first time, we could almost play and sing it, which is so unique. It's a great song to sing on stage; people in the audience know it and will sing it with you. All of them.

OH BOY – the song
by Sonny West
for Roger Daltrey
On behalf of The Buddy Holly Educational Foundation

the summer of 1956 was an exciting time for me. At age 18 while living near Lubbock, in West Texas, I had put together a 4-piece band for the purpose of a record release. We had two rockabilly songs I had written which we took to Norman Petty studio in Clovis, New Mexico in July 1956. We recorded those songs and managed to get a record release on Petty's record label, Nor-Va-Jak. I had high expectations but no realistic plans. High hopes soon turned to desperation and despair. I began looking for new ideas, searching music stores and libraries as well as experimenting on new tunes and melodies. In February 1957 as West Texas was entering it's cold, windy and dreary time of year ... it happened... "the moment" arrived. I don't know from whence it came. It was as if the gods had put it there. Oh Boy, there it was, a little ditty that rolled off the tongue, brought smiles to the face and was easy on the ears. Simplistic. It was back to the Petty Studio for me to make a demo and have Norman to make me a few acetate records to send off. Just by chance Buddy Holly, a friend and contemporary had also begun to frequent the Petty Studio. When Holly heard Oh Boy he wanted to record it. That was the best thing that could have happened for all concerned. A few months and Oh Boy was a worldwide hit thanks to Buddy Holly and the Crickets. This song now defines a part of our history and has a place in our culture.

Sixty years on ... Oh Boy
Sonny West February 2017

BOB HARRIS A lot of the acts that were coming through at that time were solo artists, and if you did get groups they were probably instrumental. You didn't have a lot of bands going out on tour and making music. The Crickets were so clearly a group. Buddy may have been the lead singer, but there was a democracy about them and their sound that predated the stuff that came out of Britain by six years. They acted as a template for The Beatles and the Rolling Stones – who covered 'Not Fade Away' so early on in their career. Clearly, that idea that Buddy Holly was in a band was a great thing.

ALBERT LEE 'Not Fade Away' has such a unique sound. We didn't understand it at the time, but now we have a far greater knowledge of the recording process, and we can picture exactly what went on during the recording of that song.

JERRY 'J.I.' ALLISON There was a group in Louisiana called the Spiders and they had a record called 'Witchcraft' that we really liked, so we thought about naming ourselves after an insect too. We looked up various insects and we must have passed over 'Beetles', because we got to C and it said 'Crickets'. That year in Lubbock there was a ton of them, swarms of crickets and locusts throughout Texas.

AGREEMENT made this 19th day of JULY 1957 between NOR VA JAK MUSIC, INC., hereinafter designated as PUBLISHER and

JOE MAULDIN of

NIKI SULLIVAN of

NORMAN PETTY of

jointly and/or severally designated as WRITER.

WITNESSETH:

(1) The Writer hereby sells, assigns, transfers and delivers to the Publisher, its successors and assigns, all of his rights, title and interest in and to a certain heretofore unpublished original work, as annexed hereto, written and/or composed by the Writer, now entitled,

I'M GONNA LOVE YOU TOO

including the title, words and/or music thereof, as well as the entire exclusive right to publicly perform and televise, together with the right to secure copyrights and renewals therein throughout the world, as proprietor in its own name, or otherwise, and to have and to hold the said work, copyrights and renewals thereof and all rights of whatsoever nature thereunder existing.

(2) The Writer hereby warrants that the said work is his sole, exclusive and original work, that he has full right and power to make the within agreement, and that there exists no adverse claim to or in the said work, which is free from all liens and encumbrances whatsoever.

(3) In consideration of this Agreement, the Publisher agrees to pay the Writer, jointly, only the following royalties:

(a) 4 ¢ per copy, in respect of regular piano copies and/or orchestrations, sold in the United States and for which the Publisher received payment.

(b) 50 % of the net amount received by the Publisher, in respect of regular piano copies and/or orchestrations sold and paid for in any foreign country.

(c) 50 % of the net amount received by the Publisher, in respect of any licenses issued authorizing the manufacture of parts of instruments serving to mechanically reproduce said work, electrical transcriptions, or to use said work in synchronization with sound motion pictures.

(d) 50 % of the net amount of performing fees received by the Publisher in the United States, only provided said fees include both Writer and Publisher shares and are payable on a fixed and determinable basis.

(4) The Publisher agrees to render to the Writer on or about February 15th, and August 15th, of each year, so long as it shall continue publishing or licensing said work, covering the six months ending December 31st, and June 30th, of each year respectively, royalty statements accompanied by remittance of the amount due.

(5) All sums hereunder payable jointly to the Writer shall be divided and paid in the following manner:

33 1/3 % to JOE MAULDIN of

33 1/3 % to NIKI SULLIVAN of

33 1/3 % to NORMAN PETTY of

(6) The Publisher shall have the right to alter, change, edit or translate the work or any part thereof, in any way it may be necessary. In the event it be necessary for the Publisher to cause lyrics to be written in other languages for and as part of the work, the publisher shall in such event have the right to deduct from the heretofore agreed royalties payable to the Writer, the cost or obligation thereof, but in no event more than a sum equal to one-half.

(7) The Writer hereby grants and conveys an irrevocable power of attorney authorizing and empowering the Publisher, its nominees, successors and assigns, to administer any and all rights in and to the said work, and collect and receive any and all the fees therefrom; also to file application and renew the copyrights in the name of the Writer, and upon such renewals, to execute proper and formal assignments thereof so as to secure to the Publisher, its successors and assigns, the renewal terms of, in and to said copyrights and/or works.

(8) The Writer hereby agrees to indemnify and save harmless the Publisher against any loss, expense or damage by reason of any adverse claims made by others with respect to the work, and agrees that all expenses incurred in defense of any such claims, including counsel fees, as well as any and all sums paid by the Publisher, pursuant to a judgment, arbitration or any settlement or adjustment which may be made in the discretion of the Publisher, or otherwise, shall at all times be borne by the Writer, and may be deducted by the Publisher from any money accruing to the Writer under this agreement or otherwise.

(9) The Writer agrees that he will not assign this Agreement nor any sums that may become due hereunder, without the written consent of the Publisher first endorsed hereon.

(10) Except as otherwise herein provided, this Agreement is binding upon the parties hereto and their respective successors in interest.

WITNESS: Joe Mauldin JOE MAULDIN Writer

Niki Sullivan NIKI SULLIVAN Writer

NORMAN PETTY Writer

WITNESS: NOR-VA JAK MUSIC, INC.

By

July 24, 1957

Mssrs. Jerry Allison, Joe Mauldin
Buddy Holly, Nicki Sullivan
INDIVIDUALLY & COLLECTIVELY COMPRISING
AN ACT P/K AS THE CRICKETS
c/o Norman Petty
Box 926
Clovis, New Mexico

Dear Sirs:

Simultaneously herewith, we are entering into Exclusive Agency Contracts on the following Forms: American Guild of Variety Artists, American Federation of Musicians #1263 F, American Federation of Television and Radio Artists & World-Wide , which contracts are scheduled to commence on July 24th, 1957.

Notwithstanding anything to the contrary contained in said contracts, it is understood and agreed that General Artists Corporation shall not be entitled to participate in any commissions from any monies earned and/or received by you as a result of your present existing contract with Coral Records, or on any renewals, extensions, options or modifications thereof.

Except as hereinabove specifically modified, all other terms and conditions of the Exclusive Agency Contracts referred-to in Paragraph One hereof, shall remain in full force and effect.

Your signatures in the space indicated below, will signify your acceptance and agreement to the foregoing.

Very truly yours,

GENERAL ARTISTS CORPORATION

BY:

ACCEPTED AND AGREED TO:

Jerry Allison JERRY ALLISON

Joe Mauldin JOE MAULDIN

Buddy Holly BUDDY HOLLY

Niki Sullivan NICKI SULLIVAN

INDIVIDUALLY AND COLLECTIVELY COMPRISING AN ACT P/K AS THE CRICKETS

LARRY HOLLEY Just before Buddy got his first hit record out, the boys and him were having a hard time keeping spending money. I was building a new home and I used Buddy quite a bit in the construction of it. My dad was a carpenter and Travis, my other brother, was good at several types of construction, so we kept Buddy busy doing various things. Digging the storm cellar was the job of Buddy, Joe B. and J.I. It was hot and the boys worked until they got blisters and began to taper off. Buddy worked the hardest, but all agreed it was not their cup of tea. I had them doing the grouting for another job. When I got there, Buddy was really working but J.I. was laying down on some cardboard and barely washing the wall, and Joe B. was playing drums on a cardboard box. I told Buddy I would have to let them go, but Buddy pled their case and I agreed to give them another chance at a different kind of work. That's when I moved them to the storm cellar digging.

Buddy was conscious of his slender build and wanted to build himself up, so he started hanging around a health club and lifting weights. He started to get some muscle then.

Top left: A publishing agreement for 'I'm Gonna Love You Too' between Buddy Holly and the Crickets and Nor Va Jak Music. Signed by Joe Mauldin, Niki Sullivan and Norman Petty, 19 July 1957.

Left: A General Artists Corporation contract with Buddy Holly and the Crickets, 24 July 1957

LARRY HOLLEY One night we were all working over at mother and dad's, installing a tile floor for them. After it was finished, Buddy and some of his friends got out their instruments and had a jam session. That was the first time I heard Buddy do 'It's Too Late', a Chuck Willis number. I thought it was the prettiest song I ever heard and asked Buddy to make me a record of it the next time he was in Clovis. Well he did and it turned out so well that they put it on an album. It was never released as a single, but it should've been. It's still my favourite song by Buddy.

NORMAN PETTY STUDIO, JULY 1957
On 2 July 1957, a large number of photos of Buddy Holly and the Crickets were taken in and around Norman Petty's studio, most of them taken by Vi Petty or Norma Jean Berry (Norman's secretary). Among them were the famous 'T-shirt' publicity photos (above and opposite, top right) that were eventually used on sheet music and promotional pictures. A day prior, they had a recording session that produced 'Peggy Sue', 'Oh Boy!', 'Listen to Me' and 'I'm Gonna Love You Too'. On 12 July, another session at Norman's produced 'Send Me Some Lovin'' and 'It's Too Late'. On 20 July, a three-day recording session at Norman's studio produced 'Moondreams'.

Left and below: Buddy Holly and the Crickets at the airport in Amarillo, TX, en route to New York City, 28 July 1957

PEER-SOUTHERN MUSIC PUBLISHING
On 30 July 1957, the group visited the offices of Peer-Southern Publishing in New York City. They met with Murray Deutch and also received copies of 'That'll Be the Day' sheet music, pictured above.

'BLACK TOUR'
Buddy Holly and the Crickets stayed at the Ambassador Hotel in Washington D.C. from 1–8 August during what has been coined the 'Black Tour', as the promoter initially believed they were a black group and booked them into black theatres. Washington was their first stop and Norman Petty joined them there. From 2–8 August, they performed at the Howard Theater on a bill that included headliner Clyde McPhatter, the Cadillacs, Otis Rush, Edna McGriff, the Hearts and Oscar & Oscar, and they received $1,000 for their week's work. Buddy sent a letter to his mother from the Ambassador on 3 August (right). During this week, Buddy lost his voice to laryngitis and Niki Sullivan had to take over on singing duties.

Below: Buddy Holly and the Crickets outside the Ambassador Hotel, Washington D.C., 4 August 1957

Bottom right: Buddy Holly and the Crickets with Jo Harper, Vi Petty and Georgiana Hagen outside the Ambassador Hotel, Washington D.C., 4 August 1957

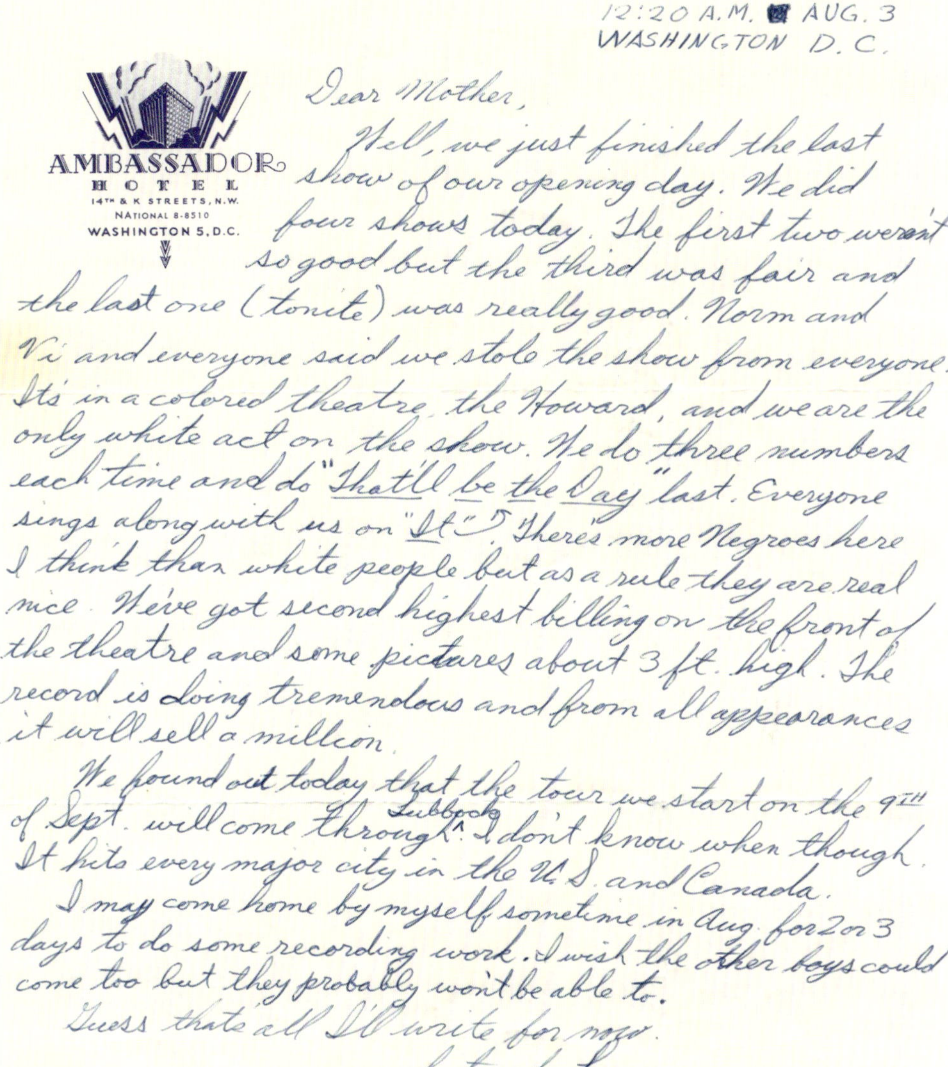

AMBASSADOR HOTEL
14TH & K STREETS, N.W.
NATIONAL 8-8510
WASHINGTON 5, D.C.

12:20 A.M. AUG. 3
WASHINGTON D.C.

Dear Mother,

Well, we just finished the last show of our opening day. We did four shows today. The first two weren't so good but the third was fair and the last one (tonite) was really good. Norm and Vi and everyone said we stole the show from everyone. It's in a colored theatre, the Howard, and we are the only white act on the show. We do three numbers each time and do "That'll be the Day" last. Everyone sings along with us on "It". There's more Negroes here I think than white people but as a rule they are real nice. We've got second highest billing on the front of the theatre and some pictures about 3 ft. high. The record is doing tremendous and from all appearances it will sell a millcon.

We found out today that the tour we start on the 9th of Sept. will come through Lubbock. I don't know when though. It hits every major city in the U.S. and Canada.

I may come home by myself sometime in Aug. for 2 or 3 days to do some recording work. I wish the other boys could come too but they probably won't be able to.

Guess that's all I'll write for now.

Lots of Love –

Buddy

500 ROOMS Completely AIR CONDITIONED ... IN EVERY ROOM — SWIMMING POOL FREE TO GUESTS

AIRMAIL

MRS. L. O. HOLLEY
1305 - 37TH
LUBBOCK, TEXAS

PAUL ANKA In 1956, after I recorded 'Diana', I became aware of Buddy. At the time, he was wondering who this little Canadian kid was that was keeping 'That'll Be the Day' from number one. His song was one of my favourite songs of that summer, but he and I were vying for the top spot.

DION DiMUCCI I'm a kid from the Bronx; we didn't have teenage music when I grew up. One of Buddy's songs came thundering through our radio one day. It was from outer space and so innovative; a new world was born for me in that moment, and it just opened everything up. It's hard to explain what 'Peggy Sue' does to you when you hear it for the first time, how the music enters your body and moves around – it's a sensation. I ran home and tried to learn it on guitar.

Southern Hotel
LIGHT & REDWOOD STREETS
Baltimore 3, Md.

SOUTHERN HOTEL CORPORATION
A. J. FINK, PRESIDENT & MANAGING DIRECTOR
HAROLD I. FINK, MANAGER

Dear Mother and folks,

I'm sitting here in the dressing room with nothing to do so I thought I'd write a few lines. We've done three shows and it's about time for the last one. Today was a little slow and the crowds were not very responsive. Tomorrow we've got an appointment with a distributor to go visit some radio stations. I dread that, too. I don't much like to talk on the radio. We've just got two more days here, thank goodness. I'll be glad to get to New York. I hope the Apollo is better than this.

Has Daddy come home yet. I hope so. It would be a lot better if he could stay there at home and work. I haven't written him on account of I think maybe he is home or going to be home before the letter could get to him.

I guess that's all I'll write for now.

Love

Buddy

Southern Hotel
LIGHT & REDWOOD STREETS
Baltimore 3, Md.

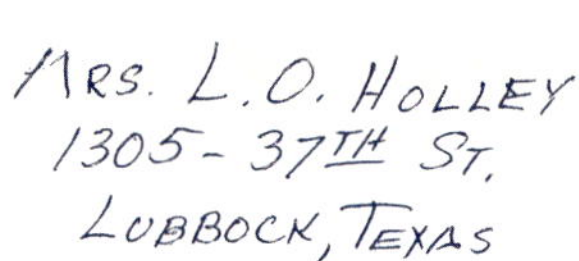

Mrs. L. O. Holley
1305 - 37th St.
Lubbock, Texas

Airmail

Southern Hotel
LIGHT & REDWOOD STREETS
Baltimore 3, Md.

SOUTHERN HOTEL CORPORATION
A. J. FINK, PRESIDENT & MANAGING DIRECTOR
HAROLD I. FINK, MANAGER

SUN., AUG. 11, 11:30 P.M.

Dear Mother,

I guess you think I don't write very much, but we don't have too much time. We get in from the theatre about 11:15 every night and try to get to bed by 1:00 as we have to get up by 10:00 in the mornings. Also with my throat being sore I've been trying to get as much rest as possible. It's about to get all right now. I just hope it doesn't get that way again.

The Royal Theatre is not as good as the Howard in Wash. D.C. and the people here are not near so nice. In fact, I think this is a "terrible" place. I guess one reason is because it's an older town and not as pretty as Wash. However we are still being recieved as well by the audiences. All the other acts call us the "house rockers" and all the people we see after the shows tell us we were the best ones and really stole the show. I told you all ready, I think, that we're the only white act on the show. It makes us feel sort of strange too. The colored guys and gals on the show are really nice. They didn't know what to think of us for a few days but we are getting to know them better now and they are real swell.

Southern Hotel
LIGHT & REDWOOD STREETS
Baltimore 3, Md.

SOUTHERN HOTEL CORPORATION
A. J. FINK, PRESIDENT & MANAGING DIRECTOR
HAROLD I. FINK, MANAGER

There's not a dull moment either, because they keep something going on all the time. I guess they are the most naturally funny people in the world because I can't quit laughing while I'm around them.

We talked to June on the phone yesterday. She was in New York and she called us at the theatre. She said she would probably get to stay and ~~cat~~ catch our opening show at the Apollo Theatre in New York. I just hope we do as well there as we did in Wash. and here. Everyone says we will though.

We ~~here~~ hear our record on the radio all the time. When we left Wash. it was no. 2 there and it's no. 4 here. The record stores have all sold out of it 2 or 3 times. All the big wheels say that we can be assured it will sell over a million. That sure does sound good, too.

I guess that's about all there is to tell right now so I guess I will end the letter here.

Love,

Buddy

EDNA GUNDERSEN Buddy created the band, which included a rhythm and a lead guitar that dovetailed together for a thicker sound. That was something that hadn't been done, especially focusing in on that guitar sound both in the studio and in live performance. Before then, the guitar was one sound within the mix, not a doubled-up sound. He made a big difference doing that.

AGREEMENT made this 13th day of August 19 57 between PEER INTERNATIONAL CORPORATION, hereinafter designated as PUBLISHER and

NORMAN PETTY of Box 926, Clovis, New Mexico

CHARLES HARDIN of

of

jointly and/or severally designated as WRITER.

WITNESSETH:

(1) The Writer hereby sells, assigns, transfers and delivers to the Publisher, its successors and assigns, all of his rights, title and interest in and to a certain heretofore unpublished original work, as annexed hereto, written and/or composed by the Writer, now entitled,

EVERYDAY

including the title, words and/or music thereof, as well as the entire exclusive right to publicly perform and televise, together with the right to secure copyrights and renewals therein throughout the world, as proprietor in its own name, or otherwise, and to have and to hold the said work, copyrights and renewals thereof and all rights of whatsoever nature thereunder existing.

(2) The Writer hereby warrants that the said work is his sole, exclusive and original work, that he has full right and power to make the within agreement, and that there exists no adverse claim to or in the said work, which is free from all liens and encumbrances whatsoever.

(3) In consideration of this Agreement, the Publisher agrees to pay the Writer, jointly, only the following royalties: An advance of $200.00.

(a) 4 ¢ per copy, in respect of regular piano copies and/or orchestrations, sold in the United States and for which the Publisher received payment.

(b) 50 % of the net amount received by the Publisher, in respect of regular piano copies and/or orchestrations sold and paid for in any foreign country.

(c) 50 % of the net amount received by the Publisher, in respect of any licenses issued authorizing the manufacture of parts of instruments serving to mechanically reproduce said work, electrical transcriptions, or to use said work in synchronization with sound motion pictures.

(d) ...... % of the net amount of performing fees received by the Publisher in the United States, only provided said fees include both Writer and Publisher shares and are payable on a fixed and determinable basis.

(4) The Publisher agrees to render to the Writer on or about February 15th, and August 15th, of each year, so long as it shall continue publishing or licensing said work, covering the six months ending December 31st, and June 30th, of each year respectively, royalty statements accompanied by remittance of the amount due.

(5) All sums hereunder payable jointly to the Writer shall be divided and paid in the following manner:

50 % to NORMAN PETTY of

50 % to CHARLES HARDIN of

% to of

(6) The Publisher shall have the right to alter, change, edit or translate the work or any part thereof, in any way it may be necessary. In the event it be necessary for the Publisher to cause lyrics to be written in other languages for and as part of the work, the publisher shall in such event have the right to deduct from the heretofore agreed royalties payable to the Writer, the cost or obligation thereof, but in no event more than a sum equal to one-half.

(7) The Writer hereby grants and conveys an irrevocable power of attorney authorizing and empowering the Publisher, its nominees, successors and assigns, to administer any and all rights in and to the said work, and collect and receive any and all the fees therefrom; also to file application and renew the copyrights in the name of the Writer, and upon such renewals, to execute proper and formal assignments thereof so as to secure to the Publisher, its successors and assigns, the renewal terms of, in and to said copyrights and/or works.

(8) The Writer hereby agrees to indemnify and save harmless the Publisher against any loss, expense or damage by reason of any adverse claims made by others with respect to the work, and agrees that all expenses incurred in defense of any such claims, including counsel fees, as well as any and all sums paid by the Publisher, pursuant to a judgment, arbitration or any settlement or adjustment which may be made in the discretion of the Publisher, or otherwise, shall at all times be borne by the Writer, and may be deducted by the Publisher from any money accruing to the Writer under this agreement or otherwise.

(9) The Writer agrees that he will not assign this Agreement nor any sums that may become due hereunder, without the written consent of the Publisher first endorsed hereon.

(10) Except as otherwise herein provided, this Agreement is binding upon the parties hereto and their respective successors in interest.

WITNESS:

NORMAN PETTY Writer

CHARLES HARDIN Writer

Writer

WITNESS:

PEER INTERNATIONAL CORPORATION

by

F M 23

CORAL RECORDS, INC.

48 WEST 57th STREET, NEW YORK 19, N. Y. • COlumbus 5-2363

August 15, 1958

Mr. Buddy Holly
c/o Norman Petty
Box 926
Clovis, New Mexico

Dear Mr. Holly:

It is hereby agreed that the contract between us dated May 16, 1957, as amended be amended in the following respects only:

(1) One master now entitled -

"HEARTBEAT"

shall be deemed to have been recorded under said contract.

(2) We agree to pay the sum of $300.00 for the aforesaid master, which shall include the advance to you under said contract together with the costs for recording.

(3) All terms and conditions of the contract shall apply to these recordings as though they had been performed under said contract and shall serve to reduce the number of record sides required to be recorded thereunder.

(4) The sum of $300.00 provided to be paid to you hereunder shall be an advance against royalties under the aforesaid agreement dated May 16th, 1957, as amended and under the master purchase agreement with Norman Petty bearing even date therewith.

Very truly yours,

CORAL RECORDS, INC.

By
Paul Cohen, Director
of Artists and Repertoire

ACCEPTED & AGREED TO:
Buddy Holly
Norman Petty

Theresa Hotel
2090 - 7th Ave.
New York, N.Y.
Phone – University 53300
Extension 729
Phone University 44490
Playing at Apollo Theatre
Phone Riverside 99114

BRIAN MAY Some people thought the Crickets were black. Though Queen were English and came a generation later, when we put out 'Another One Bites the Dust' a slew of people assumed we were black. It's odd how history repeats itself. But we owe those black blues men, all of us do, because they sang from their heart and pain, and they accompanied it with the guitar, which spoke as loudly as the voice. That's what you hear in Buddy, and most impassioned rock music.

HANK MARVIN He was different. The expectation of a rock star changed when he came along, a guy that played guitar properly, not just using it as an ornament. His whole presentation was different, as was his playing and his singing, and his songs. Perhaps that's why he stood out so much and why he was so much of an influence, because when something is good and different it hits you hard.

PETER ASHER The minute I heard Buddy, I became aware of other music that was out there at the time. I became an avid and determined fan.

BALTIMORE

From 9 to 15 August 1957, Buddy Holly and the Crickets stayed at the Southern Hotel while performing at the Royal Theater in Baltimore, MD. During his stay at the Southern Hotel, Buddy wrote another letter to his parents (opposite), stating: 'I'll be glad to get to New York. I hope the Apollo is better than this.'

NEW YORK

From 16 to 22 August 1957, Buddy Holly and the Crickets performed at the Apollo Theater in Harlem, New York, and stayed at the Theresa Hotel. By this time, the promoters already knew they were a white group; they were the first all-white band to ever take the stage at the Apollo. The Apollo opened its doors in 1913 and played a significant role in popularising jazz, bebop and R&B, and quickly became a beacon of black culture. The general contracts for a one-week appearance at the Apollo usually called for performing 31 shows. The audience were initially disappointed by the band, but by the end of the six nights, the group had won them over.

Top left: A publishing agreement for 'Everyday' between Norman Petty, Buddy and Peer International, 13 August 1957

Top right: A recording contract for 'Heartbeat' signed by Buddy, Norman Petty and Paul Cohen of Coral Records, Inc., 15 August 1958. The original agreement was made on 16 May 1957.

Fri. 4:45 P.M.

Dear Dad,

How is everything in Wichita Falls? O.K. I hope. We finished playing the Apollo last night and it sure feels good to know that we can relax for a few days. We don't have a thing to do until Monday. Then we have to go down to Philadelphia for a promotional TV appearance. It's Dick Clark's show and he's paying our expenses down there and back. Then Tuesday we have the Ted Steele show here in New York. Then we start at the Brooklyn Paramount Friday.

We are staying downtown now at the Forrest Hotel so you can drop a card here if you have time. We'll be here for a couple of weeks.

There's not much else to tell except that we found out last night that we had sold half a million as of Wed. night. Everyone says it should sell at least a million.

Well, that's all for now, I guess.

Love, Buddy

Letter To Daddy From Buddy

NEW YORK, N.Y. AUG 23 1957

VIA AIR MAIL

Mr. L.O. Holley
c/o Texas Roofing Crew
Alamo Courts
Wichita Falls, Texas

August 30, 1957

Messrs. Jerry Allison, Nicki Sullivan and Joe Mauldin
a/k/a The Crickets
2215 Sixth Street
Lubbuck, Texas

Gentlemen:

By letter dated July 23, 1957, we exercised our option to enter into a contract with you dated March 19, 1957, for your services.

It is hereby mutually agreed:

1. Two masters now entitled "OH BOY" and "NOT FADE AWAY" shall be deemed to have been recorded under the said contract.

2. We agree to pay you the sum of $300.00 for the aforesaid masters which shall include the advance to you under said contract together with the costs for recording.

3. All terms and conditions of the contract shall apply to these recordings as though they had been performed under said contract and shall serve to reduce the number of record sides required to be recorded thereunder.

4. The sum of $300.00 provided to be paid to you shall be an advance against royalties under the aforesaid agreement dated March 19, 1957, and under the master purchase agreement with Norman Petty bearing even date therewith. All royalties which shall accrue under the aforesaid agreement for your services and the master purchase agreement with Norman Petty shall be accrued under one account and all advances and recording costs under both contracts shall be deducted from said royalties.

Yours truly

CORAL RECORDS, INC.

Robert Thiele

Director of Artists and Repertoire

ACCEPTED AND AGREED TO:

Joe Mauldin

Niki Sullivan

Jerry Allison

Norman Petty

NORMAN PETTY

Above: A letter from Buddy to his father
23 August 1957

Above right: A recording agreement between Buddy Holly and the Crickets and Coral Records for the songs, 'Oh Boy!' and 'Not Fade Away'

CLOVIS NATIONAL BANK ACCOUNT

On 23 August 1957, an account in the name of Buddy Holly and the Crickets was opened at the Clovis National Bank with an initial deposit of $500. All cheques were made out and signed by Norman Petty. Cheques written on the account include one dated 24 August 1957 for $50 made out to M.M. Sullivan with a note stating 'Payment on loan made to Niki Sullivan' (right). Four other cheques were written on this day, including one to cover the first payment of $175 for Buddy's car.

Two days later, the group received $332 for an appearance on Dick Clark's American Bandstand where they performed 'That'll Be the Day'.

Opposite: Two letters from Buddy to his mother
20 and 23 August 1957

BUDDY HOLLY & THE CRICKETS
BOX 926 PHONE PORTER 3-7565
CLOVIS, NEW MEXICO

(5)

CLOVIS NATIONAL BANK
CLOVIS, NEW MEXICO

95-30
1122

CLOVIS, NEW MEXICO AUGUST 24, 1957

105
CHECK NUMBER

PAY TO THE ORDER OF M. M. SULLIVAN $ 50.00

The Sum 50 DOLS 00 CTS DOLLARS

BY ENDORSEMENT THIS CHECK WHEN PAID IS ACCEPTED IN FULL PAYMENT OF THE FOLLOWING ACCOUNT

Payment On Loan Made To
Niki Sullivan

THE CRICKETS

BY Norman Petty

NORMAN PETTY — MANAGER

FRI. 4:35 P.M.

Dear Mother,

Well we finally finished up at the Apollo. I sure was glad, too. I thought that last night would never come.

We checked into the Forrest Hotel downtown yesterday and it's real fine. Not too high, either.

We had breakfast with Murray this morning. He seems to like us real good because when we're around he won't have anything to do with anyone else. He just tells them he's busy with the Crickets right now. Celebrities, that's what.

We were going to help Dale Hawkins cut his next session this morning but we found out from Bob Thiele last night that we couldn't so he flew home to Shreveport today to cut. He should be back in a week or two, though.

We are going to buy new uniforms tomorrow. They will sure help out, too. I don't know yet what color we will get. Probably something a little brighter than those others.

Boy it feels good not to have anything we have to do until Monday. Then we go to Philadelphia for a promotion T.V. show (Dick Clark's show) Then Tuesday we make the Ted Steele TV show here in New York. Then we'll have a couple more days off.

It doesn't seem like we've been gone from home over a week until we get to thinking about it. Then it seems like 3 or 4 months. Time sure is passing fast for us. I guess because we've be so busy.

Our record has just gone over the half million mark! I just hope it does sell two million.

I guess I'll close for now and write a few lines to Daddy.

Love,

Buddy

"Letters" from Buddy
In New York – August
"Biggest Show of Stars" Tour 1957

NEW YORK, N.Y. AUG 23 8-PM 1957

SAVE THE EASY WAY BUY U.S. BONDS ON PAYROLL SAVINGS

VIA AIR MAIL

MRS. L. O. HOLLEY
1305 - 37th ST.
LUBBOCK, TEXAS

TUE. 12:00 NOON

Dear Mother,

How are things going at home? O.K. I hope. We are during our fourth day here at the Paramount. We are having a fine time, too even tho we are a little bit tired and would like to be home for a few days at least.

We got a Billboard this morning and it had a bunch of good in it. We're on all the charts that count. We haven't seen a Cashbox yet but if it's like it usually is, it will be better than Billboard.

I got a letter from Daddy a day or two ago as well as several letters from you. It sure helps to get some mail, even if its a week or two old. What counts is something out'a the ordinary everyday life up here. There is a lot of excitement and all but the letters are appreciated more than anything. If one of us gets a letter and the others don't he feels kinda like the king or chief or something like that. I don't write very much I guess because I'm so lazy, but I intend to every nite and by the time I've showered I'm so sleepy I put it off. So today just brought the Stationary to the dressing room to write in between shows. We've done our first show today and have 3 more to go. We got an encore the first show. Sure made us feel good too. Alan Freed is a pretty good boy but he's got so many people bossing him he can't do too much by us. Morris is his manager you know and Morris doesn't like us much, probably. Anyhow the first 3 days when the crowd would try to encore us we wouldn't get to do another song. Something happened tho, I guess because they're letting us do another one now. We do "That'll" first and "Oh Boy" for the encore.

I think Norman is going to be coming back home in a few days and he can tell you all about this "gig". (That's a playing job.)

There's not much else to write about so I guess I'll close for now.

Love Buddy

BRIAN MAY In those days, rock singers weren't taught to sing, but they expressed themselves in reaction to the way their parents spoke and the other music they heard. It was a rebellious time. There was a feeling that kids were marginalised, as if they didn't have a world of their own but they should. Rock and roll – from Elvis to Little Richard, and from Buddy Holly to Ricky Nelson – is rebellion.

ALBERT LEE Buddy loved Little Richard from when he did 'Ready Teddy'. We all tried to perform the songs we loved, and, in that process, we discovered what suited us best.

ALAN FREED HOLIDAY SHOW
From 30 August to 8 September 1957, Buddy Holly and the Crickets took part in the Alan Freed Holiday Show at the Paramount Theater in New York. The bill also included Little Richard, the Del Vikings, the Diamonds, Mickey and Sylvia, and the Moonglows, among many others. Just before going on stage for the first time, the group paused in the stairwell backstage for a picture with Alan Freed (left). Buddy is also pictured backstage with Little Richard (opposite, bottom left); Jerry Allison, Niki Sullivan and Jimmy Rodgers are shown outside the theatre (opposite, top left); Joe B. Mauldin, Niki Sullivan and Carolyn Hester (opposite, top right) and Jerry Allison and Josie Harper (opposite, bottom right) are shown on the New York subway.

Financial statements reveal that Buddy and the Crickets performed at the Paramount Theater for the entire run, then joined the Biggest Show of Stars for '57 – a tour already in progress – on 9 September.

BRIAN MAY You had boys with angst constructing their own music. Some of it is tough, some is about love and emotion, and some is about the way the world is, but it's all about wanting to be heard and I see that in Buddy. Buddy's melodic, and so the songs stand up very well, but there's a voice in there that has a mission.

LITTLE RICHARD When we toured together, I used to stand in the wings every night to catch his act. He was something else!

1

CABLE ADDRESS – "EDISHOTEL"

Hotel Edison.

"THE HOUSE OF HOSPITALITY"
46TH STREET TO 47TH STREET
JUST WEST OF BROADWAY
NEW YORK 36. N. Y.

MILTON J. KRAMER, PRESIDENT — CIRCLE 6-5000 — JOHN P. PRINGLE, MANAGER

10:30 P.M TUE. 30th

Hi Y'all,

We've already been ribbed about saying that so I figured it would sound good to y'all. We got here safe and sound. The plane ride was a lot of fun. We thought for awhile that it would be too cloudy to see New York from the plane but it cleared off right before we landed so we got to see it all. The Empire State Bldg., Statue of Liberty, etc. I intended to write last night but we were dead tired because we didn't get to bed until about 4:00 AM.

We've sure been busy since we arrived. As soon as we got here we checked in (7:30 AM) and slept about 4 hrs. Norm and Vi got in at noon and we showered and dressed and went down to Southern Music. It's just a couple of blocks. We were there until 6:00 and then Murray

BANQUET FACILITIES, AIR CONDITIONED RESTAURANTS & BALLROOMS — AIR CONDITIONED ROOMS, TELEVISION AVAILABLE, CIRCULATING ICE WATER — 1000 ROOMS WITH BATH AND SHOWER, RADIO IN EVERY ROOM

2

CABLE ADDRESS – "EDISHOTEL"

Hotel Edison.

"THE HOUSE OF HOSPITALITY"
46TH STREET TO 47TH STREET
JUST WEST OF BROADWAY
NEW YORK 36. N. Y.

MILTON J. KRAMER, PRESIDENT — CIRCLE 6-5000 — JOHN P. PRINGLE, MANAGER

took us all out to eat at Al and Dick's Steak House. It's real classy. The bill was $60.00. Don't get excited. It's not like that everywhere. After that we came back to the hotel and called Donnie Lanier. He came down to the room and he and Norm and us sat and talked until about 3:00. Then we went to eat again (sandwiches) and then came back and went to bed. We got up this morning and went to Southern again. Then we ate lunch and then we had an appointment at GAC (General Artists) and then an appointment with Bob Thiele. By then it was 6:00 P.M. so we ate and went to a movie and then came back to the room. We're just fixing to get in bed because we have to get up early (about 9:00) in the morning for some more appointments.

BANQUET FACILITIES, AIR CONDITIONED RESTAURANTS & BALLROOMS — AIR CONDITIONED ROOMS, TELEVISION AVAILABLE, CIRCULATING ICE WATER — 1000 ROOMS WITH BATH AND SHOWER, RADIO IN EVERY ROOM

3

CABLE ADDRESS – "EDISHOTEL"

Hotel Edison.

"THE HOUSE OF HOSPITALITY"
46TH STREET TO 47TH STREET
JUST WEST OF BROADWAY
NEW YORK 36. N. Y.

MILTON J. KRAMER, PRESIDENT — CIRCLE 6-5000 — JOHN P. PRINGLE, MANAGER

Everybody in the Music business up here is sure nice to us. Maybe ~~becaus~~ because our record is pretty hot. Everyone is singing "That'll be the Day" and we're sort of celebrities already. ~~Th~~ We had a full page picture and ad in Cash Box and I'm sending ~~on~~ a copy of that issue tomorrow to you. Billboard also had a couple of things in it which you've probably already seen. Some people (big wheels) in the high priced restaurant recognized us from the picture in Cash Box and introduced themselves to us. The record has already sold 125,000 and they've got a lot of back orders. They're shipping about 10,000 a day. I don't have time to write all I would like to so I'll close for now and write again later. Tell everyone hi for us.—

Love Buddy

P.S. Bad writing but I was sure going fast. "Bah"

BANQUET FACILITIES, AIR CONDITIONED RESTAURANTS & BALLROOMS — AIR CONDITIONED ROOMS, TELEVISION AVAILABLE, CIRCULATING ICE WATER — 1000 ROOMS WITH BATH AND SHOWER, RADIO IN EVERY ROOM

46TH STREET TO 47TH STREET
JUST WEST OF BROADWAY
NEW YORK 36, N. Y.

MRS. L. O. HOLLEY
1305-37TH
LUBBOCK, TEXAS

JERRY 'J.I.' ALLISON New York … talk about excitement. On our first trip, before we started touring, we met with music people, publishers, and ran into the Everly Brothers on the streets. It was terribly exciting to be there. While we were there, we performed on *The Arthur Murray Party* and Arthur Murray said, 'Some boys are here causing some excitement around New York,' and I just thought, wow, we're causing excitement around New York. We felt very lucky, but we didn't realise how lucky at the time. We just had so much to be excited about.

HOTEL EDISON
While performing at the Paramount in August 1957 (above), Buddy and the Crickets and Norman Petty stayed at the Hotel Edison.

Opposite: A letter from Buddy to his family, 30 July 1957

Opposite, bottom right: This baggage tag was on Jerry Allison's luggage with his Lubbock address

THE 'CHIRPING' CRICKETS

Approximately six colour photos exist of Buddy Holly and the Crickets taken on the roof, on the stairwell, and outside by the rear of the Paramount Theater in New York on 7 or 8 September 1957. Jerry had a black eye from a scuffle with Niki. One of these photographs was used for the cover of their debut album, The 'Chirping' Crickets, *released 27 November 1957. It was the group's only album to be released during Buddy's lifetime, and is considered today to be one of the classic albums of the rock and roll genre. Most importantly, it was the first album by a rock and roll band. While rock and roll had seen plenty of solo stars, the idea that a band of four musicians could share the spotlight was unheard of.*

The album saw Buddy on lead vocals, lead and acoustic guitar, Jerry Allison on drums, cardbox percussion and backing vocals, Joe B. Mauldin on contrabass and backing vocals, and Niki Sullivan on rhythm guitar and backing vocals. It also featured Larry Welborn, the Picks (Bill Pickering, John Pickering and Bob Lapham), and Ramona and Gary Tollett. Bob Thiele, who signed the band to Coral, sifted through all of their tapes to compile the best tracks for the album. It became clear they needed some new material, so during the Biggest Show of Stars for '57 package tour, the band made a stop at the Tinker Air Force Base Officer's Club, where Norman Petty set up some of his recording equipment. The album featured here is signed by all band members.

CORAL RECORDS, INC.

48 WEST 57th STREET, NEW YORK 19, N. Y. • COlumbus 5-2363

October 25, 1957

Messrs. Jerry Allison, Nicki Sullivan and Joe Mauldin and Buddy Holly
a/k/a The Crickets
c/o Norman Petty
Box 926
Clovis, New Mexico

Gentlemen:

It is hereby mutually agreed as follows:

(1) The eight master records recorded by you entitled -

YOU'VE GOT LOVE	AN EMPTY CUP
MAYBE BABY	SEND ME SOME LOVIN'
IT'S TOO LATE	LAST NIGHT
TELL ME HOW	ROCK ME BABY

shall be deemed to have been recorded under contract between us dated - March 19, 1957.

(2) We agree to pay you the sum of $1,200.00 for the aforementioned masters which shall include the advance to you under said contract together with the cost of recording.

(3) All the terms and conditions of the contract shall apply to these recordings as though they had been performed under said contract and shall serve to reduce the number of sides required to be recorded.

(4) The sum of $1,200.00 provided to be paid to you shall be an advance against the royalties and shall be deducted from royalties which shall accrue under master purchase agreement with Norman Petty dated March 19th, 1957, and the agreement with you of even datetherewith.

Very truly yours,

CORAL RECORDS, INC.

By
Robert Thiele
Director of Artists and Repertoire

ACCEPTED & AGREED TO:

Jerry Allison

Nicki Sullivan

Joe Mauldin
a/k/a THE CRICKETS

Buddy Holly

Norman Petty

CORAL RECORDS, INC.

48 WEST 57th STREET, NEW YORK 19, N. Y. • COlumbus 5-2363

November 27, 1957

Messrs. Jerry Allison, Nicki Sullivan and Joe Mauldin and Buddy Holly
c/k/a The Crickets
c/o Norman Petty
Box 926 Clovis, New Mexico

Gentlemen:

It is hereby agreed that the contract among us dated March 19, 1957, the term of which commenced as of July 23, 1957 and which has been amended and extended be further amended in the following respect only for recordings performed subsequent to the date hereof.

Paragraph 5 (c) shall be deleted and shall be replaced by the following:

Upon the acceptance by Company of each "master" record to be recorded hereunder, Company will advance to the Artist on account of royalties above provided for, the sum of $250.00 for each such "master" record. All payments hereunder shall be to the order of Norman Petty and statements rendered to him.

We hereby ratify and affirm the aforesaid agreement dated March 19th, 1957, together with all the terms and conditions provided therein.

Very truly yours,

CORAL RECORDS, INC.

By
Robert Thiele
Director of Artists and Repertoire

ACCEPTED AND AGREED TO:

Jerry Allison

Nicki Sullivan

Joe Mauldin

Buddy Holly

Norman Petty

a/k/a THE CRICKETS

Top: A recording contract between Buddy Holly and the Crickets and Coral Records for the songs on their debut album, The 'Chirping' Crickets, *25 October 1957*

Above: An agreement to extend a previous contract, 27 November 1957

JERRY 'J.I.' ALLISON We were on the road constantly in those days, so the album came out without us knowing. We didn't even know what photograph was going to be on the front. I had a copy of the first pressing and it said we were from Bullock, Texas, and Joe B.'s name was spelt wrong.

ALBERT LEE The first album I bought was *The 'Chirping' Crickets*, which happened to be the first album that Eric Clapton bought too. We were all influenced by the music on there, even just the picture of the Stratocaster on the cover. I thought that guitar was from outer space, it was a totally unique sound.

HANK MARVIN When I first saw that picture of Buddy with the Stratocaster, I was shocked. I'd never seen a guitar like that. In 1959, Cliff Richard asked me what guitar I liked, and we pored through a Fender brochure and ended up choosing the most expensive Strat, which was red with gold-plated hardware. When the guitar arrived, it was this amazing-looking instrument that no one in England had seen before. It was outrageous.

JAMES BURTON The album cover was so unique, and every song was amazing. Norman Petty was a smart man who had great talent in the studio, gathering the songs and the right accompanying musicians, then putting it all together. It was like Colonel Parker with Elvis Presley. I'm sure he saw a lot in Buddy because he was different, and that's what producers were looking for.

DON McLEAN It was my favourite album of all time. I had been listening to records since I was a child sick at home with asthma and all I had was a record player to sing along to. That was my fantasy world. I would listen to Buddy's record a hundred times and hear something different every time, which is why I felt connected to his soul. There were feelings there that weren't just created to make a hit record and that stayed with me.

GARRY TALLENT I was nine years old when I bought *The 'Chirping' Crickets* and looking back it's almost a greatest hits record. When I listen to my original record, I know where each skip and click is, and I can almost switch the record on in my brain. They were the first rock and roll band – two guitars, bass and drums – that were self-contained, made and wrote the songs, and played a part in producing them. It's a classic album by virtue of the songs and the performances on it.

BRIAN MAY One of the most magical ingredients on *The 'Chirping' Crickets* is the backing harmonies. They're incredibly atmospheric; it's almost like you're in a church and there's something supernatural happening. They're a small group and this intimacy removes the frills of an orchestra. The background vocals provide the warmth.

CLIFF RICHARD To have that many songs that were that good, that's what always makes a good album. It's at the same level as Michael Jackson's *Thriller*. An album where almost every song could have been a single is rare. Some people take years to write songs like that, and he did it all in 18 months.

BOB HARRIS The Crickets were so important. They were friends that were in it together, and that played a huge part in the expression of the songs. There was a spontaneity about their music which came from messing around in the studio and finding the right sound, and it sounds like that was very democratic. I loved that feeling of togetherness, which happened later with The Beatles.

DION DiMUCCI It was two guitars, a bass and some drums, which was popular 60 years ago and will be popular 60 years from now. It's the essence of a rock band. Buddy and the Crickets were completely self-contained, which was the nucleus for The Beatles, the Stones and Jimi Hendrix – Buddy Holly started the rock band.

The Cash Box

VOL. XIX—No. 1 SEPTEMBER 21, 1957

October 1957

October 1st, that'll be the day when The Crickets expect to be well over the million mark with their Brunswick recording of — naturally — "That'll Be The Day". Above, the high flying group, flanked on the left by Bob Thiele, A&R head of the Coral-Brunswick diskery, and on the right by Norm Wienstroer, National Sales Manager of the same organization, point to the likely date. The Crickets, in addition to achieving the first big hit for themselves with their waxing, have also delivered the first smash seller for the recently reactivated Brunswick label.

JERRY 'J.I.' ALLISON We knew 'That'll Be the Day' was a hit when we got a call to ask if we wanted to go on the road from Irvin Feld, a promoter who owned a record store in Washington D.C. He booked us for 17 weeks for a thousand dollars a week. After the agency took $100 and Norman took $100, it left the four of us with $200 apiece. We thought we were rich. We didn't know, but with the way our records started selling we could've gotten $2,000 or $3,000 a week. Still, we were tickled to death with the deal.

NEWS FROM THE BIG CITY "THAT'LL BE THE DAY" ABOUT THE BIG HIT

NOTICE

LETTERS MAILED IN HOTEL ENVELOPES IF NOT DELIVERED, WILL BE SENT TO THE DEAD LETTER OFFICE, UNLESS THE WRITER GIVES A RETURN ADDRESS.

IF NOT DELIVERED IN______DAYS, RETURN TO

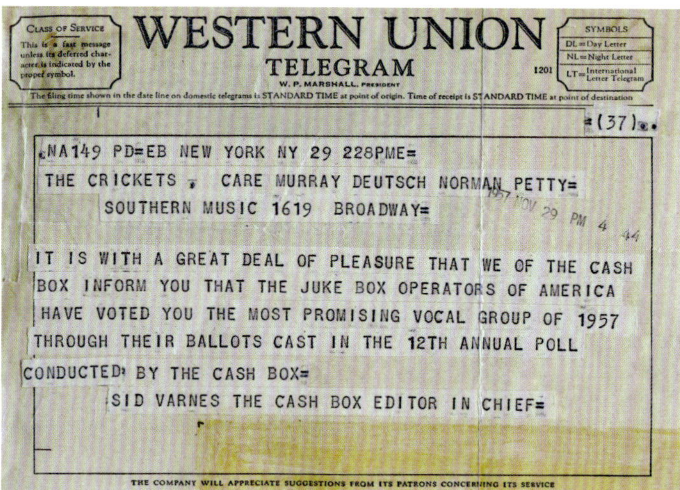

WESTERN UNION TELEGRAM

W. P. MARSHALL, PRESIDENT

CLASS OF SERVICE: This is a fast message unless its deferred character is indicated by the proper symbol.

SYMBOLS: DL=Day Letter; NL=Night Letter; LT=International Letter Telegram

The filing time shown in the date line on domestic telegrams is STANDARD TIME at point of origin. Time of receipt is STANDARD TIME at point of destination

=(37)=

NA149 PD=EB NEW YORK NY 29 228PME=

THE CRICKETS, CARE MURRAY DEUTSCH NORMAN PETTY=

SOUTHERN MUSIC 1619 BROADWAY=

1957 NOV 29 PM 4 44

IT IS WITH A GREAT DEAL OF PLEASURE THAT WE OF THE CASH BOX INFORM YOU THAT THE JUKE BOX OPERATORS OF AMERICA HAVE VOTED YOU THE MOST PROMISING VOCAL GROUP OF 1957 THROUGH THEIR BALLOTS CAST IN THE 12TH ANNUAL POLL CONDUCTED BY THE CASH BOX=

SID VARNES THE CASH BOX EDITOR IN CHIEF=

THE COMPANY WILL APPRECIATE SUGGESTIONS FROM ITS PATRONS CONCERNING ITS SERVICE

DUANE EDDY I was working in a country band playing honky-tonks in Arizona, and my friend said I had to get acquainted with rock and roll. 'That'll Be the Day' was one of the songs that came up. The country people liked to dance to Buddy's songs, so we ended up learning all of them.

RISE IN POPULARITY

Right: A rare snapshot of Buddy Holly and the Crickets in New York, dated 30 August–5 September 1957 on the reverse. They are among a number of photos that Buddy intended for a scrapbook that was never completed, and they were taken for the 21 September 1957 issue of The Cash Box *(opposite), a music trade magazine. The magazine featured an advert for 'That'll Be the Day' in August 1957 and named the Crickets as 'Most Promising Vocal Group of 1957' (opposite, bottom left) on 29 November 1957. 'That'll Be the Day' went gold in 1957 and the gold disc that was presented to Buddy is shown below.*

Right L–R: Niki Sullivan, Buddy Holly, Jerry Allison, Murray Deutch, Bob Thiele, Joe B. Mauldin and Norm Wienstroer, Brooklyn, NY, 30 August 1957

DAVID FRIZZELL The first time I heard Buddy Holly was around 1956, when I was at my brother Lefty's house in Los Angeles. I put on a demo tape of 'That'll Be the Day' and Lefty didn't like it, so I put another tape on, then played it again, played another couple of songs and played it again. Lefty said, 'You play that song one more time, I'm gonna call the cops!' Buddy made everything that he sang his own, and that's something he taught me at a young age.

I later opened Lefty's shows with 'That'll Be the Day', and in 1959, when I got the chance to audition for Columbia, it was one of the songs I performed – so it helped get me on the label. Once I heard 'That'll Be the Day' it meant a lot to me throughout my life.

JAMES BURTON Buddy had no idea 'That'll Be the Day' would cause his career to take off like a rocket. In such a short career there was so much amazing songwriting, his unique talent took over. It was fantastic music that will live forever. I played in a tribute to Buddy Holly, and it was such a wide range of people – jazz players, country players, rhythm and blues, rock and roll – they all loved him.

THE BIGGEST SHOW OF STARS FOR '57

Buddy Holly and the Crickets' tenure on the Biggest Show of Stars for '57 ran from 9 September to 24 November, when they joined the tour in Norfolk, VA. It was a gruelling run, with the artists performing a total of 80 shows across the US and Canada, getting from place to place in two Greyhound buses. On this tour, the group grossed $12,500. Other participants included Chuck Berry, Fats Domino, Dion and the Belmonts, the Everly Brothers, Paul Anka, Frankie Lymon, and the Drifters. The programme and poster displayed (below) represent the fall edition. At the time, Buddy Holly and the Crickets were so new to the scene that they did not yet have a proper publicity photo, hence the use in the programme of one of the casual 'T-shirt' images taken at Norman Petty's studio in July.

Opposite: Buddy Holly and the Crickets on stage at the Paramount in New York just before joining the Biggest Show of Stars for '57 tour, early September 1957

Left, clockwise from top left: Chuck Berry, Frankie Lymon, Paul Anka and Clyde McPhatter performing on stage for the Biggest Show of Stars for '57, 13 September 1957

Jerry Allison and myself have been playing together for about four years, and we got the other two boys and asked them if they'd like to join us and form a group ... Well, we got one [record] released the other day by the Crickets called 'Oh Boy!' ... I like 'Oh Boy!' better than 'That'll Be the Day' ... I'd prefer singing a little bit quieter now anyhow.
(This is Buddy's response when asked if he thinks rock and roll is on the wane and what he'd do if trends changed, during an interview with radio DJ Red Robinson, Vancouver, Canada, 23 October 1957)

We have three records going right now. The first one was 'That'll Be the Day', and then we have a new one out by the Crickets called 'Oh Boy!' and 'Not Fade Away'. And then there's one out, it's by the same group but it's under my name (I don't know why they did it that way): 'Peggy Sue' and 'Everyday'.

We had to think of some name that hadn't been used yet and Jerry came up with [the Crickets]. So sure enough it had already been used, but it was a good while back so it didn't matter too much.
(Buddy during the Biggest Show of Stars tour, Topeka, KS, KTOP Radio, Dale Lowery, 5 November 1957)

DON EVERLY Phil and I had heard of Buddy before he joined the Biggest Show of Stars in Montreal. We became friends immediately.

DION DiMUCCI I was in a group called Dion and the Belmonts. We'd put out a record called 'I Wonder Why' and Buddy liked it. After the Show of Stars tour, I met him again when he came to New York and I took him for pizza and egg creams, which he didn't know about, not being from the city. Then the Everly Brothers and I took him to Phil's Men's Shop on 3rd Avenue, which sold great sweaters. After that Buddy never looked the same. We then went to Manny's on 48th Street, where we brought new Stratocasters. He bought the Sunburst and I bought a white Strat.

DON EVERLY Buddy was great with the Crickets; it was hard to find musicians like that back then because nobody was playing rock and roll. I loved their music. We both liked the same artists, so our influences were quite similar, but we weren't in competition; it was a wonderful camaraderie. I could depend on him and speak to him about music, and through that we became very close.

JERRY 'J.I.' ALLISON We got to be friends with Don and Phil, and they said, 'You guys ought to wear something besides T-shirts!' So they took us to Phil's Men's Shop in New York and Alfred Norton's Rockefeller Centre, which was high dollar stuff. They dressed us up, told us what kinds of clothes and shoes were cool, and I'll always appreciate it.

DON EVERLY We bought a lot of our clothes from Phil's. Buddy bought some clothes, and we got some shoes and some long stockings that stayed up. He and the Crickets had just gotten their picture taken in white shirts, while on a break when they were setting tile in a motel. That was their first professional photograph. Later, in photographs of all of us, we all look alike because we were all buying the same clothes! It was marvellous.

We've known Norm for quite some time, down there in Clovis, New Mexico. We used to go over and make a few dubs now and then to see what we sounded like. So the last time – let's see, it was in January I believe – we went over there and were making a dub to send into various companies and see if we could possibly do anything in the line of the music business and Norm asked us if we'd like for him to send ['That'll Be the Day'] in to Brunswick Records in New York and so we told him, 'Yeah, go ahead, we can't lose.' Because we were as far behind as you could get already. So he sent it in and Bob Thiele, the A&R man for Brunswick, okayed it and put it out and the kids all over the United States did the rest.

To tell you the truth, Norm can't even get a copy. I just talked with him a while ago on the phone and he said he was wanting some awful bad but he couldn't get hold of any.

Norm has got quite a set-up [in Clovis]. I'd imagine it would be quite a bit of trouble to move it.

I might stick a little bit of a plug in here for Eddie Cochran, sitting over there, so contented like. He's starring in a picture that'll be out pretty soon. I don't know exactly when it will be out but he said that he might appear in that picture and sing a song, and so we've been buddying up to him, getting in as good as we can. (Buddy Holly in an interview with Freeman Hover, KCSR radio, NB, 2 November 1957)

INTERVIEW AT THE ALBANY, DENVER
On 2 November 1957, Buddy Holly was interviewed by Freeman Hover (above), a DJ from Nebraska-based radio station KCSR, in the Albany Hotel in Denver, CO. Eddie Cochran was in the hotel room during this interview. By the time the Biggest Show of Stars for '57 had left Canada for Denver, Buddy and Cochran had become close friends as they had a lot in common. Their hotel rooms became a communal hangout for them and their bandmates.

JERRY 'J.I.' ALLISON We finished a week gig and were paid $3,500 for it, so when we got back to the hotel, Buddy said we needed to split the money. He threw it all onto the bed and said whoever gets the most, gets the most. We started grabbing the money and sticking it in our pockets, that's how serious we were. We weren't doing it for the money.

Niki did those first tours with us. He was a good guitar player, but Chuck Berry was on the tour too and Niki would do the duckwalk because he was a big fan. We'd tell him the duckwalk was Chuck Berry's deal and we were on a show with him, so he couldn't do it too. Niki wondered why he was in a group when he could make a record himself, so at the end of the year we parted ways with him. He got a record deal right away and cut a good record.

December 14, 1957

Buddy Holly and The Crickets
C/O Norman Petty
1321 West Seventh Street
Clovis, New Mexico

Gentlemen:

This is to advise you that I hereby release you and all parties concerned of any and all obligations, financial or otherwise, concerning recordings made by BUDDY HOLLY & THE CRICKETS . . released or unreleased . . . and hereby grant to you all rights to have and to hold and to dispose of any and all material as deemed desireable.

In consideration of my releasing you for now and ever more from further obligations to me, you hereby agree to pay to me ten percent (10%) of all monies received for a recording on BRUNSWICK RECORDS by THE CRICKETS called THAT'LL BE THE DAY. Payment will be made by check to me immediately after royalty payments are made to you from BRUNSWICK RECORDS. This payment can be made payable and collected only by NIKI SULLIVAN and can be collected only by said party. This agreement shall become effective immediately and payments as stated above will continue so long as this record is sold.

Yours truly,

Niki Sullivan

NIKI SULLIVAN
3102 - 44th Street
Lubbock, Texas

Witness:

Norman Petty
NORMAN PETTY

Buddy Holly
BUDDY HOLLY

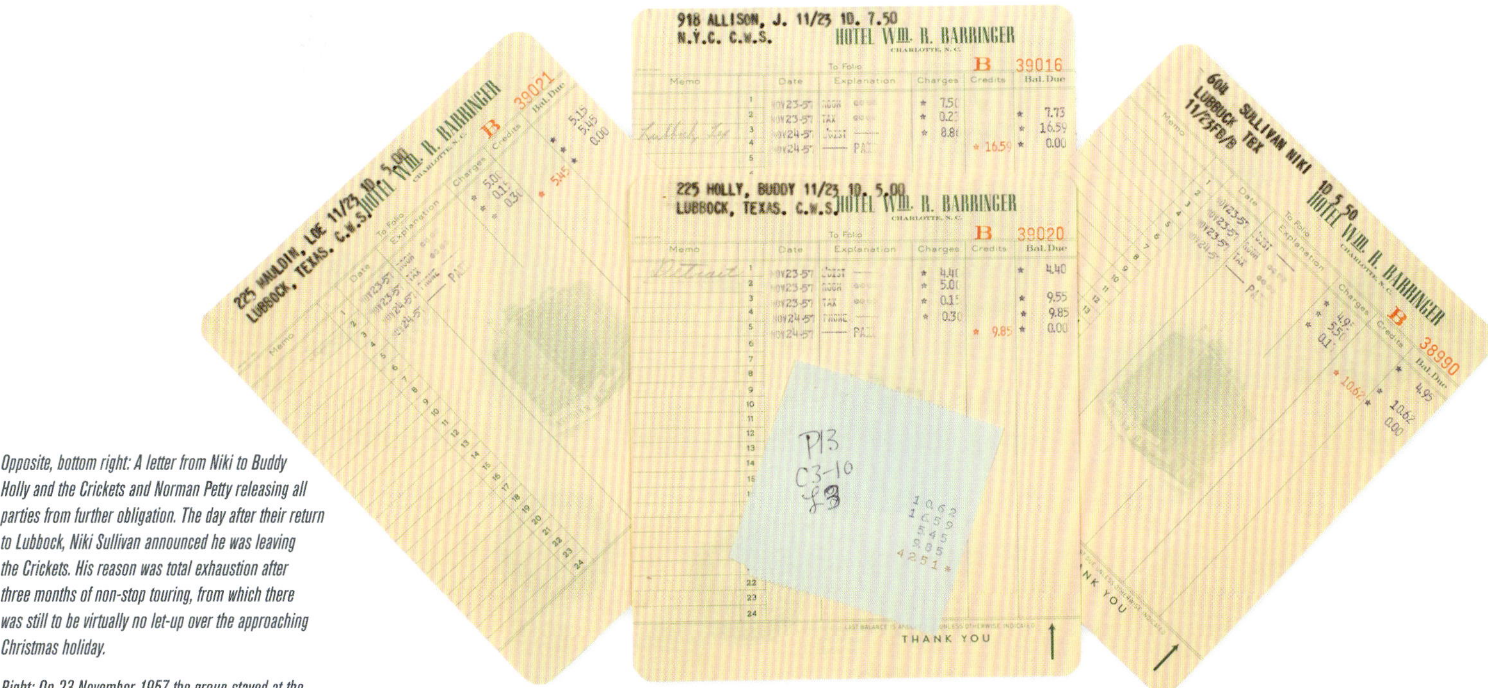

918 ALLISON, J. 11/23 10. 7.50
N.Y.C. C.W.S. HOTEL WM. R. BARRINGER
CHARLOTTE, N.C.
B 39016

225 HOLLY, BUDDY 11/23 10. 5.00
LUBBOCK, TEXAS. C.W.S. HOTEL WM. R. BARRINGER
CHARLOTTE, N.C.
B 39020

225 MAULDIN, JOE 11/23 10. 5.00
LUBBOCK, TEXAS. C.W.S. HOTEL WM. R. BARRINGER
B 39021

608 SULLIVAN NIKI 10 5.50
LUBBOCK TEX
11/23FB/B HOTEL WM. R. BARRINGER
B 38990

THANK YOU

Opposite, bottom right: A letter from Niki to Buddy Holly and the Crickets and Norman Petty releasing all parties from further obligation. The day after their return to Lubbock, Niki Sullivan announced he was leaving the Crickets. His reason was total exhaustion after three months of non-stop touring, from which there was still to be virtually no let-up over the approaching Christmas holiday.

Right: On 23 November 1957 the group stayed at the Barringer Hotel in Charlotte, NC after playing the city's Coliseum. Hotel bills for this date are displayed here.

Below: Flyer for the Biggest Show of Stars for '57

THURS. OCT. 17—SAN JOSE AUDITORIUM
Two Shows—7 and 9:30 p.m.
Tickets—Coast Radio Co., 266 So. First St., CY 5-5141
And Auditorium Box Office
CY 3-0860

SAT., OCT. 19—S. F. CIVIC AUDITORIUM
Two Shows—7 and 9:30 p.m.
Tickets—Sherman, Clay and Downtown Box Office
SU 1-1331
325 Mason St. - PR 5-2021

SUN., OCT. 20—OAKLAND AUDITORIUM
One Show—8:30 p.m.
Tickets—Sherman, Clay & Co.
Broadway at 21st - HIgate 4-8575

GENERAL ADMISSION $2.50
RESERVED SEATS $3.50
Mail orders with self addressed envelope acceptable

FOR BEST SEATS — ORDER EARLY

If it hadn't been for Elvis, none of us would have ever made it. The last time I saw him, he looked all right to me. The main thing is that he's a great vocal artist in his field.

When I was a kid back in Texas I played piano and violin. But I got sick of both, and I took up guitar. That was the start of it all. I made some dubs and sent them to Jim Denny, head of the artists bureau at WSM in Nashville, Tennessee. Mr Denny liked them and sent them to Paul Cohen of Decca Records. They gave me a Decca contract and we made some records in Nashville. Nothing happened, though, and I went back to Texas pretty discouraged.

Mr Petty made some records with us and sent them to Bob Thiele of Coral Records [which managed the Brunswick label], who bought the master of 'That'll Be the Day'. It was our first record as a group and our first hit.

It's fine with us [to tour and perform with black artists]. We don't believe there's any real difference between us anyway. We have the traditions of not going to school together, but we don't even think about it now. The people in our show are great. For me, I like the Everly Brothers as well as any of the artists. They're with us on tour and they are great boys, both of them. And Elvis is still one of my favourites. He helped us all plenty by paving the way. Eddie Cochran is another good artist. And in the old days I remember hearing records of Hank Williams and Jimmie Rodgers. Those fellows were a great inspiration for the whole country field.

I've heard good things and bad things about how it is over there [in England] from others who've been over. It'll be a brand new experience for all of us. We must have a lot of friends there because they've bought an awful lot of our records. (Buddy Holly interview for *Melody Maker*, Sheraton Lincoln Hotel, Indianapolis, IN, 7 November 1957)

Contract Blank
AMERICAN FEDERATION OF MUSICIANS OF THE UNITED STATES AND CANADA
(HEREIN CALLED "FEDERATION")

ARTIST'S COPY

General ARTISTS CORPORATION
640 Fifth Avenue, New York City, N.Y.
CIRCLE 7-7550
LOCAL NUMBER 802

THIS CONTRACT for the personal services of musicians, made this 5th day of December 19 57 between the undersigned employer (hereinafter called the "employer") and Three (3) (including the Leader) musicians (hereinafter called "employees").

WITNESSETH, That the employer hires the employees as musicians severally on the terms and conditions below. The leader represents that the employees already designated have agreed to be bound by said terms and conditions. Each employee yet to be chosen shall be so bound by said terms and conditions upon agreeing to accept his employment. Each employee may enforce this agreement. The employees severally agree to render collectively to the employer services as musicians in the orchestra under the leadership of BUDDY HOLLY & THE CRICKETS as follows:

Name and Address of Place of Engagement: Paramount Theatre, New York City, N.Y.

Date(s) of Employment: Commencing December 25th, 1957 for a period of twelve (12) days.

Hours of Employment: 35 shows weekly. Insert Exact Hours:

Type of Engagement (specify whether dance, stage show, banquet, etc.): Stage Show.

The employer is hereby given an option to extend this agreement for a period of ______ weeks beyond the original term thereof. Said option can be made effective only by written notice from the employer to the employees, not later than ______ days prior to the expiration of said original term, that he claims and exercises said option, and a copy of said notice shall be filed with the local in whose jurisdiction the engagement is to be played.

WAGE AGREED UPON $ 4000.00 for twelve day period. (Terms and Amount)

This wage includes expenses agreed to be reimbursed by the employer in accordance with the attached schedule, or a schedule to be furnished the employer on or before the date of engagement.

To be paid: Upon conclusion of engagement. (Specify when payments are to be made)

Upon request by the American Federation of Musicians of the United States and Canada (herein called the "Federation") or the local in whose jurisdiction the employees shall perform hereunder, the employer either shall make advance payment hereunder or shall post an appropriate bond.

ADDITIONAL TERMS AND CONDITIONS

APPROVED DEC 16 1957

Barracuda Music., By: Jack Hooke
Employer's Name
Signature of Employer
1619 Broadway
Street Address
New York City, N.Y.
City State
Phone

Leader's Name
Signature of Leader
1321 West 7th
Street Address
Clovis New Mexico
City State

RR/dr
Form B-3 4-1-57

JERRY 'J.I.' ALLISON One of my favourite moments was when we went to New York and played the Paramount. All our favourite musicians were playing – the Everly Brothers, Jerry Lee Lewis and Chuck Berry – and we had four records in the charts at the time: 'That'll Be the Day', 'Peggy Sue', 'Oh Boy!' and 'Everyday'. We sounded exactly like the records at those shows, so we were well received. Afterwards, we stood at the top of the Paramount Theater. Times Square was full of people, and we looked out at the crowd below and said, 'Man, ain't we the ones?' It was over on New Years, when 1957 turned into 1958.

ALAN FREED'S CHRISTMAS JUBILEE
From 23 December 1957 to 5 January 1958 Buddy Holly and the Crickets took part in Alan Freed's Christmas Jubilee Show (above and opposite, programme and ticket) without Niki Sullivan. Artists appearing in the show included Fats Domino, Jerry Lee Lewis, the Everly Brothers and Paul Anka. There were five shows per day, and during this time the group stayed at the Hotel Edison, just as they had when they played at the Paramount in August. During the residency, the band purchased three 'stage tuxedos' at Alfred Norton on 27 December, and, the following day, performed 'Peggy Sue' on The Arthur Murray Party.

JERRY 'J.I.' ALLISON Joe B. was a great, gentle guy. When we started doing our records, Buddy would say, 'Put your finger here and there' and show him the ropes, but he always got it. He played what needed playing, no more and no less, and he had great timing and a feel for music, because he was a great dancer.

SONNY WEST Buddy Holly gave an awful lot to music. He popularised the four-piece band and showed a minimum amount of music could be used to make a good song – and he had an awful lot of good songs, all of which are lasting. 'Peggy Sue' had solid chords all the way through and few lyrics; instead it's about rhythm and attitude. People loved it. In that sense, there's thousands of musicians that were influenced by Buddy. The feeling that you get from the song was Buddy's power.

CLIFF RICHARD 'That'll Be the Day' and 'Maybe Baby' are so melodic and memorable – those songs made him. He should always be remembered as a startlingly good rock writer, and he did some wonderful stuff. I cannot believe he made all that music in that short period of time. He was a very gifted man. There are a handful of people who have a true influence on thousands of others, and Buddy Holly and the Crickets are one of the handful; it's impossible to escape it.

THE BUDDY HOLLY EDUCATIONAL FOUNDATION
Ambassadors

JERRY 'J.I.' ALLISON *'That'll Be the Day'*
ERIC CLAPTON *'Mailman, Bring Me No More Blues'*
SONNY CURTIS *'Rock Around with Ollie Vee'*
BRIAN WILSON *'Everyday'*
NOKIE EDWARDS *'Everyday'*
KEITH ALLISON *'I'm Looking for Someone to Love'*
RINGO STARR *'I'm Looking for Someone to Love'*
PETER FRAMPTON *'Peggy Sue'*
JOE WALSH *'Uh Hu Hu'*
KEITH RICHARDS *'Not Fade Away'*
MICK JAGGER *'Not Fade Away'*
ROGER DALTREY *'Oh Boy!'*
SONNY WEST *'Oh Boy!'/'Rave On'*
JOHN FOGERTY *'Oh Boy!'/'Rave On'*
WILLIE NILE *'It's Too Late'*
JUSTIN HAYWARD *'Send Me Some Lovin''*
THE ZOMBIES *'An Empty Cup (And a Broken Date)'*
ALBERT LEE *'Rock Me My Baby'*
MICKY DOLENZ *'You've Got Love'*
BILLY DAVIS *'You've Got Love'*
WADDY WACHTEL *'Words of Love'*
DOLLY PARTON *'Maybe Baby'*
MIKE BERRY *'Tell Me How'*
STEVE CROPPER *'Last Night'*
JOE BONAMASSA *'Last Night'*

***THE SONGS:* 1957**
This section presents TBHEF ambassadors with guitars named after songs that were written, recorded, performed or demoed by Buddy in 1957.

BUDDY
HOLLY

JERRY 'J.I.' ALLISON *'That'll Be the Day'*

Thank the Lord.
and everyone else.
"I'm so glad Buddy, Sonny & I went
to see "THE SEARCHERS" with JOHN WAYNE -
JOHN SAID "THAT'LL BE THE DAY" five times,
Buddy & I were practicing -- Buddy said
we should write a song. I said TBTD and
here it came." Thanks to all the
rockers who enjoyed us, and who wrote
in this book. It's been a lucky life.
Thanks to the Bradleys for keepin' it
happening, and the folks who do the
Buddy Holly center.
Best to Everyone -
Jerry Allison

THAT'LL BE THE DAY

Upon release of 'That'll Be the Day' – 27 May 1957 – Billboard *reviewed the track: 'Tune is a medium beat rockabilly. Performance is better than material.' During this time Brunswick/Coral did little to promote the single, leaving Buddy in despair at the lack of action. Disc jockeys in various states (particularly Tom Clay, a Philadelphia-based DJ) played the record over and over, and by September of that year, the song was a national hit, reaching the top of the* Billboard *Hot 100. 'That'll Be the Day' served as a wake-up call to industry leaders. Across the Atlantic in Liverpool, the song was covered the following year by a young band called the Quarrymen, later to become The Beatles.*

JERRY IVAN 'J.I.' ALLISON PLAYED ON SOME OF BUDDY'S EARLY SESSIONS and became a full-time member of his group when the Crickets were formed. He wasn't just Buddy Holly's drummer; he was one of his closest friends and creative partners, and together they co-wrote the band's first hit, 'That'll Be the Day', which went to number one in the US chart in 1957. The pair's camaraderie and mutual respect laid the foundation for the band's success. Their debut album, *The 'Chirping' Crickets*, features Buddy, Jerry, Joe B. Mauldin and Niki Sullivan on the iconic front cover.

When Buddy moved to New York in 1958 to become more involved with the business, Jerry and Joe decided to return to Lubbock. Retaining the name the Crickets, they recorded new material with Sonny Curtis, who'd played with Buddy before the band was formed, and singer Earl Sinks.

Released in 1960, the group's final album for Coral, *In Style with the Crickets*, included the classics 'I Fought the Law', 'More Than I Can Say' and their version of Buddy's 'Love's Made a Fool of You'. Going on to sign for the Liberty label, Jerry, Sonny and Tommy Allsup, another musician who'd played with Buddy, became the label's regular studio musicians, backing such artists as Bobby Vee, Johnny Burnette and Eddie Cochran.

After a stint serving in the US Air Force, Jerry and Sonny Curtis provided backing vocals for Eric Clapton's self-titled debut solo album. Later the Crickets toured with Waylon Jennings, who'd played in Buddy's band on the ill-fated Winter Dance Party package tour.

In 2004, the Crickets released *The Crickets and Their Buddies*, featuring collaborations with such artists as Graham Nash, Rodney Crowell, Eric Clapton, Bobby Vee, Nanci Griffith and John Prine. As he had done on several of their previous LPs, Albert Lee played guitar on the album. In 2007, Jerry Allison was inducted into the Musician's Hall of Fame and Museum in Nashville and, as a member of the Crickets, was inducted into the Rock and Roll Hall of Fame in 2012. On 6 February 2016, the Crickets played their final gig at the Surf Ballroom in Clear Lake, Iowa, with Jerry, Sonny, Glen D. Hardin, Tommy Allsup, Gordon Payne and Albert Lee all performing. This was the venue where Buddy had played his last show almost exactly 57 years previously. Jerry died in August 2022 at the age of 82.

J.I.'s guitar was, of course, named after 'That'll Be the Day', appropriately for the guy who co-wrote the song that kicked off an incredible journey which ended too soon for Buddy, but left a legacy and inspiration for generations of musicians, singers and songwriters. – *John Firminger*

JERRY 'J.I.' ALLISON Buddy was a great record producer. He was a talented dude. I'd heard Buddy talk about doing a gospel album and using Ray Charles's arranger. He had all kinds of ideas. He would have produced a lot of good records and, hey, he discovered Waylon and produced his first record.

'The worst move I ever made was staying in Texas when Buddy moved to New York.'

ERIC CLAPTON *'Mailman, Bring Me No More Blues'*

Thanks Buddy –
for my first taste
of the real thing!

Eric

ERIC CLAPTON HAS A BLUES-SOAKED POWER and brilliance which, without Buddy Holly, we may never have got to experience.

There was an authenticity to Buddy's records that spoke to Eric. He has acknowledged many times the way those 1950s singles provided him with the inspiration he needed to take up the guitar. He first saw Buddy play live on the TV show *Sunday Night at the London Palladium* when he was 14 years old. Buddy was playing a Fender guitar and Eric was mesmerised by what he was seeing on the screen. It was the moment that changed his life.

'That Fender was the future,' he said later. 'I wanted to run away from my past.' As it turned out, his first guitar was not a Fender at all, but a Hoyer acoustic, on which he practised relentlessly, channelling the anger of his distorted childhood, thrashing the life out of this basic, hard-stringed instrument.

Soon he began to experiment with the possibilities of different sounds, using a Gibson played through a Marshall valve amp. As Eric found his way through some of the greatest bands ever – the Yardbirds, the Bluesbreakers, Cream, and Derek and the Dominos – he began to create a layered depth of playing that was as distinctive as it was sometimes dark and compelling. He was elevating the guitar to a completely new level.

Amazingly, he was yet to properly own a Fender, the guitar that had inspired his career . . . until he arrived in Nashville in the mid-1970s. He loved the city and bought no fewer than six Fender guitars while he was there, using the best parts of each instrument to morph the collection into one master guitar – a beauty called 'Blackie', which he played on stage from then on.

Since then, Eric has demonstrated his enduring love for Buddy at tribute events and concerts all over the world. He even wrote 'Wonderful Tonight' while waiting for his girlfriend – later his wife – Patti Boyd as she was getting ready to accompany him to a concert honouring Buddy, organised by fellow fan Paul McCartney on 7 September 1976, which would have been Buddy's 40th birthday.

Buddy Holly came into Eric Clapton's life through those fleeting, grainy images on an old black and white television in the analogue days of the 1950s. Buddy Holly has remained in his world ever since. – *Bob Harris*

MAILMAN, BRING ME NO MORE BLUES

Released as a B-side to 'Words of Love', 'Mailman, Bring Me No More Blues' is a song written by Ruth Roberts, Bill Katz and Stanley Clayton, and originally recorded and released by Buddy Holly in June 1957. The song was covered by The Beatles during the 'Get Back' sessions.

'Of all the music heroes of the time, Buddy Holly was the most accessible, and he was the real thing … He was one of us.'

ERIC CLAPTON One summer I got exposed to Chuck Berry and Buddy Holly. Buddy Holly made a very, very big impression on me. Because of a lot of things, but especially the way he looked and his charisma – there was something lonely and very ordinary about the guy, he gave hope to millions of kids with glasses. I was like that, and very much a loner. I didn't fit into sports or group activities as a kid, I couldn't find a niche. Music was not really part of the village curriculum – it was the one place that I could feel at home in, in a very detached and lonely life.

The first Fender I ever saw was the bass that the guy in Jerry Lee Lewis's band was playing when they made the film clip for his song 'Great Balls of Fire'. I'd never seen anything quite like it before. The next thing you know, these guys in England were using it, and Buddy Holly was using a Sunburst. I thought I'd died and gone to heaven … it was like seeing an instrument from outer space and I said to myself: 'That's the future – that's what I want.'

SONNY CURTIS *'Rock Around with Ollie Vee'*

I've always been proud of my association with Buddy Holly and The Crickets. May the music last forever.

Sonny Curtis

FROM HIS WEST TEXAS ORIGINS, Sonny Curtis has gone on to become one of America's most gifted singer-songwriters and performers. A key player in the legacy of Buddy Holly and the Crickets, he has been associated with the band for well over 60 years.

Emerging in the late 1950s, Sonny Curtis was one of the young West Texas musicians who best demonstrated the area's fertile musical environment. He formed a duo with Waylon Jennings, performing at store openings and private functions. In fact, Waylon cited Sonny as his first role model. As rock and roll started to influence these young musicians, Sonny got directly involved in the new genre by accompanying Buddy Holly both on stage around the Lubbock area and on record. The latter happened when Buddy did his first Nashville session in 1956. Cutting 'Blue Days, Black Nights' and 'Love Me', Sonny gained the distinction of being the first person to play a Fender Strat on a rock and roll record. He developed a talent for songwriting too. The Buddy Holly cut 'Rock Around with Ollie Vee' was his initial attempt at writing a rock and roll song.

Towards the end of 1958, the Crickets – drummer Jerry Allison and bassist Joe B. Mauldin – had parted company with Buddy. Continuing as the Crickets, they enlisted Earl Sinks and Sonny Curtis on vocals and lead guitar, respectively. Now reformed, the Crickets began a renewed recording career with the Buddy Holly song 'Love's Made a Fool of You', followed by 'When You Ask About Love', a Sonny Curtis/Jerry Allison co-write, both of which were minor hits in the UK. The group cut their first post-Buddy Holly album, *In Style with the Crickets*. This classic album also included 'More Than I Can Say' and 'I Fought the Law'.

By 1959, the Crickets without Buddy Holly had lost some of their impetus and had now become a trio comprising Allison, Curtis and Mauldin, at which time they also became the regular backing band for the Everly Brothers. In February 1960, Sonny and Jerry Allison played on the historic last recordings of Eddie Cochran: 'Three Steps to Heaven' and 'Cut Across Shorty'. Soon after, in March 1960, the Crickets accompanied the Everly Brothers on their first nationwide UK tour, which was a huge success. It was around this time that Sonny wrote his biggest song, 'Walk Right Back'. He sang the first verse for Don and Phil, who recorded the song before he had the chance to write a second verse. Their recording became an instant worldwide hit.

In 1961 Sonny again teamed up with Jerry Allison, who was now based in Hollywood with a new recording contract on Liberty Records. Recording as the Crickets with Sonny on guitar and vocals, the band's repertoire added more Sonny songs: 'My Little Girl', 'Parisian Girl' and 'A Fool Never Learns', which also gave Andy Williams a big hit. The mid-1970s saw the Crickets back on record with three albums showing a more contemporary side, and by 1978, the band, now consisting of Jerry, Sonny and Joe B. Mauldin, had relocated to Nashville and become part of Waylon Jennings's touring show. This saw them playing to some of the biggest audiences of their career.

As well as playing with the Crickets, Sonny also acquired several solo recording deals through the years with various independent labels. He enjoyed a series of hit singles on the US country charts. One of these was 'The Real Buddy Holly Story', written after seeing the film *The Buddy Holly Story*, which included some errors that Sonny corrected in his song. In 1985, with a new recording deal under his belt, he undertook a short solo tour of the UK. It was a success, and for the next nine years Sonny made regular visits to the UK to delight audiences with his songs, superb guitar playing and wry sense of humour.

In 1994, Sonny teamed up with Jerry Allison and Joe B. Mauldin once again as the Crickets, working until the band's retirement in 2016. – *John Firminger*

ROCK AROUND WITH OLLIE VEE

'Rock Around with Ollie Vee' was released on Decca on 12 August 1957. It was written by Sonny Curtis and first recorded by Buddy on 22 July 1956 at Bradley's Barn, Nashville, TN. There really was an Ollie Vee. She was the wife of one of the employees who worked on Sonny's father's farm.

'Music was our lives. That's all we wanted to do, and for Buddy, Bob and me, that was our existence.'

SONNY CURTIS I met Buddy Holly, Bob Montgomery and Jerry Allison when I was about 15. Buddy and Bob played guitar, of course, and Jerry played drums – even then he was a great drummer – and we all started playing together soon after. One thing I remember about that first meeting is that Buddy had black hair but, at some point, he had dyed it blond and it was growing out. I remember thinking of a black and tan coonhound when I saw Buddy the first time.

That was prior, of course, to rock and roll, so we all played mainly country music. I was playing with Buddy and Jerry when Elvis Presley came into Lubbock and we all just fell in love with Elvis, especially Buddy – he was just blown away. The next day, after Elvis left town, man, we got his records and the next night we were rocking out. We switched right over and started playing his music.

We played anywhere anyone would have us. When I was still in school, I'd play Kiwanis Club luncheons, Lions Clubs, things like that. There was a guy named Dave Stone who owned a country radio station called KDAV. They had a radio show called *Sunday Party* and Buddy, Bob and I played that just about every week. We'd play teen nights at the clubs in Lubbock and Brownsville. We played live remotes on the radio from a grocery store parking lot or automobile dealer parking lot. Music was our lives. That's all we wanted to do, and for Buddy, Bob and me, that was our existence.

We got a record deal with Decca and that's where we made those first records, in Nashville. I left the group because we weren't really making it. I went on the road with Slim Whitman and that's when Buddy got Jerry Allison and Joe B. Mauldin and they went over to Clovis, New Mexico.

Basically, the Crickets split just a year after 'That'll Be the Day'. There were a few reasons, I suppose. Joe B. always says it was because everybody got married, which is probably a bit true! But also, Buddy didn't much like the deal they had with Norman Petty, and he thought they'd do better in New York. He asked Jerry and Joe B. to come along with him but at the end of the day, they didn't want to move. So Buddy went off to New York as Buddy Holly, and the boys stayed on in Texas and with Norman Petty as the Crickets. At that point, they called me up to join the group and at the same time, Earl Sinks from Amarillo who sort of sounded like Buddy, joined as lead vocalist. So I was back in the Crickets.

I think about Buddy a lot. I think his music was good and he was great. Probably the fact that he lost his life at a very young age and was kind of a big star at the time had a lot to do with him achieving a legendary status.

BRIAN WILSON *'Everyday'*

SITUATED ON THE DOORSTEP OF LOS ANGELES, Hawthorne was the perfect childhood location for the young Brian Wilson. As his creative brilliance began to emerge, LA gave him everything he needed to grow from his family troubles and flourish as one of the most naturally gifted musicians the world has ever known.

The city had a perfect mix of cool venues, recording studios and major record labels. It was hip and uniquely glamorous. Elvis would often be seen at the RCA building on Sunset Blvd. Jerry Lee Lewis would regularly visit the city to party. The glorious beach lifestyle was attractive beyond belief – the combination of sun, sea and surf producing its own distinctive art and music.

When the teenage Brian Wilson turned the dial of his transistor radio, he was tuning into music that was to shape his life forever. He loved the vocal harmonies of the Four Freshmen. He was a massive fan of doo-wop group the Penguins, whose number one hit 'Earth Angel' grew from a demo recorded in a garage close to where Brian lived. And he loved the rock and roll records that were booming out of radio stations like KFWB and KNX in the 1950s and 93KHJ in the 1960s. Brian absorbed this breathless soundscape and blended it with LA's exciting beach culture to create the surf-rock singles that became the early Beach Boys' trademark.

Buddy Holly was hot on all of those California radio playlists and at the forefront of the incredible rock and roll revolution that was pumping across the airwaves. These were the records that made an indelible mark on the young Brian Wilson, and his love of Buddy's music has been with him ever since.

The Beach Boys released a fabulous, faithful cover version of 'Peggy Sue' on their 1978 album *M.I.U.*, and in 2011, along with Stevie Nicks, Jackson Browne, Ringo Starr and other superstars, Brian contributed to a wonderful Buddy Holly tribute album, performing the title track, 'Listen to Me', in celebration of what would have been Buddy's 75th birthday.

Then, in 2019, Brian was presented with his glorious TBHEF ambassador's guitar by Peter Bradley, in honour of his support of Buddy's music through the years. Brian was bequeathed his guitar by the original recipient, Nokie Edwards, who was the inventor of the Surfari surf rock sound. The ceremony took place at the Beverly Wilshire Hotel, a poignant full-circle moment, made all the more beautiful by its setting at the heart of the city that has given Brian's life and music so much. – *Bob Harris*

'He was a real inspiration in so many ways.'

I Love Buddy

Brian Wilson

EVERYDAY

'Everyday' was released on Coral on 20 September 1957 as the B-side to 'Peggy Sue', and features on Buddy's self-titled debut solo album. The song was recorded on 29 May 1957 at Norman Petty's studio in Clovis, NM. Buddy played acoustic guitar, Jerry Allison slapped his knees as percussion, and Joe B. Mauldin played acoustic stand-up bass. The identity of the celeste player is disputed. Some say that it was Vi Petty, but others, including the man himself, say that it was her husband, Norman.

There have since been numerous covers of the song, including versions by Bobby Vee, John Denver, Don McLean, James Taylor and Fiona Apple.

BUDDY HOLLY

NOKIE EDWARDS *'Everyday'*

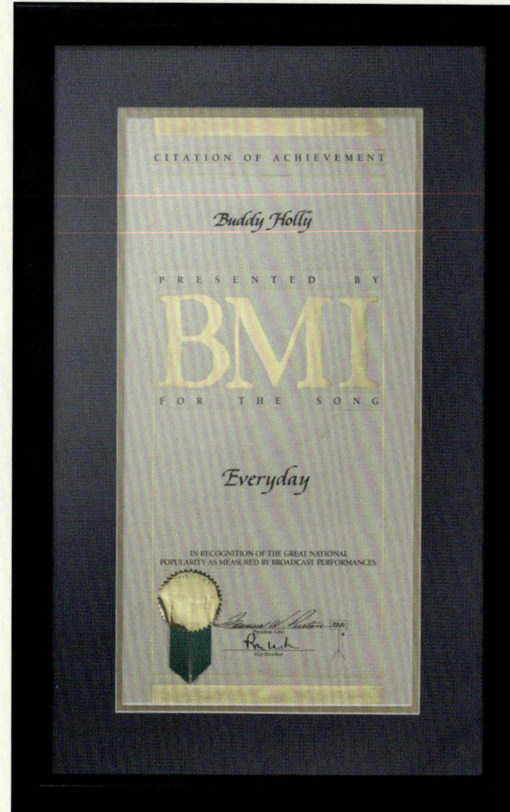

Top: Nokie Edwards recording 'Everyday' on his Buddy Holly guitar in 2012

Above: A BMI Citation of Achievement for 'Everyday' awarded to Buddy

COMING FROM A FAMILY OF ACCOMPLISHED MUSICIANS, it's hardly surprising that Nole 'Nokie' Edwards began playing a variety of instruments from the age of five, including steel guitar, banjo, violin, mandolin and bass. After a spell with the United States Army Reserve, he began playing in various country outfits including Buck Owens's band and in the house band of TV station KTNT, based in the same building as Owens's radio station, KAYE. In 1960 Nokie released a single, 'Night Run', with a band called the Marksmen. He was drafted into a Washington group that had originally been called the Versatones, founded by Don Wilson and Bob Bogle, after they heard him playing in a nightclub. By then they were the Ventures and Nokie was designated as the bass player, but would take over from Bogle on lead guitar.

The Ventures had several Top 30 hits in the US – 'Walk Don't Run', 'Perfidia', 'Ram-Bunk-Shush', 'Walk Don't Run '64' and 'Hawaii Five-O' – and four UK hit singles, with 'Walk Don't Run' and 'Perfidia' both making the Top Ten in 1960. 'Walk Don't Run' sold over a million copies and went gold. The group released a staggering number of albums, studio, live, box sets, compilations, guitar instruction and video . . . over 200 in all.

Nokie Edwards left the Ventures in 1968 but re-joined in 1972 and stayed with them until 1984, when he left to pursue a music career in Nashville and played guitar on what would be Lefty Frizzell's final recordings. By the late 1980s Nokie was back with the Ventures and would occasionally reunite with them to tour, including an annual tour of Japan, which the group undertook until 2012.

Nokie began a solo career in 1969, releasing several albums. He played sessions and performed with several bands in Nashville, receiving two Grammy Award nominations for Best Southern, Country or Bluegrass Gospel Album, for *20th Century Gospel* and *Southern Meets Soul*. In 2008 Nokie and the other members of the Ventures were inducted into the Rock and Roll Hall of Fame by Creedence Clearwater Revival's John Fogerty. The Ventures performed 'Walk Don't Run' and 'Hawaii Five-O'. At one point, Nokie landed a role in the TV Western series *Deadwood*, playing a friend of Wild Bill Hickok, for which he relocated to California.

Nokie was filmed recording 'It Doesn't Matter Anymore' and, in 2012, 'Everyday' on his copy of Buddy's J-45 at Sound Control Recording Studios, Nashville.

Nokie died in 2018 and it was his wish that his guitar presented by The Buddy Holly Educational Foundation be passed on to another musician who admired Buddy Holly and the Crickets. It was Nokie's wife, Judy, who made many of the hand-tooled leather covers for the presentation guitars, who suggested Brian Wilson would be a perfect candidate, not least because early Beach Boys music was partly influenced by the surf music sound that Nokie, and the Ventures, helped to pioneer. – *Mike Read*

'Jerry called me one day and asked if I wanted to play guitar with them, and I said I was in!'

BEST KNOWN AS A LONG-STANDING MEMBER of Paul Revere and the Raiders, Keith was the cousin of the Crickets' drummer, Jerry Allison. After leaving the Raiders in April 1975, he went on to play with the Rick Danko Band as well as working with such artists as Ronnie Hawkins, Ringo Starr, the Beach Boys, Alice Cooper, Sonny and Cher, Jerry Lee Lewis and Johnny Rivers. Keith also appeared in the 2003 film *Gods and Generals*. He performed with the Waddy Wachtel Band for over a dozen years and in 2016 he played with the Crickets at Clear Lake, Iowa for what would be their very last gig. – *Mike Read*

KEITH ALLISON When Buddy and the Crickets came to the San Antonio Municipal Theater, I dressed up in my red and black jacket and carried an empty guitar case, hoping I could get backstage. It worked and I saw Jerry Allison, who was 18. I was 15. I stood in the wings with Buddy watching Little Richard playing his new single, 'Roll Over Beethoven', and Buddy said to me 'Man, can that guy play!'

Each one of the guitars comes with a song title and mine was 'I'm Looking for Someone to Love', which was the B-side of 'That'll Be the Day'. I think that Paul McCartney has the 'That'll Be the Day' guitar.

The Crickets,

My all time favorite group,

The Highlight of my career — having being a part of them.

Keith Allison

KEITH ALLISON *'I'm Looking for Someone to Love'*

I'M LOOKING FOR SOMEONE TO LOVE
'I'm Looking for Someone to Love' was recorded on 25 February 1957 by Buddy, Larry Welborn, Jerry Allison and Niki Sullivan. Gary and Ramona Tollett provided backing vocals. It was written by Buddy and Norman Petty and released on Brunswick on 27 May 1957. It was intended to be the A-side of the record, but it was flipped over and 'That'll Be the Day' became a number one hit, while 'I'm Looking for Someone to Love' never charted.

RINGO STARR *'I'm Looking for Someone to Love'*

Buddy Was Great
Peace and Love
Ringo

'He was a big influence. He was the start of rock and roll with Eddie Cochran, Gene Vincent, Chuck Berry and, of course, Little Richard, my personal hero. He was part of that initiation into rock and roll for me.'

RINGO STARR HAS BEEN A LIGHT in the music industry for decades, both as a member of The Beatles and as a solo artist. Like Buddy Holly, Ringo hailed from humble beginnings, growing up in a working-class area of Liverpool, and, again like Buddy, he showed a passion for music at a young age.

Drawing inspiration from the burgeoning rock and roll movement that Buddy was a major part of, Ringo began his career at 17 as a drummer in a skiffle band, and then in Rory Storm and the Hurricanes. However, it was not long until he was asked to join The Beatles, a local Liverpool band that had found a degree of success in the area and in Germany. During his time in The Beatles, he wrote 'Octopus's Garden' and 'Don't Pass Me By' and sang lead on some of the band's best-loved songs such as 'With a Little Help from My Friends' and 'Yellow Submarine'.

Following the band's split, Ringo became the first solo Beatle to score seven consecutive US Top Ten singles, starting with 'It Don't Come Easy' and including the number one hits 'Photograph' and 'You're Sixteen'. In 2011, he participated in the tribute album *Listen to Me: Buddy Holly*, which celebrated what would have been Buddy's 75th birthday. Ringo contributed a cover of 'Think It Over', showcasing his enduring admiration for Buddy Holly's songwriting and performance style.

Ringo was bequeathed his guitar by the family of his good friend Keith Allison, who died in 2021.

BUDDY
HOLLY

PETER FRAMPTON *'Peggy Sue'*

If it weren't for Buddy Holly I don't think I would be playing guitar. His music was incredibly inspiring and his guitar and sound were something that really got me.
Peggy Sue was the first song I learnt to play ever! I think it was a good one to start with!!
Thanks Buddy!
[signature]

"Buddy Holly Lives"

THE FIRST TIME PETER FRAMPTON GOT UP ON STAGE and performed in front of an audience he was just nine years old. He played 'Peggy Sue' to a small gathering of people at his local Cub Scout group in Bromley, England. His interpretation of his favourite song was so good that it earned him a music merit badge which, from then on, he proudly displayed on the arm of his Scouts uniform.

It was a magic moment, one that opened the pathway towards a career that has seen him become one of the most compelling and successful live performers, first with the Herd, then with Humble Pie and ultimately as a solo artist. His successes include the 1976 award-winning album *Frampton Comes Alive*, which topped the charts across the world and sold well over 11 million copies.

Like so many young kids in Britain in the late 1950s and early 1960s, Peter was drawn to the energy and excitement of rock and roll. As well as Buddy Holly, he was a fan of Eddie Cochran, Billy Fury and Adam Faith. He particularly loved the Shadows – their music, of course, but also that their lead guitarist, Hank Marvin, wore Buddy Holly-style horn-rimmed glasses. Peter even bought himself a pair from his local Woolworths store. He knocked out the lenses, bent them to fit and proudly wore them on stage while playing with his first-ever band, the Trubeats.

The Trubeats started performing gigs at local venues just as Beatlemania was exploding right across the UK. New bands were appearing everywhere and Peter was particularly attracted to a local group called the Konrads, which featured a mesmerising sax player and vocalist called Davy Jones. Soon Peter and Davy became close friends, sharing a love of music and jamming 'Maybe Baby', 'Peggy Sue' and other Buddy Holly songs on the steps of Bromley Technical High School, where Davy was a pupil in Peter's father's art class. There began a lasting, creative friendship. Long after the charismatic Davy Jones had changed his name to David Bowie, he invited Peter to play guitar on his 17th studio album, *Never Let Me Down*, and to travel the world with him on the Glass Spider tour in 1987, a pivotal moment in Peter's career.

Peter is still performing Buddy's songs. In August 2022 I was proud to introduce him on stage at the magnificent Buddy Holly Hall of Performing Arts and Sciences in Lubbock, where he played a deeply moving set at a sell-out all-star concert, celebrating the work of one of the greatest songwriters ever. It was the perfect full circle. – *Bob Harris*

PEGGY SUE

'Peggy Sue' was released on Coral on 20 September 1957. It was recorded by Buddy Holly on 2 July 1957 at Norman Petty's studio in Clovis, NM.

When Buddy composed the song, he had called it 'Cindy Lou', after his young niece Cindy. Following several unsuccessful attempts to record the song with a contemporary calypso beat, Buddy asked Jerry Allison to play paradiddles, a rudimentary beat, on the drums. Jerry asked Buddy if he would change the title of the song so he could make an impression on his girlfriend, Peggy Sue Gerron, with whom he had fallen out. Buddy agreed. The title and beat were changed, and a hit was born. Jerry and Peggy Sue did get back together and got married.

When 'Peggy Sue' was released, the credited writers were Jerry Allison and Norman Petty even though it was Buddy who basically composed the song. He gave part of the songwriting credit to Jerry Allison, as Jerry came up with the new title and the drum beat which 'made' the record.

'He's very inspiring to many musicians still today – especially in England. I think Buddy is bigger in England, still now, than he is anywhere else.'

PETER FRAMPTON The first song I ever sang in public was by Buddy Holly – and that means so much to me.

It was really the very beginning of me learning to play guitar. At the same time as Buddy, there was Eddie Cochran and all these people that played guitar and wrote their own music or sang and played – which was the most important thing to me. Buddy was pretty techie, and he recorded a lot of his later stuff in his New York apartment on his own tape recorder, and I loved that. He always had a great sound and his playing was great; and electric guitar was coming to the fore at that time, so he was definitely a major influence for me.

Buddy made songs that appealed to everybody. At that time, it was very fresh, and it was simple. When he came out, it was just guitar, bass and drums – before he made the band bigger. Nothing was too involved in his songs, but they're classics. They were just simple – and I'm saying that as a good thing. Simplicity always wins.

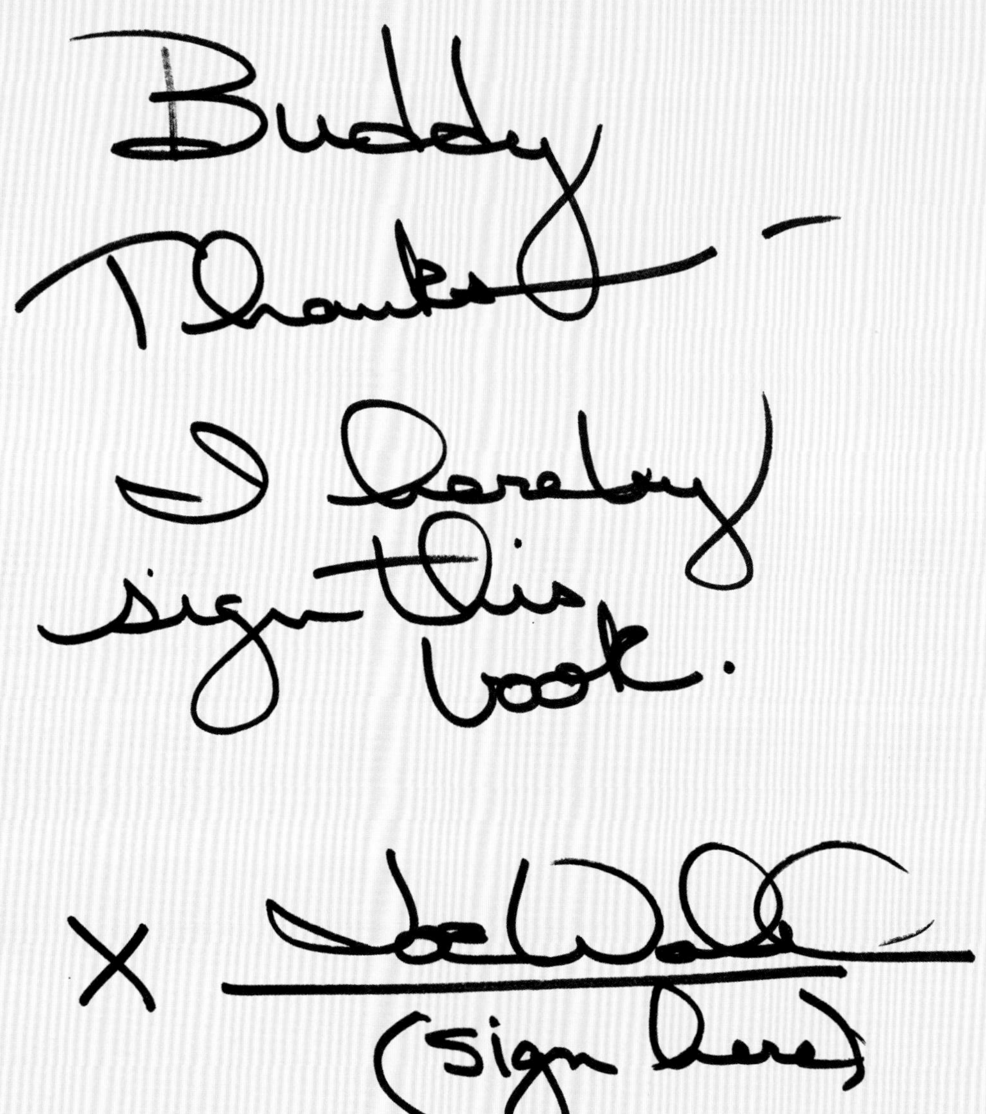

Joe Walsh is the proud recipient of a beautiful Buddy Holly guitar, which, uniquely, is not named after a song. Instead, Joe has christened it 'Uh Hu Hu' after Buddy's unique singing style. Of course he has. He's Joe Walsh.

BUDDY HOLLY HAD IT ALL. He was a singer, a songwriter, a guitarist, a solo artist, a member of a group, a compelling stage presence and a figure who commanded the respect of his peers across a multitude of genres. From country, blues and rockabilly, all the way from Lubbock to rock and roll, Buddy's music inspired an incredible new generation of world-class musicians to pick up their guitars and play.

Joe Walsh got his first guitar as a ten-year-old at the time Buddy was dominating the charts in 1957. Inspired by Buddy's music, Joe began exploring the local Ohio music scene and a few years later became a member of a local garage band, the Measles. He was networking hard and somehow managed to get a couple of songs recorded on the debut album by a neighbourhood bubble-gum group called Ohio Express, who had just scored a worldwide smash with 'Yummy Yummy Yummy'! It was the first major step on the pathway that took him to stardom.

The following year, fellow Ohio band the Lemon Pipers went into the charts with the hippie anthem 'Green Tambourine', and, through his contacts with them and others, Joe found his way to the Hit Factory studios in New York. He was just beginning his career as front man with power-trio the James Gang, creating their ground-breaking debut LP 'Yer Album' in 1969 and an instant reputation as one of the first truly great American rock bands.

Joe's heavy, riff-laden guitar style was a sensation and when the James Gang supported the Who at a local concert in Cleveland, Pete Townshend was impressed beyond belief. He immediately signed the band to support the Who on their upcoming tour of Britain, an itinerary which included a gig at the Hammersmith Palais in 1970. I was there! Jimmy Page and Eric Clapton also became big fans and international recognition followed.

Inevitably, Joe soon cut loose from the framework of the group, creating three powerful barnstorming albums which I featured on repeat on my early 1970s BBC radio shows. These were albums for the ages. Joe and his co-producer Bill Szymczyk sculpted a brilliant, distinctive, dramatic, multi-layered, swirling wall of sound, and when Bill was recruited by the Eagles to work with them on their upcoming *Hotel California* album, the band invited Joe to go with him. He arrived just in time to record the title track and play one of the most iconic dual-guitar solos ever recorded. It was a career-defining moment.

Don Henley initially thought Joe might be too wild for the Eagles, laid-back California sound and the band certainly went through various tensions over the years. But Joe remains an essential member to this day, cutting an enduring, endearing, buccaneering figure . . . blond hair bright in the spotlight, face contorted through the riffs and the roughshod, loving solos on 'Life in the Fast Lane', 'Life's Been Good' and more.

Over the years Joe has played with Ringo Starr, the Beach Boys, Bob Seger, Steve Winwood and countless other world-class musicians. He was inducted into the Rock and Roll Hall of Fame in 1998.
– *Bob Harris*

BUDDY
HOLLY

KEITH RICHARDS *'Not Fade Away'*

NOT FADE AWAY
'Not Fade Away' was released on Brunswick on 27 October 1957. It was written by Buddy Holly and Norman Petty and was recorded by Buddy on 29 May 1957 at Norman Petty's studio in Clovis, NM. 'Not Fade Away' was written with a Bo Diddley rhythm in mind, either from the song 'Bo Diddley' or, more plausibly, Diddley's 1955 song 'Pretty Thing'. Bo Diddley reciprocated much later when he recorded 'Not Fade Away' himself.

Buddy,
The very
essence
of "THE
STUFF"

KEITH RICHARDS IS THE LEGENDARY GUITARIST and co-founder of the Rolling Stones. A chance meeting with Mick Jagger on a train platform, when they bonded over the mail-order albums by Chuck Berry and Muddy Waters that Jagger was carrying, led to what would eventually become the Rolling Stones. Keith's enduring presence – both on and off stage – in the music world has left an indelible mark on rock and roll.

Buddy Holly's influence on Keith Richards is profound, and is illustrated within the group's early works, as well as their popular cover of 'Not Fade Away' – a cornerstone in the Stones' discography. The cover not only paid homage to Buddy, but helped introduce his music to a new audience. Since then, Keith has gone on the record to explain why Buddy Holly – and those great melodies – meant so much to him.

'I think doing Buddy's songs got us together to start trying to write songs.'

KEITH RICHARDS Mick had been singing with some rock and roll bands, doing Buddy Holly … He was in England as solid as Elvis. Everything that came out was a record smash number one. By about '58, it was either Elvis or Buddy. It was split into two camps. The Elvis fans were the heavy leather boys and the Holly ones all somehow looked like Buddy Holly.

Maybe it was the fact of doing Buddy's song 'Not Fade Away' that also gave us that extra propagation to start writing our own stuff. We'd done our gig, we'd recorded it, and it was great and successful, now you're a star … now what's next? I think Buddy's inspiration was that he wrote his own songs, which influenced The Beatles incredibly, and it slowly dawned on us that it would be great if one of us could write some songs, and two of us would be fantastic.

He had an influence on everybody. Everybody who is playing now and just coming up because of what they've listened to – it's been handed on. Buddy was in the union and one of the troubadours, and he passed it on via The Beatles, via us, everything he did … You still hear it on the radio today on a brand-new release, you can hear Buddy Holly on there. He's in everybody. How much? That's another thing. It's not bad for a guy from Lubbock.

'The greatest. And I mean that – the greatest.'

MICK JAGGER To English people Buddy Holly was an enormous inspiration. He was a songwriter, which Elvis wasn't. And he wrote very simple songs, sort of lesson one in songwriting. Great songs, which had simple changes and nice melodies and changes of tempo and all that. You could learn from Buddy Holly how to write songs, the way he put them together. He was a beautiful writer.

I first saw Buddy
when I was 14
he was such an inspiration

Mick Jagger

MICK JAGGER HAS BEEN WEARING HIS LOVE OF BUDDY HOLLY on his elegantly tailored sleeve for 60 years. In March 1964, already five years after Buddy's death, the Rolling Stones' irresistibly urgent version of 'Not Fade Away' became their first UK Top Ten hit, and their very first single in the US. It even shared chart space in Britain for a short time with a posthumous 45 by Buddy and the Crickets, 'You've Got Love'. The Stones' cover was an indication of the pedestal they put Buddy Holly on, and was perhaps the moment that Jagger grew into the vocal presence we have known ever since.

Long before the advent of the Rollin' (with an apostrophe) Stones, and with that unconscious synchronicity that informs so many rock and roll stories, Mick was singing with a local Dartford band doing covers of Buddy and Eddie Cochran, even as Keith Richards was buying 'Peggy Sue Got Married' and the compilation *The Buddy Holly Story*.

The US trade magazine *Cash Box* reviewed the Stones' 'Not Fade Away' as a 'wild, freewheeling full-sounding pounder that can take off in no time flat'. Norman Petty, Buddy's former manager, told *Record Mirror* in 1964: 'I was very pleased when the Rolling Stones recorded Buddy's "Not Fade Away". I'd like to see more of Buddy's songs recorded by British groups as they've still got a great sound.'

That single had a profound effect on Jagger and Richards as the writing force they were soon to become. Said manager Andrew Loog Oldham: 'The way they arranged it was the beginning of the shaping of them as songwriters. From then on they wrote.'
– Paul Sexton

Opposite: Mick Jagger welcomed Yungblud as a new ambassador for The Buddy Holly Educational Foundation when the Rolling Stones played Anfield Stadium, Liverpool, 9 June 2022

Atkin
BUDDY
HOLLY

Buddy Holly
Oh Boy!
The songs
of my teenage years.

ROGER DALTREY *'Oh Boy!'*

'When his lyrics are combined with his wonderful voice, the sincerity shines through and the songs still speak to listeners today.'

(Taken from page 408, Afterword by Roger Daltrey and Pete Townshend)

ONE EVENING I WAS INVITED BACKSTAGE AT THE ROYAL ALBERT HALL. I was welcomed into the dressing room by Roger Daltrey and his wife Heather. In true modern rock and roll style Roger offered me a cup of tea. It was hard to reconcile our diminutive host with the colossus we had just witnessed on stage as the Who headlined another fundraising Teenage Cancer Trust concert.

Roger Daltrey is one of the best front men in the world of rock. The combination of Roger's vocals with Pete Townshend's powerful guitar, John Entwistle's driving bass and Keith Moon's dynamic drumming made the Who one of the world's all-time great rock and roll bands.

Being small in stature and born and raised in the tough London areas of Acton and Shepherd's Bush, Roger had to learn to stand up for himself and he became adept at winning a fist fight, something that would cause problems later on. An exemplary, top-of-the-class pupil in primary school, Roger passed the exams to allow him to enter Acton Grammar School. The working class lad among the 'toffs' was subjected to much bullying. The teachers failed to recognise and cultivate his potential, and he ended up being expelled for smoking and various other misdeeds. His headmaster, Mr Kibblewhite, told him, 'We can't control you, Daltrey. You're out. You'll never make anything with your life.' So at the age of 15 his path changed dramatically, but expulsion was just the spur he needed to prove this teacher wrong. This was reflected in the title he chose for his autobiography: *Thanks a Lot Mr Kibblewhite*. The other big plus from his time at Acton Grammar was that it was there he met Pete Townshend and John Entwistle.

Using his woodworking skills Roger made his own guitar, modelled on a Fender Stratocaster he'd seen in a shop window. Skiffle music was all the rage with groups using home-made instruments like a tea chest bass and a washboard for percussion. He formed a band playing clubs, church halls and weddings. On the way home from work he met John Entwistle, who was carrying a huge bass guitar, also home-made. Together with Harry Wilson on drums they formed the Detours and later Pete joined on lead guitar.

With a new management team of Kit Lambert and Chris Stamp, and a new drummer called Keith Moon, the Detours became the Who and they were on their way. Pete Townshend once commented that they were 'four totally different blokes who should never have been together in a band'. But it was that dynamic tension that helped give the Who their incredible power and intensity. Sometimes this went too far: Keith's short fuse and tendency to solve disagreements with his fists led to him being fired by the group. Promising to change, he was welcomed back on probation. Later, when Pete Townshend hit him over the head with his guitar, Keith felled him with one blow, knocking him unconscious.

In 1969, the Who released Pete Townshend's ground-breaking rock opera *Tommy*. That album had a profound effect on Roger Daltrey. The variety of the songs required him to try different vocal techniques and styles and a really good vocalist became a brilliant one. In 1975, director Ken Russell chose Roger to play the lead role in the film version and subjected him to all kinds of hair-raising stunts with a careless disregard for his safety. Roger came to dread Ken's words, 'Just one more take'. Roger was nominated for the Golden Globe award for Best Acting Debut in a Motion Picture.

With the extra confidence gained from acting, together with his suede onstage outfits and fringe jackets, Roger Daltrey became a complete rock messiah to rival the likes of Jim Morrison and Robert Plant. With eight solo studio albums and over 50 acting credits in films and TV, he broadened his range to become the icon he is today.

Using his status and influence, he founded the Teenage Cancer Trust charity and Teenage Cancer America, which have raised over £20 million to help fund specialist wards for young people undergoing cancer treatment.

Pete Townshend said of his lifelong collaborator, 'I've been with him since school days. I won't pretend we always got on but I love him now. He's been so loyal to me and a great friend. I have the greatest respect for him, he's a man of honour.' – *Johnnie Walker*

OH BOY!

'Oh Boy!' was released on Brunswick on 27 October 1957. It was written by Sonny West, Bill Tilghman and Norman Petty and recorded by Buddy on 2 July 1957 at Norman Petty's studio in Clovis, NM. Right after the instrumental break, listen carefully and you can hear Buddy turn quickly from the microphone and clear his throat just after the second time he sings the word 'me'.

Sonny West recorded a demo version of the song which Buddy heard before he recorded it himself.

The
BUDDY HOLLY

Thank You Buddy
for understanding what
Rave On! actually meant.
Your Recording of that
and Oh Boy was Perfect!
Always Buddy!
Sonny West

BORN ON THE CLOVIS HIGHWAY near Buddy Holly's home town of Lubbock, Joe 'Sonny' West became a rock and roll singer and songwriter while still in his teens.

In February 1957 he recorded a demo version of one of his songs, 'All My Love'. The song was picked up by Buddy Holly and the Crickets, who recorded it under the new title of 'Oh Boy!' in the middle of 1957 at Norman Petty's studio in Clovis, with the Picks providing backing vocals. 'Oh Boy!' went to number ten for Buddy and the Crickets in the US, number three in the UK and featured on the album *The 'Chirping' Crickets*.

A year later, the band recorded another song written by Sonny, 'Rave On', which Bruce Springsteen has cited as one of the greatest rock and roll songs of all time. Springsteen even claims to pump himself up before concerts by singing it backstage. There have been over 60 covers of the song.

Sonny West was inducted into the Rockabilly Hall of Fame in 2016. He died in 2022. – *John Firminger*

SONNY WEST The first visit that I recall with Buddy Holly was at Radio KDAV in Lubbock. He was there with Bob Montgomery as they had a weekend live show. From this first encounter I could see that he and I were on the same page, having grown up culturally and geographically in this same type of family.

One year later Buddy Holly and the Crickets were on the top of the charts, and they had recorded my song 'Oh Boy!' for their second record, which also became a huge hit. A similar thing happened with 'Rave On'. He knew what the songs needed to succeed, and time has proved he was right. I was overjoyed having him do the songs. I am proud to be forever connected to Buddy and his wonderful legacy.

'He was the sort that would joke around when he was familiar with you, but he was always serious about his music.'

RAVE ON

'Rave On' was released on Coral on 20 February 1958. It was written by Sonny West, Bill Tilghman and Norman Petty and recorded by Buddy on 25 January 1958 at Bell Sound Studio in New York City.

JOHN FOGERTY *'Oh Boy!'/'Rave On'*

'There was a group pictured on the cover – a guy with a 'Strat' and three other guys. It was a group, and it was the first time you saw a group in rock and roll and I thought, "I'm gonna have a group."'

IN AMONG THE HEAVY ROCK AND PROGRESSIVE PSYCHEDELIA OF THE LATE 1960S, there was one hugely successful band whose sound hearkened back to an earlier, simpler era. That band was Creedence Clearwater Revival.

They first appeared on the UK charts in 1969 with 'Proud Mary', followed by the number one single 'Bad Moon Rising', triggering a glorious run of singles that included 'Travellin' Band', 'Up Around the Bend' and 'Have You Ever Seen the Rain' among many others. Their music was simple and direct. It spoke from the heart and it rocked like crazy, evoking the energy of the great early records that came from the Sun label in Memphis, the Starday imprint in Nashville and Buddy Holly and the Crickets in Lubbock, Texas. The leader and songwriter of CCR was John Fogerty, who grew up to the sound of those ground-breaking recordings. At the very first Rock and Roll Hall of Fame induction ceremony on 23 January 1986, he stood at the microphone and explained why Creedence sounded the way they did.

'I just want to tell you what Buddy Holly meant to me,' he began. 'I was 12 years old, and I was working at a beach resort, and that voice and guitar came up over the PA. I went out and bought "That'll Be the Day", and started learning the words. A few months later, I bought the album, and that album set a course in musical history for a series of strange events, I think. There was a group pictured on the cover – a guy with a Strat and three other guys. It was a group, and it was the first time you saw a group in rock and roll and I thought, "I'm gonna have a group."

'Over in Liverpool,' he continued, 'the same thing was going on with four other guys. They named their group The Beatles because Buddy Holly's group was called the Crickets. In 1963, these four guys chose to end their great song "I Want to Hold Your Hand" with the little syncopation Buddy Holly used in the chorus after the solo of "That'll Be the Day".' As he looked out at the audience he added, 'All you guys who play rock will know what I'm talking about.'

It was a stunning observation, and we know that the connection between Buddy and The Beatles was strong from the very start.

When John Fogerty made this speech in 1986, he had recently enjoyed his biggest chart success for many years with *Centerfield* and as he stood at the lectern, he acknowledged Buddy's influence on the title song of that brilliant comeback album. 'Well, this kid was writing a song about how it feels to be back, and he ended his song with the same riff. It came from the same place. We are all made up of the people we love and the people we admire. I think that's why we're all here tonight.'

With Buddy's widow Maria Elena and her daughter Elena by his side, John Fogerty announced Buddy Holly as one of the ten founding members of the Rock and Roll Hall of Fame. – *Bob Harris*

God Bless Buddy!
A Rocker with a true heart if
there ever was one — whose music
inspires to this day and will for years to
come —
First record I ever bought was "Peggy Sue"
Listened to it a thousand times — still do —
It changed my life —
Thanks Buddy for putting the Rock in the Roll!
And the Sock in the Soul!!
Thanks for changing the world!!
With Love + Respect —
Willie Nile

WILLIE NILE When I was in the fourth grade growing up outside of Buffalo, New York, I was over the moon with what I was hearing on the radio in the early days of rock. The first record I ever bought was Buddy's single 'Peggy Sue'. I played it over and over again on a small white plastic record player. I must have played it 200 times those first few days. It was a life-changer for me. There was something wild and innocent about it that I'd never heard before. It was alive, full of passion and it rocked!

If it hadn't been for Buddy I might not have been on this journey. His music changed the world. Its effect on a generation of kids who heard it and began their own musical journeys is well documented. I was one of those lucky kids. It set me on a course of adventure and discovery that I'm still on to this day.

There is an elegance and a majesty to Buddy's songs and recordings that speaks to something genuine and real in the human experience. They can be full of fire at one moment and tender hearted and gentle the next. There's an effortlessness to them that you just can't fake.

I'll be forever grateful to Buddy Holly for turning me on to the limitless possibilities of what can be done with an electric guitar, a bass, a set of drums and a voice that comes straight from the heart. At its best, music can be a source of healing in this world and that's Buddy for me. He was all heart! Buddy Holly was a true believer. He had a heart and soul that was made for rock and roll.

'At its best, music can be a source of healing in this world and that's Buddy for me.'

HAVING STUDIED PHILOSOPHY AT THE UNIVERSITY OF BUFFALO, Willie Nile began his musical career in Greenwich Village. After the *New York Times* music critic sang his praises, Clive Davis signed him to the Arista label. His eponymous debut album came out in 1980, one magazine writing 'Every song spins superb hooks with a Buddy Holly flair.' It also praised his breathless, beatific lyrics and crisp Buddy Holly rhythms. Willie toured with the Who that summer and his second album, *Golden Down*, came out the following year.

Willie has recorded and performed with many artists, including Bruce Springsteen, Joan Jett, Roger Daltrey, Billy Idol, Elvis Costello, Ian Hunter, Ringo Starr, Tori Amos, Carole King and Barenaked Ladies. – *Mike Read*

IT'S TOO LATE

Written by Chuck Willis, 'It's Too Late' was first recorded by Buddy Holly on 20 July 1957 at Norman Petty's studio in Clovis, NM. The song was included on The 'Chirping' Crickets, *released on Brunswick on 27 November 1957.*

Left: Willie pictured sitting outside Buddy's New York apartment

When I was very young the fashion in live pop music was to have a singer out front, doing the moves, and the group, tidy and obedient, behind them.

This was absolutely the case in Swindon where I grew up. Swindon always had a vibrant 'live' music scene, and of course Elvis was the pop idol everyone looked to for thier inspiration. I knew I would not be an Elvis; so in a way I was always a bit lost – untill Buddy came along and rescued me.

From the first moment I heard 'That'll be the Day' I knew something wonderful had happened. Buddy brought into focus what I wanted to do. I know every Buddy Holly and the Crickets song. I learnt them all for pleasure. I noted as well, from photographs of Buddy and his guitar, that he used a capo on the fifth fret on some songs. You can see the wear on the fingerboard of his original Strat. That was a 'light bulb' moment! We all owe Buddy the greatest debt – we will always love and honour him, and the records sound as good now as they did when I was at school.

Justin Hayward.

SEND ME SOME LOVIN'

Written by John Marascalo and Leo Price, 'Send Me Some Lovin'' was originally recorded by Little Richard. His version entered the charts on 27 March 1957 and reached number 54. Buddy Holly and the Crickets recorded the song on 20 July 1957 at Norman Petty's studio in Clovis, NM and included it on their album The 'Chirping' Crickets, *released on Brunswick on 27 November 1957.*

AS A TEENAGER, JUSTIN HAYWARD PLAYED BUDDY HOLLY SONGS in various groups in and around his home town of Swindon. In 1965, he answered an advertisement in the *Melody Maker* as a guitarist for Joyce and Marty Wilde. He got the job and became a member of the Wilde Three. The following year he replaced Denny Laine as lead singer of the Moody Blues. The band's first album after Justin joined, the innovative and iconic *Days of Future Passed*, has sold over two million copies. The Moody Blues' total album sales stand at well over 60 million, thanks mainly to a run of eight top ten studio albums from 1968 to 1981, from *In Search of the Lost Chord* through to *Long Distance Voyager*.

From 1967 to 1974 Justin was the Moody Blues' main singer and most prolific songwriter, writing 20 of the group's 27 singles in that period, including such classics as 'Nights in White Satin', 'Question', 'I Know You're Out There Somewhere' and 'Tuesday Afternoon'.

In 1975 Justin and fellow Moody Blue John Lodge collaborated on the top five album *Blue Jays* and the non-album single 'Blue Guitar', which became a hit. Three years later Justin had another hit with 'Forever Autumn' from *Jeff Wayne's War of the Worlds*.

Justin never forgot his roots and the early influence of Buddy Holly. He recorded a version of Buddy's 'Learning the Game', which was included on the CD re-release of his debut solo album, *Songwriter*. In August 1983, when he appeared on the Mike Read-hosted Radio One Roadshow at St Ives, he and Mike played a Buddy Holly song live on air and on stage.

In 2000 Justin was awarded the Golden Note by the American Society of Songwriters, Composers and Publishers and in 2004 he was awarded the Gold Badge by the British Academy of Songwriters, Composers and Authors for Lifetime Achievement. He is a member of the Society of Distinguished Songwriters and in 2018 he was inducted into the Rock and Roll Hall of Fame as a member of the Moody Blues. In 2022 he was awarded the OBE for services to the music industry.

The year 2024 saw Justin receive his Buddy Holly guitar from The Buddy Holly Educational Foundation, just prior to undertaking another lengthy tour. Buddy would have been proud.

'My musical and emotional life revolved around Buddy Holly.'

JUSTIN HAYWARD My biggest influence was Buddy Holly. I was devastated by his death and when I was told about it (in a chemistry lesson at school by another pupil) my future seemed empty. I am so thankful for that short time when he was giving us the best music I have ever heard. From the age of 12 or 13 onwards all the groups I was in, around Swindon, played his songs – it was our 'thing'. My musical and emotional life revolved around Buddy Holly. He taught many of us how to play properly. He will always be the greatest for me.

As soon as I came to the USA with the Moodies I visited Lubbock, Texas … and I had the pleasure of meeting his widow, Maria Elena Holly, first in the 1970s and I met her again a couple of times after that. A gentle and quiet woman – all of us English musicians loved her because he did. She came to a few of our gigs and I was always thrilled to be in her company. She told me that when you watched Buddy play guitar the most striking thing was the way he played the downstrokes with his right hand … the sheer speed of his rhythm. His guitar always carried the groove and the feel of the songs and it was through him that I came to realise what makes music truly swing.

AN EMPTY CUP (AND A BROKEN DATE)

'An Empty Cup (And a Broken Date)' was written by a young Roy Orbison and first recorded in 1956 by the Teen Kings, a band which Orbison had founded at 12 years old with his friend and schoolmate James Morrow. They recorded the song at Buddy and the Crickets' preferred studio, Norman Petty Studios in Clovis, NM, a year before Orbison started writing and recording for Sun Records. It was Petty who brought 'An Empty Cup (And a Broken Date)' to Buddy Holly and the Crickets' attention, and the group recorded it in 1957 and included it on their album The 'Chirping' Crickets.

Two guys fashioned my early Rock'n'roll life....
Elvis & BUDDY!
Rod Argent

What an honour to be associated with the late great Buddy Holly
Hugh Grundy

He taught me to write songs
Chris White

The Zombies always played Buddy's songs! We wouldn't have been the same band without his wonderful writing!!
Colin Blunstone

THE ZOMBIES, ORIGINALLY CALLED THE MUSTANGS, came together in Hertfordshire, near London, in 1961. After winning a London *Evening News* talent contest for beat groups, they signed to Decca. Their debut single, 'She's Not There', climbed to number 12 in the UK and number two in the US. A great start for any group: a transatlantic hit, a million seller and a gold disc.

Further hits like 'Tell Her No' and 'Time of the Season' cemented the band's place in the rock scene with their haunting harmonies. The Zombies' second album, *Odessey and Oracle*, released in 1967, gradually achieved critical praise and a cult following, and has since become one of the most acclaimed albums of the 1960s.

In 2019, after several nominations, the band were finally inducted into the Rock and Roll Hall of Fame. They reunite regularly to tour together and to record new, exciting sounds. – *Mike Read*

'We were hugely influenced by Buddy Holly. Who wasn't?'

HUGH GRUNDY We used to do songs like 'Peggy Sue' when we were a covers group and out on the road, before we ever wrote anything. As the drummer, I found 'Peggy Sue' quite a challenging song to play, as I had to keep that rhythm going all the way through the song. We were hugely influenced by Buddy Holly. Who wasn't? His songs were so original … loved him to bits.

COLIN BLUNSTONE Buddy Holly was a major influence on the Zombies; we played many of his songs and marvelled at his writing. They were great fun to play and of course the audiences absolutely loved them. I don't think the Zombies would have progressed in the way we did if we hadn't discovered the wonderful songs of Buddy Holly.

ROD ARGENT 'That'll Be the Day' – that groove! More sophisticated than I'd heard, yet with an instant easiness; and followed by a bewildering array of absolutely ground-breaking material: 'Rave On', 'Oh Boy!', 'Peggy Sue', 'Everyday' (which I used to wear out on the local coffee bar's jukebox!), and his later work with strings on songs like 'It Doesn't Matter Anymore' and 'True Love Ways' … such a wonderful time for music!

ALBERT LEE *'Rock Me My Baby'*

ALBERT LEE IS ONE OF THE MOST IMPORTANT GUITARISTS IN ROCK AND COUNTRY, known for his lightning-fast fingerpicking and unique hybrid picking style. Throughout his career, he's played alongside legends like Eric Clapton, Emmylou Harris, the Everly Brothers, and Joe Cocker. His talent and versatility have made him a true guitar icon, respected by fans and fellow musicians alike.

Like many other aspiring guitarists, Albert was captivated by Buddy Holly. In 1958, his parents bought him a second-hand Höfner President, the same model Buddy acquired at the start of his UK tour that same year. In 1974, Albert was chosen to replace Glen D. Hardin in the Crickets, who also at the time included Sonny Curtis and Jerry Allison. He recorded several albums with the band, the first two of which were produced by Bob Montgomery.

Albert sang 'Learning the Game' on the 2004 album *The Crickets and Their Buddies*, and later that year performed with the Crickets at a special show to celebrate 50 years of the Fender Stratocaster. They were joined by Brian May on 'I Fought the Law', 'That'll Be the Day' and 'Oh Boy!'

On 6 February 2016, the Crickets 'and their buddies' performed at the Surf Ballroom in Clear Lake, Iowa, the venue for Buddy's last show. The performers included Sonny Curtis, Glen D. Hardin, Albert Lee, Tommy Allsup and Gordon Payne. After the show Jerry Allison announced that it was to be the Crickets' final performance. What a night for Albert to be there. – *Mike Read*

I'll always regret not getting to see Buddy + the Crickets, they played near to where I was living and I got the date confused! Even missed them on the Palladium show but They were always top of my list and a great inspiration. It came to be that I joined The Crickets in 1974 and was lucky enough to record Three albums with Them.

I'm so proud to be known as a Cricket, even for a short time.

A dream come true!

ROCK ME MY BABY

'Rock Me My Baby' was originally released by Brunswick on The 'Chirping' Crickets *on 27 November 1957. The song is loosely based on the nursery rhyme 'Hickory Dickory Dock'.*

'Buddy's songs were very simple but immediately identifiable.'

ALBERT LEE Buddy had a really interesting voice and I loved the sound of his guitar and the way he played it … it wasn't very complicated but it was instantly recognisable. Whenever I play Buddy's songs I naturally play them in that same style and recreate his solos because they are an intricate part of the songs. To me there is no other way of doing them.

To my surprise, I became a Cricket in 1974 and I've had a long-term friendship with these guys, recorded three albums with them and always enjoy hanging out with them.

I've had the pleasure of playing the Surf Ballroom at Clear Lake, Iowa a few times, with people coming from all over the world to celebrate Buddy's music. To commemorate the 60th anniversary of Buddy's death I recorded a CD featuring a lot of songs from Buddy Holly and the Crickets. He was one of my earliest influences and I still love listening to his music.

MICKY DOLENZ *'You've Got Love'*

"Sine Musica,
Vita irrita" –
Thanks, Buddy –
[signature]

MICKY DOLENZ Buddy Holly quite simply captured the zeitgeist of 1950s rock and roll music – influencing everyone from The Beatles to Bob Dylan. And me. 'That'll Be the Day' is permanently ensconced in my ten favourite tunes of all time.

MIKE NESMITH 'Peggy Sue' was the first 45 I bought by Buddy Holly. Buddy had a unique style that was original and danceable. The way he dressed gave his music emphasis. For a few years Buddy was my favourite. This was when he was recording in New York and changing the face and culture of rock and roll. I was in that line. He was original! I never thought about whether he was black or white, but it was nothing I thought about too much in any case. I was swept away by his music. I still am!

HOW DO YOU DESCRIBE MICKY DOLENZ? Actor, songwriter, director, artist – he's been all of these things and more, and yet the one word that everyone will forever associate him with is 'Monkee'.

For about 18 months in the 1960s, the Monkees were the biggest pop act in the world, eventually selling around 75 million records. It's often said that they were shunned and disliked by 'serious' musicians, but that simply isn't true. Stephen Stills, Harry Nilsson, Jimi Hendrix, The Beatles – all of them not only respected, but were also friendly with Micky, Davy, Peter and Mike. Some of them even joined the guys in the studio. The songs they recorded together have matured like fine wine and are now rightfully regarded as absolute classics. The group's connection with Buddy Holly is pretty direct: no Buddy means no Beatles, no Beatles means no Monkees.

Micky was 12 when Buddy Holly had his breakthrough, and the young boy couldn't help but fall in love with the rock and roll sounds he heard through the radio: 'I was a huge fan . . . I was very young when he was big – those were my early formative years listening to music. He was incredibly influential. He started so much.'

Before joining the Monkees, like nearly every teenager in the world in the early 1960s Dolenz was singing and playing in various bands: 'I sung some of Buddy's songs in the covers bands I was in before the Monkees.'

The love for the boy from Lubbock goes even further. In 1974, Micky released a single called 'Buddy Holly Tribute'. It's a blistering medley of four of Buddy's most famous tunes. It really is something to behold – a powerhouse fusion of 1950s and 1970s rock. Micky still tours today.
– Iain Lee

YOU'VE GOT LOVE
'You've Got Love' was written by Johnny 'Peanuts' Wilson, Roy Orbison and Norman Petty and first recorded by Buddy Holly and the Crickets on 27 September 1957 at the officer's club at Tinker Air Force Base, OK. The recording was included on The 'Chirping' Crickets, *released on Brunswick on 27 November 1957.*
Also released on Brunswick in November 1957, 'Peanuts' Wilson's version of the song he co-wrote has become a collector's item today.

Atkin
BUDDY
HOLLY

BILLY DAVIS *'You've Got Love'*

I was there when Buddy Got on the plane that went down. I didnt Really get to Know him. but I Greately admired and Respected his music, and its a Great Honor to Recieve the Guitar in his Honor.

The early days of rock and roll were among the most potent in the history of music. Created by the synthesis of country music and African-American rhythm and blues, it inspired a whole new generation of would-be musicians on both sides of the Atlantic.

Driven by the beat of the drum, there was a fearless energy to this new sound. It was loud, brash and infectious. In the segregated Southern states of America they called it the 'devil's music' and tried to stop it. They made huge bonfires of 78 rpm records. Some old-style broadcasters were literally smashing these brittle 10-inch shellac discs on air.

But the force was irresistible. Young, white rock and rollers could not believe their ears. They loved the danger of this cool music, played by DJs like Alan Freed on the turntables of enlightened radio stations right across America.

Like Elvis and many of his Southern counterparts, Buddy Holly was well versed in country music. But now he was discovering new sounds. Records by Bo Diddley and Mickey and Sylvia were filling up his senses but there was one record more than any other that influenced and impacted his early playing style.

'Work with Me Annie' was the first number one single for Hank Ballard and the Midnighters, a group from Michigan who dominated the airwaves in the summer of 1954. The track was a sensation – unvarnished, raw and provocative, with a killer groove propelled by the ringing guitar riffs of Detroit's Billy Davis … and Buddy was listening. It is a straight line from 'Work with Me Annie' to 'Blue Days, Black Nights', which Buddy released in June 1956 – a record that represented that perfect synthesis of R&B, country music, rockabilly and rock and roll.

Billy toured with the Midnighters on and off for more than 30 years and it was at a gig in 1959 that he met and began mentoring a new, aspiring musician who would go on to become one of the greatest guitarists the world has ever known. His name was Jimi Hendrix. 'When I would show him something he had to perfect it,' Billy recalled. 'He would do the same thing for hours and hours. He wanted to be perfect.'

Billy's circle of friends was legendary. He hung out with John Lee Hooker, James Brown, Jackie Wilson and Sam Cooke and sought advice from B.B. King. His group the Upsetters became the in-house band for ambitious young label boss Berry Gordy, playing on records by Smokey Robinson, Martha and the Vandellas, the Supremes, the Four Tops and many others, helping to create the globally successful sound of a giant Motor City icon – the Motown record label.

In recent years, Billy has achieved an incredible grand slam as an inductee of the Rock and Roll Hall of Fame, the Doo Wop Hall of Fame and the R&B Hall of Fame. The fearless, halcyon days of the 1950s still echo today. – *Bob Harris*

WADDY WACHTEL Seeing Buddy there on *The Ed Sullivan Show*, rockin' and rollin', I knew from that moment on that any kid with glasses could be just as cool and could rock and roll just like those other guys. Buddy made it possible for me and every other little music-addicted nerd to not have to be shy any more … ever again! Thank you, Buddy, from all of us four-eyed, guitar-pickin' rock and rollers.

'That'll Be the Day'. That record drove me completely insane. Wow, what a different rockin' beat and that new style of singing. Rockabilly … that was something else entirely – it totally killed me. But that still wasn't the best part. When I saw Buddy Holly and the Crickets on TV, I thought I would lose my mind – not only because he was amazing looking, but because he had a whole band with him. A real band!

'Forever in your debt, I remain your humble student.'

Buddy,

When Donald Everly
told me you wrote
Not Fade Away for
the Everlys I knew my
life had been worth living
You have been THE inspiration
in my life and so many others
Everything I do is because of you
and every musical brother of
mine feels the same

Thank you Waddy

THE CONSUMMATE 'GUITARIST'S GUITARIST', WADDY WACHTEL has played session and live guitar for many top artists from the early 1970s onwards, including Linda Ronstadt, Stevie Nicks, Fleetwood Mac, Keith Richards, the Everly Brothers, the Rolling Stones, Jon Bon Jovi, James Taylor, Iggy Pop, Warren Zevon, Andrew Gold, Jackson Browne and Bryan Ferry.

Waddy has also played on and written many film scores and since 2000 has been performing around Los Angeles with his self-named band featuring regular members such as Bernard Fowler, Blondie Chaplin and Keith Allison, and occasional guests such as Keith Richards, Roger Daltrey and Neil Young.

In 2011, Waddy was music director for Buddy's 75th Birthday Celebration, a tribute event at the Musicbox Theater in LA, held on the evening Buddy's Hollywood Walk of Fame star was unveiled.

Since 2018, he has been in another band, the Immediate Family, which contains the elite session musicians Danny Kortchmar, Russ Kunkel, Leland Sklar and Steve Postell, and he continues to tour with Stevie Nicks.

– *Mike Read*

WORDS OF LOVE

'Words of Love' was released on Coral on 20 June 1957. It was written by Buddy Holly and recorded by him on 8 April 1957 at Norman Petty Studio.

DOLLY PARTON 'Words of Love' – such a true and beautiful description of the work and writings of one of the most loved and authentic performers of all time.

DOLLY PARTON *'Maybe Baby'*

Buddy Holly was
one of the greatest talents
ever. His songs are as
up-to-date now as they were
60 yrs. ago
I loved Buddy —
Still do
Love Dolly Parton

MAYBE BABY

'Maybe Baby' was written by Buddy Holly and Norman Petty and first recorded by Buddy on 12 March 1957 at Norman Petty's studio in Clovis, NM. On 27 September that year, Buddy rerecorded the song at the officer's club at Tinker Air Force Base, OK. It was this version that was released two months later on The 'Chirping' Crickets *and became a hit single in early 1958.*

The song was adapted from a poem written by Buddy's mother, Ella.

FROM THE DAYS GROWING UP IN POST-WAR RURAL AMERICA, sharing a one-room sharecroppers' cabin in the Tennessee hills, to the country superstardom that has taken her on to the biggest and most lucrative stages in the world, Dolly Parton has always carried her family's love with her. The support of her family has been a crucial factor all along and she has always remained proud of and inspired by the relative poverty of her upbringing. Now, with her talent, bravery, humour and sheer hard work, Dolly has established herself as one of the most globally celebrated and respected artists of all time.

Family life was musical, and Dolly grew up being massively inspired by some of the great female country music pioneers – artists such as Rose Maddox and Molly O'Day in the 1940s, Kitty Wells in the 1950s, and then Brenda Lee and Patsy Cline in the 1960s. These were empowering women who became successful on their own terms, creating a female identity in a predominantly man's world and giving voice to female perspectives.

There was no radio in the Parton household. Electricity had yet to reach the rural poor. But they entertained themselves with acoustic instruments, hand-me-down songs and rustic versions of some of the new rock and roll and rockabilly numbers Dolly's father, Lee, had been hearing. He was a fan of Elvis Presley and it seems highly likely that he also introduced the young Dolly to the songs of Buddy Holly. Certainly, she has always referred to Buddy when talking about her major influences.

Dolly's music has transcended decades of fads and fashion, genres and styles, and her fearlessness and willingness to speak her mind on behalf of the underprivileged has helped open pathways to greater understanding and harmony. More striking, even, than her brilliance as an artist, she has given confidence to those whose voices are often the hardest to hear. She brings energy, empathy, wisdom and a kindness of spirit to a world much in need of her words of love. – *Bob Harris*

MIKE BERRY *'Tell Me How'*

First saw Buddy on "Sunday Night at The London Palladium"
Was already a massive fan & couldn't believe how brilliant The Crickets were! Been a fan ever since!
Love him!
Mike Berry

'Asked what ballads I knew, I mentioned "True Love Ways", so that's what I ended up singing.'

MIKE BERRY Geoff Goddard had written this song 'Tribute to Buddy Holly', and Joe Meek told me that he wanted me to sing it and he'd put it out as a single. To give the release some credence and authenticity, Joe invited the Buddy Holly Appreciation Society to his studio to get their approval.

I recently appeared on the TV show *The Voice*. I'd learned lots of what I imagined to be really clever songs, and when they asked what ballads I knew I mentioned 'True Love Ways', so that's what I ended up singing. A great song, but not what I'd prepared!

MIKE BERRY'S CHART CAREER BEGAN with the Geoff Goddard song 'Tribute to Buddy Holly', produced by the legendary Joe Meek. Like Mike, Meek and Goddard were also big Buddy Holly fans, Mike having bought *The 'Chirping' Crickets* LP and the 78 rpm single of 'That'll Be the Day'.

Mike recorded an album, *About Time Too!*, in Nashville with the Crickets. The record – produced by Chas Hodges – was made at Jerry Allison's Tennessee studio in 2004 and included Buddy's 'I'm Gonna Set My Foot Down' and 'Fool's Paradise'. The ever-youthful Mike Berry is still associated with the Buddy Holly legacy to this day.

Mike's guitar, presented by the Foundation and Maria Elena, is 'Tell Me How', a song from *The 'Chirping' Crickets*. *– Mike Read*

TELL ME HOW
Written by Buddy Holly, Jerry Allison and Norman Petty, 'Tell Me How' was recorded in 1957 at Norman Petty's studio, and included on the album The 'Chirping' Crickets, *released on Brunswick on 27 November 1957.*

'Buddy was great – better than great. I cherish my Buddy Holly guitar.'

Buddy! thanks for all your help & inspiration
Steve Cropper

LAST NIGHT
'Last Night' was co-written with Norman Petty by future Cricket Joe B. Mauldin, who played bass for Buddy for the first time at the 12 March 1957 session during which the song was recorded (this session, at Norman Petty's studio, also produced the earliest version of 'Maybe Baby'). The song first appeared as a track on The 'Chirping' Crickets.

I MUST HAVE LOOKED LIKE A NERDY FAN deputising for a proper broadcaster, but when Steve Cropper came in to be interviewed on one of my radio shows I really wanted him to sign a couple of books that he was an important part of and he politely obliged. We went on to talk, mostly about his album *Dedicated*, a tribute to his major influence as a guitarist, Lowman Pauling of the 5 Royales.

Talking to him more recently, I run through some of his achievements, including that he was number 36 in *Rolling Stone* magazine's 100 best guitarists of all time (*Mojo* magazine named him 'the greatest living guitarist'); he was inducted into the Rock and Roll Hall of Fame and the Songwriters' Hall of Fame and won a couple of Grammys as well. Other musicians have esteemed him highly; when introduced to him, The Beatles collectively bowed. He himself has stated, 'I would hate to be a star. I just want to do the best job for the music we're making.'

I mention Buddy Holly. 'Oh, he was great,' says Steve. 'We grew up on Buddy Holly's music in the 1950s,' and he sings a few bars of 'That'll Be the Day'. We talk about his first success, the huge Mar-Keys hit 'Last Night', and he points out that Buddy Holly had recorded a song with that title a couple of years earlier. 'I like to think that I'm always the first to do things, but he beat me there.'

Of course, Steve was the guitarist of Booker T. and the M.G.'s, hit-makers of 'Green Onions' and so many more, and in effect the Stax Records house band, who played on hits by Otis Redding, Sam and Dave, Rufus Thomas, Carla Thomas, Eddie Floyd and Albert King – and on a baker's dozen albums of their own.

As a guitarist he is the master of measurement – never too little, never too much – which goes some way to explaining the vast list of artists he has collaborated with, as guitarist, keyboardist, songwriter and record producer. This includes most famously the Blues Brothers Band, as well as Etta James, John Lennon, Roy Orbison, Eric Clapton, Ringo Starr and Rod Stewart, to name a handful.

He's still at it. On 6 August 2022 at Buddy Holly Hall in Lubbock, Texas, Steve took part in Buddy Holly's 85th Birthday Bash – along with Peter Frampton and Albert Lee, among others. – *Paul Jones*

Buddy....
The game changer
The legend
Gone too soon -

'I was weaned on Bill Haley, Eddie Cochran, Gene Vincent and Buddy Holly.'

WHEN JOE BONAMASSA WAS ABOUT TO DO HIS FIRST UK GIGS, in 2005, his PR people, Frontier Promotions, sent out copies of a video about him to potentially interested journalists, broadcasters and the like. Quite a lot of it was about his being a child prodigy, including that he toured with B.B. King, aged 12. There was also footage of him demonstrating the differences between improvising in different genres – blues, rock, jazz and so on. Radio 2 producer Paul Long and I decided he was certainly worthy of encouragement and airplay. We were by no means the only enthusiasts, and soon his prolific record releases and amazing live performances had earned him the first of his appearances at the Royal Albert Hall – unforgettable for me, because he called me up to play on Sonny Boy Williamson's 'Your Funeral and My Trial' with him.

We were also informed that he had been a member of a band called Bloodline – so named because it consisted of the offspring of famous musicians like Miles Davis, Robby Krieger and the Allman Brothers' Berry Oakley. When I met Joe almost my first question was about Bloodline; he said that it was an interesting experiment, but was never going to last.

Since then, his career has been full of interesting experiments – lasting ones mostly. Things like the album *Black Rock*, on which Joe assimilated elements of Greek music; the side project Rock Candy Funk Party, where his jazz leanings get exercised; acoustic live albums at the Vienna State Opera and Carnegie Hall; collaborations with various artists such as Beth Hart and Mahalia Barnes; the albums of the hard-rock Black Country Communion; and nowadays his own label, Keeping the Blues Alive Records, supporting other artists.

Joe is famous not just as a guitarist, but also as a connoisseur, and indeed as a curator of his own guitar museum, which reputedly houses around 500 items. He enthusiastically discusses the characteristics of different woods: 'I always refer to maple-neck Strats as the Buddy Holly guitar.' (Eric Clapton and Jimi Hendrix are also well known for playing maple-neck Stratocasters.)

With 25 albums having reached number one on the *Billboard* Blues Chart, you might think Joe is entitled to some glory, but, as he says, 'History alone judges your legacy; we're still talking about Buddy Holly and Otis Redding, aren't we?' – *Paul Jones*

Top left: Bill Haley and the Comets, Eddie Cochran and Gene Vincent

HOLLY

I left her standin' there

I just walked off
An left her standin' there
Yeah, I just walked off
As if I didn't care
I dont think she knew
My poor heart was breaking too
I just said good by.
She didn't see the tear, in
my eye

I LEFT HER STANDIN' THERE
Lyrics written by Buddy titled 'I Left Her Standin' There', which were never developed further and remain unused and unreleased

PLECTRUM
A white nylon Jim Dunlop guitar pick owned and used by Buddy

Opposite, left: Buddy Holly, Jerry Allison and Joe B. Mauldin pictured with the Big Beats, Clovis, NM, December 1957

Opposite, right: Promo card from February 1958 signed by Buddy, Jerry Allison and Joe B. Mauldin during their UK tour

BRIAN MAY All of Buddy's songs reflect something in his life. It wasn't 'I love you and everything's fabulous,' but, 'I feel this stuff and it hurts me.' It was very real songwriting. He was wrapped up in being an artist on every level and living his private life in a public way. From experience, I know that's stressful. You feel very naked, yet I love Buddy because he laid his emotions on the line by opening his heart. We saw into his heart and always will. Music didn't do that before; there's some great stuff written in the 1920s and 1930s, but it was very much, 'Let's make something beautiful out of this.' It wasn't upsetting, and that's what rock and roll gave us, and still does.

CHAPTER FOUR
1958

AMERICA'S GREATEST TEEN-AGE RECORDING STARS
From 8 to 24 January 1958, Buddy Holly and the Crickets took part in a tour by General Artists Corporation titled 'America's Greatest Teen-Age Recording Stars'. It also included appearances by the Everly Brothers, Paul Anka, the Rays, Danny and the Juniors, Jimmie Rodgers, Margie Rayburn, the Hollywood Flames, the Shepherd Sisters, the Mello-Kings, the Tuneweavers, Eddie Cochran, Billy Brown, Al Jones and Jimmy Edwards. Left is a postcard depicting the Municipal Auditorium, Norfolk, VA, one of the venues on the tour.

Above left: Buddy Holly and the Crickets with Sam Donahue's band at the Municipal Auditorium, Norfolk, VA, 11 January 1958

Above: Buddy Holly and the Crickets St Joseph Armory, Hazleton, PA 14 January 1958

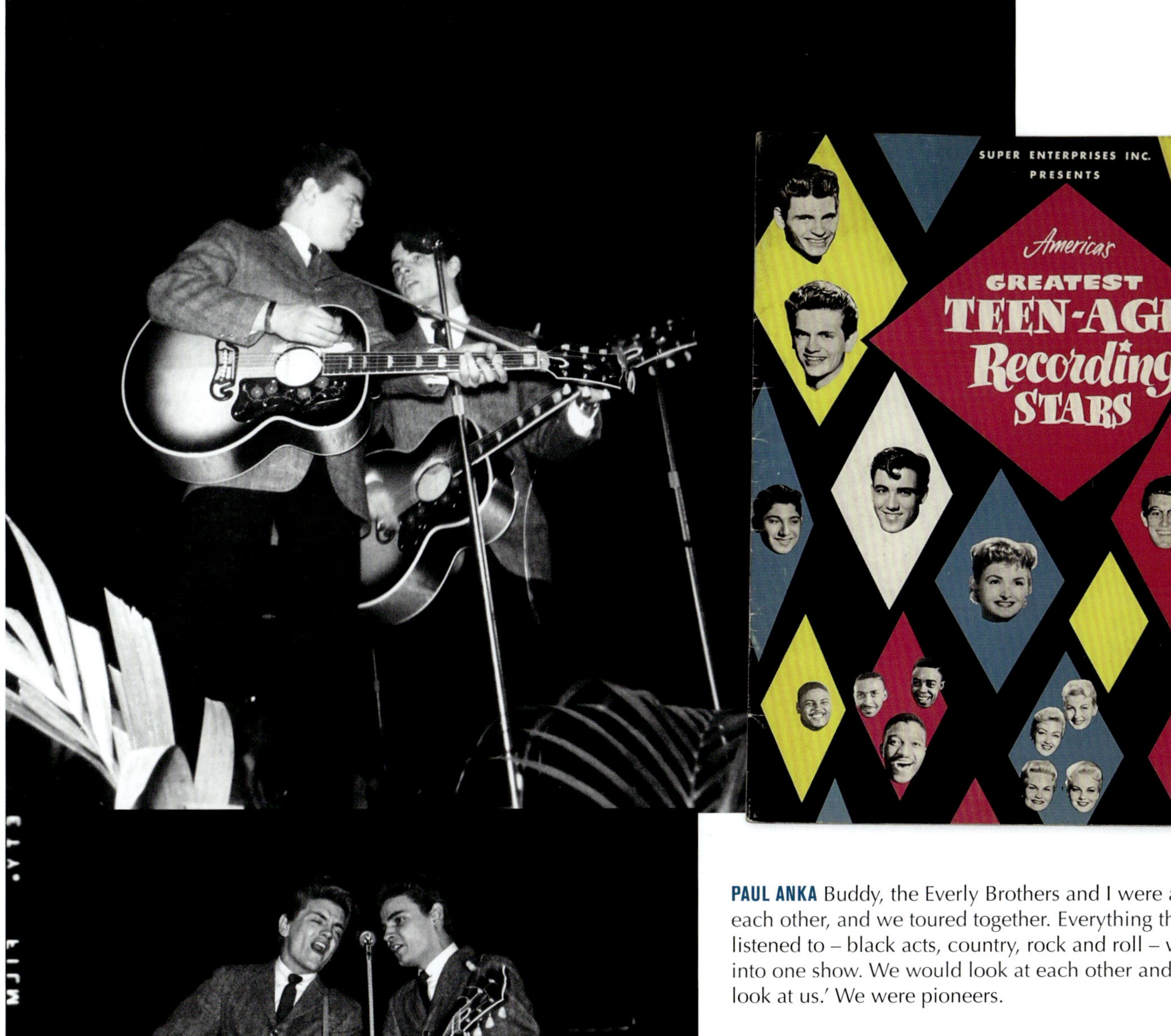

PAUL ANKA Buddy, the Everly Brothers and I were all fans of each other, and we toured together. Everything that we listened to – black acts, country, rock and roll – was merged into one show. We would look at each other and say, 'Wow, look at us.' We were pioneers.

JERRY 'J.I.' ALLISON When we were playing in Florida in March 1958, the band that showed up for the Everly Brothers wasn't working out. We knew their music because we'd heard it a million times before, and Buddy offered us to play with them, so we did our show, came back out and played their show, too. That was so fun, and the crowd liked it a lot more than the usual back-up bands that would play with them, who didn't really know their music.

DON EVERLY Often we had to use pick-up musicians. We were on tour, picking up bands in each town, when Buddy offered to play with us. He came out after his appearance and played back up for us, which was wonderful. The audience got a real treat.

This page and overleaf:
The Everly Brothers and Buddy Holly and the Crickets
Hershey Sports Arena
Hershey, PA,
17 January 1958

SAM
DONAHUE

CONTINENTAL
AIR LINES

DON EVERLY That was when rock and roll was just starting, so the only tours would be the ones with everyone on them. They were gruelling but you didn't have to play too many songs, just two or three. But we had to travel a lot.

PAUL ANKA Irvin Feld signed me to one of his tours for $300 per week, which was a lot of money. He would package lots of artists together. His trick was to see which records took off in the drugstores and call before the artist had blown up, and then he'd book us all. We were just a bunch of kids with hit records, put on these awful buses and freezing through some states during the wrong time of the year. But we were living and singing together, getting to know each other, everything that young people would do – the difference was we were famous.

EDNA GUNDERSEN Those tours were very common in the United States, revues with a long list of artists that only had one or two hits. They'd have buses full of these acts and send them out on the road, usually in horrendous conditions, and they'd do two or three shows in a town before driving overnight to the next. The idea for the artists was to get as much exposure as possible, though it didn't benefit them as much as the promoters.

1950s BUS TOURS
These photographs, from Rochester, NY, on 19 January 1958, were taken by Lew Allen for a sophomore college photography project. In a written account, he said, 'I arrived prior to the show and before the musicians had arrived at the theatre. At the stage door, I showed the show managers some of my earlier photos of Elvis Presley taken in 1956 in Cleveland, and they encouraged me to come into the theatre because they hadn't been getting any press coverage. I was the only photographer at the theatre at that time (there were no press photographers – the newspapers were not interested in the latest kids' phenomenon).

'Before and during the show, the musicians were honoured to be photographed and called me over repeatedly and gave me free rein as to where I could go. These photos were shot as the bus carrying the musicians arrived at the theatre. As they got off the bus, they were attacked by screaming girls who prevented the others from getting off, so I jumped on to see who was left on the bus and found the mood very sombre. The bus was arriving from what I believe was a long ride in the winter without having stopped at any hotels for the musicians to rest before the show. The New York Thruway wasn't finished and only two-lane highways were available for interstate travel at that time.'

DION DiMUCCI There's a difference between being entertained and having an emotional experience, and hearing 'Peggy Sue' and 'That'll Be the Day' was an emotional experience for me. Buddy Holly broke the 'nice' barrier for me; all the music I was listening to was nice, and to Buddy, nice was the kiss of death.

ALBERT LEE Buddy had a unique voice; we all wanted to sound like Elvis or the Everly Brothers, but a lot of us can't. He found a way to utilise his voice so that it suited the songs he was writing.

DION DiMUCCI From hearing his free, unrestrained music, you expect some wild man, but he was very structured, formal, stately and deliberate. He was a beautiful guy and very gentlemanly, yet when he picked up that Stratocaster he went into another world. His was a complete expression of individuality.

BRIAN MAY His guitar playing is crucial, and no one of my generation would underestimate Buddy as a guitarist. Things became much more technical later. Though it's not saturated or distorted, he makes that guitar sing. Alongside his voice, the guitar is a lead instrument, and the 1950s were very early days for that.

DON McLEAN Buddy Holly is a great interpreter who makes whatever he does his own. That's a great singer. He doesn't have to write the song, because he sings it as if he wrote it – it becomes his song. That's what a good interpreter does. Beyond that, he had a vast talent as a songwriter.

DION DiMUCCI He loved music. On the tour bus we'd always get our guitars out and play our favourite songs. He loved to express his influences; he knew where the music came from, and he loved it all.

BRIAN MAY He does a hiccupping sound which is very Buddy. It's a rock and roll thing which sounds slightly twee to us, but in those days it didn't. It was a part of the rebellious act and something that Frank Sinatra would never do.

DESMOND CHILD There was music before and after Buddy Holly, but anything that's rock came after Buddy Holly. He's the creator of punk – there'd be no Green Day without Buddy Holly. In the 1950s, country and western merged with R&B, and that collision created rock and roll – that's where Buddy Holly lives. It brought about such a distinct change in music. Buddy Holly and the Crickets created a template for all bands that came afterwards. The look, feel, energy and modernism that was in his music changed everything.

Buddy Holly and the Crickets with Sam Donahue's band, Auditorium Theater Rochester, NY 19 January 1958

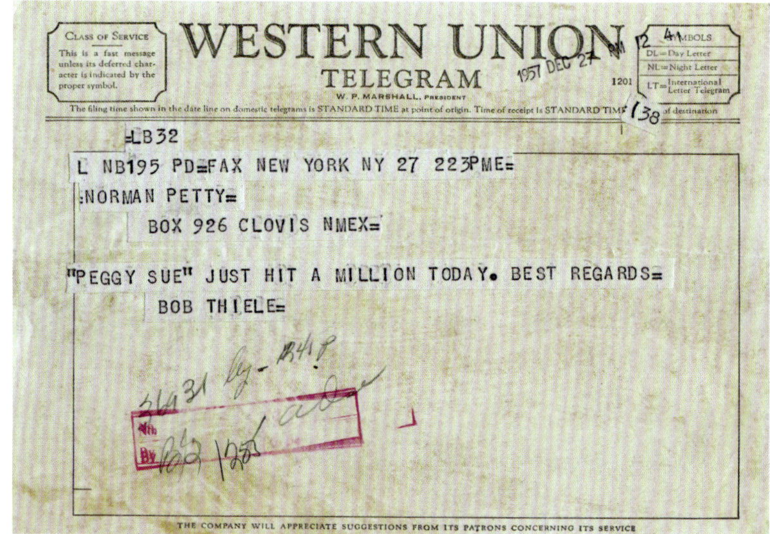

WESTERN UNION

TELEGRAM

W. P. MARSHALL, PRESIDENT

CLASS OF SERVICE — This is a fast message unless its deferred character is indicated by the proper symbol.

SYMBOLS — DL = Day Letter; NL = Night Letter; LT = International Letter Telegram

1957 DEC 27 PM 12 41

1201

The filing time shown in the date line on domestic telegrams is STANDARD TIME at point of origin. Time of receipt is STANDARD TIME at point of destination

LB32

L NB195 PD=FAX NEW YORK NY 27 223PME=

NORMAN PETTY=

BOX 926 CLOVIS NMEX=

"PEGGY SUE" JUST HIT A MILLION TODAY. BEST REGARDS=

BOB THIELE=

THE COMPANY WILL APPRECIATE SUGGESTIONS FROM ITS PATRONS CONCERNING ITS SERVICE

Top right: A page from the Buddy Holly Notebook showing Peggy Sue Gerron's initials, most likely sketched by Jerry Allison

Above: A telegram from Bob Thiele confirming 'Peggy Sue' had sold a million copies, 27 December 1957

Opposite, top: A gold disc (left) presented to Buddy Holly and Norman Petty for 'Peggy Sue'. Bob Thiele of Coral Records presenting Buddy and Norman with another gold disc (right).

Opposite, bottom right: Buddy's Coral Records contract for two masters, 'Peggy Sue' and 'Everyday', signed by Buddy Holly, producer Norman Petty and Coral Records Director of Artists and Repertoire, Bob Thiele, and dated 30 August 1957. Bob travelled to Clovis to sign the contract. Coral released 'Peggy Sue' and 'Everyday' on 20 September 1957 in the US and 15 November in the UK. They had released 'That'll Be the Day' in the UK on 10 September and it ultimately went to number one in the UK charts.

Opposite, bottom left: A Jerry Allison handwritten lyric for 'Peggy Sue'

DESMOND CHILD I was about ten years old when first I heard 'Peggy Sue'. I grew up in Miami where there was a lot of R&B, so when I heard that song it was like nothing I had heard before … the sparseness of it was captivating.

PETER ASHER 'Peggy Sue' is a great song. It's very simple, but the bridge is so unexpected, and it sets off the rest of the song perfectly. It's pop songwriting at its best.

DON EVERLY It was all about the arrangement, and 'Peggy Sue' was a great one. Listeners didn't realise the importance of arrangements back then. 'Peggy Sue' was recognisable before you'd heard the first lyric; the intro was very Buddy.

ALBERT LEE When Buddy was doing the solo in 'Peggy Sue' his Strat was set on a bassy, mellow sound, and they were all downstrokes. Niki Sullivan didn't play on it, so when it came to the guitar solo Niki switched Buddy's guitar for him to the lead position and afterwards switched it back to being mellow again.

JERRY 'J.I.' ALLISON Peggy Sue was my ex-wife. We dated in high school but she didn't like me very much, but when 'Peggy Sue' came out she liked me very much. It was originally called 'Cindy Lou', after Buddy's niece, but I asked him if we could change it. When we were recording it at Norman's studio, I messed it up and Buddy said, 'If you mess it up this time we're going back to Cindy Lou,' but next time I got it just right. I wish we'd left it as 'Cindy Lou', to be honest.

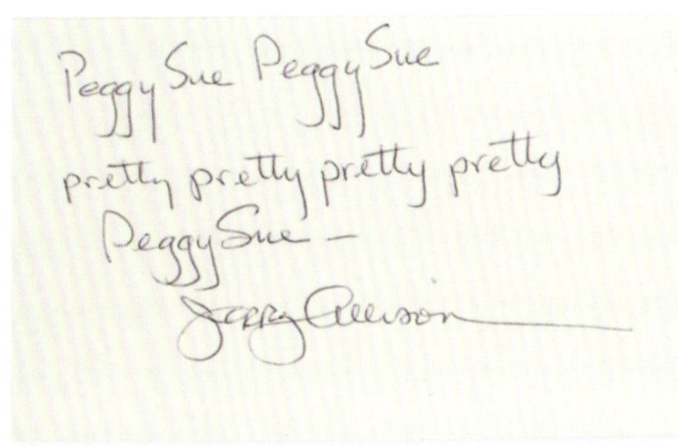

CORAL RECORDS, INC.

48 WEST 57th STREET, NEW YORK 19, N. Y. • COlumbus 5-2363

August 30, 1957

DOCUMENT
57-136

Mr. Buddy Holly
c/o Norman Petty
Box 926
Clovis, New Mexico

Dear Mr. Holly:

Pursuant to letter agreement between us dated May 16, 1957, we are hereby exercising our option to enter into the contract for your personal services bearing even date therewith, the term of said contract to commence August 30, 1957.

It is hereby mutually agreed:

1. Two masters now entitled "PEGGY SUE" and "EVERYDAY" shall be deemed to have been recorded under the said contract.

2. We agree to pay you the sum of $600.00 for the aforesaid masters which shall include the advance to you under said contract together with the costs for recording.

3. All terms and conditions of the contract shall apply to these recordings as though they had been performed under said contract and shall serve to reduce the number of record sides required to be recorded thereunder.

4. The sum of $600.00 provided to be paid to you shall be an advance against royalties under the aforesaid agreement dated May 16, 1957, and under the master purchase agreement with Norman Petty bearing even date therewith. All royalties which shall accrue under the aforesaid agreement for your services and the master purchase agreement with Norman Petty shall be accrued under one account and all advances and recording costs under both contracts shall be deducted from said royalties.

Yours truly

CORAL RECORDS, INC.

Director of Artists and Repertoire

ACCEPTED AND AGREED TO:

Buddy Holly
BUDDY HOLLY

NORMAN PETTY

SONNY WEST The weekend that Buddy was in New York for *The Ed Sullivan Show*, he recorded 'Rave On' at Bell Sound Studios. He heard Norman and I had recorded it, but it never sounded quite right. Buddy's version had rhythm and attitude. It was a great song, but it didn't catch on too much in America. Nowadays, it's probably as big as 'Oh Boy!'

EDNA GUNDERSEN Ed Sullivan was the key. He broke it wide open for The Beatles, and he was very crucial for Buddy Holly and several other acts. But not only did Ed Sullivan not understand rock and roll, he was completely mystified by it. These acts would come and go and he couldn't care less, yet there were fans that lived, breathed and died by having these acts show up.

JERRY 'J.I.' ALLISON It wasn't just Ed Sullivan, a lot of people didn't like rock and roll, but they had a rock and roller on every week at the end of the show so the kids would stay hooked. The next time we did it, they had a ju-jitsu act on before us, but they cancelled it at the last moment and put us on. Buddy went out and they were asking where the rest of the Crickets were – Joe B. and I were down in the basement karate chopping each other. Ed was standing with the audience and he said, 'Apparently the Crickets don't care much about being on *The Ed Sullivan Show*,' and Buddy responded, 'I hope they care about it more than I do.' By the time we were on stage we only had about a minute and a half. We ran out and played 'Oh Boy!' faster than we ever had before.

RAVE ON – the song
by Sonny West
for Graham Nash
On behalf of The Buddy Holly Educational Foundation

Some expressions are better sung. Some expressions are best when ~~are~~ written or spoken. Take the exclamation "Rave On", usually used as a term of affirmation. Is it possible to use it in a romantic setting? the song which became "Rave On" was written and re-written so many times I can't recall how some early versions were arranged but believe me they were quite strange. But by November 1957 the final version was cranked out and I traveled to Norman Petty Studio in Clovis, New Mexico USA to record it. the backing was supplied by The Big Beats, a rock and roll band from Dallas. this was my first record release on Atlantic Records and of course I had high hopes for success but (sigh) again it was not to be. It came to be just another step in the "rave on saga". Again it was my friend Buddy Holly who jumped in and saved the day, Holly heard my recording in Clovis and wanted to record it as part of his new solo career. He recorded it in January 1958 in New York and his new iconic version was on the streets about three months later. It soon became one of those Holly signature songs and is huge even to this day. Many fans ask me: What does it mean to Rave On? I say: Its a crazy feelin'. Its a favorite of fans worldwide.

Rave On! Sixty years On!

Sonny West February 2017

JERRY 'J.I.' ALLISON *The Ed Sullivan Show* bordered on miserable. The first time we got there they had me and the drums on a six-foot riser. There was no monitors at the time, no headphones, and in the theatre no one could hear anything. For the people out front it was just a big rattle. We're used to playing on the floor, but we were all at different heights. We told them we couldn't play the way they'd set it up and they were very disgruntled at us.

Buddy couldn't get by without his glasses; if he dropped his pick on stage he couldn't find it. He tried contacts, but I told him, 'Man, everyone loves you with glasses, so just get some big ones.' There was a fella named Ray Block, who was the musical director on *The Ed Sullivan Show*, and he had these heavy glasses. After seeing him, Buddy decided on something similar.

OH BOY!
On 26 January 1958, Buddy Holly and the Crickets performed 'Oh Boy!' on The Ed Sullivan Show. *The hour-long programme began at 8 PM. Most likely because of the problems that took place during dress rehearsal, a still upset Sullivan introduced them as 'Buddy Hollard and his Crickets'. Buddy's guitar was also turned down by the engineer. During their time in New York, they stayed at the Hotel Edison.*

RAVE ON
Shortly after the America's Greatest Teen-Age Recording Stars tour, Buddy Holly and the Crickets headed to Bell Sound Studios in New York for a recording session that lasted from 8 PM to 2 AM. This session produced 'Rave On' and 'That's My Desire'. On 20 April, Coral released 'Rave On' backed with 'Take Your Time'. Before that, though, Coral released Buddy Holly's self-titled solo album on 20 February. The album contained 'I'm Gonna Love You Too', 'Peggy Sue', 'Look at Me', 'Listen to Me', 'Valley of Tears', 'Ready Teddy', 'Everyday', 'Mailman, Bring Me No More Blues', 'Words of Love', 'You're So Square', 'Little Baby' and – before the official single release – 'Rave On'.

Hello from Hawaii. We played here last night and went over better than I thought we would. They like the same kind of music here.
(Postcard from Buddy to his sister Patricia, 28 January 1958)

PAUL ANKA Buddy was very shy, so it was hard to convince him to change his appearance. He resisted changing his glasses, and then that became his signature look. The incredible guitar, the sound that came out of it – that's where his sexuality came from, the way he approached music.

We'd be backstage doing our hair, and there was a universality as to how to comb and blow your hair, and we used to always tease Buddy or they'd tease me about the way we'd do it. There was a wave occurring out of Philadelphia with singers like Fabian and Frankie Avalon, who would comb their hair a certain way. Then we all started getting into suits; there was one place where we'd buy our clothes to get 'the look'. But it wasn't important, the music was. Buddy was so talented, and his music was inspiring.

MARIA ELENA Buddy was very quiet. He always waited to be approached and then after that he would talk quite freely.

HAWAII
Buddy Holly and the Crickets flew from Los Angeles to Hawaii on Pan American Airlines flight 805, which left Los Angeles at 9 AM and arrived in Honolulu at 4.30 PM En route to Australia for their tour, the band performed two shows on 27 January 1958 with Jerry Lee Lewis, Paul Anka and Jodie Sands at Honolulu's Civic Auditorium. Both concerts drew capacity crowds of 5,000.

Opposite, top: A postcard Buddy mailed to his parents as he was leaving Hawaii

Opposite, bottom: A colour picture of Buddy looking over the Pacific Ocean from his balcony at the Hawaiian Village Hotel. The date, 28 January 1958, was written on the back of the original photograph. Buddy, the Crickets and Norman Petty were given a guided tour of Pearl Harbour by an Air Force friend of Norman's.

HI-500
Snow on Maunea Kea taken through palms on grounds of Naniloa Hotel, Hilo Bay, Island of Hawaii.
Photo by Werner Stoy, Camera Hawaii

CHRIS-A-TONE CARD
Reproduced from Natural Color Photograph

AIR MAIL 4¢
U.S. POSTAGE

JAN 28 4:30PM 1958

POST CARD
Address

DEAR MOM & DAD,
WE'RE LEAVING FOR AUSTRALIA IN A FEW MINUTES. WE SHOULD BE HOME IN ABOUT 12 DAYS
LOVE, BUDDY

MR. & MRS. L.O. HOLLEY
1305 - 37TH
LUBBOCK, TEXAS

6841

Dear Mom and Dad, we are here on a tincy little island called Canton … it's hotter than the john down at Frank's Drive-in on a July day … They have some fine Australian beer here but since [Norman Petty] is with us, we can't drink any. (Letter from Jerry Allison to his parents written on Canton Island in the South Pacific, where their plane had to make an unscheduled landing because of engine trouble en route to Australia, 28 January 1958)

Above: Photographs of the flight from Hawaii to Australia, including (top left) Joe B. Mauldin and Jerry Allison and (top right) Jerry Lee Lewis's manager with Lee Gordon, the promoter of the Australian tour

REAL WILD CHILD
Written and recorded by Australian star Johnny O'Keefe, who joined Buddy Holly and the Crickets on their Australian tour, 'Real Wild Child' became the first song recorded by Jerry Allison as a solo artist under his middle name, Ivan. Buddy Holly sang backing vocals. It rose to number 68 in the Billboard *Top 100 chart.*

Left: Joe B. Mauldin, Jerry Allison and Buddy Holly
Beauregarde Private Hotel, Sydney, Australia, 30 January 1958

LEE GORDON PRESENTS THE BIG SHOW
Below: A souvenir programme for Lee Gordon Presents the Big Show from January to February 1958. This was a six-day run of Australian shows featuring musicians such as Paul Anka, Jerry Lee Lewis and Buddy Holly and the Crickets, which started in Sydney before travelling to Newcastle, Brisbane and Melbourne. The shows were kicked off by local talent, Johnny O'Keefe and the Dee Jays. This was Buddy Holly and the Crickets' only Australian tour.

Our drum player, Jerry Allison, thought of the [band] name back last January when our group was formed, and we didn't know that there was another group at that time by that name. We found out about it just right soon after and we had thought of the name but we found out that the other group was non-existent anymore, so nothing was done.

We're all from the same home town, and we've known each other for quite some time. Jerry and myself have been playing together for about five years, and then the other boy, Joe Mauldin, the bass player, got with us last January. [Niki Sullivan] was in the group for a while and then he decided to quit and go back to school.

I used to know Elvis quite well before he got as popular as he is now. I don't think [Elvis being in the army] alters anything real outstanding in the music business. Presley will probably be a little unpopular for a while but I think he'll come back into it, into his own, after he gets out.

(Buddy in an interview with Pat Barton for 3KO Radio, Newcastle, Australia, 31 January 1958)

We will be going home in the morning. We finished our last job here in Australia tonight. It went very well. The first few shows went very bad for us but here for the last three days we have been stealing the show, as Norm would say. We will stop over in Honolulu for another show tomorrow night, which I really can't figure out since the date changes like that. The people here are all very far behind as far as dress and modern ideas go. I'll be home by the time this letter reaches there I hope. However, I plan to spend some time with Peggy in California. I'll tell you all about it when I get home but as for now, I think I'll pack and sack … (Letter from Jerry Allison to his parents from Chevron Hotel, St Kilda, Melbourne, Australia, 5 February 1958)

Opposite: Boarding a flight from Mascot Airport in Sydney to Brisbane with Jerry Lee Lewis 2 February 1958

This page: Buddy Holly and the Crickets Lennon's Broadbeach Hotel Gold Coast, Australia, 2 February 1958

ALBERT LEE Buddy went from a pair of quite boring glasses to these outrageous, very specific glasses. Those of us in an early disposition were encouraged by somebody who looked like that, who didn't look like Elvis. I wanted a pair of black glasses like Buddy's too.

DON EVERLY Buddy looked very contemporary when he wore the horn-rimmed glasses. We told him they were a good idea – they made him look more fashionable and mysterious – and when he started wearing them he looked better on stage and it became an important part of his style. We weren't heart-throbs and we didn't want to be. He just looked like Buddy Holly.

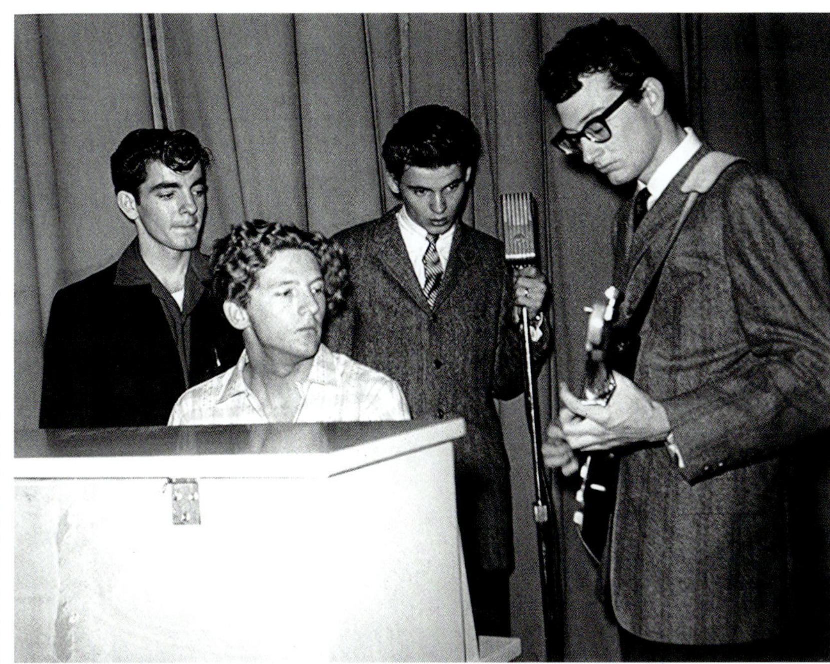

FLORIDA TOUR
Buddy Holly and the Crickets headed to Florida in February 1958 for a short tour also featuring the Everly Brothers, Bill Haley and the Comets, Jerry Lee Lewis and the Royal Teens. These unearthed, unseen photographs (left and opposite) are of the show at Fort Homer Hesterly, Tampa on 21 February 1958. Also shown here are a souvenir programme (top left) and Buddy with Jerry Lee Lewis, Jimmy Velvet and Don Everly at Fort Lauderdale, FL, 25 February 1958, on the same tour (above).

JERRY 'J.I.' ALLISON We went to England shortly after our Florida tour. That was a totally new deal, because some of the shows around the United States had 25 acts, so we'd only get to play 15 minutes, sometimes seven times a day. In England, we got to do 30 minutes and play everything we wanted to, and it went over very well. They were really nice to us.

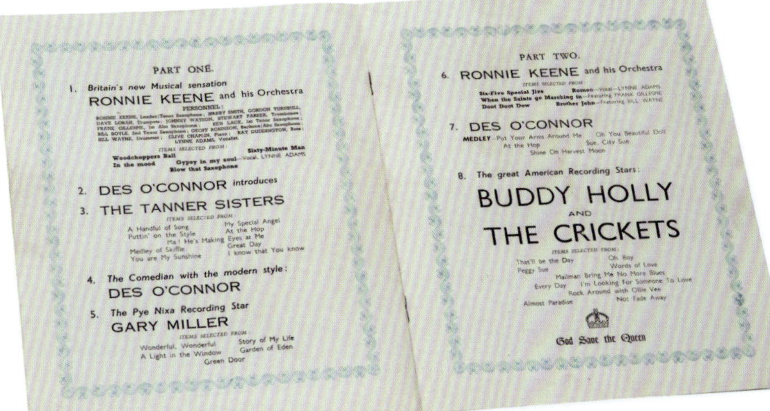

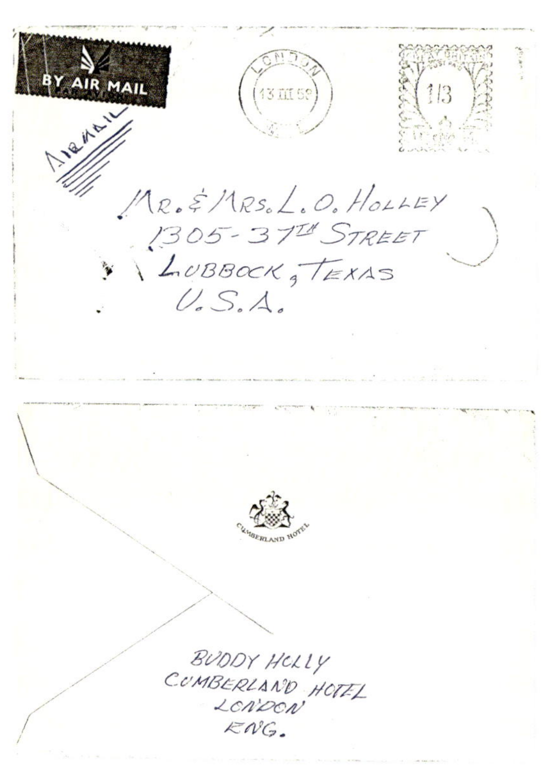

Left and top: A souvenir programme for the UK tour, which features a short biography of the group

Opposite: A letter from Buddy to his parents from the Cumberland Hotel, London, March 1958

Opposite, bottom right: Buddy Holly and the Crickets and Vi Petty on Oxford Street, London on the first day of their UK tour, 28 February 1958

Cumberland Hotel
Marble Arch
London, W.1.

Telephone: Ambassador 1234
Telegrams: Cumberotel, Wesdo, London

Dear Mother & Dad,

I haven't got any letters from you yet so I guess that if you wrote, they were lost. Jerry has had some from his mother so there shouldn't be any reason for them not being here unless they were lost.

Everything is going fine here. We are back in London for a few days. Then we start back on the road again for the remainder of the tour. It shouldn't be too much longer until we are back

Cumberland Hotel
Marble Arch
London, W.1.

Telephone: Ambassador 1234
Telegrams: Cumberotel, Wesdo, London

in the states again. I don't know why, but in a foreign country I get a lot more what could be called homesick than I do in the states even though it actually isn't too much further away from home. I'll sure be glad to get back where I can call home and talk for a while every few days. I guess that's really what I miss. It's pretty hard to call from over here and costs a lot too. It seems you have to reserve your call a few days in advance or something like that.

Cumberland Hotel
Marble Arch
London, W.1.

Telephone: Ambassador 1234
Telegrams: Cumberotel, Wesdo, London

Well there's not too much else to say other than both shows tonight went real good. Almost unbelivably good because we usually do "not so good" the first show because our spirits are kind of low about that time of the evening. It's 2:00 A.M. THUR. here but it's just 8:00 P.M. WED. there at home. Seems kinda funny doesn't it? Well, that's all for now.

Love, Buddy

P.S. Tell Larry, Trav, and Pat "hi" for me.

MARIA ELENA For Buddy and a lot of American musicians, they had to go out of the US to be recognised and then return. Buddy was more recognised in the UK than the States. The UK took Buddy – the tall, lanky kid with glasses – to heart and connected with his image as the everyman of this new music called rock and roll.

THE NEW MUSICAL EXPRESS 11

CRICKETS, BUDDY HOLLY OPEN HERE MARCH 1

25 day tour with package

AMERICA'S latest vocal group sensation—The Crickets, plus their star personality leader, Buddy Holly—have been booked to undertake their first tour of Britain, which will include at least two TV guest appearances.

Opening here on March 1, the Crickets remain for 25 days—primarily for one-night stand concert dates. However, there is a strong likelihood of one week at a leading variety theatre during their tour.

Leslie Grade (of the Lew and Leslie Grade Agency) told the NME that he contemplates lining up a package show, which will appear with The Crickets at all engagements here.

Leader of the group, Buddy Holly, is famous for his solo hit-disc "Peggy Sue."

The Crickets attained the unusual feat of securing a No. 1 best-selling record here with "That'll Be The Day." They are currently riding high with their follow-up release "Oh oy," number four in this week's Thirty Chart.

BOB HARRIS Rock and roll was coming in from America and it was by comparison much more sophisticated than skiffle, recorded in studios with electric instruments, and it can't be overstated how important that was. The group that had turned onto Buddy at that time was the Quarrymen, the nucleus of The Beatles. The first song they recorded when they went in to make their first demo in 1958 was 'That'll Be the Day' because they loved what Buddy was doing. Later, they did 'Words of Love', which is one of the nicest covers of a Buddy Holly song. So that was the deep influence that Buddy was beginning to have on the UK music scene.

UK TOUR

At 4 PM on 28 February 1958 Buddy Holly and the Crickets arrived at London Airport in preparation for their 25-day tour of the UK. On that day, the band performed for Ken Walton on the Cool for Cats *TV show, lipsyncing 'I'm Gonna Love You Too'. Ken informally interviewed Buddy for a few minutes backstage as they set up. They then headed to a press reception at the Whisky-A-Go-Go in Soho, London. Also in attendance were a group of girls from* Valentine *magazine and Godfrey Evans and Denis Compton, two notable English cricketers. This became the biggest photoshoot of Buddy's career.*

Accompanying Buddy Holly and the Crickets were Norman and Vi Petty and their road manager, Wally Stewart. The group were paid $4,000 per week and grossed almost $15,000 during this tour. Unlike their US tours, this tour was untitled and comprised a variety of musical styles. In fact, Buddy Holly and the Crickets were the only rock and roll act. Other performers included Gary Miller, the Tanner Sisters, Des O'Connor, and the Ronnie Keene Orchestra. This was Buddy's only tour of the UK.

Melody Maker

MARCH 8, 1958 World's Largest Sale EVERY FRIDAY 6d.

Jazz at Newport
See Page 15

THE ROCK SETS IN!

ROCK solid are the concert halls of Britain. Gyrating like rival sputniks round the provinces are these two rocking package shows headed by Paul Anka (top) and Buddy Holly and the Crickets (bottom left).

The Beat, like it or not, is here.

And The Beat is packing theatres, record stores, cinemas, and holding viewers to TV.

The Beat is Big Business. And it is the Music Business which is benefiting most.

Both shows are reviewed on page 3.

★ Inside—Steve Race on Drummers ★

March 8, 1958 MELODY MAKER—Page 3

BUDDY HOLLY and the CRICKETS

BRITISH disc spinners get double value for their money with the current visit of the American group, Buddy Holly and the Crickets. These three barnstorming youngsters have two hits in the charts at the moment—"Peggy Sue," under Buddy Holly's label, and "Oh, Boy!" under the banner of the Crickets.

4,500 disc fans pack Troc — despite Elvis

Breaking the ice

Gold dust

Screams

Big tour

Holly's sidemen—l: Jerry Allison (drums) and Joe Mauldin (bass).

Bill Holden

BUDDY HOLLY

PAUL ANKA

'Frozen North' thaws to his showmanship

Maurice Burman talks to Paul Anka

J. Magin

The NEW Sound... Zyn

FAST – HIGH – STINGING

AT YOUR DEALER'S NOW

Zyn CYMBAL BAR

at all the leading Drum Dealers

ELEPHANT AND CASTLE

The two headline shows Buddy and the Crickets played at the Trocadero in Elephant and Castle, London on 1 March 1958 (above and opposite) were the first of 25 dates on the UK tour. The Trocadero was the largest cinema in Britain. It was demolished in 1963, and one of the last surviving relics of pre-war Elephant and Castle was lost.

While in London, the band stayed in the Cumberland Hotel near Marble Arch, where Jimi Hendrix would stay just over ten years later. The day after playing the Trocadero they recorded a television performance for Sunday Night at the London Palladium, *where their set included 'That'll Be the Day', 'Oh Boy!' and 'Peggy Sue'. That night they played the Gaumont State Theatre in Kilburn, North London.*

MELODY MAKER

A copy of popular music newspaper Melody Maker *from 8 March 1958. Following Buddy Holly and the Crickets' performances at the Trocadero it features the group on the cover, as well as a feature headlined '4,500 disc fans pack Troc – despite Elvis.'*

TROCADERO, Elephant & Castle
BUDDY HOLLY AND
THE CRICKETS
and Full Supporting Programme
2nd Performance 8-45 (D.O. 8-15)
Saturday, March 1st, 1958
STALLS 10/6
Block 5
Seat D 26
Please enter by South Entrance
THIS PORTION TO BE RETAINED

RONNIE KEENE The Trocadero was packed to the rafters. It was obvious that no one had come to see us, or any of the other British acts. We were just cannon fodder. Still, we weren't booed: they listened to us and clapped politely. But when Buddy and the Crickets were announced, the whole place erupted. At that moment, I realised it was all over for musicians like me. This was the future.

After the show, there must have been 300 kids waiting outside the stage door, but it was all very orderly. The kids seemed to take their cue from Buddy and the Crickets. They were nice and courteous, and the kids were the same in return.

BRIAN MAY The most obvious example of Buddy's influence is The Beatles, they loved him. That wonderful explosion of sounds in Liverpool that was the Searchers, Gerry and the Pacemakers, and The Beatles – that whole movement was inspired by Buddy. The same would be true of John Mayall and Eric Clapton in London some years later. Buddy managed to distil his passion and fuse it with a great melodic sense to make rock and roll.

[In Kilburn] I broke a string for the first time. It kind of put us off balance for a while, but everything went along fine when I got it repaired.

We played at [Sheffield] City Hall and it was pretty confusing because we had people sitting behind us. We're not used to that, and another thing, the weather down there was cold, and dark, and dismal – I didn't like that. It snowed like mad when we played in Nottingham, and that wasn't too pleasant either. [In Birmingham] we were taken round the Austin Motor Works, which was quite a big kick. We spent about half a day there going right from the foundries through to the assembly rooms. [The fans] were fine – nice, enthusiastic people. Very receptive and generally well behaved. Mind you, some of them broke a couple windows in my dressing room at Worcester trying to get autographs, but they didn't mean any harm. (Buddy Holly interview with Keith Goodwin, *New Musical Express*, 28 March 1958)

BRIAN MAY I was under the covers in bed, pretending I was asleep with my headphones on, listening to Radio Luxembourg through a little crystal set that my dad and I had made. I could hear all the music coming out of America at that time, which was incredibly exciting. That's where I first heard Buddy Holly. It would have been 'Oh Boy!', 'That'll Be the Day' and 'Maybe Baby' and I was completely electrified. I thought, 'That's what I want to do, that's where I want to be.' I went down to the local record shop, a place called Waldron's in Hounslow, and that's where I bought my first records by Buddy Holly and the Crickets.

The magic happens in the first few seconds of 'Maybe Baby'. It features a guitar with these amazing, church-type harmonies behind. You haven't heard Buddy yet, but it's all set up and the magic is there. Then the whole band begins – it's only a small band, but it sounds very large – followed by this 'Oooh'. The harmonies are carefully chosen to have a haunting quality, and when Buddy comes in, the harmonies are with him. That music has been an inspiration to me all my life. If you hear Queen, the songs are full of harmonies; Freddie was influenced by this too. Buddy Holly's harmonies are just monumental, and they drive the song, which is the way he wrote it. It's very significant to me and to all of us who became obsessed with harmony vocals, from Queen to the Beach Boys to The Beatles. I think all of that comes from here. The Crickets, whatever they had at that point, was the whole universe.

MAYBE BABY

MAYBE BABY I'LL HAVE YOU

MAYBE BABY YOU'LL BE TRUE

MAYBE BABY I'LL HAVE YOU FOR ME

MAYBE BABY

In February 1958, 'Maybe Baby' backed with 'Tell Me How' was released on Brunswick. A promotional flyer (above) features reviews by Cash Box *and* Billboard*. On the 12th of that month, Buddy Holly and the Crickets returned to Norman Petty's studio to record 'Well . . . All Right'. Buddy played the guitar during this session.*

Left: A page from the Buddy Holly Notebook with 'Maybe Baby' lyrics in Buddy's handwriting

Opposite: Buddy Holly on stage
Trocadero, London, UK
1 March 1958

CLIFF RICHARD Everybody was unique at that time, but the Crickets were above them all. When they appeared at the London Palladium, it was so inspirational – they were just three guys. We hadn't heard anything like that before.

PETER ASHER It was a similar notion to a prophet being less respected in his own land. It was magically exotic to us; we were growing up in a gloomy bombsite, while America was a glossy, technicolour place with giant cars, refrigerators and perfect teeth. Television and movies made America look fabulous, and they had the music to make us fall in love with it. Americans took it for granted, whereas we felt in awe.

BRIAN MAY Buddy was more popular in England than he was in the States, and by the time he came over he was a god. I saw his performance with the Crickets on *Sunday Night at the London Palladium*, and it was incredible. It was all completely live. The bass, guitar, drums – there was no orchestral accompaniment, yet they were stupendous. I was too young to go to his shows because I was just a boy, but I would have loved to have seen him live.

ALBERT LEE I'd planned on going to a friend's house and watch him appear on the show, but I arrived late. I thought he would be top of the bill. When he played at Woolwich Granada I was determined to go, but I got the dates wrong. I ran into a friend who said they saw Buddy the previous night and how loud it was. I mentioned that to Jerry Allison years later and he said, 'Loud? Buddy had a little 40-watt amp with three 10-inch speakers.' He didn't remember any mics on the drums or bass, so I'm not sure where the volume came from.

Top: Buddy Holly on stage Gaumont State Theatre, Kilburn, London, UK, 2 March 1958

Above and opposite: Buddy Holly and the Crickets performing on Sunday Night at the London Palladium. *They played 'That'll Be the Day', 'Peggy Sue' and 'Oh Boy!', 2 March 1958.*

PAUL ANKA Buddy's style of guitar playing was unique to him. Elvis wasn't a guitar player, he strummed, but Buddy made inroads into rock and roll.

ALBERT LEE His guitar playing was simple, but he just nailed it. The best solos were the simpler ones; one of the first solos I ever learned was 'That'll Be the Day'. As a young aspiring guitar player, you could listen to that and say, 'I know what he's doing now,' so the songs were lessons in themselves. It took me a while to grasp what he was doing, but Buddy was a great stepping stone for learning your way around the guitar.

PETER ASHER The music scene in England revolved around falling in love with American culture. The Beatles were an American rock and roll tribute band to begin with, and the Rolling Stones were an American rhythm and blues tribute band. Buddy became part of our pantheon; we all performed his songs. We all adored and respected American popular music.

CLIFF RICHARD Americans gave us a change. One minute it was Frank Sinatra, and suddenly it became Elvis Presley, Buddy Holly, Little Richard and Gene Vincent. Because most musicians played guitar, Buddy was an obvious person to follow and we latched on to him. He gave us life. It was the biggest change in any art form; overnight, everything changed.

SOUTHAMPTON GAUMONT
On 3 March, Buddy Holly and the Crickets went to Southampton, where they performed two shows at the Gaumont Theatre (opposite, bottom left)

CHESTERFIELD
Above: On 4 March on the way to perform in Sheffield, some of the entourage made a stop in the town of Chesterfield. Norman Petty photographed Buddy walking with Lynn Adams, the vocalist with the Ronnie Keene Orchestra. Joe B. Mauldin can be seen in the background.

BLACK OVERCOAT
Left: A black overcoat owned and worn by Buddy Holly

HANK MARVIN Des O'Connor was the compere on Buddy's UK tour. He told me he had a guitar that Buddy Holly gave him, and I was curious as to which guitar it was, whether it was a Strat, and he came out with a Höfner that Buddy had bought in the UK as something to play around with in the dressing room.

DES O'CONNOR Buddy was a real sweet, fun guy. We'd sometimes have to share a hotel bedroom and I'd be responsible for getting him out of bed in the morning, because an early riser Buddy was not. I'd get hold of his feet and just pull. 'Don't do that, Des,' this Texan voice would say from under the blankets. 'I'm tall enough already.'

He'd ask me for jokes to tell between his songs, and I'd give him a few of my less good ones. But in that accent of his, they still went down a storm. In Harrogate, he said he wanted to have real English afternoon tea, so we went to a posh hotel and had the whole thing with dainty little sandwiches, scones and sugar tongs. One day he went out and bought an acoustic guitar for jamming on the bus, and tried out 18 different ones before he found one he liked, a Höfner. At the end of the tour, he gave it to me.

1956 HÖFNER PRESIDENT ACOUSTIC ARCHTOP
This guitar was purchased by Buddy Holly when he first arrived in London in February 1958. His own instruments were in the process of being shipped across the Atlantic for his UK tour, and so he needed a guitar to play on in the meantime until they arrived. Des O'Connor, who was acting as compere on the tour, took him to Maurice Plaquet's music shop in London, where the President was acquired for Buddy. He continued to use it on tour buses and in hotel rooms throughout his time in the UK, and, before returning to the US, he gave the guitar to Des. These photographs were taken at the Bradford Gaumont, where Buddy would have had the guitar.

Alexandra
HOTEL
HAMMONDS

Telephones:
27122/3

Great Horton Road
Bradford

19

Dear Mother & Dad,

Just thought I'd drop a few lines and tell you how things are going. Everything's just fine except that I have had a cold for about 4 days. It's not too bad though and I'm about over it now. The crowds are liking us real well and we are having a lot of fun, though we don't have much time for sight-seeing because we are so busy travelling, eating, sleeping, and playing. Tomorrow night we play at Birmingham. That's where the factories are where they make sports cars and motorcycles. We will probably buy some because they are a lot cheaper here than in the

Alexandra
HOTEL
HAMMONDS

Telephones:
27122/3

Great Horton Road
Bradford

States. So don't be surprised if and when they are delivered there. I don't guess you have done too much on the house, yet. I'm already getting anxious to get home and help on it. Probably be nearly finished when we get back, though. I'm sure looking forward to having a nice place. If you want to write before we leave England, the address is on the back of the envelope and you'll have to hurry for it to get here in time. Guess I'd better close and get some sleep, now.

Love,

Buddy

Artistry has been kicked out of the stage door and performers who can provide ephemeral thrills are taking its place. Audiences are in search of the momentary gimmick, of which they tire whenever another novelty is introduced.

At least it would seem so from the fanatical reception given to a screeching guitar player and his two colleagues when they headed the bill at the Gaumont Theatre, Bradford last night. They were American Buddy Holly and the Crickets.

Unless they had previously read the lyrics or heard them sung by an articulate vocalist, I would have defied anyone in the audience to tell me what 70 per cent of the words which issued from the lips of this foot-stamping, knee falling musician were. Where on earth is show business heading?

The tragedy often is that many of the performers, like the trio last night, have a basic talent which they distort in order to win an audience's favour. On an elaborate display board at the Gaumont announcing a forthcoming musical contest, is fixed a washboard. What a pitiful symbol it is of present-day entertainment. Like its worshippers, it would be better employed in the dolly-tub! ('Perhaps the audience is to blame!' Review of the show on Sunday 9 March 1958, Peter Holdsworth, Bradford *Telegraph & Argus*)

BRADFORD GAUMONT

On 9 March, Buddy Holly and the Crickets played two shows at the Gaumont Theatre, Bradford. The group performed 'That'll Be the Day', 'Peggy Sue', 'Everyday', 'Maybe Baby', 'Oh Boy!', 'Money Honey', 'Be-Bop-A-Lula', 'She's Got It' and 'Ready Teddy'. During their time in Bradford, they stayed at the Alexandra Hotel, where Buddy wrote a letter to his parents (above).

BIRMINGHAM TOWN HALL

Right and opposite: On 10 March, Buddy Holly and the Crickets played the Town Hall in Birmingham

ALBERT LEE He was a huge influence on a lot of us. He influenced Eric Clapton, and obviously he was a big influence on The Beatles, which Paul recognised when he bought Buddy's catalogue.

PAUL ANKA I met The Beatles in the 1960s and hung out with them. They'd all say to me, 'Chuck Berry!' and 'Buddy Holly!' You could hear them copying each other. All the guys I've met, from Elton John to Clapton, Buddy was an influence.

JERRY 'J.I.' ALLISON We worked better as a trio. If you can make the same amount of noise with three people, it's more impressive than when you have five. Through the years, we've been everything from a three-piece to a 12-piece, but three of us has always worked best. Joe B.'s bass wasn't mic'd a lot of the time, so if someone knew the records then they'd fill in the bass mentally. I played as loud as I could, so I'd break a drum skin at least once a night, and Buddy always turned his amp all the way up. People would say, 'I don't know how you like them, they're entirely too loud for three people,' but it worked well.

OFF THE RECORD
Buddy Holly and the Crickets performing 'Maybe Baby' on BBC's Off the Record
14 March 1958

What's the best sports car on the road today? We've been arguing about this ever since we got to Britain, so maybe you can help us now. Personally, I'd like a Jaguar or a Mercedes.

But Jerry Allison, who plays drums with the Crickets, is sold on M.G.s, and Joe Mauldin, our bass player, fancies an Austin Healey. You see, we all want to take a car back home with us.

You know what happened after our concerts at Kilburn – our third day in Britain? Well, I'll tell you.

We spent most of the day along with Keith Goodwin of the New Musical Express, *and Allan Crawford, managing director of Southern Music, who publish a lot of our songs. Keith was going on about Jaguars and Allan was recommending the Mercedes, and in the end, we just couldn't make up our minds. And that's how, at around two o'clock early on Monday morning, the five of us came to be touring London in Allan's car inspecting all the automobile showrooms.*

That's typical, by the way, of the sort of crazy things in which the Crickets always seem to get involved! Anyway, we still haven't made up our minds, so if any of you have got any suggestions, please let us know!

As I write this, we've only been in England a matter of days, so the Crickets and I haven't yet managed to see much of the country. But what little we've seen, we like, and we know we're going to have a real ball here!

The people we've met have all been just wonderful to us, and we especially appreciate the many courtesies shown us by stage managers, stage hands, electricians, etc., at all the theatres we've visited. It's so refreshing to find such co-operative people!

The equipment you have in your theatres puts most American halls to shame. We're really impressed by the technical aspect of show business in Britain, and the smooth running of the London Palladium TV show, which we did on our second day here, was something to be marvelled at.

We (I mean the Crickets – Jerry, Joe and myself) like British audiences too. They're always very receptive, and really make us feel at home. They listen while we're playing, don't scream and holler out, and then reward you at the end with good, hearty applause. That's good! Also they seem to like all kinds of music, which is another very good thing.

We came to Britain with our manager, Norman Petty, who brought along his wife, Vi. Norman, as you probably already know, more or less 'discovered' us, and we still make all our records at his studio in Clovis, New Mexico, before they are released on the American Coral and Brunswick labels.

I'll tell you another thing which happened after our Kilburn concert. Norman, you see, has his own trio back home, and he plays mighty fine organ. Well, as we were getting ready to go, Norman located the theatre organ and started to play. So we stayed at the theatre an extra half-hour! Vi, by the way, plays great piano, and if she'd have got going, I don't think we'd ever have got away!

A lot of people have asked me why Niki Sullivan, one of our original members, isn't here with us. Well, Niki decided a little while ago that he wanted to go back to school, and when he left, we just decided to carry on as a trio.

In answer to another question, I first started playing guitar when I was in the seventh grade at junior high school back home in Lubbock. It cost me around 45 dollars, and I taught myself to play it through a process of trial and error. More recently, I've taken up composing, and things like 'That'll Be the Day', 'Peggy Sue' and 'Listen to Me' are my songs.

We like to think that we play rhythm and blues, with country and western overtones, and my personal favourites in this field (the boys agree with me on this, by the way) are Elvis Presley, Ray Charles, the Everly Brothers and Eddie Cochran. We also like Little Richard, and do some of his numbers in our act.

Back home in the States, most of our time is taken up with big package shows that tour from coast to coast. You may be interested to know that as soon as we arrive in the States again we're going to spend six days touring around Florida with a show that will also star people like Jerry Lee Lewis and the Everly Brothers. We've also got some TV shows lined up, like the Bob Hope and Steve Allen shows.

These package shows I mentioned a few words ago are really mammoth affairs. Sometimes there are as many as 18 or 20 acts in the show. Some artists do only one number, but this of course depends entirely on how many records that particular artist has got moving at the time. The starring acts usually do about four songs without encores. The encores, of course, are dependent on audience reaction. The travelling distances in the States probably sound enormous to you. We look upon journeys ranging from 200 to 300 miles as 'small hops', and do these either by bus or rail. Anything over 400 miles is made by air.

So you see, the journeys we are making between dates in Britain are really small to us, and aren't any bother at all. The shows are different in many ways – for instance, we are doing at least a dozen songs at each appearance here. Still, it's a wonderful experience, and we're all enjoying ourselves immensely.

We (once again, I mean the Crickets) never do any night club dates in America. The point is that we feel our kind of music appeals principally to young people – and the fans just can't afford to go to these places even if they wanted to. Night clubs appeal primarily to the middle age group, and although we might go down quite well in a niterie, we're happier doing the one-night-stand circuits!

About our music – well, we try to show creativeness and go out of our way not to copy any other artist – intentionally or otherwise. Our aim is to concentrate on original material and to produce a distinctive sound of our own. Between us, Norman and I have written quite a lot of songs, and we hope to open our own music-publishing house some time in the very near future.

Many of the English fans I've met so far have asked me about hobbies. Well, as you can imagine, I don't really get much time for them. But when I do get the opportunity, I like to go water-skiing and swimming. I'm mad on motorcycle riding, too, and used to have a Triumph, but I sold it a couple of years ago to get a car. I'm running a Chevrolet right now ... Hey, seems to me we've talked enough about automobiles already. ('Buddy Holly Writes' article, *Hit Parader*, April 1958)

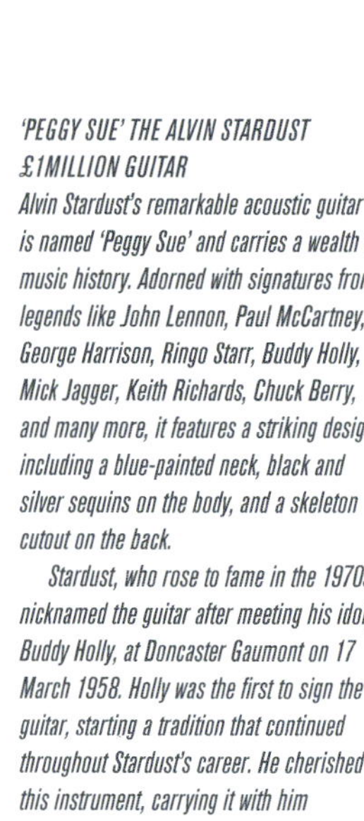

'PEGGY SUE' THE ALVIN STARDUST £1MILLION GUITAR

Alvin Stardust's remarkable acoustic guitar is named 'Peggy Sue' and carries a wealth of music history. Adorned with signatures from legends like John Lennon, Paul McCartney, George Harrison, Ringo Starr, Buddy Holly, Mick Jagger, Keith Richards, Chuck Berry, and many more, it features a striking design including a blue-painted neck, black and silver sequins on the body, and a skeleton cutout on the back.

Stardust, who rose to fame in the 1970s, nicknamed the guitar after meeting his idol, Buddy Holly, at Doncaster Gaumont on 17 March 1958. Holly was the first to sign the guitar, starting a tradition that continued throughout Stardust's career. He cherished this instrument, carrying it with him everywhere as he collected autographs from fellow rock and roll greats while delivering hits like 'My Coo Ca Choo' and 'I Feel Like Buddy Holly'. Though the guitar has no maker or serial number, its history and signatures make it an invaluable piece of music history.

Signatures clockwise from top left: Joe B. Mauldin, Jerry Allison and Buddy Holly, Paul McCartney, George Harrison, Cliff Richard, Jeff Beck

DONCASTER GAUMONT

Prior to performing at the Gaumont in Doncaster on 17 March 1958 (a poster for this date is shown opposite, top right), Buddy made time to jam with Alvin Stardust. After they all played a rendition of 'Peggy Sue', Buddy and the Crickets signed his guitar.

ALVIN STARDUST My parents bought me a three-quarter size guitar for my 12th birthday, and I never put it down. In April 1958 I caught the bus to Doncaster to see my hero Buddy Holly perform. I thought I'd take my guitar with me to show how keen I was. The staff saw me and took me backstage to meet Buddy and the Crickets. Buddy asked me if I could play the guitar and I played and sang 'Peggy Sue'. It was amazing. I'm singing and playing my guitar and Buddy was strumming along too. All too soon it had to end but there was no paper with which to get an autograph. Luckily I had a pencil in my guitar case, and Buddy and the Crickets signed the guitar. On my way home I decided to give my guitar a name. I thought, B.B. King has called his guitar 'Lucille', so I'll call mine 'Peggy Sue'.

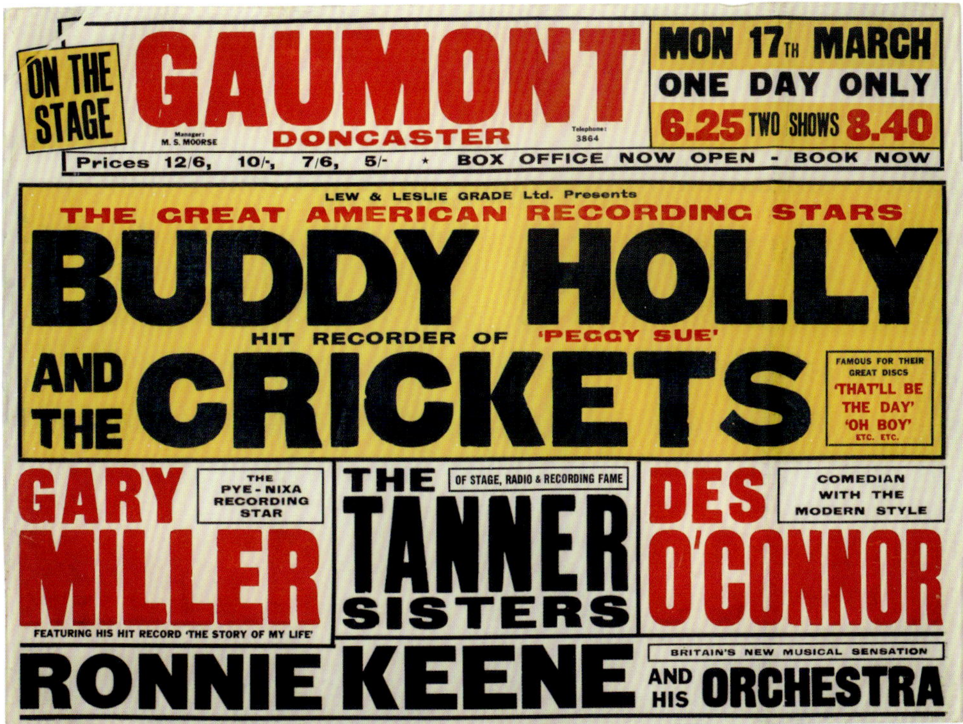

MIKE READ It was many years ago that Alvin Stardust first showed me the guitar his mum had bought him as a young teenager. At first it looked just like the first instrument any of us would have had – inexpensive, not flashy and never easy to keep in tune. But on closer inspection and if you saw it in the right light, there were names on it. And as Alvin pointed them out one by one, it became clear that they weren't just any names. The Beatles, the Rolling Stones and the Who had held this battered old guitar … and not only held it, but signed it. The journey for this six-string autograph book started with Buddy Holly. Buddy and the Crickets only toured the UK once, in March 1958. It was a great opportunity for the music-mad Bernard Jewry, as Alvin was then, to head to his nearest theatre. Hanging round by the stage door in the hope of getting a glimpse of his idols, he was noticed by the doorman, who saw the guitar he was carrying and asked who he was looking for. Rather boldly, he said 'Buddy Holly', thinking the doorman might let him know when the singer was due to come out.

Instead, he ushered him in. 'Second door on the left.' More naive times. The doorman simply assumed he was part of the show. He found the door. Knocked. Buddy opened it. Had a strum on the guitar and signed it. The Crickets followed suit. Young Bernard reasoned that if it worked with Buddy, it might also work with Eddie Cochran. It did. And with many others. Many artists used to stay at his mother's small hotel in Mansfield, so he was ahead of the game. Early British rock and rollers like Cliff Richard, Billy Fury and Marty Wilde signed it, as did US legends such as Chuck Berry, Gene Vincent and Bill Haley. I know at one time the guitar was insured for £1.25 million as I did a TV programme with Alvin talking about its history and provenance.

No other guitar has been on a journey like this … I'm sure all of us who picked it up and played a song or two felt history coursing through our veins and hoped the magic would rub off. Thank goodness the signatures didn't.

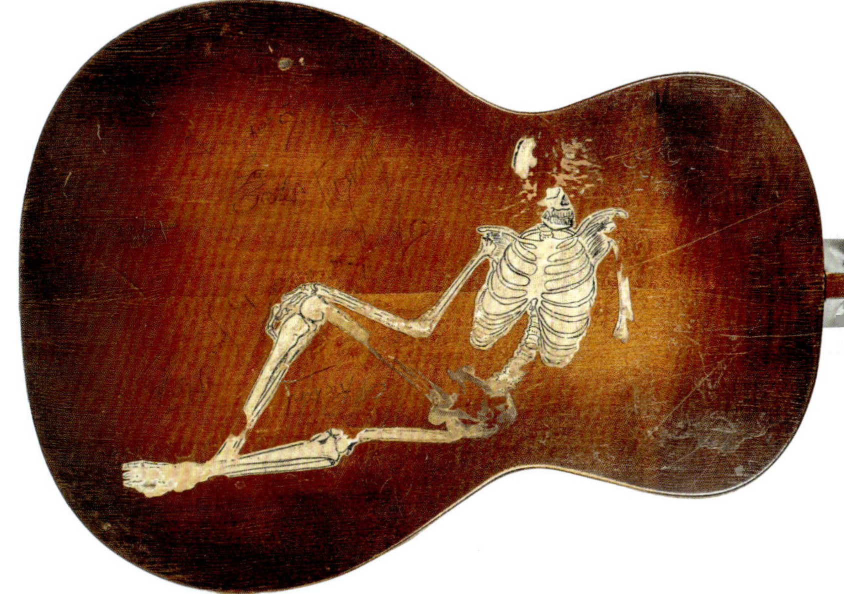

LIVERPOOL PHILHARMONIC HALL
Right: A promotional poster for Buddy Holly and the Crickets' headline show at Liverpool Philharmonic Hall on 20 March 1958

LONDON FOG JACKET
Below: Buddy Holly's London Fog jacket, which he bought during his time overseas. Maria Elena has stated that it was this jacket Buddy was wearing when he returned from the UK in March 1958.

SALISBURY GAUMONT
Opposite, top: A letter from Buddy to his parents, 22 March 1958

LEICESTER DE MONTFORT HALL
Opposite, bottom right: On 16 March, Buddy Holly, the Pettys and the Crickets came to Leicester, and Buddy and the Crickets performed two shows, at 5.40 PM and 8 PM. That night they stayed at the Grand Hotel, and Buddy wrote a letter to his parents.

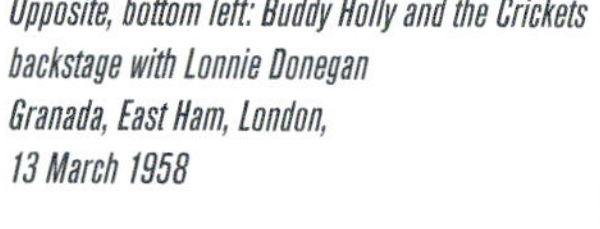

Opposite, bottom left: Buddy Holly and the Crickets backstage with Lonnie Donegan
Granada, East Ham, London,
13 March 1958

MARIA ELENA When Buddy came back from the tour in England he said he was thinking of doing more tours over there. The main reason he wanted to go back was because he heard so much talent out there. He was also thinking about opening a recording studio in England, bringing talent in and developing it. With The Beatles and everybody that followed, he was on the right track.

Sat. Mar. 22
Salisbury, England

Dear Mother & Dad,

I thought I would drop one more letter to you before we leave England and I figured it had better be now or we would get to the states before the letter. We probably will anyhow but — there you are.

We had three good shows today. The last one especially. We are getting to where we can carry on pretty good on the stage what with a few little jokes and all. Everyone comments on how my jokes get bigger laughs than the comedian on the show, Des O'Conner. Who knows, we might change and be comedians instead of rock & roll stars.

I guess you are wondering by now why I am writing this way. Jerry and I bought some new pens today, and they write good this way so I thought I'd try it.

Norman and Jerry are sitting over by the fireplace (this is a real old, quaint place) talking about dreams. Norman was just telling about a dream he had where all his teeth came out. I guess he's just getting old?

I was glad to hear that you are getting something done on the house. I wonder what it will look like when it's finished. Just have to wait, I guess.

Well, I guess I'll close for now and talk to you when we get to New York. Til' then, bye for now.

Love,

Buddy

GAUMONT SALISBURY
Lew & Leslie Grade Ltd. present
BUDDY HOLLY AND THE CRICKETS
1st Performance at 6-20
Saturday, March 22nd, 1958
BACK CIRCLE 5/6
P 4
THIS PORTION TO BE RETAINED

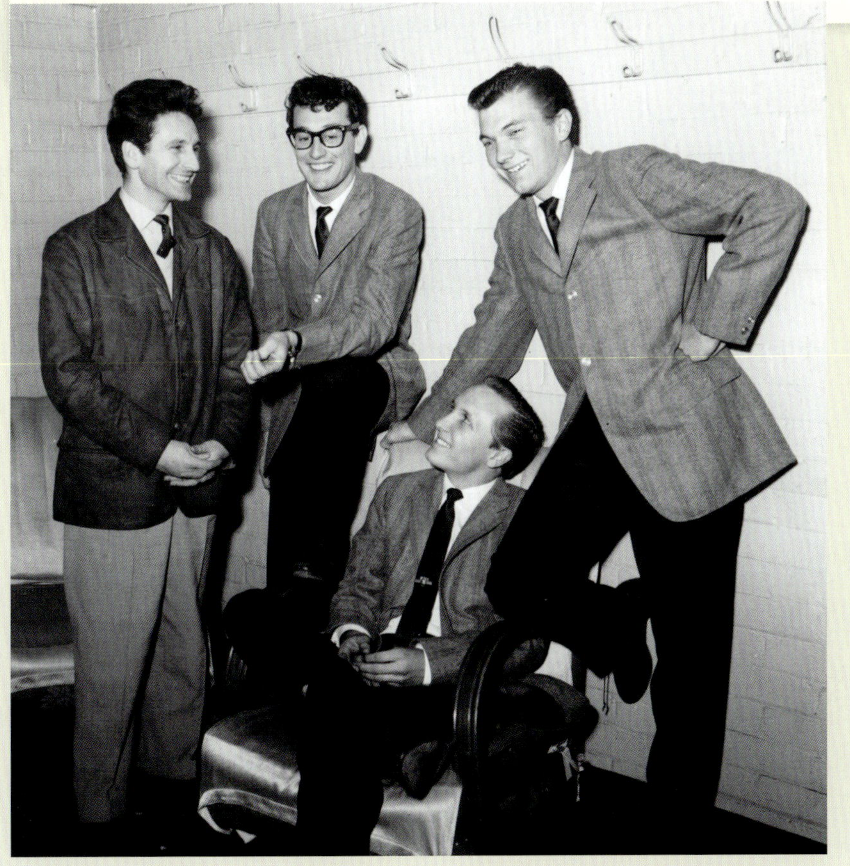

TELEPHONES
5222, 5223, 5224

TELEGRAMS
GRANDHOTEL, LEICESTER

GRAND HOTEL
LEICESTER

Adjacent to
L.M.R. & E.R. Stations
150 Bedrooms

King's Hall Rooms
available for
Receptions, Dances,
Banquets, etc.

Dear Mother & Dad,

We just checked into a hotel and I thought I would write a few lines before I have to go to the theatre. I guess everything is going all right at home? All's fine here except we want to get back to the U.S. We had a long bus trip today but are none the worse for wear. This is the nicest hotel we have stayed in over here and we are in a pretty good mood. Good hotels make happy "recording stars". That's all for now I guess. Tell everyone hello.

Love, Buddy

PROPRIETORS: THE GRAND HOTEL (LEICESTER) LTD.

ALAN FREED BIG BEAT TOUR

Shortly after returning from England, Buddy Holly and the Crickets embarked on a 43-day tour that began at the Paramount Theater, New York on 28 March and concluded in Hershey, PA on 9 May 1958 (a show in Newark, NJ scheduled for 10 May was cancelled). Other performers included Chuck Berry, Jerry Lee Lewis, Frankie Lymon, Danny and the Juniors, the Diamonds, Screamin' Jay Hawkins, Billie and Lillie, the Chantels, Larry Williams, Billy Ford, the Pastels, Jo Ann Campbell, Dicky Doo and the Don'ts, Ed Townsend, the Velours, the Shirelles, the Twin Tones and the Alan Freed Orchestra featuring Sam 'The Man' Taylor.

Below: A colour film reel of a very rare eight-minute home movie shot in Flint, MI in 1958 without sound of Buddy performing on the Alan Freed Big Beat Tour. Stills from this film are shown opposite.

Bottom: Frankie Avalon (left); the Royal Teens (centre); and Jimmy Dell, Sam Cooke and Frankie Avalon (right), Auditorium, Kitchener, ON, Canada, 11 April 1958

ALAN FREED PRESENTS THE BIG BEAT

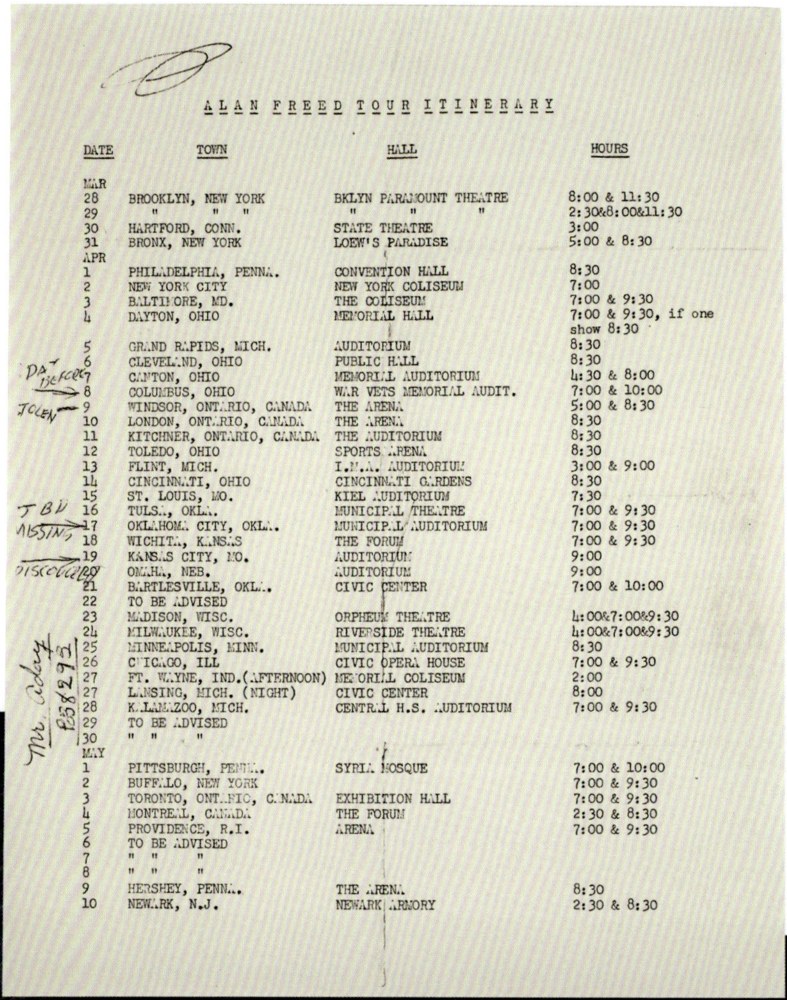

ALAN FREED TOUR ITINERARY

DATE	TOWN	HALL	HOURS
MAR			
28	BROOKLYN, NEW YORK	BKLYN PARAMOUNT THEATRE	8:00 & 11:30
29	" " "	" " "	2:30&8:00&11:30
30	HARTFORD, CONN.	STATE THEATRE	3:00
31	BRONX, NEW YORK	LOEW'S PARADISE	5:00 & 8:30
APR			
1	PHILADELPHIA, PENNA.	CONVENTION HALL	8:30
2	NEW YORK CITY	NEW YORK COLISEUM	7:00
3	BALTIMORE, MD.	THE COLISEUM	7:00 & 9:30
4	DAYTON, OHIO	MEMORIAL HALL	7:00 & 9:30, if one show 8:30
5	GRAND RAPIDS, MICH.	AUDITORIUM	8:30
6	CLEVELAND, OHIO	PUBLIC HALL	8:30
7	CANTON, OHIO	MEMORIAL AUDITORIUM	4:30 & 8:00
8	COLUMBUS, OHIO	WAR VETS MEMORIAL AUDIT.	7:00 & 10:00
9	WINDSOR, ONTARIO, CANADA	THE ARENA	5:00 & 8:30
10	LONDON, ONTARIO, CANADA	THE ARENA	8:30
11	KITCHNER, ONTARIO, CANADA	THE AUDITORIUM	8:30
12	TOLEDO, OHIO	SPORTS ARENA	8:30
13	FLINT, MICH.	I.M.A. AUDITORIUM	3:00 & 9:00
14	CINCINNATI, OHIO	CINCINNATI GARDENS	8:30
15	ST. LOUIS, MO.	KIEL AUDITORIUM	7:30
16	TULSA, OKLA.	MUNICIPAL THEATRE	7:00 & 9:30
17	OKLAHOMA CITY, OKLA.	MUNICIPAL AUDITORIUM	7:00 & 9:30
18	WICHITA, KANSAS	THE FORUM	7:00 & 9:30
19	KANSAS CITY, MO.	AUDITORIUM	9:00
20	OMAHA, NEB.	AUDITORIUM	9:00
21	BARTLESVILLE, OKLA.	CIVIC CENTER	7:00 & 10:00
22	TO BE ADVISED		
23	MADISON, WISC.	ORPHEUM THEATRE	4:00&7:00&9:30
24	MILWAUKEE, WISC.	RIVERSIDE THEATRE	4:00&7:00&9:30
25	MINNEAPOLIS, MINN.	MUNICIPAL AUDITORIUM	8:30
26	CHICAGO, ILL	CIVIC OPERA HOUSE	7:00 & 9:30
27	FT. WAYNE, IND.(AFTERNOON)	MEMORIAL COLISEUM	2:00
27	LANSING, MICH. (NIGHT)	CIVIC CENTER	8:00
28	KALAMAZOO, MICH.	CENTRAL H.S. AUDITORIUM	7:00 & 9:30
29	TO BE ADVISED		
30	" " "		
MAY			
1	PITTSBURGH, PENNA.	SYRIA MOSQUE	7:00 & 10:00
2	BUFFALO, NEW YORK		7:00 & 9:30
3	TORONTO, ONTARIO, CANADA	EXHIBITION HALL	7:00 & 9:30
4	MONTREAL, CANADA	THE FORUM	2:30 & 8:30
5	PROVIDENCE, R.I.	ARENA	7:00 & 9:30
6	TO BE ADVISED		
7	" " "		
8	" " "		
9	HERSHEY, PENNA.	THE ARENA	8:30
10	NEWARK, N.J.	NEWARK ARMORY	2:30 & 8:30

Above: The tour programme came in at 28 pages and featured individual bios and black and white images of each performer. During this tour, the group began flying to some of the venues. In venue-to-venue advertising, Buddy Holly and the Crickets were mistakenly perceived as two separate acts and were billed separately.

STOLEN STRAT

Buddy's Fender Stratocaster was stolen during this tour. He immediately replaced it with a new one, which was shipped to him via air express. The date pencilled on the back of his replacement guitar was '4/58'. One of the Crickets remembers that the theft took place while they were in St Louis. In a photo taken on 22 April it's apparent that his guitar is new, as the wear marks near the pick-ups, seen on many earlier photos, are not there.

On Buddy's itinerary sheet for Alan Freed's Big Beat tour (top right) handwritten notes by Buddy can be seen in the margins. He wrote the word 'stolen' next to the 9 April date in Windsor, Ontario. If he also had a guitar stolen in St Louis, then he may have lost two Strats on this tour.

Opposite, bottom left:
Civic Auditorium
Grand Rapids, MI,
5 April 1958

Opposite, bottom right:
Auditorium, Kitchener,
ON, Canada,
11 April 1958

Left and below:
Hippodrome Auditorium
Waterloo, IA,
22 April 1958

ALAN FREED
PRESENTS
THE BIG BEAT

WITH
JERRY LEE LEWIS
BUDDY HOLLY & THE CRICKETS
CHUCK BERRY
FRANKIE LYMON
THE DIAMONDS
BILLIE FORD & THE THUNDERBIRDS
DANNY & THE JUNIORS
DICKEY DOO & THE DONT'S
THE CHANTELS
LARRY WILLIAMS
SCREAMIN' JAY HAWKINS
THE PASTELS
JO-ANN CAMPBELL
ED TOWNSEND
ALAN FREED & His Orchestra
featuring
SAM (THE MAN) TAYLOR

BUDDY HOLLY & THE CRICKETS

The high flying Crickets hail from Lubbock, Texas, and the group consists of Leader Buddy Holly on guitar, Joe Mauldin on bass, Jerry Allison on drums, and Niki Sullivan on guitar. They were organized in Lubbock by Holly.

Buddy Holly was born on September 7, 1936, in Lubbock, and his musical career started at the ripe old age of eight at which time he started taking violin lessons. However, several squeaks later, Buddy decided his interest should be changed to the guitar. At the age of 15 this change was made and Buddy began singing while accompanying himself on guitar at various clubs around the Southwest. He then went to Nashville, Tenn., where he was signed by Decca Records and recorded a few Western tunes.

After this, he visited the Norman Petty Recording Studios in Clovis, New Mexico, where with the help of Petty, who, incidentally, had a hit record of his own in "Almost Paradise," Bud recorded a few of his own compositions. Petty took the demonstration records to Murray Deutsch of the Southern Music Publishing Company in New York, who in turn brought them to Bob Thiele of Coral and Brunswick Records. Thiele signed Bud Holly and The Crickets to a recording contract with the Brunswick label, a subsidiary of Decca Records.

When Impresario Irvin Feld first heard them, he and his assistant, Allan Bloom, started telephone wires singing (humming) to sign them up for the Fall Edition of "Biggest Show of Stars for '57." We feel sure that The Crickets will prove one of the reasons that "Super Enterprises" shows are the SHOWS of STARS.

APR • 58

APR • 58

APR • 58

APR • 58

Onstage photos of Buddy Holly and the Crickets; Danny and the Juniors (bottom left); Alan Freed with unknown (bottom centre); and Chuck Berry with fans (opposite, centre right) are all from Central High School Auditorium, Kalamazoo, MI, 28 April 1958

Opposite, bottom right: Alan Freed, Larry Williams, Ben DaCosta and Buddy, New York Coliseum, NY, 2 April 1958

CLIFF RICHARD We played Buddy Holly all the time at parties in London, that was the thing. Buddy showed us that three or four chords were enough to write songs. In an octave there are only eight notes, yet thousands of songs are written with them, alongside those three or four chords.

DUANE EDDY Harlan Howard and Hank Cochran were two of the earliest successful songwriters, and one of them said, 'All you need for a country song is three chords and the truth' – maybe that's where Buddy got it from.

BRIAN MAY There's true magic in those records. They feature a guitar that is incredibly incisive. The context is very different because in those days there wasn't guitar music, so to hear a guitar up front on a record was revolutionary. We were coming out of the big band era of swing and Frank Sinatra. If a guitar was featured, it would be in the background chugging away acoustically. You didn't have a guitar kicking in at the beginning of the record, but now it was the backbone.

GARRY TALLENT Buddy was a terrific guitar player, a rhythm guitar player who would take the lead. His lead was very monumental, especially because he and the Crickets mainly worked as a trio, so if he stopped playing it all fell away. His solo in 'Peggy Sue' is what he's playing throughout the song with some embellishments, which was so rock and roll. Nothing fancy, but it drives the song.

DON McLEAN He was very creative. He used a capo a lot, so he would capo up five or six frets and play on the first fret. He was an excellent guitar player; like a lot of good guitar players, he did things that were simple and brilliant.

LARRY WELBORN He got that high sound through his capo. We used to call him 'Clamp' back in the day.

AGREEMENT made this 25th day of MAY 1958 between NOR VA JAK MUSIC, INC., hereinafter designated as PUBLISHER and

BUDDY HOLLY of Box 936 – Clovis, New Mexico

.... of ....

.... of ....

jointly and/or severally designated as WRITER.

WITNESSETH:

(1) The Writer hereby sells, assigns, transfers and delivers to the Publisher, its successors and assigns, all of his rights, title and interest in and to a certain heretofore unpublished original work, as annexed hereto, written and/or composed by the Writer, now entitled,

LONESOME TEARS

including the title, words and/or music thereof, as well as the entire exclusive right to publicly perform and televise, together with the right to secure copyrights and renewals therein throughout the world, as proprietor in its own name, or otherwise, and to have and to hold the said work, copyrights and renewals thereof and all rights of whatsoever nature thereunder existing.

(2) The Writer hereby warrants that the said work is his sole, exclusive and original work, that he has full right and power to make the within agreement, and that there exists no adverse claim to or in the said work, which is free from all liens and encumbrances whatsoever.

(3) In consideration of this Agreement, the Publisher agrees to pay the Writer, jointly, only the following royalties:

(a) ..4..¢ per copy, in respect of regular piano copies and/or orchestrations, sold in the United States and for which the Publisher received payment.

(b) ..50% of the net amount received by the Publisher, in respect of regular piano copies and/or orchestrations sold and paid for in any foreign country.

(c) ..50% of the net amount received by the Publisher, in respect of any licenses issued authorizing the manufacture of parts of instruments serving to mechanically reproduce said work, electrical transcriptions, or to use said work in synchronization with sound motion pictures.

(d) ..50% of the net amount of performing fees received by the Publisher in the United States, only provided said fees include both Writer and Publisher shares and are payable on a fixed and determinable basis.

(4) The Publisher agrees to render to the Writer on or about February 15th, and August 15th, of each year, so long as it shall continue publishing or licensing said work, covering the six months ending December 31st, and June 30th, of each year respectively, royalty statements accompanied by remittance of the amount due.

(5) All sums hereunder payable jointly to the Writer shall be divided and paid in the following manner:

90 % to BUDDY HOLLY of Box 936 – Clovis, New Mexico

10 % to NORMAN PETTY of Box 936 – Clovis, New Mexico

...... % to .... of ....

(6) The Publisher shall have the right to alter, change, edit or translate the work or any part thereof, in any way it may be necessary. In the event it be necessary for the Publisher to cause lyrics to be written in other languages for and as part of the work, the publisher shall in such event have the right to deduct from the heretofore agreed royalties payable to the Writer, the cost or obligation thereof, but in no event more than a sum equal to one-half.

(7) The Writer hereby grants and conveys an irrevocable power of attorney authorizing and empowering the Publisher, its nominees, successors and assigns, to administer any and all rights in and to the said work, and collect and receive any and all the fees therefrom; also to file application and renew the copyrights in the name of the Writer, and upon such renewals, to execute proper and formal assignments thereof so as to secure to the Publisher, its successors and assigns, the renewal terms of, in and to said copyrights and/or works.

(8) The Writer hereby agrees to indemnify and save harmless the Publisher against any loss, expense or damage by reason of any adverse claims made by others with respect to the work, and agrees that all expenses incurred in defense of any such claims, including counsel fees, as well as any and all sums paid by the Publisher, pursuant to a judgment, arbitration or any settlement or adjustment which may be made in the discretion of the Publisher, or otherwise, shall at all times be borne by the Writer, and may be deducted by the Publisher from any money accruing to the Writer under this agreement or otherwise.

(9) The Writer agrees that he will not assign this Agreement nor any sums that may become due hereunder, without the written consent of the Publisher first endorsed hereon.

(10) Except as otherwise herein provided, this Agreement is binding upon the parties hereto and their respective successors in interest.

WITNESS: .... Writer
BUDDY HOLLY

.... Writer

.... Writer

WITNESS: NOR VA JAK MUSIC, INC.
By ....

FM-27

HERSHEY, PENNSYLVANIA
Opposite, above and overleaf: Buddy Holly and the Crickets backstage at the Arena in Hershey, PA, 9 May 1958

Opposite, bottom right: Jerry Lee Lewis on stage during the same show

Left: A recording contract for 'Lonesome Tears' between Buddy Holly and Nor Va Jak Music, Inc. signed by Buddy and Norman Petty, 25 May 1958

JERRY 'J.I.' ALLISON Our flight got cancelled on the way home from a tour, so we were stuck in Dallas. We put our luggage on the next flight and had the idea to buy some motorcycles and ride them home, which was about 350 miles. Buddy had $8,000 in his pocket, a lot of money, so we went over to the Harley Davidson dealer and asked the salesman about three of the bikes. He said we couldn't afford the first payment on them, so Buddy whipped out the money and told him we could. He asked us to wait so we went back outside, got a taxi and went to the Triumph dealer. We rode them a lot, often from Lubbock to Clovis.

LARRY HOLLEY After they came into a little money from their first records, they all went to Dallas and bought new motorcycles. They rode them around a lot and were getting real good.

ARIEL CYCLONE MOTORCYCLE

On 13 May 1958, on their way home from the Alan Freed Big Beat Tour, Buddy and the Crickets visited Ray Miller's Motorcycle Shop in Dallas and each bought a motorcycle. Buddy chose an Ariel Cyclone 650cc (left), a limited edition model of which only 200 were ever built; Joe B. Mauldin and Jerry Allison both went for Triumphs. They bought matching Levi's jackets and peaked caps (above, left), and rode the rest of the way to Lubbock on their new purchases. That summer, between tours and television appearances, Buddy, Joe B. and J.I. were often seen riding around town on their motorcycles.

After Buddy's death, the Ariel motorcycle stayed in the Holley family until 1970, when it was sold. In 1979, the Crickets approached the new owner and put in an offer to buy it back. They then gave it to Waylon Jennings as a birthday present. Waylon is shown above on Buddy's motorcycle.

MARIA ELENA I'd met Buddy when I was working as a receptionist in the Brill Building in New York. I replaced the receptionist that quit and I'd only been there about five days when Buddy came in through those doors. It was a magical moment for both of us. We fell in love immediately. I didn't even know who he was, as I'd never seen a picture of him. The thing I remember is the name – 'I'm Buddy Holly, I have an appointment with Mr Deutch.'

People in the office said this was the young man whose 45 ('That'll Be the Day') I'd been mailing to disc jockeys. He was on his way to meet Murray Deutch and I said, 'Sit down, I'll let him know you're here.' The other two Crickets were there too, but Buddy was the one who started a conversation with me.

He asked me where I was from and I told him I was from Puerto Rico but that I lived in New York. He said, 'Cool, you have an accent,' and I turned around and said, 'You do too.' It was a Texas twang. He said he spoke Spanish and called me 'senoriti'. I replied, 'You mean "señorita".'

Buddy was called into his meeting, and the secretary came running out and said, 'Call your aunt, Buddy wants to take you out to dinner.' My aunt had told me not to date musicians, so I told him I couldn't go out with him, company policy. I was 25 and I had never gone out with anybody before, but I liked him – there was an immediate connection.

Buddy never took no for an answer, so he spoke to Murray Deutch who phoned my aunt and gave him a reference, told her that he was a nice young man. She eventually let me go, if I was home by midnight.

He came into P.J. Clarke's, we sat down, and he said 'Would you excuse me? I'll be right back.' He came back with his hands behind his back, sat down and pulled out a red rose. My aunt always said that musicians are not all there, they're crazy. That thought came into my mind – these people are crazy! Five hours after we'd known each other he popped the question. I was sarcastic and said, 'Well, do you wanna get married now or after dinner?'

MARIA ELENA Buddy wrote 'True Love Ways' for me, which is my favourite. I loved all his songs, but that was a special and beautiful moment. A lot of people play that song at their wedding. 'It Doesn't Matter Anymore' and 'Raining in My Heart' are sad yet beautiful records.

Above: Maria Elena Santiago, June 1958

Opposite: On 11 June 1958, Buddy and Joe B. Mauldin were interviewed on The Ted Randal Show *on KPIX TV in San Francisco*

DION DiMUCCI There was nothing tentative about Buddy's guitar playing. It was a free abandon – no solos or single notes, he just came down on his guitar however felt right. He didn't produce his music, he expressed it. It came off the record and into my head, soul, heart and spirit … it plastered me against the wall.

PAUL ANKA The volume of work and the number of hits that he had was amazing. If he were still with us – and we all wish that he was – he would have gone on to write an enormous body of work, not unlike Leiber and Stoller, in which he was a writer first. But it was already an amazing body of work, and I was glad to be a part of it.

MARIA ELENA This (opposite) is my favourite photograph of Buddy.

SUMMER DANCE PARTY
In July 1958, Buddy Holly took part in the Summer Dance Party. This was not a big tour like the Winter Dance Party, but did include Tommy Allsup and his Western Swing Band, who also participated in the Winter Dance Party alongside Buddy.

Above and opposite: Buddy tuning his guitar backstage at the Electric Park Ballroom with Eddie Randall in Waterloo, IA on 8 July 1958, during the Summer Dance Party tour. When photographer Dick Cole asked Buddy to take off his glasses, he replied: 'I never take my glasses off for photos.'

GIBSON J200
Buddy purchased this 1958 Gibson J200 at Manny's Music in New York. It is believed Buddy used this acoustic guitar to write his last songs in his Greenwich Village apartment in New York City.

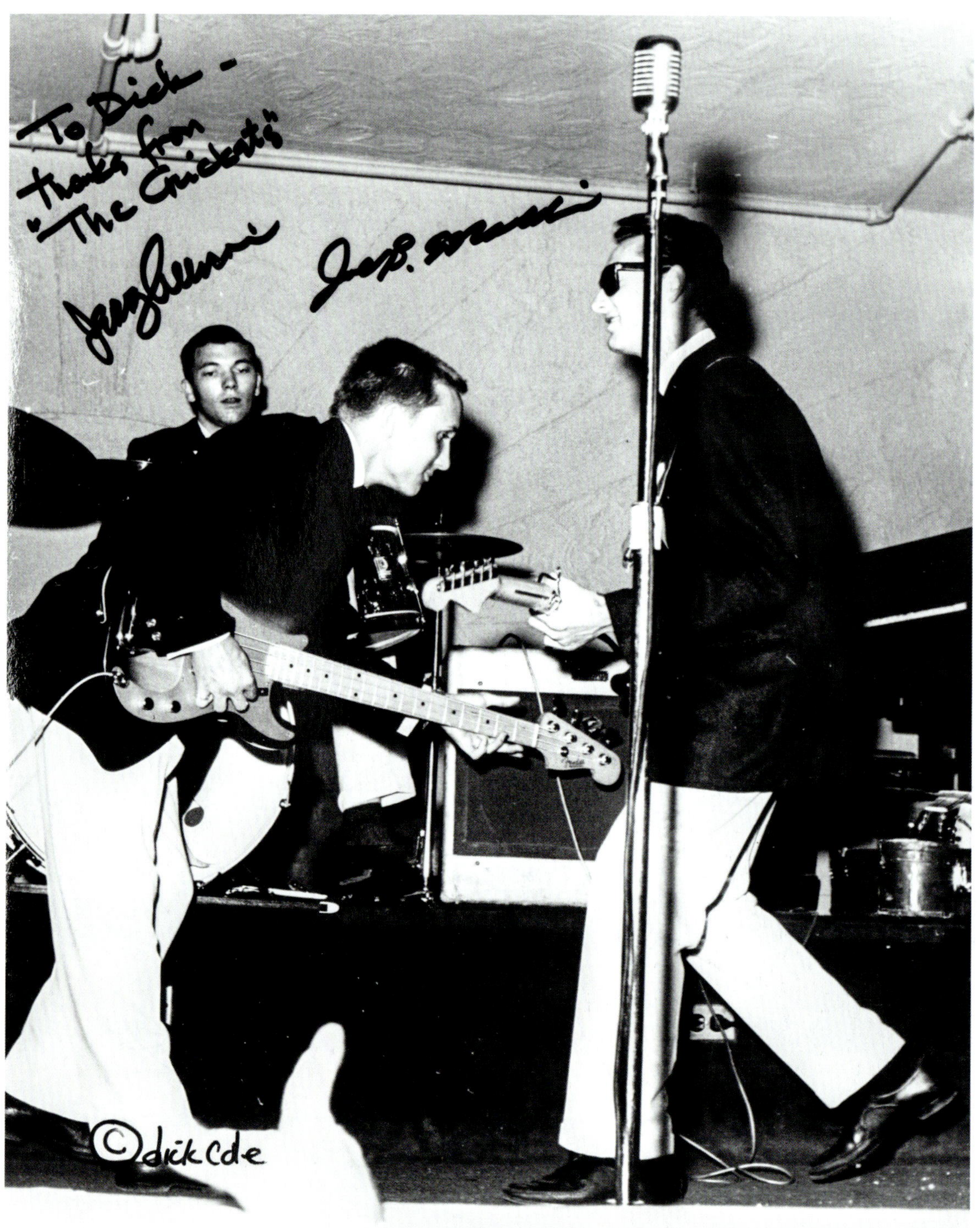

PETER ASHER Buddy Holly influenced both the Rolling Stones and The Beatles, who were from different musical worlds, and there aren't many musicians who did that. You could take 'Not Fade Away' and make a rhythm and blues song out of it or take 'Words of Love' and make a brilliant Beatles track out of it.

EDNA GUNDERSEN The Beatles, the Rolling Stones, the Kinks, Eric Clapton, all these musicians came over and spoke about Buddy Holly, which sparked this excitement in America.

Buddy Holly and the Crickets
Electric Park Ballroom
Waterloo, IA, 8 July 1958

CRYSTAL
ROCK
RHINELANDER, WISCONSIN
Presents the teen-age sensation
BUDDY HOLLY AND THE 'CRICKETS'
top Recording Stars of
• Oh Boy! • Maybe Baby! • That'll Be The Day!
• Fool's Paradise. • Think It Over.
SUN. JULY 13, 1958
4 MILES WEST OF RHINELANDER ON U. S. HIGHWAY 8
Admission $1.75 Dancing from 9 to 1

TOMMY ALLSUP Buddy collected the money from the promoters each night and kept it in the glove compartment of his car. We'd be going down the road and Jerry Allison would say, 'Hey, I need some money.' Buddy would open up the glove compartment, get out a handful of bills and pass 'em back.

Above: Promotional posters for the Buddy Holly and the Crickets shows in Wausau, WI and Rhinelander, WI on 12 and 13 July 1958. The 2 PM outdoor stage show in Wausau was cancelled due to rain, but the evening dance show went ahead as scheduled. Pictured right is Buddy on stage at the Crystal Rock Ballroom in Rhinelander.

Opposite: Buddy Holly on stage with Eddie Randall, front man of Iowa band the Downbeats, Electric Park Ballroom, Waterloo, IA, 8 July 1958

GENERAL ARTISTS CORPORATION
NEW YORK · CHICAGO · BEVERLY HILLS · CINCINNATI · DALLAS · MIAMI BEACH · LONDON
640 FIFTH AVENUE · NEW YORK 19, N. Y. · TELEPHONE CIRCLE 7-7543

OFFICE OF
CY DONNER
TREASURER
VICE PRESIDENT · OPERATIONS

August 5, 1958

Mr. Norman Petty
Box 926
1321 West 7th Street
Clovis, New Mexico

Dear Norman:-

Harry Bloom had discussed with me the feeling that BUDDY HOLLY & THE CRICKETS Tour - July 4th through the 13th should be at ten per cent commission since you were not aware that fifteen per cent was the applicable rate on one-niters. Since there are extenuating circumstances, I am going along reducing the commission to ten per cent on this Tour only.

In making such reduction, it is not be construed as a precedent. All future one-niters, in accordance with the permissible commission rates under the American Federation of Musicians Management Contract, will be fifteen per cent.

Enclosed please find check in the amount of $1916.16 together with statement showing breakdown.

Kindest regards.

Sincerely yours,

CY DONNER

CD:AS
ENC.

GENERAL ARTISTS CORPORATION
ARTISTS REPRESENTATIVES · AMERICAS BLDG. • ROCKEFELLER CENTER
NEW YORK
CIRCLE 7-7550

To BUDDY HOLLY & CRICKETS - STATEMENTS 7/31/58

Date 19

DATE	EXPLANATION	Miscellaneous Charges	Commissions	DEPOSITS and CREDITS	BALANCE
2/27	Photos	19 31			
3/3	Mats	15 96			
w/e 5/8 & 5/9-10	Freed Tour (6 days)		428 57		
7/4	Angola		100 00	500 00	
5	Spring Valley		85 00	425 00	
6	Fruitport		75 00		
8	Waterloo		85 00		
9	Decorah		90 00	450 00	
10	Oelwein		85 00	425 00	
11	Duluth		100 00	500 00	
12	Wausau		65 00	425 00	
13	Rhinelander		85 00	425 00	
		35 27	1198 57	3150 00	
			428 57		
			770 00		
	BALANCE DUE BUDDY HOLLY & CRICKETS AS OF 7/31/58				1916 16

SONNY WEST It's hard to imagine the world without his music. It was the way he crafted his songs, and each one sounded different from the previous. He didn't fit into a category, while creating a lot of sounds that were lasting. Simplicity works and future bands followed that; so many people have been encouraged by his life and music and some of Buddy's songs are remembered better today than when he was here. He showed us that a small group could achieve anything if they had the right attitude and songs.

BUDDY HOLLY & THE CRICKETS
BOX 926 PHONE POrter 3-7565
CLOVIS, NEW MEXICO

CLOVIS NATIONAL BANK
CLOVIS, NEW MEXICO

95-30
1122

223

CLOVIS, NEW MEXICO JULY 21, 1958

PAY TO THE ORDER OF JERRY ALLISON $3,000.00

THREE THOUSAND and 00/100 DOLLARS

Advance On Record Royalties

THE CRICKETS

BY NORMAN PETTY — MANAGER

Opposite and top left: Crystal Rock Ballroom, Rhinelander, WI, 13 July 1958

Above: A royalty cheque made out to Jerry Allison from Norman Petty, 21 July 1958

Top right and right: A covering letter and commission statement from booking agent C.Y. Donner at General Artists Corporation to Norman Petty for Buddy Holly and the Crickets, touring up to the end of July 1958

PHOTOGRAPHIC
SOUVENIR
of your visit to the
TAVERN ON THE GREEN
in Central Park
TAVERN ON THE GREEN
NEW YORK CITY PRICE 50¢

MARIA ELENA After we'd gotten engaged, Buddy, his parents, my aunt and I went out for dinner. Afterwards we went to see the movie *Mr. Roberts* starring Henry Fonda. It was Mr and Mrs Holley's first time in New York, so they were excited. We took them to the Waldorf Astoria for dinner, then to Radio City for the movie.

Top left: Maria Elena's engagement ring

Top right and right: Maria Elena Santiago, 1955

WEDDING PREPARATIONS

On 14 August 1958, Buddy Holly and Maria Elena Santiago applied for a marriage licence to Arlona Short, a clerk of the county court in Lubbock. They gave their names and ages: 21 for Buddy; 25 for Maria Elena. In preparation for the wedding, Maria Elena wrote out a list of items she needed: 'Wedding dress, hose, 2 pr shoes, cosmetics, 2 bags, powder, slacks & shirt, lipstick, 3 gowns & 1 pyjamas, rouge, 7 panties & 1 white bra, perfume, 3 dressy dresses, 2 cotton shirts & blouses.'

LARRY HOLLEY Buddy brought Maria Elena down to Lubbock in August of '58 and they were married in Mother and Dad's home by our preacher. We were all pleased with his pretty wife and they started living in New York.

Christmas of '58 they came to Lubbock and they really spent a lot of money on presents for all the kinfolks. It was a wonderful time. Buddy was interested in helping other artists get started. We were out at the edge of town at some people's house and listening to a fellow sing and play. Buddy was wanting to help him get a start. Then Buddy picked up the guitar and said, 'Wanna hear what my next song is gonna be? It's gonna be the best one yet.' So he sang and played 'Raining in My Heart' with just his guitar. It was beautiful and I agreed that it would be his best. When it was released later it had a symphony orchestra with it. But I liked it best when he did it in Lubbock. Well, when he left Lubbock this time we all went to the plane and saw them off and that was the last time we saw him.

PAUL ANKA Buddy was a changed guy after meeting Maria Elena. He was shy, but when Irvin Feld and I would talk with him there was a new confidence and a different feeling you got from him. He was still growing into his image but suddenly he'd found love for the first time in his life, of a great magnitude. He was ready for a new world.

MARIA ELENA We got married at Buddy's house by the local Lubbock pastor. Peggy Sue and Jerry were there, along with Buddy's family. Peggy Sue couldn't stand that I was marrying Buddy. She pulled him aside and said, 'I don't know why you're marrying this woman from New York,' and I heard Buddy respond, 'Peggy Sue, I really dislike you, and now I dislike you more.' I don't think that Jerry would have said anything about it, but she was in love with Buddy.

DON McLEAN Maria Elena's a fun and very smart lady. She likes doing the work that is necessary and appreciated by Buddy Holly fans. She could've shunned it and said it was a past life.

THE WEDDING
On 15 August 1958, Buddy married Maria Elena at the Holley family home located at 1606 39th Street in Lubbock. Among those attending the small ceremony were Buddy's parents, Ella and L.O. Holley (pictured top right with Buddy and Maria), his brothers and sister, Larry, Travis and Patricia, and their spouses, as well as Peggy Sue Gerron and Jerry Allison (pictured top left with Buddy and Maria) and Joe B. Mauldin. Buddy wrote a cheque for $100 to Rev. Ben Johnson of the Tabernacle Baptist Church for performing the home ceremony. Jerry put Buddy's latest record on the record player and played the B-side, 'Now We're One'.

After the wedding ceremony, Buddy drove Maria Elena, Jerry and Peggy Sue to El Paso, TX in a yellow DeSoto station wagon, staying overnight in the city. The next morning, the four flew to Mexico for a two-week honeymoon (Jerry and Peggy Sue having got married less than a month earlier). Arriving in Acapulco, the two newlywed couples checked into the Las Brisas Hotel and immediately noticed that they did not have rooms overlooking the water. A few nights later they transferred to the El Cano, located right on the beach.

Top left: Maria Elena, Buddy, Jerry and Peggy Sue at dinner on their double honeymoon Acapulco, Mexico, August 1958

Above left: Buddy Holly's sunglasses

Above: Buddy Holly and Maria Elena Holly, Phil Everly, and Everly's date, taken during a meal at the El Chico restaurant in New York City, 1958

Left: Peggy Sue's wedding ring

LUCILLE BARILLA My father, Louis Giordano, always loved music. His favourite artists were Alan Dale, Vic Damone and Frank Sinatra, and he learned how to play guitar in his teens. Determined to make it in the music business, Lou began writing songs and performing in clubs in and around New York City, including Club 802 (famously renamed the 2001 Odyssey for the film *Saturday Night Fever*), various USO shows, and appearances on the Joe Franklin and Bea Kalmus radio shows. Lou wrote dozens of songs before acquiring a record deal with the now-defunct Brunswick Records, which in 1952 was put under the management of Decca's Coral Records subsidiary. That same year, Brunswick resumed releasing new material, initially as a rhythm and blues speciality label, before adding pop music in 1957.

Lou first came into contact with Buddy Holly and Phil Everly via an introduction by Joey Villa, the lead singer of the Royal Teens. Joey and Lou were close friends. The session that produced the songs 'Stay Close to Me' and 'Don't Cha Know' took place on 30 September 1958 at the Beltone Recording Corporation in New York and was produced by Buddy Holly and Phil Everly. Murray Deutch of South Publishing was also present. The group met in a room at the Hotel Wolcott to discuss the session. The contract between Lou Giordano and Coral Records was dated 13 November 1958, and was signed by Lou and Paul Cohen. It was a six-month contract, with an option of a contract between Lou and Buddy Holly. My father signed the agreements as Lou Jordan.

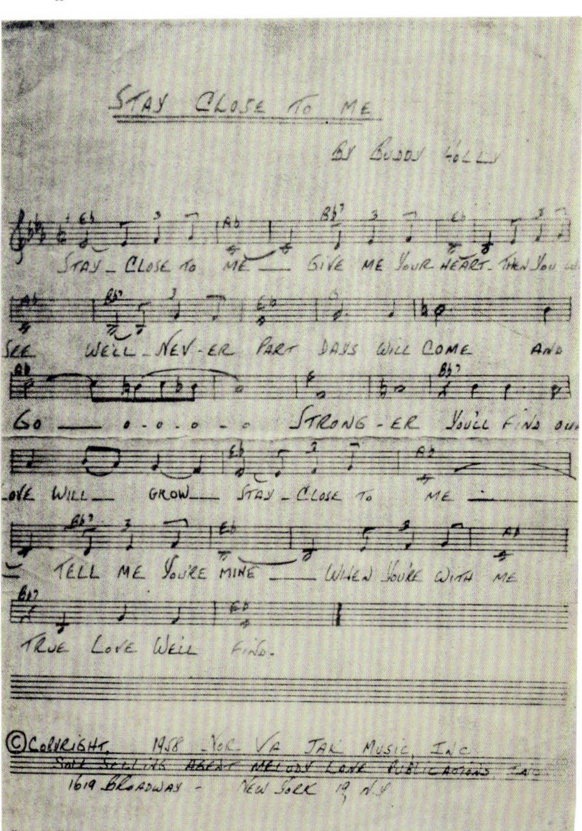

The record was released in January 1959. The female-sounding background performers were none other than Buddy Holly and Phil Everly, as they could not afford actual female background singers for the session. After the release of 'Stay Close to Me', Lou had several other records, which were released under the name of Lou Jordan.

MARIA ELENA Buddy knew he wouldn't get anywhere with his music if he stayed in Lubbock. We had nowhere to live until I suggested we go to New York to be near my aunt. We didn't have much money so I called her and she got us an apartment. It wasn't far from her place: she lived on Tenth Street and Fifth Avenue and our apartment was on Eleventh Street and Fifth Avenue. That's how we ended up in New York.

PAUL ANKA I became very friendly with Buddy, and there was a time where we'd talk about starting a music company together. We were aware of the components that made us successful. When Buddy evolved from the early, experimental music and began producing and writing, I was doing the same. We'd talk about the future, the business, and where we wanted to go. We were very aware of longevity. When he was living in New York and needed money, it was Irvin Feld and me that created the Winter Dance Party for him. I was very much a part of all of that.

MARIA ELENA Living with Buddy was a constant challenge because he was always thinking of the things he wanted to do. He wanted to open offices in New York, a recording studio, a publishing company. Even at that time he was thinking about developing other artists. He wanted to be able to deal with every facet of the industry. He was producing Waylon Jennings and Lou Giordano at that time. He also mentioned he wanted to score for movies. I said, 'Buddy, do you think you're going too fast?' and he replied, 'Oh no, I'd like to write a score for a movie and study acting.' He was a very laid-back individual but driven about his career. He wasn't afraid of doing new things.

DION DiMUCCI I was amazed by his character. Buddy was a fearless businessman; his trajectory was like a rocket ship. He wanted to start a record company called Taupe, the colour of his Cadillac, and had plans to begin publishing music. All while he was writing. He was an incredible, old soul for 22 years old, and I learned a lot from him because he was very centred around his principles. He could make decisions that overwhelmed me, because I was 19 and tentative, but Buddy was very sure of himself and knew what he wanted. They grow 'em up in Texas!

EDNA GUNDERSEN Buddy doesn't get enough credit for resisting control from suits, unions and the corporate structure that controlled record making. He wanted to do it himself, and that made his records sound better. In the studio he could do things his way, and you can hear it in how great some of these records sound because he got to the point where he had the right amount of reverb or echo. It was all on his terms.

MARIA ELENA Buddy loved it in New York. In the day, he would walk over to my aunt's house where he'd play and write on her piano. At night, he would come back to the apartment and continue writing on the guitar. He would always have his tape machine with him, and I didn't understand what it was he was doing at the time. He'd come back and say, 'OK, I've got it now.'

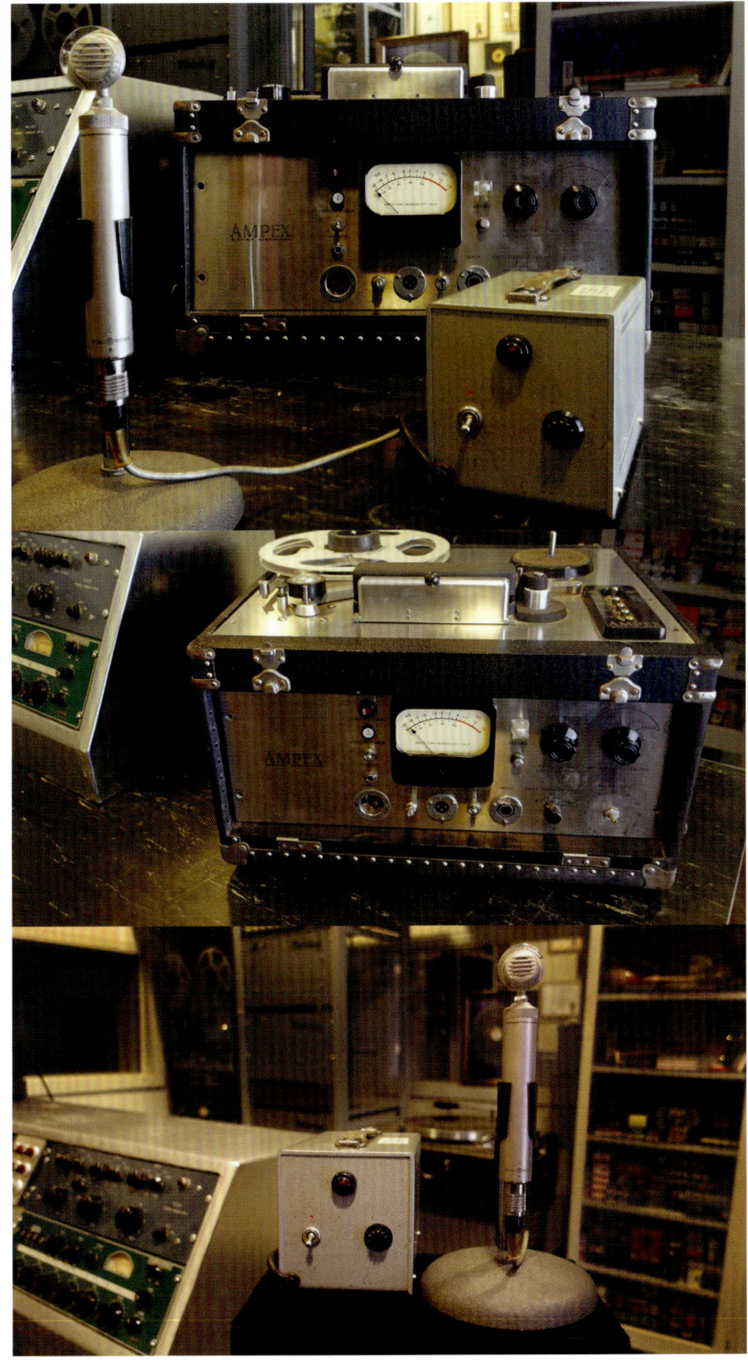

PRISM RECORDS

In September 1958, Buddy formed a recording and publishing company called Prism Records with Norman Petty and Ray Rush. Two recording sessions for release on Prism were known to have taken place: Waylon Jennings recorded two songs at Norman Petty's studio on 10 September 1958, which were eventually released on Brunswick in May 1959; and Lou Giordano recorded two songs at Beltone Studios in New York on 30 September 1958. Buddy played guitar on both of these sessions. Because Waylon had never recorded before, Buddy had some instrumental tracks laid down first, then Waylon added his vocals.

Prism Records was part of Buddy's plan to control his music, while also signing and producing new artists – an indication of the future career he had mapped out for himself.

Opposite, bottom left: Sheet music for the Buddy Holly song 'Stay Close to Me' recorded by Lou Giordano on 30 September 1958

THE WORLD'S MOST FAMOUS TAPE RECORDER

In the fall of 1958 massive change was on the horizon in Clovis, New Mexico. Buddy Holly was moving to New York to live with his new bride Maria Elena and, as such, was reassessing his life. Meanwhile, the Crickets decided to stay in Clovis with producer/manager/recording engineer Norman Petty. While much has been written about the final months of Buddy Holly's life and the last fateful meeting between Holly and Petty in Clovis, many questions will be left forever unanswered.

But one thing that we do know is that when Holly left Clovis, New Mexico for the last time in early November 1958, he took with him the now-famous Ampex 401A tape recorder along with a new Telefunken/Schoeps microphone, the CM61.

Holly was writing new material and needed a way to get these new ideas on tape while in New York and he turned to Petty for advice. Lucky for us, Holly and Petty decided that these recordings should be made with some of the best gear available at the time.

The Ampex 400 series of tape recorders were first released in 1950 and, while records aren't completely clear, it appears that Petty purchased his Ampex 401A, serial number 5065, in the fall of 1951 with a second Ampex recorder purchased shortly after. At this point in history tape recording was very new technology, with the first commercially available tape recorders emerging in the late 1940s. The Ampex 400 series was a major step forward in technology. It was smaller, lighter and less expensive than previous models. The Ampex 401A was a portable machine and Petty purchased it with an eye to taking it on the road. In the early part of the 1950s, the Norman Petty Trio was a going concern, performing in luxury hotels and army dance halls around the country. Petty decided it was wise to be able to record whenever and wherever he wanted. It was this foresight that allowed the Norman Petty Trio to record their first hit record, 'Mood Indigo', on 1 April 1954, in Jackson, Michigan at the Hayes Hotel. And it was that hit record that, in part, allowed Norman to build his recording studio at 1313 West 7th Street back in Clovis.

When construction of the Norman Petty Studio began in 1953, the trusty Ampex 401A became a centrepiece and would be used on almost every hit song that came from the studio between its opening in 1954 and when it left for New York with Holly in 1958. When remote recordings were needed the portability of the recorder came in handy. After the success of 'That'll Be The Day' more hits were being demanded from Holly's label in New York. Instead of waiting for Holly to return to the studio in Clovis, Petty met Holly and the Crickets while they were on the road and in September 1957 they recorded 'Maybe Baby' at the Tinker Airforce Base in Oklahoma. It was this versatility that made the Ampex 401A the obvious choice for Buddy to take with him to New York on his latest adventure.

The Telefunken CM61 was also a great choice for Holly to record these solo demos in New York. The slim microphone was ideal for the type of recording Holly was planning and its unique front-facing capsule made the perfect placement between Holly's guitar and vocal easily attainable. The CM61 was distributed by Telefunken in the US but the microphone was manufactured by the Schoeps Mikrofone company in Germany. According to records kept by Schoeps Mikrofone, this particular microphone, serial number 830, was manufactured in late 1956 and was shipped to Telefunken in a batch of 16 on 14 May 1957, for branding and eventual sale. Petty purchased the microphone shortly after that. To put the quality of the Telefunken/Schoeps CM61 into perspective, 1957 product catalogues show that the price of the CM61 was slightly higher than that of the famous Telefunken/Neumann U47.

When Holly returned to New York from Clovis with the microphone and tape machine he didn't waste any time and went to work recording what would eventually be known as 'The Apartment Tapes'. Between 3 December and 17 December 1958, Buddy recorded demos of six newly written compositions which could have easily been the backbone of his next album. After the Christmas break, Holly returned to recording and experimenting with a series of cover songs. His very last recording, coming on 20 January 1959, was a cover of Lieber and Stoller's 'Smokey Joe's Café'.

In the aftermath of Holly's death these demo recordings were turned into hits, first with the overdubbing sessions in New York by producer Jack Hansen. Unhappy with the results and wanting future Buddy Holly productions to be done closer to home, Holly's family chose Norman Petty as the producer of all future Buddy Holly releases and these apartment tapes became the basis for several posthumous releases, all overdubbed by Norman Petty in Clovis, New Mexico.

The famous Ampex 401A and the Telefunken/Schoeps CM61 also returned to their rightful home with Petty in Clovis. After Buddy's death, Crickets drummer Jerry Allison purchased them from Holly's widow Maria Elena, took them to California and sometime in 1964 sold them back to Petty. Today these two amazing pieces of rock and roll history are still at their original home at the Norman Petty Studio, 1313 W 7th Street in Clovis, New Mexico. – *Ron Skinner*

Dear Mother & Daddy:

I hope when you receive this letter both are in the best of health.

You will have to forgive us for not writing sooner and more often but you probably know what it takes to get a house ready. We have been going to bed 3 & 4 o'clock in the morning. During the day we go out shopping and sometimes Buddy has to go and see some of the "people".

He is really working on different ideas. As he tells you in his letter Murray Deutch gave him a pretty good deal & I think is going to work out alright. Provi is our "adviser" (ha, ha).

As soon as everything gets stablished we will give you more details.

II

How is grandmother? Tell her that I missed her very much and that very soon I'll see her to give her "corn flakes" with butter milk" (ha, ha).

Give my regards to everyone & tell them that we will see them around Christmas.

Well, I guess I better say good-bye because I have to get dressed to go to the grocery stores.

Don't forget to take it easy so you can get in shape for your trip to New York. We are going to have a pretty tough schedule.

I missed both of you very much. Keep well!!

Love

Maria Elena

MARIA ELENA I went with Buddy on the tours that he had at that time. But he wasn't touring that much, because he was starting to do other things. We were actually departing from being with his manager, Norman Petty. We were beginning to do other things, to get Buddy back on his own.

Going on tour was nothing like nowadays. We had to set up, pick up the instruments, collect the money. We had to wash our underwear in the sink. The pay wasn't great either.

Now managers make sure it flows smoothly when you travel distances, but back then it would be one end of the world to the other because it wasn't organised. Wherever you could get a gig from promoters – that's where you went. Consequently, we were exhausted. As a matter of fact, I had to learn how to drive. Buddy at that time was so exhausted, that he'd said, 'You have to drive.' I told him I didn't know how, and he said, 'Don't worry, I'll show you. It's very easy. Just go straight.' I did it out of desperation. He was so tired.

I never told fans that I was his wife. I always said I was the secretary of the group. He didn't like that. He would say, 'You have to say you're my wife,' and he'd tell everybody that I was. I'd say, 'No, I'm the secretary of the group.' At that time the teeny-boppers didn't like their idols to be married.

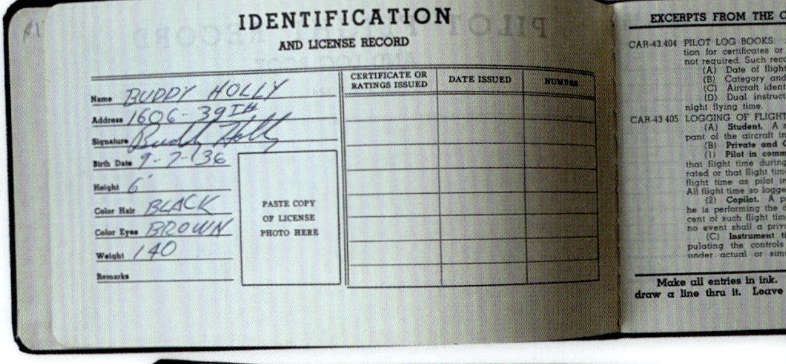

IDENTIFICATION
AND LICENSE RECORD

Name BUDDY HOLLY
Address 1606-39th
Signature Buddy Holly
Birth Date 9-7-36
Height 6'
Color Hair BLACK
Color Eyes BROWN
Weight 140
Remarks

PASTE COPY OF LICENSE PHOTO HERE

CERTIFICATE OR RATINGS ISSUED	DATE ISSUED	NUMBER

We met in high school in Lubbock, Texas, that's our home town, and we all went to the same high school there, and we started playing together.

We've always made a point to not like jazz, it's kind of in conjunction with rock and roll in one way and then it's against it in another way.

We don't know what's coming up for us after this tour. The last night of this tour is three nights from tonight and then we don't have anything in bookings afterwards. Our new release will be out in a few days. It's a Coral release entitled 'Heartbeat' backed with 'Well ... All Right'.

I prefer the one-nighter tours, such as the one we're on. The large rhythm and blues type package shows. You can do your four or five songs and it feels good to play to an audience that's watching instead of an audience that's interested in something else, like nightclubs. There's a lot going on that sometimes they're interested in something besides the act on stage and then, with dances, they're more interested in their dancing, of course.

(Buddy in an interview with Ronnie King for WGH Radio, Norfolk, VA, 16 October 1958)

CERTIFICATE OF TITLE TO A MOTOR VEHICLE

The State Highway Department certifies that the applicant herein named has been duly registered in the office of the Department as the lawful owner of the Motor vehicle described below.

DUPLICATE ORIGINAL

Cadillac 58M 055107 20995223
BT 9539 1958 60 Special Sedan 5200
Alderson Cadillac Company Lubbock Texas
Buddy Holly
1606 39th Street
Lubbock, Texas
9/5/58 Alderson Cadillac Company 1210 19th Street
1101 61 Lubbock, Texas

Buddy Holly

SEPT. 12, 1958

D. C. Greer, State Highway Engineer
By D. T. Harkrider, Director Motor Vehicle Division

STATE OF TEXAS

Opposite, top: A letter from Maria Elena to Buddy's parents, in which she writes about her married life with Buddy

Opposite, bottom: Buddy and Maria Elena pictured backstage on tour, late 1958

Above right: Buddy's pilot flight record and logbook. In late 1958, Buddy took some flying lessons, intending to qualify as a pilot and fly his own Cessna around the country. It cost $9 for one half-hour lesson.

Left: A motor vehicle certificate from the State of Texas for a '58 Cadillac owned by Buddy

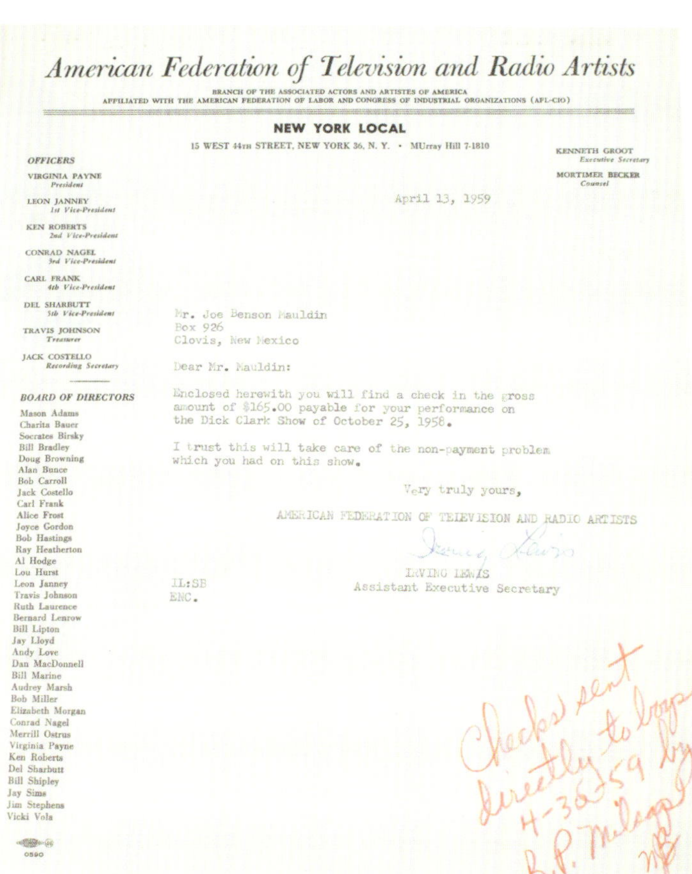

American Federation of Television and Radio Artists

BRANCH OF THE ASSOCIATED ACTORS AND ARTISTES OF AMERICA
AFFILIATED WITH THE AMERICAN FEDERATION OF LABOR AND CONGRESS OF INDUSTRIAL ORGANIZATIONS (AFL-CIO)

NEW YORK LOCAL
15 WEST 44TH STREET, NEW YORK 36, N. Y. • MUrray Hill 7-1810

KENNETH GROOT, Executive Secretary
MORTIMER BECKER, Counsel

OFFICERS
VIRGINIA PAYNE, President
LEON JANNEY, 1st Vice-President
KEN ROBERTS, 2nd Vice-President
CONRAD NAGEL, 3rd Vice-President
CARL FRANK, 4th Vice-President
DEL SHARBUTT, 5th Vice-President
TRAVIS JOHNSON, Treasurer
JACK COSTELLO, Recording Secretary

BOARD OF DIRECTORS
Mason Adams
Charita Bauer
Socrates Birsky
Bill Bradley
Doug Browning
Alan Bunce
Bob Carroll
Jack Costello
Carl Frank
Alice Frost
Joyce Gordon
Bob Hastings
Ray Heatherton
Al Hodge
Lou Hurst
Leon Janney
Travis Johnson
Ruth Laurence
Bernard Lenrow
Bill Lipton
Jay Lloyd
Andy Love
Dan MacDonnell
Bill Marine
Audrey Marsh
Bob Miller
Elizabeth Morgan
Conrad Nagel
Merrill Ostrus
Virginia Payne
Ken Roberts
Del Sharbutt
Bill Shipley
Jay Sims
Jim Stephens
Vicki Vola

April 13, 1959

Mr. Joe Benson Mauldin
Box 926
Clovis, New Mexico

Dear Mr. Mauldin:

Enclosed herewith you will find a check in the gross amount of $165.00 payable for your performance on the Dick Clark Show of October 25, 1958.

I trust this will take care of the non-payment problem which you had on this show.

Very truly yours,

AMERICAN FEDERATION OF TELEVISION AND RADIO ARTISTS

IRVING LEWIS
Assistant Executive Secretary

IL:SB
ENC.

Checks sent directly to [illegible] [illegible] by B.P. [illegible]

0590

PETER ASHER Buddy Holly made it acceptable to be a slightly nerdy pop singer. People thought you had to look like Elvis, or a handsome, clean-cut American like Fabian or Bobby Rydell. It made a difference that you could look a little studious and wear glasses, so he became a personal hero to me in that respect alone. The moment I stopped wearing wiry National Health spectacles, I went to the opticians with a Buddy Holly album and said, 'I want these glasses.'

LARRY WELBORN The last time I saw Buddy was in New York. He looked a little nerdy, but he'd got his hair straightened out, had new glasses and a tight suit. He looked sharp and very uptown, but it was still natural. He knew he was going to do it, and nothing would stand in his way.

EDNA GUNDERSEN His decision to go to New York was brave, but it was also a fresh backdrop and new people to work with. He'd outgrown where he'd come from; everything in Lubbock and Clovis had become too small for him. New York represented a new challenge.

Opposite, top left: A cover letter to Joe B. Mauldin with payment for his performance on The Dick Clark Show *on 25 October 1958*

Opposite, top right and bottom left: Publicity photos taken by Bruno of Hollywood

Opposite, centre right: Buddy Holly performing 'Heartbeat' on Dick Clark's American Bandstand, *28 October 1958*

BUDDY'S GLASSES
When Buddy's local Lubbock optometrist, Dr Armistead, visited Mexico City, he found what he believed to be the perfect pair of glasses and brought back two pairs for Buddy. These became an important part of his signature style.

Following the air crash in which Buddy died on 3 February 1959, his glasses were nowhere to be found among the wreckage. They lay undiscovered until 7 April 1959, when the farmer who owned the field began work on the land for that year. It was then that he found some of the passengers' belongings, including a watch engraved with the Big Bopper's initials, and Buddy's glasses. The authorities placed Buddy's effects in an envelope marked 'Charles Hardin Holley, rec'd April 7, 1959' and filed them away in a steel cabinet for 21 years.

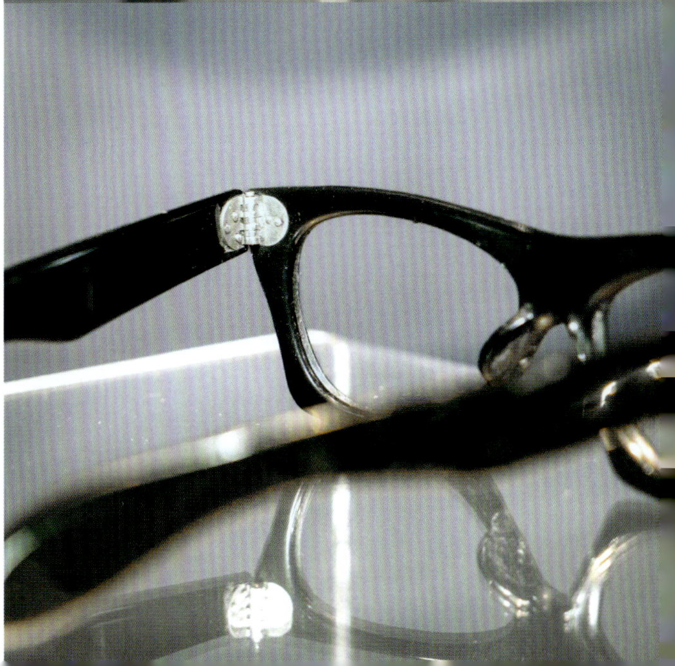

HANK MARVIN It was encouraging to see Buddy. Elvis was always presented as something that was exciting and exotic, but Buddy wasn't. He was a guy that wore glasses and looked like most of us when we were kids. Not everyone is a matinee idol.

We thought if he could do it wearing glasses, maybe we can too, and we had confidence that we didn't have to look like Elvis or a young Cliff Richard. The Shadows did a show in 1959 with Cliff, and Denny Wright took me over to one side in a fatherly fashion and said, 'Hank, can I give you a bit of advice?' And then he said, 'Do not wear your specs on stage. It's not showbiz, we don't wear specs on stage.' I told him that I was almost blind and I'd fall over. I thought if Buddy Holly could get away with it, so could I. And I'm glad I did because it became a trademark.

DESMOND CHILD Roy Orbison's widow, Barbara, once said to buy a hundred pairs of glasses, because they're your signature. If you put them on a lead sheet people should know that it's you. And there isn't anything more distinctive than the look of Buddy Holly and his glasses.

EDNA GUNDERSEN Elton John would have never put on those glasses if Buddy Holly hadn't done so first. He was giving permission for every dorky kid to pick up a guitar; you didn't have to be a gorgeous pin-up boy like Elvis. Buddy also made strides in winning over male audiences, which hadn't fully happened before him.

DUANE EDDY In 1958 I went on my first bus tour on an ex-Greyhound with 13 other acts piled on there. Myself and the three guys in my group got the bus at 8 AM in New York City, which was where I first met Buddy. He had a car because Maria Elena was coming on tour with him and the bus insurance didn't cover family members.

The tours would last four to six weeks, and we worked every night. Sometimes two shows a night; it was unusual to do just one. Buddy seemed to be happy, but we were just kids. You don't get exhausted when you're 22 years old. With Maria he couldn't wipe the smile off his face, they were both happy to be together. He had his birthday on that tour and we all got together in the dressing room.

Top left: Duane Eddy, 24 September 1959

Above: Duane Eddy on tour, 6 February 1959

Top right: Publicity photo taken by Bruno of Hollywood

Right: A burgundy tie from Zeeman's, owned by Buddy. This tie would typically be worn by Buddy for concerts and other public appearances.

Opposite: Buddy Holly and Jerry Allison Community War Memorial Building Rochester, NY, 15 October 1958. Duane Eddy is present in an uncropped version of this photo.

IN
OUT
DRINK
THE BOTTLER OF COCA COLA
DRINK

BUDDY'S PERSONAL RECORD COLLECTION

Angelic Gospel Singers: *'Jesus Never Fails Me'/'I'll Be Alright'*
Toni Arden: *'Padre'/'All at Once'*
Ray Campi with Johnny Maddox, Henry Hill and the Debs: *'With You'/'My Screamin' Screamin' Mimi!'*
Valerie Carr with Hugo Peretti and His Orchestra: *'Look Forward'/'Bad Girl'*
Wynona Carr: *'Should I Ever Love Again?'/'Till the Well Runs Dry'*
The Channels: *'Stay as You Are'/'That's My Desire'*
Ray Charles: *'Mary Ann'/'Drown in My Own Tears', 'What Would I Do Without You'/'Hallelujah I Love Her So', 'Swanee River Rock'/'I Want a Little Girl', 'You Be My Baby'/'My Bonnie', 'I Want to Know'/'Ain't That Love', 'Come Back'/'I've Got a Woman'*
Nat 'King' Cole: *'Bend a Little My Way'/'Non Dimenticar'*
Doris Day with Frank De Vol and His Orchestra: *'Everybody Loves a Love'/'Instant Love', 'A Very Precious Love'/'Teacher's Pet', 'Heart Full of Love'/'The Sound of Music'*
De John Sisters: *'(My Baby Don't Love Me) No More'/'Theresa (The Little Flower)'*
Bo Diddley: *'Hey! Bo Diddley'/'Mona', 'Before You Accuse Me (Take a Look at Yourself)'/'Say (Boss Man)'*
Eddie Fontaine: *'Nothin' Shakin''/'Don't Ya Know'*
Everly Brothers: *'Bird Dog'/'Devoted to You', 'Problems'/'Love of My Life'*
Johnny Fuller and Band: *'All Night Long'/'You Got Me Whistling'*
Hugo & Luigi: *'Honolulu Lu'/'La Plume De Ma Tante'*
Mahalia Jackson: *'Have You Any Rivers'/'For My Good Fortune'*
Roland Johnson: *'Traded Her Love'/'I'll Be with You'*
The Jones Boys: *'No One Home'/'Mary Smith'*
Kitty Kallen: *'Come Live with Me'/'Be True to Me'*
Buddy Knox with the Orchids: *'Party Doll'/'I'm Stickin' with You'*
Peggy Lee: *'You Don't Know'/'Fever'*
Mantovani: *'Love Song from "Houseboat" (Almost in Your Arms)'/'Almost in Your Arms (Love Song from "Houseboat")'*
Skeets McDonald: *'I Can't Stand It Any Longer'/'Number One in Your Heart'*
The McGuire Sisters: *'Banana Split'/'Sugartime'*
The Midnighters: *'Work with Me Annie'/'Until I Die', 'Don't Say Your Last Goodbye'/'Sexy Ways', 'Annie Had a Baby'/'She's the One'*
Jimmy Reed: *'Honey, Don't Let Me Go'/'You've Got Me Dizzy', 'You Got Me Crying'/'Go on to School'*
Little Richard: *'Good Golly, Miss Molly'/'Hey-Hey-Hey-Hey!'*
Shirley & Lee: *'Now That It's Over'/'I Feel Good'*
The Slades: *'No Time'/'You Gambled'*
Little Walter and His Jukes: *'Thunder Bird'/'My Babe, I Got to Go'/'Roller Coaster'*
Larry Williams: *'Dizzy, Miss Lizzy'/'Slow Down'*
Roger Williams: *'Take Care'/'Autumn Leaves'*
Chuck Willis: *'Thunder and Lightning'/'My Life'*
Peanuts Wilson: *'Cast Iron Arm'/'You've Got Love'*

L.O. HOLLEY I really don't know which song was his favourite, because he never expressed a preference. However, I knew the type of songs he liked best, just by listening to the ones he was usually singing around the house and the records he brought home. He really loved some of Ray Charles's songs … I just wish all of his fans could have heard him on these, if only we had gotten some on tape. He was planning a Ray Charles album. He had no musical training to speak of, a few piano lessons for about six months when he was ten years old, but nothing more than that. His was just a natural talent and ability.

HANK MARVIN He cut four sides while in New York, and one became a huge posthumous hit single in the UK and US, 'It Doesn't Matter Anymore', which was quite an interesting title given the events that followed. He was moving away from guitar-based rock and roll into a big band sound. Perhaps he foresaw rock music moving in that direction. If he continued with the guitar-led music, it might have kept him in a rock and roll niche.

BOB HARRIS The production and sound on those four tracks were so different from what Buddy had been doing before. It's often discussed whether they represented the watering down of Buddy's rock and roll sound, but there isn't an answer to that. Buddy died just a few weeks afterwards, so what direction he would've taken following those recordings is unknown.

I DEC. 11, 1958

Dear Mother & Dad,

We're sitting here with not much to do and I thought I would drop a line or two, even tho' I'll probably call in the next day or two. I would have written sooner but we have been pretty busy getting the house fixed up and getting these pub. co's started. We still don't have our furniture but I suppose it will get here in a few days. I hope so. The lawyer is sending that property deed with a note to Daddy in it. I don't know much about those kind of transactions but I suppose Daddy knows what to do

II

about title searches and things like that. That's what the Lawyer's note is about. It may have already been done.

The publishing companies are gradually shaping up. I told you on the phone about the deal I made with Murray Deutch through Southern Music. We haven't completed the deal yet. Murray is getting the papers drawn up. It will probably be named Flaka Music tho I don't know for sure. The other one is named Maria Music. Be sure not to mention either of them to anyone. The gossip down there ~~gest~~ gets around faster than radio or telephone.

III

I've been writing a few songs. Some of them are fairly good. The best one to date is a "top secret" one titled "Peggy Sue Got Married". Please don't mention it to anyone either. I want it to be a complete surprise.

I don't want to describe our apartment to you in detail because I want it to be a surprise to you when you come in to New York. I think you all will like it. I couldn't resist saying "you all". No one up here knows what that ~~means~~ but we do, don't we.

The weather up here has really been cold. It ~~snowed~~ snowed 2 in. the other night and another snow

IV

is expected tonight. The temperature has been down to nearly zero just about every night. Consequently we stay home just about every night. Maria Elena is turning out to be a real good cook. She can fix anything I want. We cooked some fried okra tonight ("we" meaning I tried to show her how and I didn't know how myself) but it didn't turn out so well. I think it was because it was canned and not fresh okra. Anyhow we realized some good experience out of it. Namely not to use canned okra.

That's about all that's happening here now so I guess I'll close. Be ~~sure~~ sure to tell everyone hello for us.

Love Buddy

A letter from Buddy to his parents from his and Maria Elena's New York apartment 11 December 1958

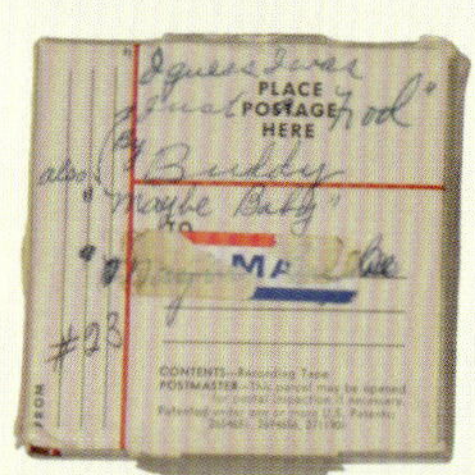

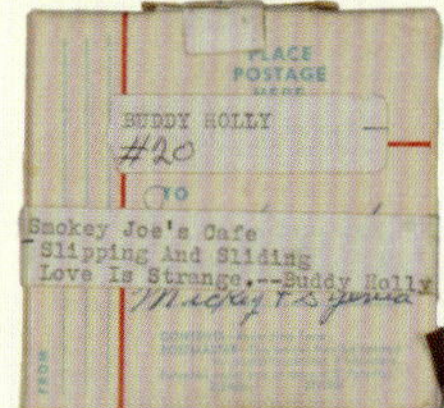

ALBERT LEE There wasn't a dud among those tapes; they were classics, and he was able to turn them into his own with his voice. Who would have thought that they would work after hearing his early stuff, that he'd be able to make such a record? They were perfect.

BOB HARRIS Those songs came from an element of loneliness in Buddy's life. There he was in New York, and you get the sense that he was very much on his own in this big city. Things hadn't been going well with his record label, and he hadn't had the royalties that he earned. He was in a lonely place, and 'Raining in My Heart' expresses that.

'True Love Ways' is one of the greatest songs ever written. You can judge the way a song will translate through generations and whether it will be lasting, and 'True Love Ways' has really lasted – it's as relevant today as the moment Buddy recorded it.

THE APARTMENT TAPES

At the end of 1958, Buddy bought an Ampex tape recorder from Norman Petty, who had used it to record everything from the Dorsey Brothers to the Petty Trio. Buddy used it to make demo tapes of songs that he was writing at home, which was Apartment 4H, Brevoort Apartments, 11 Fifth Avenue in Greenwich Village. After his passing just two months later, the tape recorder was found in his apartment, together with tapes of 14 songs, most of which were recorded using only vocals and guitar. These were Buddy's last ever recorded songs.

The tapes were given to producers Jack Hansen and Norman Petty, who overdubbed some of the songs with a full band. In June 1959, Coral Records overdubbed two of the songs with backing vocals from the Ray Charles Singers and studio musicians in an attempt to recreate the Crickets sound. These became one of the first posthumous Buddy Holly singles: 'Peggy Sue Got Married' backed with 'Crying, Waiting, Hoping'. All the finished songs were included on The Buddy Holly Story Vol. II, *released in 1960. The original raw recordings never saw an official release, though they have been found on fan websites and bootleg albums.*

ARCHIVE OF ORIGINAL TAPES
These tapes contain a wide range of recordings, from demos to new working songs, to radio interviews and live performances. They were comprehensively catalogued in 1999 at MCA Music Media Studios at a listening session with Bill Griggs, Kenneth Broad, Maria Elena Holly, Jerry Allison and Larry Holley and other representatives of MCA Records and the Petty Estate all present.

BRIAN MAY His voice has matured. Buddy has gone full circle here, he's a guy who's reacted against crooning and his parents' generation, but he's come back around to songs that are unashamedly romantic. I could imagine Frank Sinatra singing 'True Love Ways', which is very romantic. It's a beautiful tune.

CLIFF RICHARD He was still rock and roll, but it was a ballad. The string arrangement on 'True Love Ways' was different and very influential and it demonstrated you could do something different without rebelling from your rock roots. I don't think he forgot about 'Peggy Sue' and 'That'll Be the Day', he was just writing a different type of song within the boundaries of rock and roll. That was very influential for the Shadows, so they wrote wonderful ballads for me that were still rock and roll. People forget that rock and roll is not just a tempo, it's a whole genre of music and the umbrella of rock and roll covers so much. Buddy's career was so short and it was a huge loss to our industry that he died so young. I think he would've continued writing those great pop songs.

EVERLY BROTHERS' ROOM AT THE PARK SHERATON HOTEL

Buddy spent an afternoon with the Everly Brothers, their road manager and Lou Giordano, while they were performing on the Alan Freed Christmas show at the Paramount in New York, which ran from 25 December 1958 to 6 January 1959

THE BUDDY HOLLY EDUCATIONAL FOUNDATION
Ambassadors

THE SONGS: 1958
This section presents TBHEF ambassadors with guitars named after songs that were written, recorded, performed or demoed by Buddy in 1958.

EMMYLOU HARRIS *'Come Back Baby'*
DONOVAN *'Listen to Me'*
CHARLIE GRACIE *'I'm Gonna Love You Too'*
JOE BROWN *'Valley of Tears'*
DARREL HIGHAM *'Valley of Tears'*
CHRIS DIFFORD *'Take Your Time'*
GORDON PAYNE *'Real Wild Child'*
SAM FENDER *'Ready Teddy'*
BRENT MASON *'Midnight Shift'*
GRAHAM GOULDMAN *'Look at Me'*
GRAHAM NASH *'Rave On'*
DON EVERLY *'Love's Made a Fool of You'*
PHIL EVERLY *'Wishing'*
SIR CLIFF RICHARD *'Early in the Morning'*
RAY BENSON *'Now We're One'*
ED SHEERAN *'Ting-A-Ling'*
BRAD PAISLEY *'Don't Come Back Knockin''*
DEBBIE HARRY *'I'm Changing All Those Changes'*
SHOOTER JENNINGS *'Jole Blon'*
KEITH URBAN *'When Sin Stops (Love Begins)'*
PETE TOWNSHEND *'It's So Easy!'*
KIMMIE RHODES *'Lonesome Tears'*
WILLIE NELSON *'Lonesome Tears'*
ELVIS COSTELLO *'Reminiscing'*
MARIO VALENS *'La Bamba'*
JOHN JORGENSON *'Well … All Right'*
LINDA RONSTADT *'Heartbeat'*
BRIAN MAY *'Moondreams'*
PETER ASHER *'True Love Ways'*
DION DiMUCCI *'That Makes It Tough'*
GLENN TILBROOK *'That Makes It Tough'*
BRIAN POOLE *'What to Do'*
DAVID FRIZZELL *'Learning the Game'*
JULIAN LENNON *'Learning the Game'*
HANK MARVIN *'You're the One'*
THE STRYPES *'Fool's Paradise'*

EMMYLOU HARRIS 'Come Back Baby'

AT THE TIME OF THE TRAGIC PLANE CRASH THAT TOOK HIS LIFE, Buddy was a solo performer. He and the Crickets always had been marketed separately by their producer Norman Petty and, in 1958, that distinction became reality when Buddy moved to New York and the Crickets returned to Lubbock to rethink and reset.

Soon they enlisted vocalist Earl Sinks, who sang on 'I Fought the Law' and 'Love's Made a Fool of You', two of the band's best-known numbers, before leaving Lubbock for Nashville. Both songs were written by multi-talented Sonny Curtis, whose work was covered by the Clash, Bobby Vee, Leo Sayer and more – great songs that helped create a musical legacy that endures to this day.

My own personal favourite post-Buddy song by the Crickets is 'Don't Ever Change', released in 1962. It's an amazing record and now sounds like a prototype for the UK guitar groups headed by The Beatles that flooded into the charts a few months later.

By this time, the Crickets were sporadically featuring an amazing young piano player, whose CV went on to include work with Bing Crosby, Linda Ronstadt, Roy Orbison and Elvis Presley – Glen D. Hardin.

In 1970, Elvis recruited him into his backing group the TCB Band, in which he played for the next six years. A high-profile gig that led to other wonderful opportunities, including production and arrangement work with a beautiful young country rock artist called Gram Parsons on *GP* and *Grievous Angel*, two of the most deeply important albums of the 1970s.

It was this collaboration that opened the pathway to Glen's connection with Gram's protégée Emmylou Harris. When Emmy began to put her own group together, she invited Glen to join James Burton, Rodney Crowell, Hank DeVito, Emory Gordy Jr. and John Ware in her famous and massively influential backing group the Hot Band. I introduced their live performance on *The Old Grey Whistle Test* in 1977, when Emmy was touring her magnificent album *Elite Hotel*, and the level of musicianship that day was as good as anything I've ever heard.

Since then, Emmy has gone on to become one of the true greats of country music. She has elegantly respected the core values of the genre while pushing at the boundaries of where it can go. Her support of young emerging artists is one of countless demonstrations of her deep generosity as an artist and as a person, and she truly deserves the Grammy-winning success her glorious, enduring work has brought her. – *Bob Harris*

'Buddy – you live in my heart forever.'

COME BACK BABY

Written by Norman Petty and Fred Neil, 'Come Back Baby' was recorded by Buddy Holly and the Crickets with King Curtis on saxophone at Norman Petty's studio in Clovis, NM on 10 September 1958. It was released by Coral as part of the Showcase *compilation album on 18 May 1964. Buddy flew King Curtis in especially for this session, which also included 'Reminiscing' and two songs by Waylon Jennings.*

DONOVAN *'Listen to Me'*

LISTEN TO ME

The song 'Listen to Me' was written by Buddy Holly and Norman Petty and first recorded on 2 July 1957. It was released as a B-side to 'I'm Gonna Love You Too' on 5 February 1958.

Crickets First then
E.P.s of Buddy
each one
a gem ~
I knew how to do
Production from
you Buddy ~
Thank You!
Donovan

BORN IN SCOTLAND AND RAISED NEAR LONDON, Donovan began to play folk clubs in and around the capital during the mid-1960s before taking to the road, a romantic inspiration for many young guitar players. While he was out touring, guitar on his back, writing songs and poetry, Buddy Holly was one of his early influences.

He soon had a record deal. 'Catch the Wind', Donovan's first single, was a big hit and won an Ivor Novello Award for the Outstanding Contemporary Folk Song of 1966. With Brian Jones's former wife Linda Lawrence as his muse, Donovan followed his debut success with a string of hits including 'Colours', 'Jennifer Juniper', 'There Is a Mountain' and 'Sunshine Superman', the latter going to number one in the US and selling over a million copies. His sessions featured many top musicians, including Jimmy Page, Big Jim Sullivan, Jack Bruce, Danny Thompson and John Paul Jones.

Donovan moved with ease from folk to psychedelia before progressing to slightly heavier material. In 1968, he travelled to India to meet the Maharishi Mahesh Yogi with other western musicians including The Beatles and Mike Love of the Beach Boys. While there, he famously taught Lennon and McCartney how to play fingerpicking on their guitars. – *Mike Read*

'Buddy's song "Listen to Me" was a direct encouragement for me to ask my generation to listen when I became a recording artist.'

DONOVAN The whisper vocals on 'Listen to Me', the hiccup and Buddy's 3-4 chord playing were filled with possibilities. All this, and me at 14 years young on a Saturday morning down at Hatfield Market. This was where I helped my dad on the cake stall he tended each week for his Glasgow pal Joe Hale, who'd been a big band leader in Scotland in the 1940s. With the money I earned on the stall, I went up to the record shop in the market for Buddy's latest EP. Only later did I find out Buddy was producing his sound too. Now I have the demos from his Greenwich Village flat.

Later in my life, I went on a tour of Texas and visited the Dallas branch of the Hard Rock Café chain, founded by Isaac Tigrett. Located in an old Baptist church, it had stained glass windows of Elvis, Bo Diddley and Chuck Berry, and a giant Fender guitar sat at the top of the bar. That night, the Crickets played and Isaac took me upstairs to the VIP area where an English barman pulled pints in a room that looked like Pete Townshend's lounge … and it was! Isaac had just married Maureen Starkey, Ringo's ex-wife. She was dressed in Bohemian black. My stepson, Julian – Brian Jones's son – was my roadie then, and in came Buddy's wife, Maria Elena. Julian and Maria Elena danced to the Crickets (she danced Julian under the table), I was there on stage singing 'Rave On', and I was so pleased! Earl Sinks, who was at one time the singer with the Crickets, closed that amazing evening and the last tune that night was just right … we all sang along to 'Not Fade Away', as we all knew that Buddy never would fade away.

Before I was presented with a Buddy Holly acoustic guitar, I was asked what song the guitar should highlight, and I chose 'Listen to Me'.

CHARLIE GRACIE *'I'm Gonna Love You Too'*

ENCOURAGED TO PLAY GUITAR BY HIS FATHER, Charlie Gracie made his first TV appearance on *Paul Whiteman's Goodyear Revue* at the age of 16 and won numerous talent shows in the Philadelphia area. After graduating in 1952, he signed to Cadillac Records and released his first single, 'Boogie Woogie Blues', which led to his first appearance on *American Bandstand*. In 1956, the new Cameo label in Philadelphia signed him, and his first single for them, 'Butterfly', went to number one for jukebox plays on the *Billboard* chart. The song sold over two million copies and earned Charlie a gold disc. It was followed by 'Fabulous', a Top 20 hit in the US and a Top Ten hit in the UK, and 'Wanderin' Eyes' provided his third *Billboard* hit and another Top Ten hit in the UK.

He appeared on *The Ed Sullivan Show* and in the 1957 rock and roll film *Jamboree*, and played on major tours with such artists as Chuck Berry, the Everly Brothers, Bo Diddley and his close friend Eddie Cochran. Charlie was also a great admirer of Buddy Holly. In 1957, he became only the second American rock and roll artist to tour Britain, returning the following year and headlining major UK venues including the Liverpool Empire and the Birmingham Hippodrome. Future members of the Hollies and The Beatles were among his audiences, including lifelong fans Graham Nash and George Harrison, who was a big admirer of his guitar technique.

Charlie was an inductee of the Broadcast Pioneers of Philadelphia Hall of Fame, the Rockabilly Hall of Fame and the British Rock and Roll Hall of Fame. He was welcomed into The Buddy Holly Educational Foundation in 2018 while performing at a UK festival in Pakefield, Suffolk. He returned to play the same venue less than a month before he died in December 2022. – *Mike Read*

I'M GONNA LOVE YOU TOO

'I'm Gonna Love You Too' was released as a single on Coral on 5 February 1958, having been recorded on 12 July 1957. While it is credited to Niki Sullivan, Joe B. Mauldin and Norman Petty, Jerry Allison later stated the song was actually written by Buddy Holly, with Jerry helping to compose the bridge. At the end of the song you can hear the chirping of an actual cricket, which had got into the studio. The lyric 'Drunk man, street car, foot slip, there you are' was a favourite saying of Buddy's mother, Ella, whenever she stumbled over something. The song was later covered by Blondie on Parallel Lines *and chosen as the album's lead single.*

'In my mind, Buddy Holly was without a doubt the greatest rock and roll innovator of his time.'

CHARLIE GRACIE I have always loved everything about Buddy Holly. A great majority will say that Elvis made the biggest impact of all 1950s recording artists, and I take nothing away from that. However, being a musician and a guitarist myself, I've always found the music that Buddy created a lot more fascinating. He accomplished in the studio what most of us could only dream of. What he did in such a short period has stood the test of time. Buddy was never manufactured or 'prettied up'. His legacy is built upon genius and ingenuity.

My heartfelt appreciation goes out to everyone associated with the Foundation – and especially to Buddy's devoted widow, Maria Elena. I'm grateful too that my fans got to witness the presentation of my Buddy Holly guitar before my concert performance at Pakefield, England. This truly made it extra special.

JOE BROWN Like everyone else I bought 'That'll Be the Day', 'Oh Boy!' and all the other stuff by Buddy and the Crickets. I not only learned the songs but worked out the solos. When Buddy Holly died, we all felt terrible. We knew he had so much more to give.

You always wonder what Buddy would have gone on to do and how his music, songs and productions would have changed and whether they would have continued to influence young writers and musicians.

'Before Buddy Holly, I mainly played skiffle, but then I heard this amazing sound from America. From then on, I just wanted to play Buddy Holly songs.'

Buddy Holly
THE MAN.
What a terrible Tragedy
he was such an Inspiration
I often wonder what
would have happened had he
survived – Taking into account
all the Inovations he
developed in the recording
World I dont know
anyone in this business
that didnt Love him
Joe Brown

JOE BROWN WAS HIRED BY TV PRODUCER JACK GOOD in 1958 to be the lead guitarist for his new series *Boy Meets Girls*, and he was also in demand to play on the road with touring artists such as Gene Vincent and Eddie Cochran. Here, at just 17 years old, was where Joe Brown cut his teeth.

In the spring of 1960, Joe played lead guitar on Billy Fury's debut LP, *The Sound of Fury*, which would later be recognised as the first true British blend of rock and roll and rockabilly. Later, Joe began to have hit singles under his own name, including 'The Darktown Strutters' Ball', 'A Picture of You', 'It Only Took a Minute' and 'That's What Love Will Do'.

A highly respected guitarist, Joe also played the ukulele, including in his incredibly moving version of 'I'll See You in My Dreams', performed for his close friend George Harrison at *A Concert for George*.

Joe has also been in six films, starred in shows in London's West End, continues to write songs and undertakes over a hundred gigs a year. He remains a steadfast Buddy Holly fan. – *Mike Read*

DARREL HIGHAM Having been born in 1970, I grew up in a decade that saw a tremendous revival of interest in 1950s music and the artists that defined that music. So I know I first heard Buddy's music at a young age because he was still being played on national radio back then!

However, in the early 1980s the rockabilly revival was in full swing and it was during this period I discovered the recordings Buddy had made prior to his hit records. 'Midnight Shift', 'Rock Around with Ollie Vee', 'Love Me', 'Don't Come Back Knockin'', 'Modern Don Juan', etc. Those records blew me away! They are virtually perfect rockabilly: the incredible slap bass from Don Guess, the excellent lead guitar picking from Sonny Curtis and Buddy's confident and assured vocals – not trying to copy Elvis but matching his enthusiasm for this new form of music Elvis had been so instrumental in creating while at Sun Records. Buddy made some of the greatest rockabilly recordings ever committed to tape. If rock and roll is 50 per cent country and 50 per cent blues, then rockabilly is 50 per cent rock and roll and 50 per cent country.

Artists like Elvis, Buddy, Carl Perkins, Eddie Cochran and numerous others seemed to instinctively understand this and that's why their names are so intrinsically intertwined with the genre. Many of these erstwhile country boys went on to record some of the greatest and most enduring rock and roll records of the era. Buddy, like most of his contemporaries, was a country boy at heart so rockabilly was already in his blood. Rockabilly was never the poor man's rock and roll but rather the stepping stone for many young artists in the 1950s onto the more lucrative path of rock and roll.

Throughout my career, I've returned to Buddy's early recordings time and time again in order to study them, always discovering something new that I've overlooked but always being hugely impressed with how exciting they still are. I've made a career out of being a rockabilly guitarist and I thank the greats for their continued inspiration and the immense joy their music has brought to my life. Buddy's up there with the very best of them.

Long Live the music
and memory of Buddy Holly –
May his influence continue to
inspire for many generations
to come!
His Rockabilly recordings continue to inspire me –
If someone was to ask me to play one song that
defines the genre, it would be Midnight Shift
God bless 'Ol Annie and the mighty
Buddy Holly!!
Darrel Higham

VALLEY OF TEARS

Written by Dave Bartholomew and Fats Domino, the original was released in 1957. Buddy's version of 'Valley of Tears' was released on Coral in March 1958 on the Buddy Holly *LP and posthumously in 1961 as a B-side to 'Baby I Don't Care' and charted shortly after. It features Buddy on vocals and guitar, Joe B. Mauldin on bass, Jerry 'J.I.' Allison on drums, as well as producer Norman Petty on organ and his wife, Vi Petty, on piano, both of whom were members of the Norman Petty Trio.*

CHRIS DIFFORD Buddy Holly has been in and out of my life forever. Firstly when I was a young lad at home in a prefab in south-east London with my elder brother playing his music on the stereogram. These songs embraced happiness and a simple life. Buddy's music resurfaced again when I first met Glenn Tilbrook and Glenn played his music and recorded some fine demos of a few of his songs.

In 2014, I was invited to a Buddy Holly Foundation presentation day at Abbey Road Studios. Together with the Foundation we hatched a plan to make Buddy's legacy an important part of my songwriting retreats, which are now sponsored by the Foundation. I was lucky enough to be given a guitar, one I take on tour with Squeeze. The workshops roll on and for me they signify the gentleness of the songwriting of this man who was sadly taken in the prime of his life. His music and his kindness will last forever.

'If Buddy were alive today the music industry would possibly be a more inclusive and wonderful place to be. I hear the passion in the music he created in such a short space of time, which is so much part of all of our lives today. We need gentle songwriters to hold our hands in rough times, and to guide us when the lights go out on our own journey showing us the way forward. Today this kind of songwriting is lacking in our world.'

Buddy Holly was the backing track of my childhood life – how beautiful to have this music as part of my early life

A FOUNDER MEMBER OF SQUEEZE WITH GLENN TILBROOK, Chris Difford continued to write songs for other artists, including Jools Holland, Elvis Costello and Elton John, after the band broke up in 1983. In partnership with Glenn Tilbrook and John Turner, Chris also created the 1983 musical *Labelled with Love*, based on Squeeze's classic 1981 album *East Side Story*. The show ran for three months and sold out every performance along the way.

Squeeze reformed in 1985 with a different line-up. To date, some 24 musicians, including Jools Holland, Paul Carrack and former Attractions Pete Thomas and Steve Nieve, have stood in the band's ranks during their different incarnations, but only Chris Difford and Glenn Tilbrook have remained constant members. They have released 15 studio albums with Squeeze and one as a duo.

Alongside his ongoing touring and recording with Squeeze, Chris has released five solo studio albums and from time to time curates shows at the Barbican Centre in London. For over 30 years, he has also hosted songwriting retreats, most notably for The Buddy Holly Educational Foundation, in Glastonbury, Somerset.

TAKE YOUR TIME

The Buddy Holly composition 'Take Your Time' was released in the US on 20 April 1958 as the B-side to 'Rave On'. Paul McCartney and Denny Laine recorded the song for Denny's 1977 album of Buddy covers, Holly Days.

GORDON PAYNE *'Real Wild Child'*

IT WAS THROUGH WORKING WITH WAYLON JENNINGS that Oklahoma-born guitarist and singer Gordon Payne became part of the Buddy Holly legacy with the Crickets. As a boy he recalled that he first heard Buddy Holly on records that his brother had bought, which led Gordon to do the same.

Obtaining his first guitar at around the age of 13, Gordon soon got involved in music, playing rock and soul numbers in local combos. Later moving to Tulsa he became part of the area's vibrant music scene along with others like Leon Russell and J.J. Cale.

Gordon first met the Crickets in the early 1970s when they were based out on the West Coast. Working with Freddy Weller and then Tanya Tucker, Gordon moved to Nashville in 1975 then went on to work with Johnny Rodriguez before landing the gig with Waylon as guitarist, singer and harmonica player. Between 1978 and 1983, at Waylon's invitation, the Crickets opened the shows for the country superstar. During this period Gordon would also occasionally augment the Crickets on guitar. He also stood in for Sonny Curtis once following an accident in which Sonny broke his arm.

After leaving Waylon in 1985 Gordon officially became a member of the Crickets, joining the band following Sonny's departure to concentrate on his solo career. For nearly ten years Gordon fronted the Crickets on stage and on record, including a series of memorable tours of the UK, beginning in 1986. On record Gordon is featured on the band's 1988 recording of 'T-Shirt' which became a minor hit on the UK's independent charts. Keeping the music of Buddy Holly and the Crickets alive, Gordon and Co. continued to perform some of Buddy Holly and the Crickets' old classics along with newer material. With his soulful vocal style, solid guitar playing and talent as a songwriter, Gordon Payne certainly made some major contributions to the Crickets' longevity. – *John Firminger*

GORDON PAYNE The first time I played an Atkin Guitar was at Jerry Allison's house. J.I. handed me the guitar and asked me to try it. I was blown away by the sound and the feel of it. By the feel I mean the way it vibrated the bass and midrange and how perfectly it fit my hand. I fell in love with a guitar, and I had never felt that before.

Once I got back home to Texas I kept thinking about that great-sounding guitar I played at J.I.'s. I asked him if he could get me one. That's when John Beecher of Rollercoaster Records got involved. He spoke to Atkin and they asked me to name the guitar. We settled on 'Real Wild Child' to honour J.I.: 'Real Wild Child' was first released in the US in 1958 by Ivan, J.I.'s stage name.

My Atkin 'Real Wild Child' arrived Christmas Eve morning. From the first strum, I got that same feeling I fell in love with at J.I.'s. From my days with Don White and J.J. Cale in Tulsa, to Waylon and Willie and the Outlaw years, then spending ten years singing for the Crickets with J.I. and Joe B. Mauldin, I have played a thousand guitars, but I don't remember ever being so impressed with a guitar.

Buddy
Will always
be under rated.
Oh Boy is one of
the greatest Vocal
performances of
all time.
Gordon Payne

REAL WILD CHILD
'Real Wild Child' was written by Australian artist Johnny O'Keefe and was recorded by Jerry Allison in 1958 under his middle name 'Ivan'. It reached number 68 in the US charts and Jerry occasionally performed it during the Biggest Show of Stars for '58 tour. 'Real Wild Child' was made a hit again by Iggy Pop in the 1980s.

‘It’s the music of my grandparents. Being a Buddy Holly ambassador connects me back to it.’

SAM FENDER *‘Ready Teddy’*

WHAT DOES ROCK AND ROLL MEAN TO SAM FENDER? ‘It’s freedom of expression,’ he says, ‘defiance of oppression. It combats depression and it makes you wanna session!’

The BRIT Award-winning, chart-topping North Shields singer-songwriter has found the guitar ‘intriguing’ ever since he first laid eyes on one. ‘It was the first hobby I ever had and I never needed another – it stole my heart!’ he admits. Surrounded by guitars, with his father and brother both players, he got hooked when he saw his dad playing in bands as a kid and wanted to be part of the gang. By the age of 13, he couldn’t put his guitar down.

After years of learning his craft by jamming songs by the likes of Jimi Hendrix, Bruce Spingsteen and Jeff Buckley, he got discovered by Ben Howard’s manager while performing in a pub and soon took to touring the UK with his own gritty gut-punch songs that turned the harsh realities of his poverty and drug-stricken home town into arena-ready anthems.

It was also around that time he discovered Buddy Holly through being a superfan of The Beatles, with Paul McCartney often referencing Buddy as an influence. ‘What stood out with Buddy was that he wrote all of his own stuff and played all the lead parts on guitar,’ he says. ‘“That’ll Be the Day” was the first tune that really caught my ear. I used to play guitar in the Lowlights Tavern in North Shields. Those were some of the happiest times of my life.’

Sam’s hand-painted Buddy Holly Atkin parlour guitar has different artwork from the other ambassador guitars that is inspired by the branding for Newcastle Brown Ale – his onstage drink of choice. He played it on his third album to ‘add a lot of sparkle to the tracks’. The ‘Seventeen Going Under’ star continues to carry Buddy’s rock and roll creative spirit with him. ‘I take great pride in writing all my stuff alone. Buddy made that normal.’ – *Andrew Trendall (News Editor,* NME*)*

Buddy Holly,
I’ll get you a pint
on the other side
big love brother.
Sam Fender

READY TEDDY
Written by Robert Blackwell and John Marascalco, ‘Ready Teddy’ first entered the charts in June 1956 when Little Richard’s version reached number 44. Elvis Presley also recorded the song that year, though it is likely Buddy heard the Little Richard version first. Buddy recorded ‘Ready Teddy’ in May or June 1957 at Norman Petty’s studio in Clovis, NM and included it on his self-titled debut solo album, released on Coral on 20 February 1958.

ONE OF AMERICA'S TOP SESSION GUITARISTS, Brent Mason taught himself to play from the age of five. After leaving high school in his native Ohio, he was drawn by his love of country music to Nashville. There he was discovered by Chet Atkins, who asked him to play on his album *Stay Tuned*, and he has gone on to contribute to more than a thousand albums by artists including Neil Diamond, David Gates and Shania Twain. As well as playing sessions, Brent has produced many artists and has an online education site for aspiring guitarists.

Brent was voted Nashville Music Awards Guitarist of the Year in 1995 and Country Music Association Musician of the Year in 1997 and 1998, winning a Grammy in 2008. Incredibly he has been voted Guitarist of the Year 14 times by the Academy of Country Music and *MusicRow* Session Guitarist of the Year ten times between 1994 and 2010. He was also inducted into the Thumbpickers Hall of Fame in 2011. – *Mike Read*

I WAS Greatly influenced
By Buddy's Music...
A music Style That will Always
Be Cool Beyond its years!!
Thanks for the Music!
Brent Mason

'I play the Buddy Holly J-45 constantly and it sounds beautiful, especially in the studio.'

BRENT MASON The fact that Buddy Holly is as popular as he is today is a testament to his talent as a singer-songwriter and guitar player. I can only imagine what he might have done had his career and life been able to run its full course. To think about what he was able to accomplish in the short time he had is amazing. It all stands the test of time.

MIDNIGHT SHIFT

The Jimmy Ainsworth and Earl Lee song 'Midnight Shift' was recorded during Buddy Holly's first Decca session on 26 January 1956 at Bradley's Barn, Nashville, TN by Buddy, Sonny Curtis, Grady Martin, Don Guess and Doug Kirkham. It was released as a track on the Decca album That'll Be the Day *on 14 April 1958 and then as a single on Brunswick, which came out posthumously on 5 June 1959.*

GRAHAM GOULDMAN IS ONE OF THE UK'S GREATEST SONGWRITERS, having written classic tunes for the Hollies, such as 'Bus Stop', as well as 'For Your Love' for the Yardbirds, along with hits for Herman's Hermits and Wayne Fontana and his own bands 10cc and Wax.

Graham's Buddy Holly guitar is a nod to his first group, the Whirlwinds, who released their cover of Buddy's 'Look at Me' on HMV in June 1964. Whereas Buddy's original was keyboard based, Graham's band of Salford lads gave 'Look at Me' the guitar-laden British treatment, with an almost country-style instrumental break.

Buddy Holly was, and still is, a major influence on me both as a songwriter and musician. I still hear echos of his music in my work today. He will always be with me as will his legacy for generations to come.

Graham Gouldman

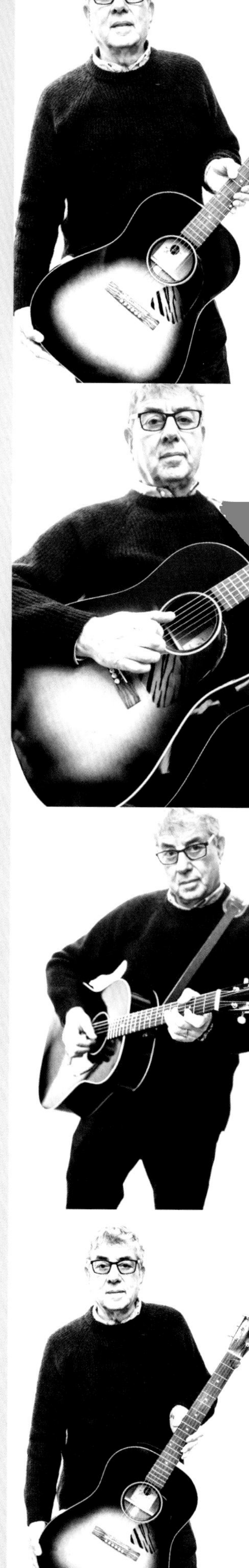

LOOK AT ME

'Look at Me' was written by Buddy Holly, Jerry Allison and Norman Petty and recorded on 19 December 1957 at Norman Petty's studio. C.W. Kendall, a friend of Norman Petty, played piano on the song. It was included on Buddy's debut solo album, Buddy Holly, *released on 20 February 1958.*

'Buddy will always be with me, as will his musical legacy for generations to come.'

GRAHAM GOULDMAN I would have been 11 years old when I first heard Buddy Holly. The record was 'That'll Be the Day'. I fell in love with Buddy, that song, and, when I first saw pictures of him, his sunburst Fender Stratocaster. All the records he released were absolute gems.

When I list my musical heroes, he is there, and his importance cannot be overestimated. Buddy Holly was a major influence on me both as a songwriter and a musician. I still hear echoes of his music in my work today.

Buddy —

What is there to say
that hasn't been said
Before

He's the reason I'm writing
these humble words
Long live Buddy
and his music!

G

RAVE ON

'Rave On' was written by Sonny West, Bill Tilghman and Norman Petty and first recorded by Sonny West for Atlantic Records. Buddy's version was recorded on 25 January 1958 at Bell Sound Studio, New York City and first released as a track on his self-titled debut album for Coral on 20 February 1958.

FANS OF BUDDY HOLLY AND THE EVERLY BROTHERS, Graham Nash and his school friend Allan Clarke once hung out in the street to try and meet Don and Phil after a concert. Later, when they formed their chart-topping group the Hollies they chose the name based on their admiration for Buddy Holly, as Graham confirmed in a 2009 interview.

Departing from the Hollies at the end of 1968, Graham moved to Laurel Canyon in Los Angeles and formed Crosby, Stills and Nash with David Crosby and Stephen Stills. He wrote some of the group's classic songs, including 'Teach Your Children', 'Our House' and 'Marrakesh Express'. For their second album, *Déjà Vu*, their line-up now included Neil Young. Released in 1970, the record topped the US chart and sold over 8 million copies. The following year Graham released *Songs for Beginners*, the first of seven solo albums to date.

CSN didn't play together again until a 1974 reunion and regrouped again in late 1976. Over the ensuing decades they have reconvened at various points to tour and record together, sometimes with Neil Young, sometimes as a trio, before returning to solo projects.

Graham has twice been inducted into the Rock and Roll Hall of Fame, first as a member of Crosby, Stills and Nash in 1997 and then as a member of the Hollies in 2010. That same year he received an OBE and he holds four honorary doctorates awarded by universities in the US and UK. Graham's autobiography, *Wild Tales: A Rock and Roll Life*, was published in 2013. - *Mike Read*

'I end my show these days with "Everyday". Need I say more?'

GRAHAM NASH Buddy Holly was my friend. I never knew him, never met him, but he was my friend, he was one of us. He wore thick-rimmed glasses … He didn't need to shake his backside to get attention. All he had was his voice and his music. Music that is so incredibly simple yet effective, and I say 'is' because Buddy's songs stand the test of time today.

He died on my birthday in 1959. Allan Clarke walked over to my house to tell me, because it had been in the paper. I remember that we were crying on the street corner. Fifty years later, to the day, I played the Surf Ballroom in Clear Lake, Iowa, which was the last place that Buddy played. Every year they have a concert for him. Of course, I was all over it, so me and my son Will went to Clear Lake – which is one of the coldest places I've ever been in my life – but to stand at the site where that plane crashed was insanely emotional for me. I was so sad. I saw a shot of Buddy when he was just months from death and he looks so lonely, as if to say, 'I'm here on the road, but everything I love is back in Manhattan with Maria Elena.' To me, he just doesn't want to be there. I don't know how you react to it, but it's a beautiful shot.

DON EVERLY 'Love's Made a Fool of You'

Buddy was a friend of mine

Don Everly

DON EVERLY We got to be very close friends with Buddy Holly and the Crickets and he wrote a couple of things for us. 'Love's Made a Fool of You' might have been one. We had just learned to dress a little sharper ourselves and they noticed it, so we took them to all the places.

'We took Buddy and the Crickets down to our clothes stores in New York.'

DON AND PHIL EVERLY TOURED WITH BUDDY HOLLY in 1957 and 1958 and, it seems, were responsible for getting Buddy and the Crickets to wear suits. One of the items by which they were able to identify Buddy Holly after the plane crash was a sapphire ring, Buddy, Don and Phil having bought identical rings from a jeweller backstage on *The Ed Sullivan Show*.

Back in the day, Don and Phil didn't travel with their own band and had to use local musicians, but at one concert in Florida there were only amateur players, so Buddy and the Crickets stepped in to back them. That must have been a very special night for those who had a ticket.

The Everly Brothers were inducted into the Rock and Roll Hall of Fame in 1986, and in 1997 they were given the Grammy Lifetime Achievement Award. They were also inducted into the Country Music Hall of Fame, Vocal Group Hall of Fame, Iowa Rock and Roll Hall of Fame and were recognised by the Rockabilly Hall of Fame. In 1986 they received a star on the Hollywood Walk Fame. – *Mike Read*

LOVE'S MADE A FOOL OF YOU

'Love's Made a Fool of You' was written by Buddy Holly and Bob Montgomery in 1954, but the song was not recorded until 2 June 1958 when Buddy made a demo version for the Everly Brothers at Norman Petty's studio in Clovis, NM. This demo version was released posthumously in 1964 on the Showcase *compilation. However, the Crickets, led by Sonny Curtis, also recorded the song without Buddy and this version was released in 1959. Twice the Crickets' version was accidentally included on Buddy Holly compilation albums: first in 1972, on* Buddy Holly: A Rock and Roll Collection*; and again in 1997, on* The Very Best of Buddy Holly*. In 1966, the Bobby Fuller Four released a cover of the song, which became one of their biggest hits.*

Above: Buddy with Don Everly outside Carnegie Hall, circa 1958

GENERAL ARTISTS CORPORATION
GAC
NEW YORK • CHICAGO • BEVERLY HILLS • LONDON
8 SOUTH MICHIGAN AVENUE • CHICAGO 3, ILL. • STATE 2-6288

CH

Mr. Miles Adams, Secretary
Musicians Protective Union
204 Guaranty Bank Bldg. Cedar Rapids, Mich.

Local No. 137

THIS CONTRACT for the personal services of musicians, made this 4th day of March, 1966, between the undersigned employer (hereinafter called the "employer") and Five (Including the Leader) musicians (hereinafter called "employees").

WITNESSETH, That the employer hires the employees as musicians severally on the terms and conditions below. The leader represents that the employees already designated have agreed to be bound by said terms and conditions. Each employee yet to be chosen shall be so bound by said terms and conditions upon agreeing to accept his employment. Each employee may enforce this agreement. The employees severally agree to render collectively to the employer services as musicians in the orchestra under the leadership of Don & Phil Everly EVERLY BROTHERS as follows:

Place of Engagement: Danceland Ballroom Cedar Rapids, Iowa

Date(s) of employment: Saturday, July 30, 1966 — EMPLOYER TO FURNISH BAND TO PLAY THE DANCE PORTION AT NO COST TO THE EVERLY BROTHERS.

Hours of employment: 2 Shows Bet. Hrs. 9-12:45 A.M.

Type of engagement (specify whether dance, stage show, banquet, etc.): Show/Dance Combination

Price agreed upon $ 1500.00 vs. 60% (Terms and amount)

This price includes expenses agreed to be reimbursed by the employer in accordance with the attached schedule, or a schedule to be furnished the employer on or before the date of engagement.

DEPOSIT: $ NONE (Certified Check, Money Order or Bank Draft) payable to General Artists Corporation upon signing of contract. (In the event that, contrary to contract specifications, an uncertified check is tendered by employer, same will be received and deposited for clearance purposes only. If check is not paid upon presentation, this contract, even if signed by all parties, shall be of no force and effect.)

Received $........ ...., 19.... by ....

BALANCE to be paid in United States currency to General Artists Corporation or Leader on or before conclusion of engagement. There are to be no deductions for any reason whatsoever.

Overtime Charge ....

The employer is hereby given an option to extend this agreement for a period of .... weeks beyond the original term thereof. Said option can be made effective only by written notice from the employer to the employees, not later than .... days prior to the expiration of said original term, that he claims and exercises said option, and a copy of said notice shall be filed with the local in whose jurisdiction the engagement is to be played.

Upon request by the American Federation of Musicians of the United States and Canada (herein called the "Federation") or the local in whose jurisdiction the employees shall perform hereunder, the employer either shall make advance payment hereunder or shall post an appropriate bond.

If any employees have not been chosen upon the signing of this contract, the leader shall, as agent for the employer and under his instructions, hire such persons and any replacements as are required for persons who for any reason do not perform any or all services. The employer shall at all times have complete control over the services of employees under this contract, and the leader shall, as agent of the employer, enforce disciplinary measures for just cause, and carry out instructions as to selections and manner of performance. The agreement of the employees to perform is subject to proven detention by sickness, accidents, or accidents to means of transportation, riots, strikes, epidemics, acts of God, or any other legitimate conditions beyond the control of the employees. On behalf of the employer the leader will distribute the amount received from the employer to the employees, including himself, as indicated on the opposite side of this contract, or in place thereof on separate memorandum supplied to the employer at or before the commencement of the employment hereunder and take and turn over to the employer receipts therefor from each employee, including himself. The amount paid to the leader includes the cost of transportation, which will be reported by the leader to the employer.

All employees covered by this agreement must be members in good standing of the Federation. However, if the employment provided for hereunder is subject to the Labor-Management Relations Act, 1947, all employees, who are members of the Federation when their employment commences hereunder, shall be continued in such employment only so long as they continue such membership in good standing. All other employees covered by this agreement, on or before the thirtieth day following the commencement of their employment, or the effective date of this agreement, whichever is later, shall become and continue to be members in good standing of the Federation. The provisions of this paragraph shall not become effective unless and until permitted by applicable law.

To the extent permitted by applicable law, nothing in this contract shall ever be construed so as to interfere with any duty owing by any employee hereunder to the Federation pursuant to its Constitution, By-Laws, Rules, Regulations and Orders.

Any employees who are parties to or affected by this contract are free to cease service hereunder by reason of any strike, ban, unfair list order or requirement of the Federation, and shall be free to accept and engage in other employment of the same or similar character or otherwise, for other employers or persons without any restraint, hindrance, penalty, obligation or liability whatever, any other provisions of this contract to the contrary notwithstanding.

Representatives of the local in whose jurisdiction the employees shall perform hereunder shall have access to the place of performance (except to private residences) for the purpose of conferring with the employees.

The performances to be rendered pursuant to this agreement are not to be recorded, reproduced, or transmitted from the place of performance, in any manner or by any means whatsoever, in the absence of a specific written agreement between the employer and the Federation relating to and permitting such recording, reproduction or transmission.

The employer represents that there does not exist against him, in favor of any member of the Federation, any claim of any kind arising out of musical services rendered for any such employer. No employee will be required to perform any provisions of this contract or to render any services for said employer as long as any such claim is unsatisfied or unpaid, in whole or in part. If the employer breaches this agreement, he shall pay the employees, in addition to damages, 6% interest thereon plus a reasonable attorney's fee.

The employer, in signing this contract himself, or having same signed by a representative, acknowledges his (her or their) authority to do so and hereby assumes liability for the amount stated herein.

To the extent permitted by applicable law, there are incorporated into and made part of this agreement, as though fully set forth herein, all of the By-laws, Rules and Regulations of the Federation and of any local of the Federation in whose jurisdiction services are to be performed hereunder (insofar as they do not conflict with those of the Federation), and the employer acknowledges his responsibility to be fully acquainted, now and for the duration of this contract, with the contents thereof.

THIS CONTRACT SHALL NOT BE BINDING UNLESS SIGNED BY ALL PARTIES HERETO.

Name of Employer: Mr. Darlowe Oleson, Danceland Ballroom
Street Address: 124-Third St. N,E.
City & State: Cedar Rapids, Iowa
Phone ....

Accepted by Employer: Darlowe Oleson
Accepted .... (Orchestra Leader)

Return all copies signed to GENERAL ARTISTS CORPORATION 8 SOUTH MICHIGAN AVENUE CHICAGO 3, ILL.

If this contract is made by a licensed booking agent, there must be inserted on the reverse side of the contract the name, address and telephone number of the collecting agent of the local union in whose jurisdiction the engagement is to be performed.

OFFICE COPY — Form B-2a 3-61

WISHING

'Wishing' was written by Buddy Holly and Bob Montgomery for the Everly Brothers. However, the song was rejected by the Everlys' producer on the basis that the demo was too good. This had been recorded at Norman Petty Studios, Clovis, NM on 2 June 1958 by Buddy, Tommy Allsup, George Atwood and Bo Clarke. It was released on Coral posthumously on 23 July 1963 on the EP Brown-Eyed Handsome Man.

Top: Phil Everly was presented with his 'Wishing' guitar during the events commemorating Buddy's 75th Birthday in Hollywood, Los Angeles, CA

Above: A performance contract between the Everly Brothers and General Artists Corporation for two shows at Danceland Ballroom, Cedar Rapids, IA on 30 July 1966

THE EVERLY BROTHERS PLAYED A VITAL ROLE in my early appreciation of the possibilities of music. Their songs were strong and powerful and their driving, acoustic sound was exciting beyond belief – the well-spring of what later became known as country rock. And their beautiful sibling harmonies ... well, they sounded like voices from another planet.

Don and Phil's records helped form the spine of my early investment in music, a collection that lines the walls of my studio to this day. I bought their first two releases, 'Bye Bye Love' and 'Wake Up Little Susie', on 78 rpm discs and played them on repeat on my parents' beautiful stereogram, mixing them with my Buddy Holly and the Crickets records, creating my first rock and roll playlists.

I loved the fact that Phil, Don, Buddy and the Crickets were all friends, travelling together on the massive package tours that criss-crossed the Southern States. 'I wouldn't swap those memories for a million dollars,' said Phil later. The bond between them all was huge and when Buddy passed away in 1959, Phil flew down to Lubbock for the funeral.

It was in 1959 that I finally realised a huge ambition and got myself a Dansette record player and, not surprisingly, the first 45 single I bought was by the Everly Brothers. It was released in Britain on the legendary London American label and not only did it have a great sound, but with its triangular centre and distinctive striped sleeve design, it looked amazing too.

I was so enamoured by the image of this glorious record that I propped it up under the light at the side of my bed so that I could gaze at it as I fell asleep. It didn't go well. By the time I woke up the following morning that gorgeous piece of vinyl was unrecognisable – warped and unplayable from the heat of the lightbulb. I had no idea this could even happen! A very harsh lesson. 'Problems' turned out to be an appropriate title of my first-time buy!

It was a great double-sided single with 'Take a Message to Mary' on the other side, but perhaps the most exciting of all the Everly Brothers, music was the huge sound of their biggest hit, 'Cathy's Clown'. It was the first ever release on the newly launched Warner Brothers record label, with the UK catalogue number WB1. Like all of us, The Beatles were listening and it was with warm recognition that I later heard the huge influence that the Everly Brothers and Buddy Holly had on the music of the Fab Four.

We've always loved the Everly Brothers here in Britain and it was with great joy and respect that The Buddy Holly Educational Foundation presented Phil with his bespoke guitar at the Hollywood Star All-Star evening concert in Los Angeles in 2011, one of his final public appearances. It was a very lovely, emotional and full-circle moment because, as he did at Buddy's funeral all those years before, he sat beside Buddy's widow Maria Elena. – *Bob Harris*

SIR CLIFF RICHARD *'Early in the Morning'*

CLIFF RICHARD We were all fans of Buddy and the Crickets. In a way, Buddy introduced us to the fact that you can get away with just three or four chords on the guitar, play them in different keys, and still be able to write songs. Thousands of songs are written with those three or four chords that Buddy showed us. Buddy was a very obvious person to follow … that's why we latched on to him, because he gave us life.

There are only a handful of artists who have a true influence on thousands of others and Buddy and the Crickets are one of those. It's impossible to get away from the fact.

'He should always be remembered as a startlingly good songwriter.'

EARLY IN THE MORNING

Written by Bobby Darin and Woody Harris, 'Early in the Morning' was originally recorded by Bobby Darin for Brunswick under an assumed name, the Ding-Dongs, to try to hide Darin's identity from his contracted record company, Atco. However, Atco realised what was happening and they reclaimed the masters and released the record under the name the Rinky-Dinks.

Buddy Holly's version, recorded on 19 June 1958 at Decca's Pythian Temple studios in New York City, was released on Brunswick on 5 July. It was intended to compete with the Bobby Darin record, which did much better in the US. Buddy's version was more successful overseas.

CLIFF RICHARD WAS A 19-YEAR-OLD WITH TWO TOP TEN HITS when Buddy Holly died, but today, with 14 UK number one singles and seven number one albums behind him, he still acknowledges Buddy's incredible influence on him.

Cliff holds an all-time UK chart record as the first artist ever to score a Top Five album in eight consecutive decades, a testament to his amazing longevity. His debut album in 1959 included a cover of Buddy's 'That'll Be the Day', recorded in the presence of hundreds of fans at Abbey Road Studios. In 1983, Cliff's version of 'True Love Ways', recorded at the Royal Albert Hall, made the UK Top Ten. He played his Foundation guitar, named 'Early in the Morning', on stage on his 2018 60th anniversary tour, performing Elvis Presley's 'Heartbreak Hotel', Buddy's 'Peggy Sue' and the Everly Brothers' 'Wake Up Little Susie'.

'A West Texas poet and guitar slinger singer brought pop songwriting and rock and roll to new heights in the 1950s and inspires thousands of songwriters and singers still today.'

RAY BENSON *'Now We're One'*

Buddy,
That'll be the day I
write you a letter;
Today!!
Love to you and the
Crickets!
Ray Benson

HUGE IN STATURE AND PERSONALITY, Ray Benson has been the ever-present frontman of Asleep at the Wheel since he formed the renowned western swing band with two friends in 1970.

Starting with their 1972 debut *Comin' Right at Ya*, the band have released more than 20 albums. They've received numerous awards, including nine Grammys, and have had as many as 90 musicians pass through their ever-changing line up. Ray has been the one constant keeping the music of Bob Wills and his Texas Playboys alive by releasing two hugely acclaimed tribute albums of songs by the king of western swing, while providing many new songs with the distinctive swing of country, blues and jazz.

In addition to his work with the band, Ray has also produced for Dale Watson, Suzy Bogguss, Merle Haggard, Aaron Neville, Brad Paisley and his great friend Willie Nelson, who also provided his distinctive vocals to the 2009 collaboration *Willie and the Wheel*. Ray and 'the Wheel' continue to tour extensively and he features in many music documentaries talking about the history of country music and those who keep it alive by introducing it to new audiences on both sides of the Atlantic. – *Bob Harris*

NOW WE'RE ONE

Buddy's version of the Bobby Darin song 'Now We're One' was recorded on 19 June 1958 at Decca's Pythian Temple studios in New York City and released on Coral on 5 July 1958 as the B-side of another Bobby Darin cover, 'Early in the Morning'.

After Buddy was married at his family home in Lubbock on 15 August 1958, the song was played on the phonograph.

Thank you so much for this wonderful guitar! Lots of love Ed

ED SHEERAN *'Ting-A-Ling'*

CELEBRATED SINGER-SONGWRITER ED SHEERAN shares with Buddy Holly a great ability to blend storytelling with memorable melodies in a way that resonates with millions across continents and generations. Also like Buddy, he became successful at a young age; his UK chart-topping debut album, *+*, was released in 2011 when he was just 20 years old.

Known for his remarkable guitar skills and innovative loop pedal performances, Ed captivates audiences with his dynamic live shows. With his grounded demeanour, he remains a beloved figure, connecting with fans through the universal language of music.

Often incorporating influences from classic rock, folk and R&B into his songwriting, Ed continues to reflect the sounds of artists like Buddy Holly, Bob Dylan and Van Morrison. He has also previously covered musicians such as Stevie Wonder, Nina Simone and Elton John, paying tribute to the elder statesmen and women of his craft.

Ed Sheeran's guitar was presented to him backstage at the Teen Cancer America 'Backyard Concert' in 2018 by Don McLean. Ed was there with his parents, who are huge Buddy Holly fans. He was particularly pleased that it was an Atkin guitar as he has quite a few back in his home in Suffolk.

TING-A-LING

'Ting-A-Ling' was written by co-founder of Atlantic Records Ahmet Ertegun for the Clovers, who had a hit with the song in 1952. It was recorded by Buddy Holly on 22 July 1956 at Bradley's Barn, Nashville, TN, and released on 14 April 1958 on the Decca album That'll Be the Day.

Top: Ed with his Buddy Holly guitar with John Fogerty
Middle and bottom: Having been presented with his Buddy Holly guitar, Ed rehearses and performs a duet of 'Vincent' with Don McLean, Teen Cancer America 'Backyard Concert', Los Angeles, 24 August 2018

BRAD PAISLEY *'Don't Come Back Knockin'*

Buddy,

I don't want to even imagine rock and roll, country, or any kind of modern recorded music if you hadn't led the way. Rave on in the great beyond,

Your fan

DON'T COME BACK KNOCKIN'

'Don't Come Back Knockin" was written by Buddy and Sue Parrish and recorded on 7 December 1955 at Nesmen Studio, Wichita Falls, TX with Sonny Curtis, Don Guess and Jerry Allison. It was originally released on 14 April 1958 on the Decca album That'll Be the Day. *It was one of the demos sent by Buddy to Eddie Crandall* *(see page 52).*

'Covering Buddy's song "Maybe Baby" was a way for me to honour his legacy and what he has done for the world of music.'

BRAD PAISLEY AND I HAVE BEEN FRIENDS FOR MANY YEARS. My first visit to Nashville in 1999 as host of the Radio 2 *Country Show* exactly coincided with the release of Brad's first album, 'Who Needs Pictures', and from the opening guitar riff of 'Long Sermon' it was clear that this was a debut release created by someone very special.

Brad Paisley has a sound. There is a distinctive twang to his incredible guitar playing. Fire on the strings. Few guitarists in the world can combine his phenomenal speed and deep emotional expression but Brad makes it look almost effortless ... while at the same time creating possibly the most distinctive playing style in the whole of country music.

Seemingly out of nowhere, Brad brought a vibrancy and a fantastic energy to Nashville. Here was a major new artist crashing into what had previously been a slow-moving country scene, bringing great songwriting, an open mind and a unique, infectious sense of humour to Music Row. Brad brought country music into the 21st century and helped push open the door to a whole new generation of country stars. And for many years he brought a wonderful spirit of irreverent laughter and joy as co-host with Carrie Underwood of country music's biggest night – the Country Music Association Awards.

His unique sense of humour is brilliantly expressed in a songwriting style that combines lyrical sharpness with a wry and quirky sense of fun and his songs represent a progressive world view that has inspired many other Southern artists to engage with fans from way beyond their own county line. It's a mindset best expressed in the words of 'Southern Comfort Zone' – a huge production, open-minded hymn to world exploration and travel. 'I've walked the streets of Rome and been to foreign lands. I know what it's like to talk and have no one understand.'

His eclectic influences transcend musical genres. At last count, his record collection included Merle Haggard, Randy Travis, Eric Clapton, Huey Lewis and the Rolling Stones and he has collaborated with artists as diverse as Alison Krauss, Mick Jagger, B.B. King, LL Cool J and Sheryl Crow.

Over the years Brad and I have talked many times about the music he loves and many times the conversations have come back to Buddy Holly. 'He was way ahead of his time,' Brad told me. 'He made music that was magic in its simplicity and genius in its accessibility. He was one of the greats who paved the way for so many of us.'
– Bob Harris

DEBBIE HARRY IS AN ICON. As the lead singer with the band Blondie she is one of the most recognised women on the planet. With her signature platinum-blonde hair and punk-inspired fashion choices she's an edgy, glamorous, global megastar.

Blondie came together in 1974 at exactly the time punk and new wave bands were taking over the New York underground music scene in Manhattan and on the East Side of the city, bringing a whole new generation of impatient fans to their music. Change was in the air and the energy was incredible.

Ground zero was CBGB, a legendary venue located in the Bowery district. The atmosphere inside the packed club was rebellious and exciting – a launch pad for some massive careers. Blondie were rubbing shoulders with the Ramones, Talking Heads, Patti Smith, Lou Reed and Television . . . but when Deborah Harry took to the stage, she transcended. She was stunning under that smoky spotlight – the shimmering, charismatic lead singer, who brought a unique range of musical styles into the band.

Debbie has always acknowledged how much she loves Buddy Holly's songs and the catchy, heartfelt, storytelling appeal of his lyrics. Blondie even acknowledged Buddy on their multi-million-selling break-out album *Parallel Lines*, in 1978, recording a fabulous version of 'I'm Gonna Love You Too', which Buddy had released as a double A-side with 'Listen to Me' 20 years earlier.

Like Buddy, Debbie is blessed with a natural lyrical skill, able to touchingly express emotion and experience through her songs. And, like Buddy, she has been inspired by music from many different genres. She's a fan of soul music, blues, pop, punk and disco. Her first recording was a folk album, and she loves the girl groups and the British bands of the 1960s.

Blondie outgrew the ground-breaking moment that birthed them, staging a major takeover of the charts in the late 1970s, putting out some of the greatest records ever made and rocketing to global stardom. At a time when girl lead singers were still a relative rarity, Debbie became the first woman to take a rap track to number one when 'Rapture' topped the US charts in 1981.

More than 40 years later she is still regarded as one of the most fascinating women in the world – seminal rock star, complex songwriter, incandescent front woman, actor and fashion icon. And she and Blondie are part of the Rock and Roll Hall of Fame, joining one of her greatest influences – Buddy Holly. – *Bob Harris*

I'M CHANGING ALL THOSE CHANGES
'I'm Changing All Those Changes' was written by Buddy and recorded on 22 July 1956 at Bradley's Barn, Nashville, TN with Sonny Curtis, Don Guess and Jerry Allison. It was originally released on 14 April 1958 on the

SHOOTER JENNINGS *'Jole Blon'*

SHOOTER JENNINGS IS A GIANT OF THE NASHVILLE MUSIC SCENE. Over the past 20 years he has established a peerless reputation as a major musician, storyteller, songwriter, podcaster, producer and record label CEO.

As an artist, he debuted on the American charts with the driving '4th of July' in 2005, released from his first full-length album, *Put the O Back In Country*, featuring a cameo appearance by 'The Possum' George Jones. The track is a classic – soaked in Shooter's love of traditional country music and powered by a rebel spirit inherent in his attitude to life.

He has worked many times with Grammy-winning producer Dave Cobb, whose raw, analogue, unvarnished Southern sound adds so much soul to the deep authenticity of Shooter's brilliant records. He is a self-proclaimed 'studio nerd' and in recent years has, among many other blue-chip projects, helped revive the career of Tanya Tucker, co-producing her beautiful *While I'm Livin'* album with the glorious Brandi Carlile. He is a massively gifted and fiercely independent spirit.

Born into country music royalty, he grew up surrounded by music. 'I had great parents. My mom and dad were very close. I had a really fun childhood. We travelled all the time.'

His mother, Jessi Colter, was a major country hitmaker. The highlight of her ten-year chart career was the haunting 'I'm Not Lisa', which reached number one in 1975, while his father, Waylon Jennings, was a straight-up country music legend. Known as one of the outlaw country pioneers, Waylon's career was huge. His hits included country music's first ever platinum album, *Wanted! The Outlaws!*, the classic country song 'Luckenbach Texas' and chart success in the supergroup the Highwaymen with Kris Kristofferson, Willie Nelson and Johnny Cash.

Waylon's journey began in 1958 at a recording session organised by Buddy Holly, who then invited him to tour the Southern states with him as bassist in his band. It has been many times told that it was Waylon who gave up his seat to Buddy on the fateful plane ride on 3 February 1959 and when Waylon's first son was born just over a year later, he named him after Buddy.

So, it is deeply touching that Shooter Jennings has received a beautiful Buddy Holly guitar from the Foundation in his new studio in Los Angeles and that the guitar bears the title of the iconic song that Buddy produced with Waylon at that famous session all those years ago. That song was 'Jole Blon'. – *Bob Harris*

JOLE BLON

It was Hi-Pockets Duncan who saw Waylon Jennings's potential when he was working as a DJ at KDAV and performing around Lubbock, and in late 1958 Buddy, agreeing with Duncan, set out to launch his career and arrange for his first record. 'Jole Blon' was the song Buddy and Waylon chose for his first single. A Cajun classic and popular country dance tune written by Harry Choates, it was recorded by Jennings with Buddy on guitar, George Atwood (bass), Bo Clarke (drums), King Curtis (saxophone) and the Roses (backing vocals) on 10 September 1958.

KEITH URBAN *'When Sin Stops (Love Begins)'*

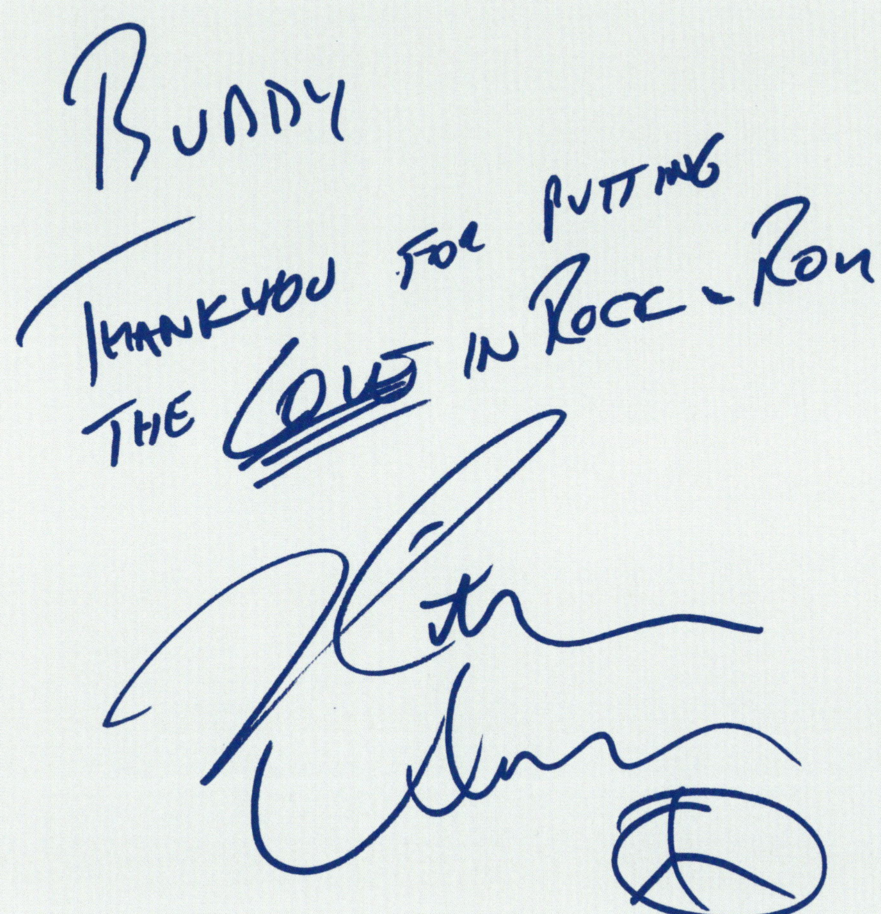

COUNTRY SUPERSTAR KEITH URBAN IS WHAT IS DESCRIBED in the industry as a 'gear head'. In other words, if there's a new type of guitar pedal, a new type of string, even a new type of guitar, Keith is all over it. But there is one piece of music-making equipment above all others that holds a special place in his heart – a magnificent vintage amplifier. To be precise, it is a 1958 Magnatone Custom 280, which Keith acquired in 2010.

Why did he want it? Why does he still love it so much? Well, the answers are simple and endearing. The 1958 Mag was the same kind of amp that Buddy Holly used to make his now famous home recordings at his Brevoort apartment on Fifth Avenue in New York.

1958 was a very important year for Buddy. He had parted company with the Crickets and moved, with his new wife Maria Elena, more than 1,600 miles across America from his home town of Lubbock, Texas to seek fresh opportunities in the Big Apple. It was a huge, brave step.

Buddy's time in New York was incredibly prolific. The Brevoort apartment was situated in the bohemian district of Greenwich Village, a vibrant and exciting place to be. There were coffee houses, poetry readings, folk and jazz performances. He and Maria Elena were visited by friends like Phil Everly and Waylon Jennings, and Buddy was energised and constantly working on new songs.

He began recording demos of the songs onto his Ampex 401A reel-to-reel tape machine and amplifying his guitar using the '58 Mag, famous in guitar circles for producing a fantastic vibrato – a classic twangy sound. As Magnatone themselves described it in their 1957 catalogue, the beast was 'the ultimate in modern amplifiers – the Custom 280 has a sound as Big As All Outdoors – the vastness of the sky combined with Magnatone's Big "V" Electronic True Vibrato . . .' What a description!

But don't just take their word for it – you can hear Buddy using the amp on 14 of those home demos from January 1959 that have been released commercially over the years. And the work is incredible. Songs like 'Peggy Sue Got Married', 'Learning the Game', 'Crying, Waiting, Hoping' and spooky, intimate recordings that show us a whole other side of Buddy, recorded late at night while Maria Elena slept in the other room.

So, it is not surprising that Keith Urban would be entranced by this amazing sound. After all, he has been a Buddy Holly fan for all his life! Growing up near Brisbane, Australia, Keith was already an accomplished guitar player, and as a member of a children's group called Kids Country (complete with matching T-shirts!) he was a regular on the popular Aussie TV show *Reg Lindsay's Country Homestead*.

Luckily for us, one of those pre-teen appearances has survived to delight YouTube users the world over. And what is the song they are performing? Well, it's Buddy Holly's 'It's So Easy!' And yes, as he always has done, 11-year-old Keith makes it look just that!
– Bob Harris

WHEN SIN STOPS (LOVE BEGINS)
On 10 September 1958, Buddy returned to Clovis for a new recording session at Norman Petty's studio, which yielded 'Reminiscing' and 'Come Back Baby'. During this session, he also ventured into producing by recording two songs for Lubbock DJ Waylon Jennings: the single 'Jole Blon' and 'When Sin Stops (Love Begins)'.

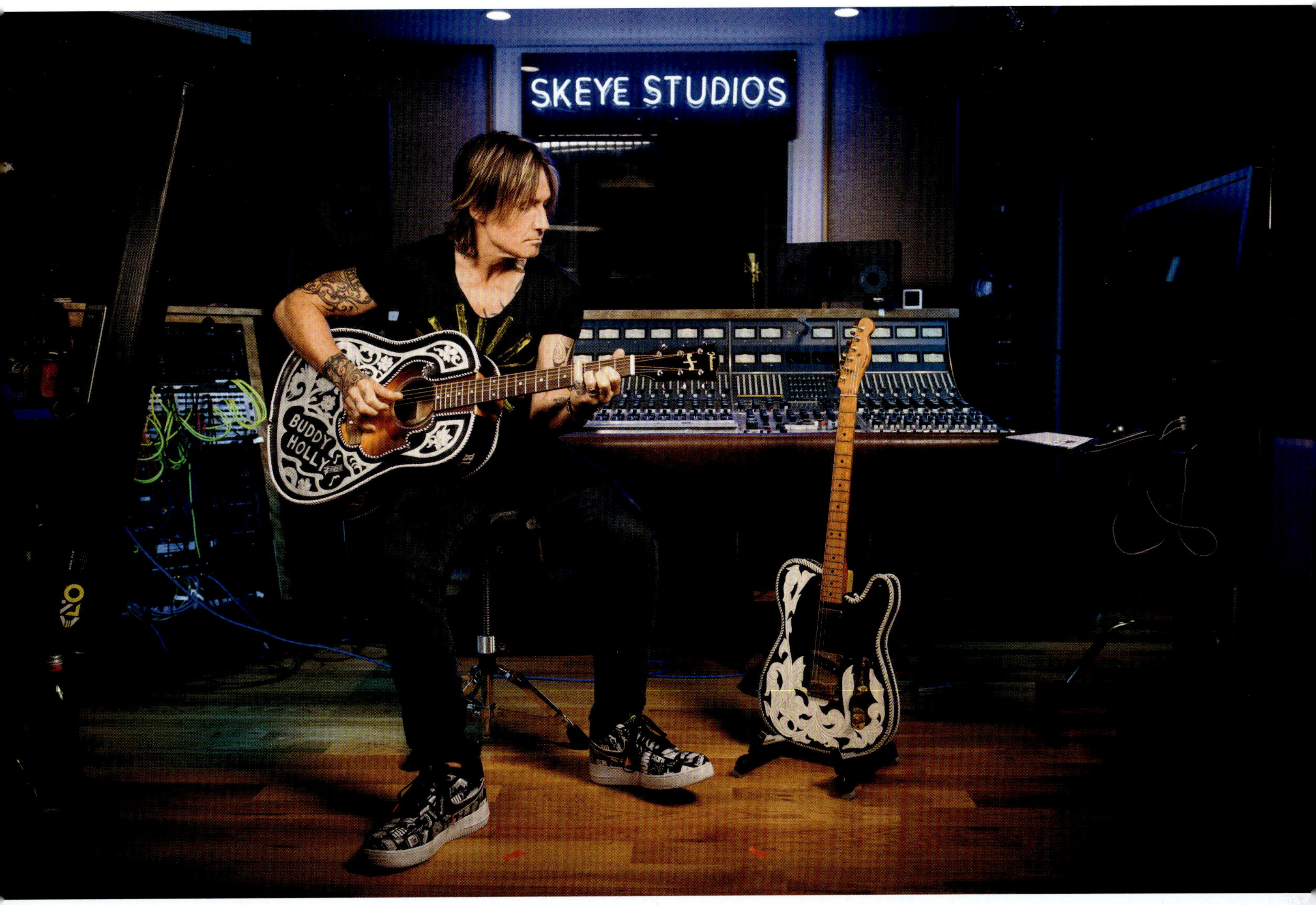
SKEYE STUDIOS
BUDDY HOLLY

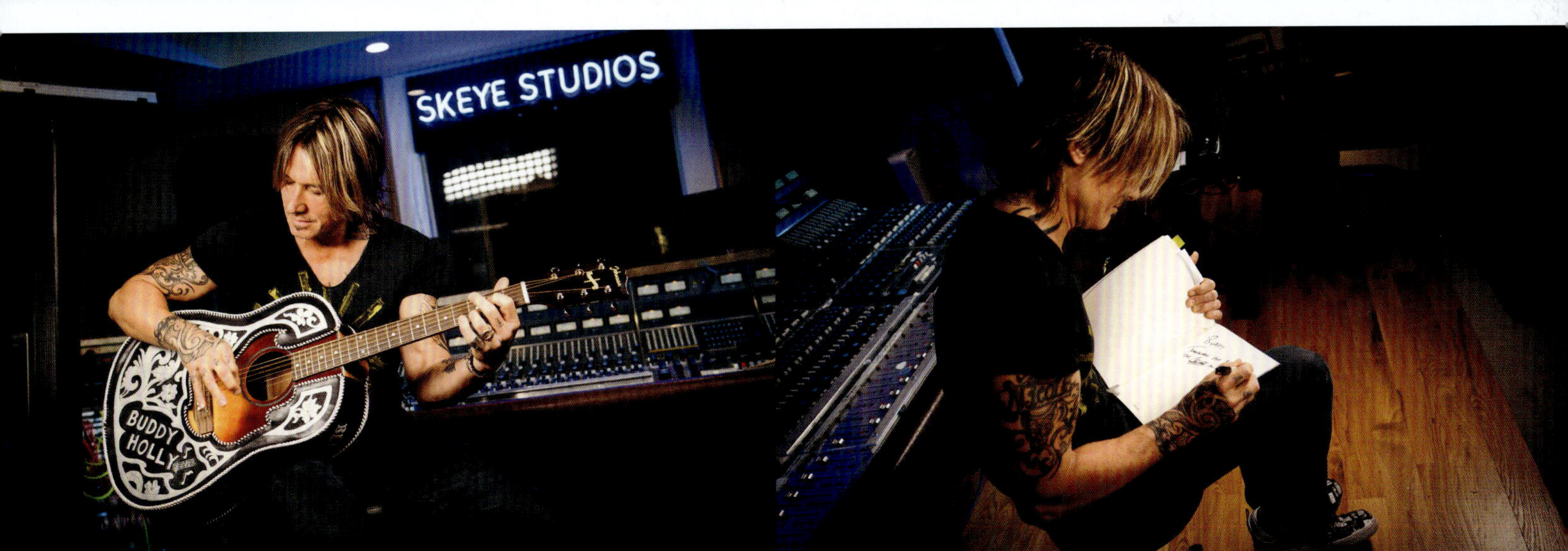

SKEYE STUDIOS
BUDDY HOLLY

PETE TOWNSHEND IS MY GENERATION. We were born within a year of each other and were fortunate, beyond belief, to grow up with rock and roll as the soundtrack to our lives.

This was music that was changing the world. It burst into life like a fire. It was new and it was dangerous and, unlike the music it was replacing, it was all about energy and sexuality. Growing up in the 1950s, we were hearing some of the greatest and most exciting records ever made … in real time. Like all of us, Pete was an Elvis fan. He also bought Eddie Cochran's singles – famously recording his song 'Summertime Blues' on the Who's *Live at Leeds* album in 1970 – and he loved black rhythm and blues. But most of all, he loved the music of Buddy Holly. Pete loved the rawness of Buddy's early records and admired the fact that he wrote and produced his own songs – very rare in those days. Buddy's independence and DIY ethos inspired Pete to insist on always having artistic control of his own work.

There was a tone and an expressive freedom about Buddy's technique that touched Pete's soul. He was massively inspired by the unusual combination of strumming and picking that characterised Buddy's playing and, as his own style evolved, he began to weave Buddy's rhythmic patterns into the Who's early music, fuelling the power chords that became their statement sound.

He worked with the great Jim Marshall to make the turbo-charged amplifiers that boosted the stage volume to 11 and the feedback to the limit. The result was the huge, violent wall of sound that underpinned the anarchic chaos of the band's mid-1960s gigs. They were incredible, and I know. I was there.

Pete and Roger Daltrey are founders of the Teenage Cancer Trust and Teen Cancer America and they are still touring with the Who. And now, all these years later, Pete has become an ambassador for The Buddy Holly Educational Foundation and been presented with a personalised guitar. A proud moment for the Foundation and for a musician who has been inspired by Buddy since those amazing pioneering days of the 1950s.

– Bob Harris

I love Buddy!
My dream was to write as simply as he did but with so much potency.

Pete Townshend

IT'S SO EASY!

Written by Buddy Holly and Norman Petty, 'It's So Easy!' was recorded in May 1958, at Norman Petty's studio, with Tommy Allsup supplementing the Crickets on lead guitar. When released in September 1958, backed with 'Lonesome Tears', the single failed to chart, but 'It's So Easy!' is highly regarded as a favourite by many fans, and is notable as the final release by the Crickets while Buddy was still in the band.

The song has been covered by numerous artists, including Bobby Vee, Skeeter Davis, Connie Francis and Hot Tuna. Paul McCartney recorded the song for the Rave On *tribute album, released in 2011 to commemorate the 75th anniversary of Buddy's birth. The Beatles also performed the song at the 1969* Let It Be *sessions. Perhaps the most notable cover was by Linda Ronstadt, whose 1977 version reached the Top Five in the US.*

On 28 October 1958, Buddy performed 'It's So Easy!', along with 'Heartbeat', on American Bandstand*, which turned out to be his last major television appearance.*

Above: Pete was presented his Buddy Holly guitar by James Burton

PETE TOWNSHEND Buddy Holly was a hero to me. One of the great rhythm players like Eddie Cochran. Both were influenced by the blues, of course, but when I was a kid I didn't really know that. Buddy was a bit of a geek, but so elegant and cool. No frills, just great songs and a great sound.

'I regard myself as a great rhythm player rather than a shredder, so I am a true disciple of Buddy.'

KIMMIE RHODES *'Lonesome Tears'*

"The Yellow Radio"

Before my family moved from Wichita Falls, TX to Lubbock (because a tornado blew my Dad's car lot away) I listened to Buddy on my Baby sitter Bobby Count's yellow radio everyday! My first and favorite musical memory is of singing "That'll Be The Day" and "Peggy Sue" with Bobby & Buddy!

Love & Happiness

Kimmie Rhodes

KIMMIE RHODES IS A TEXAN BY BIRTH who moved with her family to Buddy's home town of Lubbock at the age of five.

Kimmie tours extensively, has written three musicals, appears on TV, headlines concerts, and has worked in films on both sides of the camera. Her songs have appeared on several movie soundtracks, and she has co-written with such eminent songwriters as Waylon Jennings, Beth Nielson Chapman and Emmylou Harris. Artists who have recorded her songs include Peter Frampton, Mark Knopfler, Amy Grant, Trisha Yearwood and John Farnham.

Kimmie has released 16 solo albums since her 1981 debut, named after her band Kimmie Rhodes and the Jackalope Brothers, which was recorded at the studio of the musician she credits as her mentor, Willie Nelson. Her further album releases have also seen duets with Joe Ely, Townes Van Zandt and Willie Nelson. Kimmie has long been a mainstay of the Buddy Holly Educational Foundation songwriting retreats, and in 2018 she was asked by Maria Elena Holly to deliver an acceptance speech for Buddy Holly's induction into the Texas Heritage Songwriters Association Hall of Fame. 'I am grateful to have met Maria Elena Holly, who has honoured me as an ambassador for The Buddy Holly Educational Foundation. I cherish the opportunity to educate and co-write songs with aspiring new young talent. My beautiful Buddy Holly guitar brings great joy and inspires me to remember the spirit of magic and fun that is at the soulful heart of all things Buddy!'

LONESOME TEARS

'Lonesome Tears' was originally released on Brunswick on 12 September 1958. It was written by Buddy Holly and was first recorded by him on 25 May 1958 at Norman Petty Studio, Clovis.

KIMMIE RHODES My earliest musical memory is of a big plastic yellow radio on the windowsill of the home of my babysitter, Bobby Carol. From that radio, Buddy Holly sang 'That'll Be the Day' and 'Peggy Sue' and 'Heartbeat'.

I sang along with Bobby and Buddy, parroting the harmony parts as if they were the melody. My daddy was a Depression-era, self-made boy with a second-grade education. By the time I was five, he had worked his way up from shining shoes on the streets of Wichita Falls, Texas, to owning a used car lot, until the day the sky turned a toxic shade of green and a tornado spun down and blew his cars away. Daddy Ray packed up the family and moved us to Buddy's home town of Lubbock, Texas.

On 9 February 1964, I was ten years old, sitting cross-legged on the living room floor of our little rented house in Lubbock as The Beatles made their American debut on *The Ed Sullivan Show*, influenced in name and musical style by Buddy and the Crickets. I never dreamed that someday I'd be standing on the stage where John Lennon stood that night, singing my own song, West Texas, Heaven, inspired by those early memories.

A couple of decades later, I arrived home in Austin to find a message on my answering machine from Waylon Jennings. Waylon and I became friends and co-writers, and he shared many Buddy stories with me. He gave my daughter Jole his only copy of his first single, a recording of 'Jole Blon', produced by Buddy.

'My beautiful Buddy Holly guitar brings great joy and inspires me to remember the spirit of magic and fun that is at the soulful heart of all things Buddy!'

WILLIE NELSON *'Lonesome Tears'*

BUDDY HOLLY WAS BORN IN LUBBOCK, TEXAS IN 1936. Three years earlier and 300 miles to the south east, another giant of Texas music came into the world. The great Willie Nelson was born in Abbott, a little south of Fort Worth, and although he and Buddy moved in similar musical circles during the 1950s, sadly their paths never crossed.

The nearest they would probably have come to meeting was during Willie's stints as a radio DJ, firstly on KCNC out of Fort Worth in 1956 and then on KVAN in Vancouver, Washington throughout 1957, after which Willie quit the radio business to become a full-time musician. It's entirely probable that among the songs he played during those radio times were Buddy's latest singles!

However, there are some connections that are much more clearly defined, particularly their mutual friendship with Waylon Jennings, who was Buddy's protégé and played bass for him on the Winter Dance Party tour, and who gave up his seat on that fatal plane to the Big Bopper. It was Willie who then helped transform Waylon into the outlaw country superstar that he became.

And there's perhaps the most important link between Buddy and Willie – the Texas spirit. It's a mix of individualism, stubbornness and a total determination not to compromise. Both men had it in spades. The critics didn't matter.

It's a mindset that comes from history and the rich heritage of Texas that is still prevalent today. It was, after all, an independent country for the decade between 1836 and 1845, before joining the Union. Texas has forever had its own identity and the energy of rebellion is still a huge part of the culture of the Lone Star state.

And there are few better examples of that free spirit than Buddy and Willie. Both were pioneers in their own field, neither was willing to compromise their music and both were prepared to walk away from something they didn't want to do. They were Texan titans and musical ground-breakers.

Who knows what would have happened if they'd ever had the chance to work together . . . – *Bob Harris*

ELVIS COSTELLO Despite the coincidence of sharing the same taste in spectacles, I was really too young to be hit full force by the music of Buddy Holly.

In 1960, I was a kid relying on the BBC Light Programme broadcasts. I almost certainly heard someone imitating Buddy's vocal mannerisms and even the pizzicato string accompaniment of the arrangements before I even registered any of his own records. But that was flimsy English rock and roll for you; more of a facsimile than a thrill.

That all changed with the arrival of The Beatles. Their faithful and affectionate version of 'Words of Love' and their acknowledgement of Buddy, along with Little Richard, Chuck Berry, the Everly Brothers and even the Miracles, was a miracle in itself. Less confident, more arrogant songwriters might have covered their tracks in pursuit of the illusion of originality. John and Paul never hid what they had learned from Buddy and all their other favourites.

I didn't have any older brother or sister to tell me to listen to Buddy Holly, so I was alone with my small stack of records and a fistful of fingers that wouldn't always obey me when I picked up the guitar. But as I learned to play and then to write, the drive of Buddy's songs filtered through versions of 'Not Fade Away' by both the Rolling Stones and the Grateful Dead. Then I understood the singular nature of his ballads and his brilliance as an arranger of both singers and small groups, responding to larger orchestrations. I just wish we could hear where this all would have led in time.

The only one of Buddy's songs I have ever performed is 'True Love Ways', which I would sing in the finale of shows around 1987. These featured my own recent compositions alongside selections from the Great American Songbook – but not the familiar exclusive club that only extends to George Gershwin and Irving Berlin but one that would cheerfully and rightfully welcome Hank Williams, Mose Allison, Allen Toussaint, Dan Penn, Willie Dixon and, of course, Buddy Holly.

Whenever I struggled to find a closing sentiment in among my own love songs, filled as they were with crooked lines and trapdoors, the straightforward, heartfelt tone of Buddy's 'True Love Ways' would be exactly what I needed to sing at that moment.

I will be forever grateful to him.

This beautiful guitar will always lead me to 'True Love Ways'
We are all in Buddy's debt
Elvis Costello

REMINISCING

'Reminiscing' was recorded by Buddy Holly on 10 September 1958 at Norman Petty's studio. Buddy flew saxophonist King Curtis in especially for this session, which also included 'Come Back Baby' and two songs by Waylon Jennings. Although Buddy actually wrote 'Reminiscing', he gave the writing credit to Curtis for the favour of coming to Texas to perform. The song features Buddy on vocals and guitar, George Atwood on bass and Bo Clarke on drums.

It was first released on Coral on 20 August 1962 as the B-side of the posthumous 'Wait Till the Sun Shines Nellie' single.

THE SON OF A JAZZ TRUMPETER, London-born Declan MacManus, better known as Elvis Costello, came to prominence as a post-punk singer-songwriter in the 1970s. His critically acclaimed debut album, *My Aim Is True*, was released in 1977 followed by *This Year's Model* in 1978, by which time he had added the Attractions as his backing band.

With his oversized glasses giving him a Buddy Holly look, Elvis went on to have many more single and album successes over the subsequent decades. Differences between Elvis and the Attractions caused them to part company in 1986 (although they came back together for two albums in the mid-1990s), and much of his work since then has been as a solo artist. He has co-written several original songs for motion pictures in collaboration with Burt Bacharach and T-Bone Burnett. He has also ventured into different musical genres, including country, jazz and classical.

In 2019, Elvis received an OBE for his services to music.

Link Wray once told me that Ritchie was indian wrestling + knocking every one out on the tour. He always played from his heart and soul

MARIO VALENS *'La Bamba'*

THE LATE GREAT RITCHIE VALENS WASN'T THE ONLY MUSICAL TALENT IN THE FAMILY. Mario, who was only 18 months old when his big brother passed away, knows Ritchie through his music and through stories told by Mama, other family members, and fellow musicians who toured with Ritchie, like Tommy Allsup, Link Wray, and Chris Montez. Daniel Valdez – the younger brother of Luis Valdez, who was the writer and director of the Ritchie Valens biopic *La Bamba* – also played an important role inspiring Mario through his music.

Ritchie's fire and drive fuelled a passion for music in Mario, who plays harmonica, writes for and sings in his own group, the Backyard Blues Band.

Mario's band has appeared as an opening act for many well-known artists including John Lee Hooker, Los Lobos and George Thorogood and the Destroyers. Dick Dale, famous surf guitarist who toured with Ritchie, told Mario that he called Ritchie 'Ricardo, my latin buddy'.

Mario performed at the Viva Las Vegas Rockabilly Weekend with the Chop Tops as part of their farewell tour and was invited to perform as part of the All Star Jam at Ritchie's induction into the Rock and Roll Hall of Fame, at the Waldorf Astoria in New York City.

With his family's encouragement, Mario now performs some of Ritchie's songs in his concerts.

'My memories of Buddy and Ritchie come from my brother Bob and Mama, telling me about Ritchie creating songs in the bedroom that came from the heart, with soul. I love all of Buddy's music too and like to play some Buddy tunes and try to put my own heart and soul into it.'

LA BAMBA

In October 1958 Del-Fi released Ritchie Valens's rock and roll version of the Mexican folk song 'La Bamba'.

A Top 40 hit in the US charts, Valens's 'La Bamba' is ranked number 345 on Rolling Stone *magazine's list of the 500 Greatest Songs of All Time and it is included in the Rock and Roll Hall of Fame's list of 500 songs that were influential in shaping rock and roll. Valens was performing this song during the ill-fated Winter Dance Party tour which he joined alongside Buddy Holly and the Big Bopper.*

TO HEAR THE MAGICAL SOUND OF
"PEGGY SUE" COMING OUT OF MY
RADIO AS A YOUNGSTER WAS
MIND-BLOWING, AND PUSHED ME TO
LEARN ABOUT RECORDING & PRODUCTION.
"WELL ALRIGHT" HAS GIVEN ME SO MUCH
JOY AS A SONG AND AS A GUITAR.
BUDDY'S GIFT TO THE WORLD REALLY
CAN'T BE MEASURED ...
I ASPIRE TO CARRY A FRACTION
OF THAT JOY FORWARD FOR GENERATIONS
TO COME ——

John Jorgenson
HOLLYWOOD, CA

JOHN JORGENSON COMES FROM A MUSICAL FAMILY, his father an orchestral conductor and college music professor and his mother a piano teacher. He began playing professionally at the age of 14 and has become a hugely respected multi-instrumentalist, winning the Academy of Country Music's Guitarist of the Year award three years running.

John formed the Desert Rose Band in 1986 with former Byrd Chris Hillman and their success propelled him from being a local musician to a national and international recording artist with five US number one singles and seven more in the Top Ten.

In 1993, John formed the Hellecasters with Will Ray and Jerry Donahue, and what was intended as a short-term collaboration resulted in four albums over the next 12 years. In 1994, he joined Elton John's band for an 18-month tour and stayed with them for six years. He has also recorded and toured with many other major artists, including Willie Nelson, Roy Orbison, Emmylou Harris, Luciano Pavarotti, Johnny Cash, Barbra Streisand and Bob Dylan.

His love of 'gypsy jazz' inspired him to form the John Jorgenson Quintet in 2004 and in the same year he portrayed Django Reinhardt in the film *Head in the Clouds*. In 2009, he won a Grammy, with several other top guitarists, for the song 'Cluster Pluck'. – *Mike Read*

WELL ... ALL RIGHT

Inspired by one of Little Richard's favourite expressions, 'Well ... All Right' was written by Buddy Holly, Jerry Allison, Joe B. Mauldin and Norman Petty and recorded on 12 February 1958 at Norman Petty's studio. The song was chosen as the B-side of the 'Heartbeat' single, released on Coral on 5 November 1958.

JOHN JORGENSON As a youngster growing up in Southern California in the 1960s, I became obsessed with pop music and rock and roll early on. I was drawn to 1950s records that were considered 'oldies' even then – songs by the Everly Brothers, the Coasters, Elvis, Chuck Berry, Eddie Cochran and especially Buddy Holly and the Crickets.

As the years went by, I learned to play guitar and write songs, and began to understand Buddy's huge musical influence on not only The Beatles, but on many other artists of the day. Equally astonishing is the timelessness of Buddy's songwriting and its ability to be interpreted over the decades by artists as varied as Blind Faith and Linda Ronstadt. As I learned about production, I also became aware of how ground-breaking and influential the recording techniques pioneered by Norman Petty on Buddy's records were, and how important they would become to the overall sound of the pop music that followed.

'As the years went by, I began to understand Buddy's huge musical influence.'

That'll Be the Day
woke me up on my
clock radio most mornings
in 4th grade. I've had a
crush on him and his music
ever since!

Rave On Buddy Holly

Linda Ronstadt

HEARTBEAT

Written by Bob Montgomery and Norman Petty and recorded by Buddy on 25 May 1958 at Norman Petty's studio, 'Heartbeat' was first released as a single on Coral on 5 November 1958.

Right: Sheet music for 'It's So Easy', written by Buddy and Norman Petty and released by Linda Ronstadt in 1977

'"That'll Be the Day" woke me up on my clock radio most mornings in fourth grade. I've had a crush on Buddy and his music ever since. Rave on, Buddy Holly!'

FEW ARTISTS ARE MORE UNIVERSALLY LOVED AND MORE DEEPLY RESPECTED THAN LINDA RONSTADT. Blessed with a voice from the stars, she has become one of the most successful and influential female artists of all time.

Linda burst onto the Southern California music scene in the late 1960s, blazing a trail for the next generations of female artists to follow. She was a successful woman in a male-dominated world. From 1975 to 1978, she scored no fewer than six Top Five albums in the US, success that opened the pathway to record-breaking arena tours, taking her onto stages with Jackson Browne, the Eagles and the Rolling Stones and earning her the title of the 'Queen of Rock'.

Linda was inducted into the Rock and Roll Hall of Fame in 2014, has received 11 Grammys and two Academy of Country Music Awards, among many other honours that acknowledge the beautiful, interpretive brilliance she brings to locating the emotional heart of a song. She has always loved to craft reinterpretations of numbers from the past, having topped the US charts with songs previously recorded by Betty Everett, the Everly Brothers and Roy Orbison, but she is particularly passionate about the work of Buddy Holly, a massive influence on her music. She released 'That'll Be the Day' in 1976, 'It's So Easy' a year later, 'Rave On' in 1980, 'Oh Boy!' in 1989, 'Well ... All Right' in 1995 and 'Maybe Baby' in 2011, all of them proud interpretations of the music she adores. Linda's musical interpretations underscore her beautiful connection to Buddy. Her ground-breaking covers of some of his most famous songs stand, to this day, as glorious endorsements, not only of his lasting impact on the music industry, but also of our enduring love of the woman who has brought new life to a catalogue of timeless classics. – *Bob Harris*

BRIAN MAY *'Moondreams'*

My Inspiration!

My Dream!!!

Buddy Holly and the Crickets changed my life forever – and are still with me every day – EVERY DAY!!!

Eternal THANKS!!!

Bri

BRIAN MAY FORMED THE BAND SMILE with Tim Staffell in 1968, later to be joined by drummer Roger Taylor, but the line-up only lasted a few years before Staffell's departure and the arrival of Smile fan Freddie Mercury. Freddie suggested a name change to Queen and bassist John Deacon was recruited before the band's eponymous debut album of 1973. With the release of *A Night at the Opera* and the single it spawned – 'Bohemian Rhapsody' – Queen became one of the biggest bands in the world. Through Queen, Brian became regarded as a virtuoso musician and was identified by a distinctive sound created through the layering of guitars. He often used a home-built electric guitar called the Red Special. He also contributed as a songwriter; some of the hits Brian penned for the band include 'We Will Rock You' and 'I Want It All'.

Brian topped the list of the 100 Greatest Guitarists of All Time, as voted for by *Total Guitar/Guitar World* readers in January 2023. He was cited for 'timeless riffs that will forever remain as exhilarating as the first time we ever heard them'. In 2001 he was inducted into the Rock and Roll Hall of Fame as a member of Queen and in 2018 the band received the Grammy Lifetime Achievement Award.

Away from music, Brian has a PhD in astrophysics, which enabled him to serve as a science team collaborator with NASA's 'New Horizons' Pluto mission, while he is also an ardent animal rights campaigner through his Save Me Trust organisation.

MOONDREAMS

Written by Norman Petty, 'Moondreams' was originally released by the Norman Petty Trio in 1957. One year on, it became one of four songs recorded by Buddy Holly during a session on 21 October 1958 at Decca's Pythian Temple studios in New York City, where he was accompanied by the Dick Jacobs Orchestra. It was released posthumously on the album The Buddy Holly Story Vol. II, *and, in the UK, as a B-side to 'True Love Ways', in May 1960.*

'Buddy's persona, his songs, his guitar playing, and those awesome harmonies still resonate with me today.'

BRIAN MAY Buddy Holly was my absolute hero as a kid. Those first Crickets singles on 45 rpm discs with black labels, slipped into plain brown paper sleeves, were probably the most exciting acquisitions of my whole childhood. They're still some of my most treasured possessions. The moment when I learned of Buddy's tragic death remains etched indelibly in my mind. I heard the words 'Buddy Holly has been killed in a plane crash' and I rushed downstairs to tell my mum and dad, hardly able to speak. In that moment of grief, I think something inside me decided that the world that Buddy Holly and the Crickets had carved out was where I wanted to be.

I can't even begin to detail how many and how strong are the influences on my musical path from Buddy. The guitar that The Buddy Holly Educational Foundation presented to me is now another of my treasured possessions, and a material symbol, if I ever needed it, of the fact that I still feel like I carry a piece of Buddy inside me.

BUDDY HOLLY IS MY FAVOURITE POP SONG WRITER IN SO MANY WAYS. SIMPLE MELODIES AND CHORDS BUT ASSEMBLED WITH MYSTICAL SKILL AND PRECISION. MASTERPIECES OF MUSICAL + LYRICAL ELEGANCE

Peter Asher

PETER ASHER HAS CONTRIBUTED MUCH TO BUDDY HOLLY'S LEGACY throughout his illustrious career in music. He and his schoolfriend Gordon Waller formed the duo Peter and Gordon in 1962 and they had a hit on both sides of the Atlantic three years later with their beautiful rendition of 'True Love Ways'.

Their first and biggest hit was with Lennon and McCartney's 'A World Without Love', which was followed by another of their songs, 'Nobody I Know'. Paul McCartney wrote another song for them, 'Woman', under the pseudonym of Bernard Webb.

Peter would work with and produce many top artists after Peter and Gordon split up in 1968, initially taking charge of the A&R Department at The Beatles' Apple Records. He signed and produced many multi-platinum albums for James Taylor, the first non-British artist to be released on the Apple label. Peter's work with James led to further work with his sister Kate Taylor, who recommended him to Linda Ronstadt. As manager and producer, he oversaw further landmark releases with Linda, including several much-loved Buddy covers.

In 2011 Peter was the executive producer for *Listen to Me: Buddy Holly*, a compilation album which featured a cavalcade of musicians, many of whom subsequently joined The Buddy Holly Educational Foundation as ambassadors. He was also music supervisor, producer and co-host of the award-winning accompanying concert, which celebrated Buddy's 75th birthday.

'The creative and extraordinary body of work with which Buddy left us is unequalled.'

PETER ASHER I became a devoted fan of Buddy and his records. In the first place, he broke the mould of the traditional pop star, proving that one could be a bit nerdy looking and still be cool; for some reason I found this deeply reassuring! I think he was the first rocker to ever wear glasses – and I tried to find exactly those frames for myself.

One of my favourite songs was 'True Love Ways', which is a strange phrase and a beautiful song I much enjoyed singing with my old partner Gordon Waller, and it became a big hit for us. The work that Buddy did in the studio was as ground-breaking as his songwriting – little pitter-patter percussion parts instead of a regular drum beat, a celeste in place of the expected keyboard part, the little vocal hiccups which became a much-imitated element of his singing style.

TRUE LOVE WAYS

'True Love Ways' was first released on Coral on 11 April 1960. It was written by Buddy Holly and Norman Petty and was recorded by Buddy on 21 October 1958 at Decca's Pythian Temple studios in New York City. The melody was based on Buddy's favourite gospel song, 'I'll Be Alright', which was played at his funeral.

There has been much discussion about who really wrote this song. It is agreed that Buddy composed the basic melody, but did he write the lyrics? Norman and Vi Petty have both stated that Buddy stopped by one day to leave the melody with them and that Norman then gave Buddy a songsheet with a completed version of the song with lyrics by Petty. The Pettys had also made a demo of the song, with Vi singing, but a record of her version wasn't pressed until 1960 and then wasn't commercially sold, only given away to fans and others. As the New York 'string session' at the Pythian Temple was pretty much Norman Petty's idea, and Buddy did record another of Petty's songs ('Moondreams') during the session, this account of how 'True Love Ways' was written is very plausible.

To Buddy
Friends Forever!!
Rock on.... Always
With Great Love,
Dion

THAT MAKES IT TOUGH

Recorded in Buddy Holly's New York apartment on 8 December 1958, 'That Makes It Tough' was first released on Coral on 25 June 1959 as part of the US 'Peggy Sue Got Married' EP. Buddy sings vocals and plays acoustic guitar.

'If Buddy was around today, he'd be producing young artists and championing the cause.'

DION DiMUCCI Buddy Holly – what an amazing talent. He had it all: he was a great friend, guitar player, songwriter, entertainer and visionary. We travelled the country back in 1958 and 1959 … we rocked some towns. I was fortunate to be presented with my Buddy Holly 'That Makes It Tough' guitar, which I will cherish forever, my epic keepsake. I miss him.

I remember Buddy as a great guy, a gentleman, statuesque, decisive, passionate and focused. A man on a mission. He was very thoughtful. He was one of a kind and I'm blessed to have known him. Friends forever, Dion.

DION DEVELOPED A LOVE OF MUSIC AT AN EARLY AGE, having toured with his father, Pasquale DiMucci, who was a vaudeville entertainer. Keen on the blues and what would become known as doo-wop, he learned his vocal skills singing a cappella on street corners in the Bronx, New York. Dion's first record release, 'The Chosen Few', was credited to Dion and the Timberlanes, with backing vocals from a group he'd never met. It motivated him to find three more like-minded singers, who became the Belmonts, taking their name from the street on which some of them lived.

The breakthrough for Dion and the Belmonts came in April 1958 with 'I Wonder Why', which made it to number 22 on the US chart. Further singles earned them a place on Alan Freed's Biggest Show of Stars for Fall 1958, and then the Winter Dance Party tour. Despite the tragic events of 3 February 1959, the tour continued on for another 13 dates.

The following month, 'A Teenager in Love' became a hit on both sides of the Atlantic for Dion and the Belmonts. By the time Dion made the decision to go it alone, the group had run up a string of eight consecutive US hit singles. 'Runaround Sue' and 'The Wanderer' were high points of his solo career, along with the distinction that he and Bob Dylan were the only rock artists to be featured on the cover of The Beatles' *Sgt. Pepper's Lonely Hearts Club Band*. – *Mike Read*

PROBABLY THE ONLY RECIPIENT OF A BUDDY HOLLY GUITAR to have performed at base camp on Mount Everest, Glenn Tilbrook is a founder member of Squeeze with Chris Difford, whom he met after Chris put an ad in a local sweet shop window in Greenwich, London. Difford and Tilbrook have written many classic hits together for the band throughout its various different incarnations over more than four decades.

Having broken up in 1983, Squeeze reunited in 1985. However, during those two years Glenn and Chris continued to work together, creating the Squeeze-based musical *Labelled with Love* with John Turner and releasing a self-titled album as a duo.

When the band parted ways again in 1999, Glenn pursued a solo career, touring the US and UK and releasing two albums. His 2001 US tour was filmed for the 2006 documentary *Glenn Tilbrook: One for the Road*. A year later, Squeeze were back performing once again and have continued to do so, on and off, ever since.

Glenn supports Mike Peters's Love Hope Strength Foundation, a charity that promotes innovative music-related, outreach and awareness programmes for leukaemia and cancer sufferers, survivors and their families.

When I was 14 years old
I learned, & fell in love with.
Everyday. One great song
out of many, & still so Fresh!
with love & much respect

Glenn Tilbrook xxxx

Buddy
Soon as We Saw Him
Had to Look Like and be like
Never Stopped Eh!!
B Poole
TREMELOES

'I wore glasses at school so the lads suggested I wear the horn-rimmed ones for "playing", as we called it.'

BRIAN POOLE When the Tremeloes and I were all at school in Barking, Essex, we heard Buddy Holly on Radio Luxembourg and decided then and there that the set we performed at American Air Force bases would be all Buddy Holly and Crickets songs. Good times. Do your A-level homework, then travel to maybe Brize Norton or Bentwaters, play, then drive home for school next day.

We wrote to Buddy Holly and the Crickets through Norman Petty and he sent us songs over the years, including one of our biggest hits, 'Someone, Someone'. We played this song for years before recording it. Norman sent us many songs and we were even asked to play them at Douglas House, the American Air Force headquarters in London.

The guitar was really presented to Ally McErlaine, my son-in-law, and Shelly Poole, my daughter, as Ally used it on stage with his bands Texas and Red Sky July.

IN THE MID-1950S, BRIAN POOLE, HEAVILY INFLUENCED BY BUDDY HOLLY and the Crickets, started performing with friends Alan Blakley and Alan Howard. They went on to form the Tremeloes, who predominantly covered Buddy Holly and the Crickets records, with Brian as lead vocalist. With their unique sense of harmony, the Tremeloes soon developed a wide fanbase and following. In 1964, a long-standing correspondence with Buddy's manager and producer Norman Petty led to Brian and the Tremeloes covering 'Someone, Someone', which had been the Crickets' first release after separating from Buddy. Norman went on to play piano on two other Tremeloes recordings, 'The Three Bells' and 'After a While'.

Brian Poole received his replica of the Buddy Holly J-45 in conjunction with his daughter, Shelly Poole, and her husband, Ally McErlaine.

WHAT TO DO

Recorded in Buddy Holly's New York apartment on 3 December 1958, 'What to Do' was first released in 1960 on the Coral compilation The Buddy Holly Story Vol. II. *Buddy sings vocals and plays acoustic guitar.*

Above left: An image of Brian Poole with Norman Petty shown on a phone screen

DAVID FRIZZELL *'Learning the Game'*

My Brother Lefty & I heard "That'll Be the Day" at the same Time, I think I learned To sing that day -

David Frizzell

DAVID FRIZZELL The Buddy Holly Educational Foundation called me and asked if I could write a song for Maria Elena for her birthday. After that, we started doing some songs, and I asked some of my friends to come in and join me. I didn't want to do it all by myself. We had some great artists and musicians … I called Sonny Curtis and got him involved with it. He's an amazing person and such a great songwriter. He was so gracious. We did one of his early songs, 'Rock Around with Ollie Vee', which Buddy had recorded in 1956. We just had a ball.

'When I started out in the business working for Lefty, opening his shows, I was singing Buddy Holly songs.'

BORN IN EL DORADO, ARKANSAS, DAVID FRIZZELL began performing in 1953 at the age of 12. He toured with his brother, country singer Lefty Frizzell, during the 1950s and 1960s before serving in the US Air Force during the Vietnam War.

In 1981, David had his first number one country hit with 'You're the Reason God Made Oklahoma', duetting with Shelly West, daughter of country star Dottie West. The song won the Country Music Association's Song of the Year and Vocal Duet of the Year. It was also nominated for a Grammy and featured in the Clint Eastwood movie *Any Which Way You Can*. David and Shelly also won the Academy of Country Music award for Vocal Duo of the Year in 1981 and 1982. In 1981, David had another number one on the country chart with his solo single 'I'm Gonna Hire a Wino to Decorate Our Home'. Between 1981 and 1984 he had five hit country albums with Shelly West and two solo albums, and the duo toured regularly up until Shelly's retirement in 2015.

In 2013, David Frizzell breathed new life into the Buddy Holly songs he sang as a boy, when The Buddy Holly Educational Foundation invited him to produce a very special album dedicated to the music of Buddy Holly and the Crickets. David kindly agreed, gathered some wonderful country artists, including Sonny Curtis, T. Graham Brown, Helen Cornelius, Jimmy Fortune and Merle Haggard, and created *Buddy Holly Country Tribute: Remember Me*.

Buddy Holly, was of course, One of the Singer/Songwriters That Dad First heard, back in his youth, along with McCartney. So impressed by Buddy's abilities, That likely Buddy was certainly One of the Triggers, for Dad and the boys to start writing their own Material...

And it is evident of Dad's love & respect for Buddy Holly, by virtue of the fact, That Dad plaid tribute to his hero, by recording Peggy Sue on his Rock'n'Roll Album, and in turn, I have come to love Buddy's work, through Dad...

Julian Lennon

x

JULIAN LENNON IS A LOVELY GUY AND AN AWESOME TALENT. He is a Grammy-nominated musician, whose compelling seven-album catalogue spans four decades. From his brilliant debut, *Valotte*, released in 1984, to his 2022 soundscape *Jude*, he has been his own musical master.

He has an extraordinary eye, announcing his arrival in the fine art photography space in 2010 with a beautiful and triumphant debut exhibition, 'Timeless', at the Morrison Hotel Gallery in New York. It was a take-notice moment, since when he has exhibited his visual work all over the world.

As the author of a children's book trilogy, *Touch the Earth*, and its follow-up, *The Morning Tribe*, he is the recipient of the World Literacy Award for his significant contribution to the promotion of literacy and the protection of the environment.

Julian founded the White Feather Foundation in 2007 to help preserve and protect indigenous cultures, a vision which has now expanded to support projects worldwide in the areas of education, health and clean water, work that contributed to his being named a Peace Laureate by UNESCO in 2020. Like his father, he has done work to be proud of.

I am extremely fortunate to have met John Lennon. My producer Mike Appleton and I got to spend a couple of days with him in 1975, filming an interview with him for our BBC television music show *The Old Grey Whistle Test*. He had the *Rock 'n' Roll* album coming out and we filmed a wonderful, relaxed conversation, in which he talked about his family, his life and the songs on the record, one of which was a great cover of 'Peggy Sue'. John was a massive Buddy Holly fan. He'd recorded 'That'll Be the Day' during his first ever recording session with Paul McCartney and George Harrison in a little studio in Liverpool in 1958 and had carried his love of Buddy's records into The Beatles, making sure that every one of the band's new singles sounded slightly different from all the others – a true Buddy Holly trademark.

Because of his green card issues at the time, John was unable to leave America and he was missing Julian. The interview between us was part of a postcard he was sending to his lad back in Blighty.

It is fabulous and fitting that Julian has received his Buddy Holly guitar. It's an important moment and a circle completed. He and his dad embody a brave and caring spirit. Truly they are a force for good in the world.
– *Bob Harris*

LEARNING THE GAME
Recorded in Buddy Holly's New York apartment on 17 December 1958, 'Learning the Game' was first released by Coral on 25 June 1959 as part of the US 'Peggy Sue Got Married' EP. Buddy sings vocals and plays acoustic guitar.

HANK MARVIN *'You're the One'*

When the "CHIRPING CRICKETS" L.P was released, I rushed out, bought it, and played it to within an inch of its life while drooling over the guitars shown on the cover. I learned all the songs, and I spent hours learning to copy Buddy's lead guitar solos, Buddy & the Crickets still have a special place in my heart.

EAST PERTH WA 6004 (D)

AS A YOUNG TEENAGER, HANK MARVIN PLAYED THE BANJO and the piano, but after hearing Buddy Holly, he knew that he had to learn the guitar.

In late September 1958, Cliff Richard's manager John Foster – in an attempt to find a lead guitarist for Cliff's first professional tour – came to Soho looking for Tony Sheridan, who had been recommended. Fortunately, John heard Hank play and told him, 'The gig's yours if you want it.' On hearing they also needed a rhythm guitarist, Hank recommended his friend Bruce Welch, and they, along with Jet Harris and Tony Meehan, became the Drifters. However, in 1959, to avoid confusion with the American vocal group of the same name, they renamed themselves the Shadows. Following the phenomenal success of their first number one, 'Apache', they also had a long career in their own right. Knowing how much Hank had wanted a Stratocaster, Cliff brought a fiesta red one back from the States as a present for him. It was an inspired gift.

'That first Strat made an appearance in 1959,' said Hank later. 'My guitar had a horribly bent neck, so Cliff wanted to buy me a good guitar. We decided that the Fender was the way to go.' And why was that? Why did Hank and so many other young players dream of owning that magnificent instrument? 'Because we'd seen Buddy Holly with one on the Crickets album cover!' Hank used it to create an instantly recognisable tremolo sound and between them, Cliff and the Shadows went on to dominate the UK charts for years to come.

In the mid-1990s Hank recorded *Hank Plays Holly*, an instrumental album of Buddy Holly and the Crickets songs, including 'It Doesn't Matter Anymore', 'Peggy Sue' and 'Raining in My Heart'. Fittingly for the original iconic Strat player in the UK, Hank's Buddy Holly guitar is entitled 'You're the One'. – *Mike Read*

YOU'RE THE ONE

'You're the One' was written and recorded by Buddy Holly, Ray 'Slim' Corbin and Waylon Jennings on 27 December 1958 at the KLLL radio studio in Lubbock, TX. Someone bet Buddy that he couldn't write a new song in 30 minutes. This is the result – done in 20 minutes and then recorded on KLLL's acetate machine. It was first released on the Coral compilation Showcase *on 18 May 1964.*

HANK MARVIN I first heard the Crickets hit 'That'll Be the Day' on a local café jukebox. It began with Buddy's guitar intro … what a sound, what a record. It was sonic heaven! The song just stopped me in my tracks. Well, it would have if I hadn't been sitting down.

I became an instant fan, so when *The 'Chirping' Crickets* was released in the UK I rushed out and bought it. The LP was played within an inch of its life while I drooled over the guitars shown on the cover, one of which was Buddy's sunburst Fender Stratocaster. Bruce Welch and I learned all the songs and I spent hours trying to copy Buddy's lead guitar solos. In 1959 Cliff bought me a red Fender Stratocaster with a Bird's Eye Maple neck, a whammy bar and gold-plated hardware. It looked better than Buddy's – it certainly caught your attention.

To revisit those songs and interpret them as guitar instrumentals on *Hank Plays Holly* was a challenge that made all of the creative juices flow. It was a pleasure to work on new arrangements with Warren Bennett, who grew the ideas into reality and did a wonderful job. I am very proud of that album and would like to think that Buddy would have approved.

'Buddy was a major influence on my musical development.'

THE STRYPES *'Fool's Paradise'*

THE STRYPES WERE STILL SCHOOLBOYS in Cavan, Ireland, when they signed a major record deal with Mercury Records and a management deal with Rocket Music.

From 2013 until their split in 2018 the band released three albums, two of which charted Top 20 in the UK. Ross Farrelly, Josh McClorey, Pete O'Hanlon and Evan Walsh shared a passion for 1950s rock and roll and their breakout track 'You Can't Judge a Book' was a Bo Diddley cover, an artist they discovered listening to Buddy's Bo-influenced 'Not Fade Away'. Buddy's music was a constant on tour bus journeys with the lads loving his 'edgier' side – 'Midnight Shift', 'Rock Around with Ollie Vee' and 'Well … All Right' were particular favourites.

The Strypes toured all over the world playing iconic venues and festivals, their passion for music always fuelled by a love of true pioneering genius from greats like Buddy Holly. Love for real, not fade away … – *Niall Walsh (The Strypes' manager)*

FOOL'S PARADISE

Recorded by Buddy Holly, Joe B. Mauldin and Jerry Allison at Norman Petty's studio on 13 February 1958, 'Fool's Paradise' was written by Horace Linsley, Sonny LeGlaire and Norman Petty. It was first released on Brunswick as the B-side of 'Think It Over' on 27 May 1958.

Right: Josh McClorey at the Chris Difford Songwriting Retreat, 2014

CHAPTER FIVE

1959

WINTER DANCE PARTY POSTER
Probably the only surviving poster for a concert which took place on 3 February 1959 in Moorhead, Minnesota, the day after the three headlining musicians, Buddy Holly, Ritchie Valens and the Big Bopper (J.P. Richardson) died in a plane crash en route. In 2022 this precious artifact became the most expensive poster ever auctioned when it sold for $447,000.

JOHN THOMAS The bell above the door to Adair Music Company in Lubbock, Texas clangs again. But this time, the young man who entered the shop only half an hour ago exits. While he had shuffled in minutes ago, shoulders slumping, appearing reticent, looking at his feet, he now walks with a spring in his step, head up, and he sports a broad smile. He's holding one key to his future in his right hand. That's a 1954 sunburst Fender Stratocaster he's carrying. Or maybe it's a 1955 model. If you enjoy a good internet wormhole, try googling 'Was Buddy Holly's first Stratocaster a 1954 or a 1955 model?' You'll land upon a heated debate, split roughly 50/50, based on a few grainy photographs and a lot of speculation. Whatever its provenance, Buddy's futuristic guitar would soon be turning heads at sock hops and high school dances.

Buddy Holly and his guitar would turn even more heads with the 27 November 1957 release of *The 'Chirping' Crickets*. By most accounts, Buddy wasn't playing that 1954 or 1955 Stratocaster when he made his debut on *The Ed Sullivan Show* on 1 December 1957. The guitar, story after story on the internet proclaims, had been stolen and Buddy quickly purchased what most consider a 1957 Stratocaster from a Detroit music shop just in time for the gig. Curiously, though, a few weeks later, he appears on *The Ed Sullivan Show* playing what looked like a well-used instrument. Fender equipped pre-1957 Stratocasters with pick-up covers formed from polystyrene, a brittle material that often cracked when struck by a guitar pick. Chunks of the polystyrene have chipped off the pick-up covers, likely because Buddy used those vicious downstrokes to pound out songs like 'Peggy Sue'.

Holly historian Bill Griggs had a conversation with a bus driver for Buddy's spring 1958 tour. On 9 April, Buddy's Fender Stratocaster was stolen off the bus in Canada during a stop in Windsor, Ontario. Buddy quickly purchased a replacement. On 22 April 1958, its replacement was stolen at a stop in East St Louis, Missouri. Though Chris Rees, another Buddy Holly authority, thinks that there may only have been one theft.

This brings us to the one existing verified Buddy Holly Stratocaster, which resides in the Buddy Holly Center in Lubbock, Texas. It's the guitar he played during his last gig, at the Surf Ballroom in Clear Lake, Iowa. Buddy, of course, boarded the airplane on 3 February 1959, but his instrument stayed on the tour bus. Tommy Allsup, who had recently joined Buddy's band as second guitarist, delivered the guitar to the Holley family in Lubbock. The guitar features a sunburst finish. However, it's not the two-tone sunburst of earlier guitars but the three-tone finish that Fender introduced in 1958. The guitar bears serial number 028228 and a pencilled date of 4/58 on its neck.

FENDER STRATOCASTER

Apart, perhaps, from his glasses, Buddy Holly's Fender Stratocaster is the object most closely associated with him. He acquired and played three, or possibly four, Strats over the course of his career, this being the last that remains. This 1958 model was the guitar Buddy played during his last ever concert, at the Surf Ballroom, Iowa on 2 February 1959. The guitar is a three-tone sunburst with an alder body and 'slim C' profile neck. The serial number is 028228.

PAUL ANKA Buddy Holly, Fats Domino, Chuck Berry and I had gravitas because we wrote our own hits, which separated us from other musicians. Buddy planned on going out on his own and gave me a guitar, taught me some chords and asked me to write a song for him. Songwriters try to take on the profile and dynamics of the artist they're writing for. With Sinatra, I used things that you wouldn't normally write in a song – 'ate up', 'chew' and 'spit out' – because that's the way he was. With Buddy, I had a strong sense of his vocal magic and I wrote for his style and range, then he added some of his own stuff. It was a feeling I had for a great artist.

MARIA ELENA Buddy and Paul were great friends. Paul Anka's manager Irvin Feld was in discussions to bring on Buddy as a client, and Paul and Buddy were working on 'Raining in My Heart' and 'It Doesn't Matter Anymore'. Buddy was figuring out how to make them his own, and so he went to Dick Jacobs and told him he wanted violins for the songs.

PAUL ANKA We wound up in the studio in New York to record 'It Doesn't Matter Anymore'. Buddy was in the studio with this huge string section, which may have been his first experience with a big band. Buddy was used to a studio that had a few pieces – drums, guitar and a bass. Dick Jacobs knew to add pizzicato. Writing my own stuff has always been a kick, but to have Buddy Holly sing one of my songs was amazing. It was a very warm and heartfelt moment.

DAVID FRIZZELL His approach to writing and how to put a song together was completely different from other artists. Everything I heard by Buddy turned me on because of the way he approached and delivered it.

WINTER DANCE PARTY
Eagles Ballroom
Kenosha, WI,
24 January 1959

Above, from left to right: Jim Lounsbury (local DJ), J.P. Richardson (the Big Bopper), Debbie Stevens, Frankie Sardo, Buddy Holly

Left, from left to right: Frankie Sardo, Jim Lounsbury, J.P. Richardson, Ed Oxnar (local DJ), Buddy Holly

WINTER DANCE PARTY
Eagles Ballroom
Kenosha, WI,
24 January 1959

This page: Ritchie Valens and Waylon Jennings (top left), Dion and the Belmonts (top right and above), Ritchie Valens (left and far left), Ritchie Valens with Waylon Jennings (centre left)

Opposite: The Big Bopper signing autographs with fellow musicians

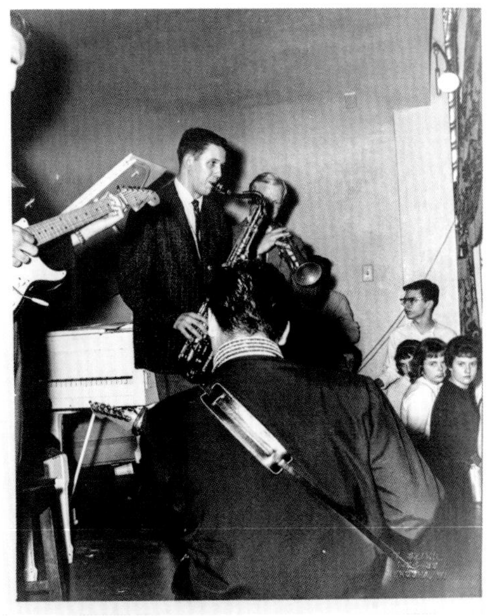

Waylon Jennings and Buddy Holly in a photo booth January 1959

MARIA ELENA When Waylon Jennings was recording with Buddy, he told Buddy he was certain he wanted to make rock and roll music. Buddy would tell him, 'I don't hear you making rock and roll, I hear you making country music.' Waylon disagreed, so Buddy asked him to record two versions of the same song, one in a fast tempo and the other slow. Afterwards Waylon said to him, 'I don't know, I still want to make rock and roll.' As you know, Waylon became a country singer.

ALBERT LEE Buddy was a great performer, writer and innovator. To come up with all that in such a short space of time is astounding. There are so many kids making records now and they're nothing in comparison. Rarely do you find someone at that age who has been able to grasp what it takes to make great music like that.

SONNY CURTIS He was miles ahead of the rest of us; he wanted to get into the business, publish and build a recording studio in Lubbock, while continuing to write and sing. He would've achieved a great deal of that because he was a visionary. He was a great singer and rock and roll artist, unique in many ways. His songs are simple yet complicated. Young pickers felt like they could pick up the guitar and sing those songs, and he had a gift for writing them. He pumped out so much music over a few years. It would have taken somebody else 15 years. He would have been a real force in the music business, had he lived.

PETER ASHER Buddy's songwriting is very unusual. They're simple songs with basic chords, but he puts them in an unusual order, which makes some songs hard to learn because they're so simple that it's easy to get wrong. It's very clever. It's the same with the lyrics. 'True Love Ways' is a strange lyric that uses ordinary words. We know 'true love ways' is slightly off-kilter; it's not a typical phrase and that makes it very memorable. Buddy was one of the first true singer-songwriters. He wrote so much of what he sang initially, then became very interested in how records got made and the business itself.

WINTER DANCE PARTY
Kato Ballroom
Mankato, MN,
25 January 1959

Above: Buddy on stage with Waylon Jennings (above left) and Tommy Allsup (above right)

WINTER DANCE PARTY
Fournier's Ballroom
Eau Claire, WI,
26 January 1959

BRIAN MAY Buddy had such a glittering yet tragically short career but he changed the world, and we're still listening to and performing his music. I did a couple of covers – 'Maybe Baby' and 'That'll Be the Day' – as another persona called T.E. Conway, which some people didn't realise was me. I did his songs with great love and tried to recreate his sound and feel, which was very difficult.

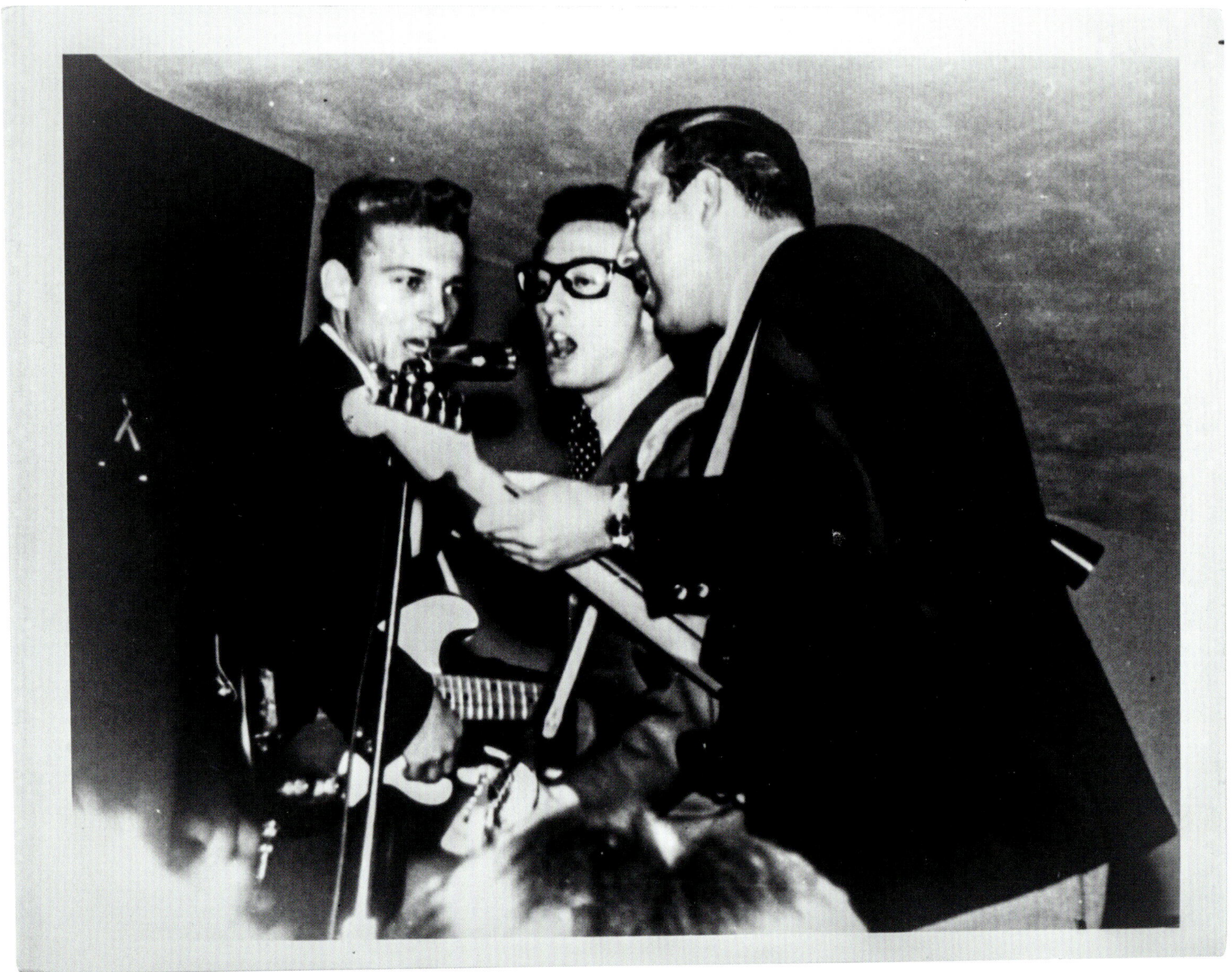

BRIAN MAY When you hear 'Peggy Sue Got Married' you can see how his writing evolved. He had an incredibly short active period in the music business, but he was already evolving. 'Peggy Sue Got Married' is quite provincial; he's talking about this girl that he was in love with years ago and she got married to someone else. It's romantic, and there's so much of Buddy's passion in it. The first time I put it on it was foreign to me, and I was slightly scared off, but I ended up loving it.

DION DiMUCCI During the Winter Dance Party tour in '59, I used a white Strat that I had purchased with Buddy in 1957, but a lot of the time I played his. Ritchie Valens, Buddy and I would get into a battle of who could make them ring for the longest. I can't remember who won. We became close during that tour.

It was very creative at the back of the bus. We'd play songs we knew and jam, a Chuck Berry or Fats Domino song. We'd all jump in and harmonise. It was a fun time; the best thing that happened in my life. The plane crash felt like the rug was ripped out from under me. I was a 19-year-old Italian kid from the Bronx. We don't exploit or talk about anyone's death; you grieve privately.

WINTER DANCE PARTY
Fiesta Ballroom
Montevideo, MN,
27 January 1959

Opposite: Buddy performing on stage with Tommy Allsup and Waylon Jennings

Above: Buddy and Waylon Jennings

WINTER DANCE PARTY
Prom Ballroom
St Paul, MN,
28 January 1959

Opposite:
Laramar Ballroom
Fort Dodge, IA,
30 January 1959

& NEWS

VMT
& NEWS

DAVID FRIZZELL He was an original. When you hear Buddy Holly, even just the beginning of a song, you know who it is. His songs had signature licks, and he did that by the way he attacked the guitar. It was all rhythm back in those days, like 'Peggy Sue'. He didn't copy off anybody else and instead we all tried to emulate him, but there was only one Buddy Holly. It came from his heart. I don't hear a lot of original stuff around anymore, but you sure heard it in those days.

BRIAN MAY It was a colossal career. You're looking at a genius, yet a very modest guy. He had a way of cutting through the frills and conventions to come up with something that was fresh and expressed the feelings of a whole generation.

BUDDY HOLLY'S OVERNIGHT BAG

On 30 January 1959, the bus carrying the stars of the 1959 Winter Dance Party rolled into Fort Dodge, Iowa for a concert at the Laramar Ballroom.

Bob Meyers, a photographer backstage that night, captured Buddy Holly (opposite) wearing his tan winter coat and carrying his personal overnight bag under his right arm. The Big Bopper is seen with his back to Buddy, signing an autograph for a fan.

On the morning of 3 February 1959, the overnight bag was discovered in a snow-covered cornfield on Albert Juhl's farm, following the plane crash earlier that day that took the lives of Buddy Holly, Ritchie Valens, the Big Bopper and pilot Roger Peterson.

The additional photos seen here are Buddy's overnight bag as it appears today. Originally, there was a hidden compartment located in the bottom of the bag where Buddy kept his money and a pistol. The bottom of the bag was ripped off during the plane crash. Many of Buddy's personal toiletry items, such as his toothbrush, toothpaste, a comb and a hairbrush (above), were found inside the bag. Sixty-five years later, the hairbrush still contains strands of Buddy's hair.

WINTER DANCE PARTY
Riverside Ballroom
Green Bay, WI,
1 February 1959

It was on the way to this show that the tour bus broke down in Pine Lake, WI, as described by Dion (right)

DION DiMUCCI Irvin Feld put the Winter Dance Party together for Buddy. We all met in Chicago at the end of January and rehearsed. I noticed the Crickets weren't there; Buddy had a pick-up band with Tommy Allsup and Waylon Jennings, who was just a kid, and Carl 'the Goose' Bunch on drums and they augmented the band with three guys from the Midwest: a trumpet player, a sax player and a piano player.

The next day we jumped on a bus, a yellow 1950s school bus they must have borrowed from a Baptist school. That tour criss-crossed the Midwest, and we were working armouries and skating rinks – they'd put planks down on the ice and set up chairs. The ballrooms were better, but still cold. It was the dead of winter, which wasn't a problem until the bus started breaking down.

One day we broke down in Pine Lake, when a piston rod went through the engine. It was a blinding snowstorm and some of the musicians from the Midwest started to freak out, because they knew how dangerous it was. The trumpet player said, 'We're gonna die. People die on these roads all the time.' On our way to Clear Lake, we broke down again when a belt broke on the bus, which wasn't a big deal and we got it fixed quickly. But Buddy decided that when we got to Clear Lake he was going to try to charter a plane.

DION DiMUCCI Prior to the show, Buddy found someone who would help him and gathered the headliners, the Big Bopper, Ritchie Valens and me, into the room. Heads, you fly, tails, you have to ride the golden chariot. The Bopper and I won the coin toss, and Buddy told us it was $36 to fly from Mason City to Fargo. That money resonated with me, because my parents in the Bronx argued about the rent all my life, so I told Ritchie that he could go. After the show, they went to the airport.

When we got to the hotel, the locals from the town were sitting around a black and white television in the lobby, and they were talking about three rock and roll artists who'd died in a plane crash. It was all over the news. I couldn't take it in. I walked out to the bus and sat on there. It didn't make sense. I'm sitting there with Buddy Holly's guitar on one of the seats, after he'd told me to take care of it. Ritchie Valens's little blue vest is hanging up, and the Bopper's hat is on the hat rack.

WINTER DANCE PARTY
Riverside Ballroom
Green Bay, WI,
1 February 1959

Opposite: Frankie Sardo, Buddy and Dion DiMucci talking backstage

MARIA ELENA Buddy was working towards creating film scores, so we had decided to go to California – to get him closer to Hollywood. When they presented him with a star on the Hollywood Walk of Fame, I wrote, 'Here you are Buddy. You wanted to be in Hollywood, and now you are.'

PETER ASHER He created a body of work that is the envy of everyone in rock and roll. The more you live with the songs, you understand that clarity and simplicity stands the test of time. Something simple and beautiful is often harder to make than something that's complicated and beautiful, and he pulled that off again and again. It's extraordinary.

WINTER DANCE PARTY
Riverside Ballroom
Green Bay, WI,
1 February 1959

Buddy and the Big Bopper are pictured with twins Joan and Judy Bender, who performed as the Jayettes

Opposite, bottom left: Ritchie Valens on stage with Tommy Allsup and Waylon Jennings. After a show in Duluth, Minnesota on 31 January 1959, Buddy's drummer, Carl Bunch, was hospitalised with frostbite due to the band's unheated tour bus breaking down in subzero temperatures near Ironwood, Michigan. To fill in for him, Buddy, Ritchie and Dion took turns playing drums for each other in Green Bay, Wisconsin and Buddy's final performance at the Surf Ballroom in Clear Lake, Iowa..

PETER ASHER If Buddy had not died so tragically early, he wouldn't be fat and playing Vegas, he'd be writing programmes for Pro Tools, running a record label and discovering new bands. He was intellectually and musically hungry, while wanting to be a star – which he did, no musician gets there by accident. He was one of the most brilliant of the bunch and would've gone on to have an extraordinary career beyond writing some of the best pop songs ever written.

PAUL ANKA Buddy Holly was one of the greatest influences of rock and roll. He was emerging as a great artist, especially in terms of performing. He was one of the key influential artists in rock and roll, as well as pop music. If you look at the full landscape of music, Buddy Holly was one of the guys that painted that picture and allowed the rest to learn from it.

North Iowa's Daily Newspaper

MASON CITY GLOBE-GAZETTE

HOME EDITION

"The Newspaper That Makes All North Iowans Neighbors"

Four Killed in Clear Lake Plane Crash

Bodies of two victims (arrows) lie near the demolished plane in corn field

Nationally-Known Rock 'n' Rollers, Lake Man Victims

BUDDY HOLLY

3 Singers Made Top Recordings

Russ Hold U.S. Army Convoy

Iowa House in Fiery Debate Over Right-to-Work Law

Contest by Messer Dismissed

Light Snow Falls Over Iowa as Mercury Climbs

VINCENT ASTOR

Heart Attack Takes Life of Astor, 67

7-Year-Old Iowans Head Heart Fund

Cigarette Vending Machine Bill Offered

Car-Train Collide, Redfield Man Killed

TRAFFIC DEATHS IN IOWA 56

RITCHIE VALENS

PLANE'S WRECKAGE

Daily Mirror

WED FEB 4 1959

FORWARD WITH THE PEOPLE No. 17,150

Tragedy of 'Jape' Richardson

THEY CALLED HIM 'THE BIG BOPPER'

TOP 'ROCK' STARS DIE IN CRASH

From BARRIE HARDING, New York, Tuesday

THREE of America's top rock 'n' roll stars were killed in a plane crash today, a few hours after delighting teenagers at a "big beat" concert.

They were BUDDY HOLLY, whose recording of "That'll Be The Day" sold more than a million and a half copies; BIG BOPPER (Jape Richardson), singer of the current hit "Chantilly Lace," and RITCHIE VALENS, composer of the Tommy Steele favourite "Come On, Let's Go."

On TV Here

Buddy Holly . . . as Britain saw him

7 days FREE Viewing

D.E.R. 21st ANNIVERSARY OFFER

. . . only 7'6 a week

600,000 JOBLESS?

By ROLAND HURMAN

Mirror Industrial Editor

Decedent was killed in an airplane crash in Iowa. At the time, decedent was part of an Act that was touring the country with a group which had been "packaged" by the employer. Contract between decedent and the employer covered one night engagements over a period of three weeks and two days. Employer's vice-president testified that the show was sold as a package; that the employer rehearsed and arranged the show; that the employer provided the itinerary for the trip and provided a bus to take the group from one engagement to another. He further testified that the stars were not prohibited from using other means of transportation. Employer's road manager testified that he was in charge of the troupe of which decedent was a member; that on the evening of 2/2/59 the troupe played an engagement at Clear Lake, Iowa; that this engagement was completed about 11:30 P.M. with the next stop the following evening being at Moorehead, Minnesota, some 300 miles away; that he became aware that decedent had chartered a flight out of Clear Lake and he questioned decedent about it; that the bus had developed trouble enroute to Clear Lake and had completely broken down in zero degree temperature; and that decedent and two other stars, who had accompanied him on the flight, had indicated that they wanted to go ahead of the bus to get their clothes cleaned and to get set.

MARIA ELENA The night before Buddy left for that tour we both had similar dreams. It seemed like a premonition we had, and we woke up at the same time. I didn't want him to go. I was two months pregnant at the time. My aunt would come and check in on me, and a young man – whose music was being produced by Buddy at the time – would sometimes call me to see if I needed anything. One day he called and said, 'Please do me a favour, stay in bed and don't put the television on. I'll be there in a little while.' I wasn't sure why he said that, so naturally I got up and put the television on. It was everywhere. It was the same way Buddy's mother had found out.

When I arrived in Lubbock, the whole family were beside themselves, preparing for the funeral, but I didn't want anything to do with it. I just stayed in the house. At the funeral, people asked where I was, and later, when people asked me why I didn't go, I told them it was because Buddy wasn't there and nor was his spirit.

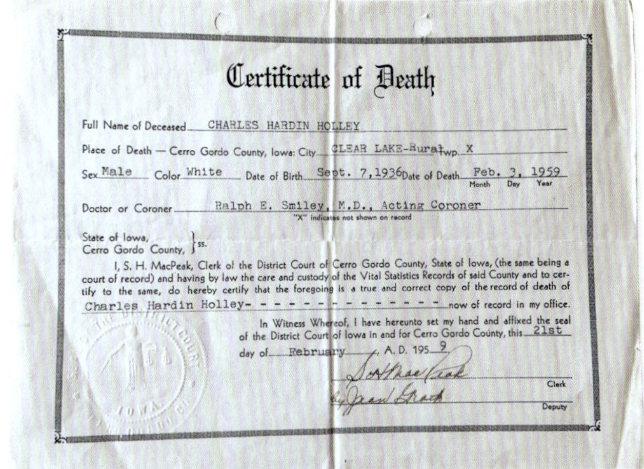

Certificate of Death

Full Name of Deceased CHARLES HARDIN HOLLEY

Place of Death — Cerro Gordo County, Iowa: City CLEAR LAKE-Rural twp. X

Sex Male Color White Date of Birth Sept. 7,1936 Date of Death Feb. 3, 1959
Month Day Year

Doctor or Coroner Ralph E. Smiley, M.D., Acting Coroner
"X" indicates not shown on record

State of Iowa,
Cerro Gordo County, } ss.

I, S. H. MacPeak, Clerk of the District Court of Cerro Gordo County, State of Iowa, (the same being a court of record) and having by law the care and custody of the Vital Statistics Records of said County and to certify to the same, do hereby certify that the foregoing is a true and correct copy of the record of death of Charles Hardin Holley- - - - - - - - - - - - - - - - now of record in my office.

In Witness Whereof, I have hereunto set my hand and affixed the seal of the District Court of Iowa in and for Cerro Gordo County, this 21st day of February, A. D. 1959

Clerk

Deputy

THE DAY THE MUSIC DIED
Pictured opposite are the front pages from Mason City Globe Gazette *on 3 February 1959 and England's* Daily Mirror *on 4 February 1959 and a Memorandum of Decision from 1960 (bottom). On this page is a photograph from the aftermath of the crash (above); memorials at the crash site (below); and Buddy Holly's death certificate (above right).*

EDNA GUNDERSEN Buddy's death was the first true tragedy in rock and roll music, and the first real tragedy that a lot of young people experienced in the public forum. It was tremendously sad, because the media was not interested in rock and roll, so his death was not reported as a huge event in society. There was no tribute or national recognition of what had happened. A lot of young people who loved Buddy Holly had no idea how to handle and channel the feelings they had over someone they so closely identified with.

It took America a while to recognise what a hero they had in their own backyard. There was a box set released in 1979 of six LPs, which came out in England and Germany first, and then America. That kindled some recognition. There was the movie, which was not very good, and that generated some more appreciation. The building of Buddy Holly's status was a very slow-moving event.

PAUL ANKA When I heard the news of Buddy's death, I was on another tour close by, and Irvin told me in the middle of the night. It was jolting to all of us. It's one thing to hear about the death of a fellow artist, but we were all family and had life experiences with each other; Buddy was one of our own ... That night was horrific, as were the days and years that followed.

SONNY CURTIS The night before Buddy died, Jerry Allison, Peggy Sue and I drove to Lubbock from Clovis and spent the night at J.I.'s parents' house. The next morning, a lady from across the street came over and said she'd heard the news on the radio about Buddy dying in a plane crash. I had the sad task of telling J.I. He didn't want to believe it. They were very close; even though Buddy lived in New York and we lived in Texas, everything was amicable. At that age you don't think about mortality much, and it was a very sad occasion. We just couldn't believe it, a good friend dying like that. It's hard to accept.

JERRY 'J.I.' ALLISON Our neighbour Oleta Hall came over that morning and told Sonny the news, who told me. I felt as bad as you can feel, and I immediately went over to his folks' house. I felt guilty too, because I believe if I had been there I wouldn't have let Buddy get on that plane. We hadn't spoken in a while because he was in New York, which we'd planned on doing together, but Norman Petty talked Joe B. and me out of it – we were like his workers at the time.

Waylon Jennings later told me that Buddy had planned to get Joe B. and me together to do another tour of England. He planned on having Waylon open the show. This was just two days before he died.

KEVIN MONTGOMERY My dad didn't talk too much about Buddy regarding the music they made together. He viewed him as one of his best friends and he was very hurt by his passing. He thought a lot of Buddy and respected him and recognised that he lost a best friend, and the world lost a powerhouse of a musician and songwriter.

LARRY WELBORN I was touring with Charlie Phillips when I heard about Buddy's death. We heard it on the radio when we were out in New Mexico. I couldn't believe it. I went down to his funeral, where I was an honorary pallbearer. It was hard for everybody to take, especially his folks. Everybody couldn't believe it; he died so young. He'd already done more than most people do in ten years.

DON McLEAN At that time, I was a paperboy. I opened the papers that morning and read, 'Buddy Holly, Ritchie Valens, the Big Bopper, killed in a plane crash'. I couldn't move. I went to junior high school the next day, and nobody cared; he hadn't been on the charts for two years, and rock and roll wasn't thought of as important. But prior to that, everything was black and white. I never forgot that reaction. I was 14 and everything affected me. Buddy's songs were written for kids whose emotions were tender.

JIMMY PAGE I shall never forget the day that the morning paper came through the door and there it was: a photograph of Buddy Holly, Ritchie Valens and the Big Bopper, all killed in a plane crash. It was devastating.

I had learned guitar from the records of Buddy Holly. He had been such a major part of my growth as a musician. And Ritchie Valens's record 'La Bamba' was also just extraordinary.

It was the vibe of the whole thing. You wanted to be sitting there at a concert one day, hearing all these guys make this wonderful music. And then they were gone.

I went to school with a heavy heart. I remember asking a friend if he had heard that Buddy Holly had died. He said, 'Oh yeah, it was in the paper wasn't it?' For me, it was such a tragedy because I knew what we'd lost musically. But for other people, it wasn't such a big deal. That's when I realised my passion was radically different from other people's.

HANK MARVIN One of our heroes had gone and it felt like he'd only been around for five minutes. It was 18 months and he created so many sounds we were excited by. We were all really shattered by that, and I remember it on the front page of the paper. We lost an innovator in rock and roll music, someone who influenced so many other people that followed him.

JAMES BURTON I was playing guitar for Ricky Nelson at the time, and we were driving down Hollywood Boulevard when we heard about the airplane crash. It was a very sad day; we both loved Buddy and his music, which was completely unique.

SONNY WEST I was working a dreaded shift job in a mill in New Mexico, and I'd gotten off my shift when I heard the news on the radio. Everybody can say they were shocked, and it affects everybody differently, but it was a sad day. It shows you how fragile we are.

Though I wasn't very close to Buddy, it felt personal. We ran into each other a lot while he recorded in Clovis, and I hoped we might collaborate again. But his death was much deeper than that. It wasn't just sad for me, but for the world of music. He was a young man with a big future in front of him.

BRIAN MAY It's a moment you never forget. I remember Kennedy's death, Lennon's death, but the first I remember was sitting under the covers in the bed listening to Radio Luxembourg, when the announcer comes on and says, 'Buddy Holly has been killed in a plane crash.' I felt a wave of shock and horror and rushed downstairs to tell my mum and dad, and they were just as shocked because they knew how much I was a disciple of Buddy. You couldn't confirm it in those days until the newspapers came out the following day. I hadn't been bereaved that way until then and it's something I'll never forget. I thought, 'So there won't be any more music, how can that be?' It was a hard thing for me.

DON EVERLY I went into my bedroom, shut the door, and that was it for about two weeks. I felt so bad. It was a very terrible feeling. Phil went down to the funeral, but I couldn't even get on a plane for a while. Occasionally I had to fly on small planes, but I never wanted to.

I think about Buddy when I'm having a good time on the road. I think, Buddy missed this. He would've continued to do very well and be one of the few that lasted in rock and roll. It's a shame.

DAVID FRIZZELL My brother and I were on tour in New Mexico. He called me in the room and said, 'You better sit down for this one.' Everybody knew that I loved him. If you've ever had your heart broken and dreams destroyed … it all came down on me right then. I could not believe it. I still have trouble with it.

DON McLEAN I was always trying to find out more about Buddy. I would go to the public library in New York City and look up microfilm to see whether the *New York Times* had further information regarding his death, but they didn't. It was hard to find out anything about anybody in 1959.

LARRY WELBORN One time Buddy and I went down to KDAV and there was another show recording. Buddy called them and requested a song called 'I'll Be Alright', which was a very bluesy song. He liked that song so much it was played at his funeral.

BRIAN MAY It's strange when somebody dies because they become crystallised in that moment. In a strange way, some good comes out of it, because what followed was a realisation of what Buddy Holly had been; that we'd lost something wonderful and significant. But we lost his further development. If he could go that far in three years, what on earth would he have been doing in another ten? He had an incredibly creative mind and he moved through all the different styles in that short time. You can only dimly imagine what heights he might have reached.

THE BUDDY HOLLY EDUCATIONAL FOUNDATION

Ambassadors

THE SONGS: 1959
This section presents TBHEF ambassadors with guitars named after songs that were written, recorded, performed or demoed by Buddy in 1959. 'Stay Close to Me' was written by Buddy before 1959 but the Lou Giordano recording was released in 1959. Don McLean's 'American Pie' was, of course, written much later, but was inspired by Buddy's death in 1959.

JOHN LODGE *'Gotta Travel On'*
DAVID GILMOUR *'Gotta Travel On'*
PAUL ANKA *'It Doesn't Matter Anymore'*
MARTY WILDE *'It Doesn't Matter Anymore'*
NOEL GALLAGHER *'Slippin' and Slidin''*
DAVE STEWART *'Raining in My Heart'*
MARK KNOPFLER *'Stay Close to Me'*
ALLAN CLARKE *'Peggy Sue Got Married'*
BRUCE WELCH *'Crying, Waiting, Hoping'*
STING *'Salty Dog Rag'*
KIEFER SUTHERLAND *'Smokey Joe's Cafe'*
DON McLEAN *'American Pie'*

JOHN LODGE *'Gotta Travel On'*

JOHN LODGE I first heard 'That'll Be the Day' on a TV programme. I remember rushing to my little record shop called the Music Box in Birmingham and excitedly asking if they had the record. 'No,' was the reply, 'But we can order it.' A couple of weeks later I collected the record and rushed home to play it on my turntable. The record was a 78 rpm 12-inch recording on Coral, which I played over and over, totally in awe of the song, guitar, and vocal harmonies. I still have the record and faithfully play it on my 1945 Wurlitzer 1015 jukebox. It sounds as good today as it did then!

In 1958 Buddy Holly and the Crickets came to the UK on tour and appeared at the Birmingham Town Hall. I was lucky enough to be given a ticket, which was in the front row of the circle. Unbelievable! The concert was pure magic … I bought a programme, a treasured possession which I still have.

On my tour of the UK in 2015, I said to my agent, 'The last concert of my tour has to be at the Birmingham Town Hall.' I would be standing on the stage where Buddy Holly once stood, and I could look up to the circle and see a young Johnny Lodge there.

On a Moody Blues tour in early 2000 we ended our tour in Lubbock. After the concert, Justin and I arranged to visit the cemetery where Buddy was buried. The curator opened the gates for us at about midnight and there we were in the quiet of the night looking at Buddy's grave. Here was the singer, songwriter and musician who had lit up my life so many years before. I had to do something to say thank you. I had a plectrum in my pocket from the concert that night and I placed it on Buddy's gravestone. In the moonlit night, when the stars were shining over Texas, a cricket flew by and landed on Buddy's gravestone … a magical end to a most memorable night that will stay with me forever.

Dear Buddy,
'That'll Be the Day' was the first record I bought and showed me the way to my musical life… that's my "That'll Be the Day"
Thank you… for your inspiration
John Lodge

A PART OF THE BIRMINGHAM MUSIC SCENE in the mid-1960s, John Lodge joined the Moody Blues on bass and vocals in 1966, having known one of the group's founding members, Ray Thomas, since he was 14. John's early inspiration was Buddy Holly. Many artists would have loved to see Buddy and the Crickets on their UK tour in 1958 but most, like The Beatles, missed out. John Lodge made the cut.

Justin Hayward was drafted into the Moody Blues at the same time as John, both of them going on to write many of the band's classics. John contributed dozens of songs, including 'Peak Hour', 'Emily's Song', 'Isn't Life Strange', 'I'm Just a Singer (In a Rock and Roll Band)' and 'Gemini Dream'; he won major songwriting awards for the last three of these.

In 1985, the Moody Blues picked up the Ivor Novello Award for Outstanding Contribution to Music, and in 2018 they were inducted into the Rock and Roll Hall of Fame. In September 2019, John was given a Lifetime Achievement Award by *Prog* magazine. In *Bass Player* magazine, John was voted one of the top ten bass players of all time.

As well as being a 'lifetime Moody Blue', John has undertaken many solo projects, including albums and tours, and has produced records for other artists. In 1975, he and Justin Hayward collaborated on the album *Blue Jays*, released on Threshold Records, the Moody Blues' own label.

During the Covid lockdown in 2020, John wrote and recorded 'In These Crazy Times' in his home studio. The song was a big hit on the Heritage Chart, as was the follow-up, 'The Sun Will Shine', the following year. But the journey began, as it did for so many artists, with the inspiring songs of a young man from Lubbock called Buddy Holly. – *Mike Read*

DAVID GILMOUR IS A MUSICAL GIANT. For more than half a century he has entranced us with guitar playing from another planet, within one of the most innovative and successful bands the world has ever known – Pink Floyd.

Few have melded ground-breaking musical intelligence and record-breaking chart success as brilliantly as Pink Floyd. Since their inception in the mid-1960s, they have established an almost unbroken occupation of record charts in the UK and across the world, selling more than 250 million copies in the process. Now a new generation of fans has discovered their music, a reflection of their incredible relevance and endurance.

David was born just after the Second World War and, like many of us baby-boomers, he was massively inspired by the energy and fire of the new American music that hit our shores in the mid-1950s – 'Rock Around the Clock' by Bill Haley and the Comets and 'Heartbreak Hotel' by Elvis Presley were among the first in his collection.

He was immediately determined to express his feelings through music. Soon he borrowed a guitar from his next-door neighbour and began to experiment with the chords and styles of the blues, rhythm and blues and rock and roll records he was now discovering – Leadbelly, B.B. King, Pete Seeger and Buddy Holly's Fender Stratocaster were the sounds that fired his ambition.

David founded and played in a few cover bands before joining Pink Floyd in 1968 at the height of the psychedelic era, where he dived into liquid light shows and mixed-media happenings, forging an indelible bond between experimental music and visual art. It was a multicoloured combination that the band used to express their music through their live performances from then on, including a truly mind-blowing charity concert at the Rainbow Theatre in London in 1973. The centrepiece of this show was a performance of *Dark Side of the Moon*, their most successful album ever.

A quiet man, David has always expressed emotions mainly through his music. From those early days of rock and roll through the world domination of Pink Floyd to the release of his expressive and beautiful solo recordings, carefully crafted in his houseboat studio, David Gilmour has created a legacy that will last forever. – *Bob Harris*

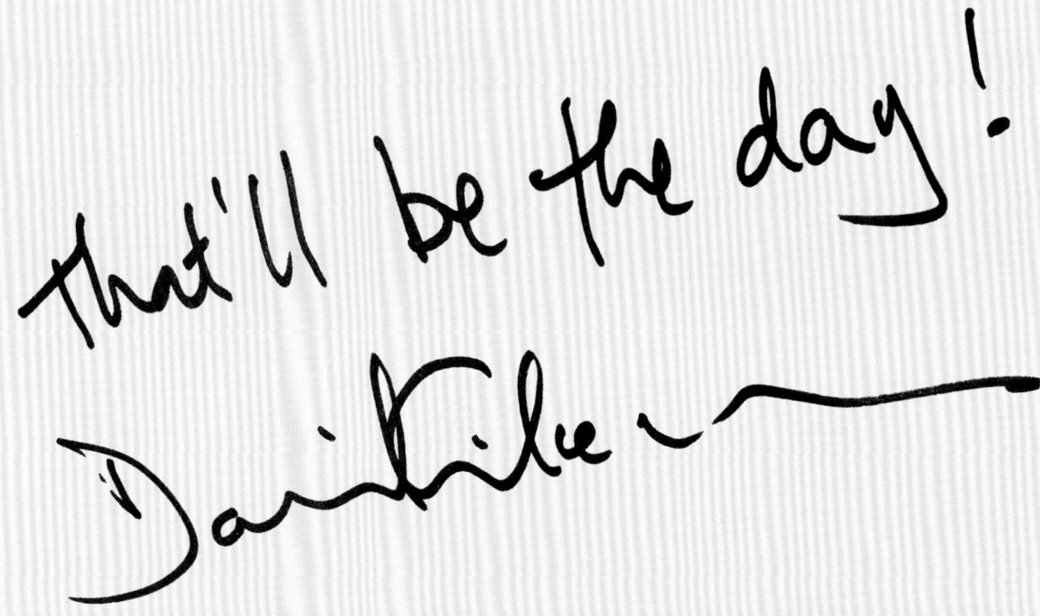

GOTTA TRAVEL ON

'Gotta Travel On' is an American folk song which was performed by Buddy Holly as an opening number on his final Winter Dance Party tour.

PAUL ANKA *'It Doesn't Matter Anymore'*

What an
Honor – all
of us for our
man!
Buddy
Paul

IT DOESN'T MATTER ANYMORE
'It Doesn't Matter Anymore' was written by Paul Anka expressly for Buddy Holly. The song was recorded by Buddy on 21 October 1958 at Decca's Pythian Temple studios in New York City. When released on Coral on 5 January 1959, it reached number 13 in the US charts and number one in the UK.

PAUL ANKA HOLDS A VERY SPECIAL PLACE IN MY HEART. The first record I ever bought was 'Diana', his first hit single, in 1957. I was 11 years old, and I can still vividly remember the spine-tingling feeling of hearing that record for the first time. It was blasting from a coffee-shop jukebox, and I was transfixed. I changed all my pocket money into threepenny bits and played it over and over until my money ran out. It was exciting beyond belief to hear it pumping out of those massive Wurlitzer speakers and I can honestly say that it was *the* life-changing moment that opened the pathway to the rock and roll music that I grew to love. I couldn't wait to get to my local record shop and buy the single – a 78 rpm Columbia disc (catalogue number DB 3980) that sits proudly framed on the wall of my home studio. A place of honour.

As I got to know Paul Anka's music more ('I Love You Baby', 'Lonely Boy' and 'Put Your Head on My Shoulder' – now famous through a million random TikTok clips), I began learning about his growing friendship with Buddy Holly. They were thrown together on seemingly endless tours, some as long as 80 days, playing countless cities across America, often with Eddie Cochran and Jerry Lee Lewis sharing the bill. Broken-down tour buses, late-night drinking parties and thousands of miles. But somehow Buddy always stayed separate from the madness. 'He had a soft shyness about him,' said Paul. 'He was a country boy, very raw, simple, modest and sensitive. He and I were neck and neck with our hits "That'll Be the Day" and "Diana" and, like me, Buddy wrote his own songs. He also had his own group, the Crickets. We were all buddies.'

They began to talk about collaborating and creating a different, more orchestral sound for Buddy's records and when Buddy relocated from Lubbock to New York, leaving his southern twang behind, their serious work together began. Soon Paul came up with the song that gave Buddy one of the biggest hits of his career – 'It Doesn't Matter Anymore'. It was recorded on 21 October 1958 at the Decca Studios in New York City, with an 18-piece orchestra and string players brought in from the New York Symphony. It was incredibly sophisticated and totally different from everything Buddy had recorded before. During the time of the studio session Buddy had been constantly talking to Paul about his lovely new wife Maria Elena and by the time the record came out, on 5 January 1959, she was pregnant. They were very much in love – happy, excited and optimistic about the future.

Less than a month later, Buddy was dead. A few weeks after that, 'It Doesn't Matter Anymore' topped the UK charts and Paul Anka donated every penny of his royalties to Maria Elena, to protect her future. Mine is not the only life changed by the sound of Paul Anka's music. – *Bob Harris*

'"It Doesn't Matter Anymore" has a tragic irony about it now, but at least it will help look after Buddy's family. I'm giving my composer's royalty to his widow. It's the least I can do.' (Paul Anka, quoted in the *NME*, 1959)

Above: Paul Anka on stage October 1957

Right: Paul Anka backstage 13 January 1958

MARTY WILDE *'It Doesn't Matter Anymore'*

One of the biggest influences in my rock'n'roll life. He helped me, and millions of others to see what could be achieved in music – he will always be....

Special!!

Marty Wilde

CLIFF RICHARD'S FATHER FAMOUSLY SAID TO HIM, 'Why can't you sing properly like that Marty Wilde.' Of course, they are both great singers. Performing as Reg Patterson (although his birth name is actually Reg Smith), Marty was spotted at London's Condor Club in 1957 by Larry Parnes, who dubbed him 'Marty', after the 1955 film of that name, and 'Wilde' because he liked to give his stable of singers 'powerful' names.

Marty became a regular on late-1950s TV music shows *6.5 Special*, *Oh Boy!* and *Boy Meets Girls*, during which time he met and married Joyce Baker, who was a member of vocal group the Vernons Girls. His run of hit singles began in 1958 with 'Endless Sleep', and the following year he had Top Ten hits with 'Donna', 'A Teenager in Love', 'Sea of Love' and 'Bad Boy'. The last of these he wrote himself, which was unusual at the time; apart from Buddy Holly, few 1950s artists wrote their own material.

In the early 1960s, Marty had more hits, including 'Rubber Ball' and 'Jezebel', but he was now moving more into acting and songwriting. He co-wrote 'Jesamine', a big hit for the Casuals, 'I'm a Tiger' for Lulu, and the early Status Quo single 'Ice in the Sun'.

His family are all talented musicians and singers. His daughter Kim Wilde had eight UK Top Ten hits in the 1980s, including three – 'Kids in America', 'Chequered Love' and 'Four Letter Word' – that were co-written by Marty and his son Ricky. – *Mike Read*

'Buddy Holly is, and will always be, one of my greatest inspirations.'

MARTY WILDE From that early *'Chirping' Crickets* album, which we all loved, so many young songwriters were inspired to try and come up with new-sounding material. People like The Beatles, and almost every artist you can think of, owe a huge debt to the great man, and also to his wonderful band, the Crickets.

Left: Marty's 1958 diary showing 22 March 1958, the day he saw Buddy Holly and the Crickets at the Gaumont in Salisbury, Wiltshire during Buddy's only tour of the UK

NOEL GALLAGHER *'Slippin' and Slidin''*

Well Alright!!
Yes Buddy..
the King of the
3 Minute Masterpiece
Big ♥
x

'BUDDY TEACHES US TO KEEP IT SIMPLE,' SAYS NOEL GALLAGHER of Buddy as an inspiration for his own iconic and universal songwriting through Oasis into his solo work with the High Flying Birds. 'You don't need fancy chords or obtuse lyrics. Buddy's songs are direct, short and to the point. It's fair to say he wasn't a big influence on "Champagne Supernova"!'

But it's clear to see there's a bit of Buddy in Gallagher's most direct works. Ever since he found a guitar lying around his house on a council estate in Manchester, Gallagher's destiny was to entertain the world – and music his way out. Now his are some of the most instantly recognisable and well-known songs in stadiums, festivals, pubs and weddings the world over. To him, rock and roll simply means 'freedom', and Buddy's take on it endures because it's 'pure': '"That'll Be the Day" will *never*, *ever* get old,' Gallagher adds.

His Buddy Holly Atkin, named 'Slippin' and Slidin'', is, as he puts it, 'a rather unexpected treat. I'm even considering wearing glasses now, and getting a quiff!'

Now that he's put bad blood with his brother Liam behind him to reunite Oasis, you'll be hearing a lot of that no-frills Buddy-touched magic from Gallagher, keeping it straight and to the point. He's still making history, not that the guy who wrote 'Wonderwall' and 'Don't Look Back In Anger' cares too much about legacy. 'I truly, truly couldn't give a f**k about that,' he admits. 'I live in the here and now. And right now, today, I'm happy with what I've done and indeed what I'm doing.' – *Andrew Trendall*

SLIPPIN' AND SLIDIN'
The Little Richard song 'Slippin' and Slidin'' was recorded by Buddy in his New York apartment in 1959 and released on the Coral compilation Reminiscing *on 18 February 1963.*

BUDDY HOLLY
BLACK NIGHTS

I first heard "Raining In My Heart" in Rainy Sunderland in N.E. of England..... needless to say I immediately wanted to know more about Buddy and joined millions of others in being a massive fan and started to try write songs myself...... I'm still learning the game!

DAVE STEWART WAS BARELY OUT OF HIS TEENS when he got his first record deal. His folk-rock group Longdancer were the first act signed to Elton John's Rocket label in 1973, but he did not have any commercial success until he co-founded the Tourists in 1977. Three years later, he formed the Eurythmics with fellow Tourist Annie Lennox. Together, they enjoyed a string of hit albums and singles, including the US number one 'Sweet Dreams (Are Made of This)' and the UK number one 'There Must Be an Angel (Playing with My Heart)'. Like all successful musicians and writers, Dave Stewart is quick to acknowledge his early influences – including Buddy Holly. – *Mike Read*

DAVE STEWART Buddy Holly's first television appearance was in 1952, the year I was born, but I only became aware of his music in 1966. My brother, or perhaps my mother, bought *The Buddy Holly Story* album and as I was learning guitar I was ploughing through all the vinyl I could find in the family's collection.

In the UK in 1966 we already had The Beatles, the Rolling Stones, the Animals, the Kinks and the Who, blasting out of the radio but something happened when I first put the needle down on side one, track one of *The Buddy Holly Story*. 'Raining in My Heart', with its complex orchestral arrangement, kicked in and then the purest, most honest-sounding voice came in singing the saddest lyrics with that beautiful melody against those wonderful chord changes. This was at a time my mum and dad had separated and I was alone in the house. I sat there in front of the record player and cried for the first time about everything I'd kept bottled up inside. I found out later Buddy didn't write that song but it didn't matter. On every song on that album I heard the influences of early rock and roll, country and blues, but mostly I heard a beautiful melancholy; a sweetness that had a sadness too.

I had already heard 'Peggy Sue' and 'Rave On' on the radio when I was younger and even seen a performance on television while eating the usual beans on toast after school, but it wasn't until I actually was alone and chose to put on a whole album that I had that 'aha' moment. The realisation that the soul of Buddy Holly was embedded in those grooves and that I was so fortunate to hear and feel that, all the way from Lubbock, Texas, cutting through to a young a kid up in Sunderland in the North East of England, seven years after he had that fatal plane crash. Somehow my life was changed forever too.

'I was only six or seven years old when Buddy Holly was knocking out song after song and changing the way music sounded on the radio.'

RAINING IN MY HEART

'Raining in My Heart' was written by husband-and-wife songwriting team Felice and Boudleaux Bryant. Buddy recorded his version on 21 October 1958 at Decca's Pythian Temple studios in New York City with orchestral backing arranged by Dick Jacobs. It was released as a single on Coral on 5 January 1959 and later included on Buddy's first greatest hits album, The Buddy Holly Story, *which came out the following month.*

MARK KNOPFLER *'Stay Close to Me'*

STAY CLOSE TO ME

Written by Buddy Holly, 'Stay Close to Me' was recorded by Lou Giordano on 30 September 1958 at the Beltone Studio in New York City, with Buddy producing and playing guitar. The single was released in February 1959. The song was covered by Mike Berry in 1979.

Buddy Holly was a huge influence on me – I loved his records, songs and sound. He would have gone on to do amazing things. There will always be a special place in my heart for Buddy.

Mark Knopfler

MARK KNOPFLER'S LOVE OF BUDDY HOLLY is deeply embedded in his musical DNA. The four-time Grammy winner has himself been a guitar hero for millions through the immortal catalogue of Dire Straits, as well as decades of his own distinguished solo albums and unforgettable film soundtracks. But it all comes back to Buddy, one of the first American artists he heard as a teenager growing up in Newcastle upon Tyne in North East England.

Mark speaks often of his formative influences as a would-be guitar player, such as Hank Marvin and Duane Eddy, who inspired him endlessly as he pressed his nose against the window of local instrument shops. But when that first wave of rock and roll came crashing across the Atlantic and into his front room, there was nothing quite like Charles Hardin Holley and the golden songbook he created in little more than 18 months.

Many years later, on the multi-artist 1996 tribute album *Not Fade Away*, Mark had the opportunity to pay his respects to Buddy in a poignant collaboration. He played beautifully on a warm and tender remake of 'Learning the Game' with vocals by Buddy's great friend and collaborator and latter-day country giant Waylon Jennings, who of course narrowly avoided that fateful accident on the day the music died. Mark was delighted when Waylon told him that they had nailed the song definitively.
– Paul Sexton

'Everybody knows I've always loved Buddy.'

MARK KNOPFLER Everybody knows I've always loved Buddy. Here's another example of it. About 20 years ago, I was at a street café somewhere, sitting outside on the pavement. They had the Dire Straits song 'Telegraph Road' playing, which is a big, long, tortuous thing. I was listening to it, thinking of ways that I would improve it now, and so on.

Then Buddy's 'Rave On' came on and blew my song into the weeds. Two minutes of 'Rave On' destroyed it. And I asked myself, 'When am I going to write a song as good as Buddy's? That'll be the day.'

ALLAN CLARKE *'Peggy Sue Got Married'*

PEGGY SUE GOT MARRIED

Buddy Holly wrote 'Peggy Sue Got Married' in late 1958 after his father suggested he write a follow-up to his big hit 'Peggy Sue'. Peggy Sue had indeed got married, to Jerry Allison, on 22 July 1958, but they waited until after Buddy and Maria Elena's wedding on 15 August before going on honeymoon. The two couples honeymooned together in Acapulco, Mexico.

Buddy recorded the song on 5 December in his New York apartment and an overdubbed version was released as a single on Coral on 20 July 1959.

Left: The song title attributed to Graham Nash's Buddy Holly guitar is 'Rave On', however in this image he is using a Buddy Holly guitar with the song title 'Because I Love You'

SUCH A SHAME TO HAVE MISSED
SEEING THE MAN WHO CHANGED
SO MANY LIVES WITH HIS MUSIC.
HIS SONGS WILL ALWAYS
LIVE ON SO I CAN ALWAYS
HEAR THOSE FAMOUS CHORD
CHANGES WE ALL LEARNED
IN OUR EARLY DAYS OF
ROCK & ROLL
THANKS BUDDY

ALLAN CLARKE BEGAN SINGING with childhood friend Graham Nash while they were still at school. Later they formed the Hollies together, first charting in 1963 with '(Ain't That) Just Like Me' and 'Searchin''. The hits kept coming through the 1960s, some of them written by fellow Mancunian Graham Gouldman, others by Allan and Graham with lead guitarist Tony Hicks.

Graham Nash left the Hollies in 1968, but they continued to flourish. Allan also left the band in 1971 to make his first two solo albums, but rejoined in 1973 and thereafter managed to continue his solo work while remaining a member of the band.

In 1980, the Hollies released a whole album of their takes on Buddy Holly songs, simply called *Buddy Holly*. In 1996, the Hollies and Graham Nash collaborated on a new version of 'Peggy Sue Got Married', dubbing harmony vocals and instrumental backing over Buddy's lead vocals. The resulting recording, credited to 'Buddy Holly and the Hollies' was the opening track on that year's *Not Fade Away* tribute album.

Allan retired from music in 1999 due to problems with his vocal cords. He was inducted into the Rock and Roll Hall of Fame in 2010 as a member of the Hollies. In 2019, he picked up his solo career again with a new album called *Resurgence* and released a follow-up in 2023. – *Mike Read*

ALLAN CLARKE Buddy appeared alongside all the other great rock and rollers of that time and was a great influence. Most of those tunes featured the three most important chords needed to play rock and roll. Buddy's superb songwriting and playing of the now famous Fender Stratocaster enabled the transition of those three chords to play and sing most of his songs as rock and roll took over.

Graham and I joined the Foundation at the beginning and felt it quite a privilege to be asked. The memories of those early days of rock and roll greet me every morning and I just can't stop myself taking my guitar, playing 'Peggy Sue' and smiling. Thanks, Buddy.

'When asked what my favourite Buddy song is, I can't answer. They're all my favourite.'

BRUCE WELCH *'Crying, Waiting, Hoping'*

Don McLean wrote in 'that' song
he couldn't remember if he cried
the day 'the music died'.
I can and I did, reading the news
over breakfast.
I can't begin to tell you the
influence Buddy had on my life
and especially my playing style
Loved him then and still do
today!

Bruce Welch

CRYING, WAITING, HOPING
Buddy Holly recorded 'Crying, Waiting, Hoping' in his apartment in New York on 14 December 1958. Producer Jack Hansen hired studio musicians and the Ray Charles Singers to play alongside Buddy's original recording in an attempt to match the sound of Buddy Holly and the Crickets as closely as possible. This overdubbed version was released as the B-side to 'Peggy Sue Got Married' on 20 July 1959.

IN 1956, BRUCE WELCH AND BRIAN RANKIN were two 14-year-old schoolkids in grey Newcastle upon Tyne, who got caught up in the birth of rock and roll. Elvis, Little Richard, Fats Domino and Gene Vincent were all new and exciting sounds.

Fast forward to April 1958, Bruce and Brian – or Hank Marvin, as he now called himself – had moved to London, and that's when the sun came out, as *The 'Chirping' Crickets* was released in the UK. On the cover was Buddy Holly with a guitar they had never seen before, a Fender Stratocaster.

They were hooked on all things Holly. Bruce studiously copied all of his rhythm parts and Hank learned all his licks. Here was a unique talent who played the guitar wonderfully, had a distinctive 'hiccupping' vocal style and wrote most of his own material.

Later that summer, still only 16, they joined the Drifters, the backing band of an emerging star called Cliff Richard, but soon found they had to change the name to avoid confusion with the American vocal group of the same name. And so, the Shadows were born. The story of Cliff importing the 'Red Strat' for Hank to play is legendary now. That first Stratocaster in the UK became Hank and the Shadows' trademark and is still revered today. A stream of Shadows hits followed, both backing Cliff and as an instrumental band in their own right.

This partnership continued until the end of 1968, when the Shadows took a break. Bruce continued to play, write and produce for various artists, including Olivia Newton-John, Cliff Richard and Marvin, Welch & Farrar, his next musical enterprise with Hank Marvin. In 1989, Bruce became the musical consultant for the highly successful stage musical *Buddy: The Buddy Holly Story*, which ran on the London stage for 13 years.

While visiting New York before the Broadway opening of the show, Bruce visited Buddy's apartment building on Fifth Avenue, where his last songs were written. It seems fitting that to thank Bruce for his contribution to Buddy's legacy, his guitar is named 'Crying, Waiting, Hoping'.

BRUCE WELCH I was sitting having lunch in New York with Maria Elena and Laurie Mansfield – the producer of *Buddy: The Buddy Holly Story* – as the show was about to open on Broadway. Why don't you go down to the apartment block on Fifth Avenue where we lived?' Maria Elena suggested. So I did. Walking into the reception hall, the porter approached me and asked, 'Can I help you, sir?' 'Thanks, but I just wanted to see the place where Buddy lived, left and never came back. Where he wrote, among others, "True Love Ways" and "Crying, Waiting, Hoping".'

'This story has gone full circle thanks to Buddy Holly, the man and his music.'

As a 7 year old boy
in the North of England
I listened to Buddy's records
on Coral with my mother.
Buddy changed our lives -
Oh Boy!

Love & Appreciation

SALTY DOG RAG

The Salty Dog Rag is a traditional American country dance. The country singer Red Foley had a hit in 1952 with a song of the same name, whose lyrics gave directions for the moves of the dance. Buddy Holly performed a cover of 'Salty Dog Rag' during the Winter Dance Party tour in 1959. According to Waylon Jennings, who was in Buddy's band during that tour, audiences reacted well when they played the song.

THE WORK AND SONGS OF BUDDY HOLLY AND STING are woven together in many ways. Some creative strands are instantly visible, others are more subtle and unexpected. These two great artists share a gift of prolific and memorable lyrical brilliance.

Their respective bands, the Crickets and the Police, performed their music in group arrangements of stunning and often stark simplicity, highlighting the power and clarity of the words to create a timeless energy and a legacy that includes some of the greatest records ever recorded.

But the connection goes deeper than their shared hit-factory genius. In 1979, as the Police were approaching their peak, Sting was given his screen debut in an indie, ultra-cool UK road movie called *Radio On*, in which he played the part of Just Like Eddie, a massive Eddie Cochran fan who happened to be the forecourt attendant of a neglected garage close to the location of Cochran's fatal car accident in 1960.

It's a bleak, sometimes depressing but always compelling film, made on a shoestring. The highlight for me is a performance by Sting of 'Three Steps to Heaven', the song that posthumously and ironically took Eddie Cochran to the top of the UK chart a few weeks after he died. Sting is leaning up against an old-fashioned petrol pump, strumming an acoustic guitar and singing from the heart. It's a short but casually fantastic performance, doleful and soulful and captured in grainy black and white, and it's a moment that tells us everything about how much the song means to him. I share the love. The original version is one of my favourite records ever.

Buddy and Eddie were great friends, so it was fitting and poignant that two of the guys from Buddy's group the Crickets, guitarist Sonny Curtis and drummer Jerry Allison, were the backing musicians on that fabulous record. 'Three Steps to Heaven' was Eddie's biggest-ever hit single and was the song that provided Sting with such a memorable monochrome moment in a truly fascinating film.

The ties that bind brought the music of Buddy Holly, Eddie Cochran and Sting together in an amazing way and it's wonderful that, all these years later, Sting is now a proud ambassador for The Buddy Holly Educational Foundation and a deeply respected recipient of the Buddy Holly guitar. – *Bob Harris*

KIEFER SUTHERLAND *'Smokey Joe's Cafe'*

Dearest Buddy.

I will never be able
to thank you enough for
your songwriting and arranging
your music is a constant
inspiration to me.

You left this world more beautiful
than your found it

Deepest Respect

Kiefer Sutherland

KIEFER SUTHERLAND There are so many things that have moved me about Buddy Holly. His music, his producing and his style, but the thing that stands out the most to me is his love and devotion to his wife and the strength of their partnership.

I believe the first song I ever heard of Buddy Holly's was 'Peggy Sue'. I was always struck by the hooks in his songs; they would get you right out of the gate and you would find yourself singing along before the song finished.

His impact as a producer is still felt today and, sadly, I think he was just hitting his stride as a composer when he was taken. I believe very strongly that he would have made an even greater impact on all contemporary music.

'I think the sky was the limit for Buddy Holly.'

KIEFER SUTHERLAND HAS HAD MANY LIVES: actor, country recording artist, rodeo champion, record label owner – now ambassador for The Buddy Holly Educational Foundation.

The first single Kiefer ever bought was Buddy Holly's 'Raining in My Heart'. While he didn't grow up listening to country music – he was 'the only kid in kindergarten who had an Aerosmith T-shirt' – it was this genre he later endeavoured in. During a break from acting in 1998, Kiefer became a rodeo rider and found himself travelling around America with cowboys. It was at this time he discovered the music of Johnny Cash, Merle Haggard, Waylon Jennings and Willie Nelson. The storytelling that weaves through both country music and acting was a recurring theme in Kiefer's passions. But Buddy Holly, his first musical love, persisted throughout.

His fascination with music has persisted throughout his successful acting career – which has included 11 number one box office hits, as well as a Golden Globe and an Emmy for his leading role in *24* – and came to fruition in 2016 when he released his debut album, *Down in a Hole.* Since then, he has released two more albums and toured across the US, Canada and beyond. In 2019, Kiefer busked on the streets of Los Angeles with his Buddy Holly guitar in the video for his song 'Something You Love'.

SMOKEY JOE'S CAFE

'Smokey Joe's Cafe' was written by Jerry Leiber and Mike Stoller and first recorded by the Robins in 1955. Buddy recorded his version in his New York apartment on 21 January 1959, shortly before leaving for the Winter Dance Party tour. This version was overdubbed and first released on the Coral compilation Giant *almost exactly ten years later, on 20 January 1969.*

In the mid-1990s, Leiber and Stoller created a long-running Broadway musical revue named after this song.

DON McLEAN *'American Pie'*

FEW PEOPLE HAVE DONE MORE since Buddy Holly's sad passing to keep his music and memory alive than Don McLean. His classic 1971 single 'American Pie' has reminded successive generations of Don's own early musical hero and coined the enduring phrase 'the day the music died'.

Don began playing guitar at the age of 16 and dropped out of university to become a musician. His early career saw him playing the Newport Jazz Festival and the legendary Troubadour club in Los Angeles and learning the art of performing from his mentor, Pete Seeger, with whom he appeared in 1969 to raise awareness about environmental pollution.

By the time Don's second album, *American Pie*, was released, his record label had been taken over by United Artists, so for the first time he had major promotion for his songs. The title track, an abstract story of his life set against the development of American youth culture, was partly inspired by Don's memory of hearing of the deaths of Buddy Holly, Ritchie Valens and the Big Bopper. The song became an international hit despite being more than eight and a half minutes long. 'American Pie' was ranked number five in the RIAA list of the Songs of the 20th Century and the original manuscript of the song sold for more than $1.2 million in 2015, the third highest price ever paid for an American literary manuscript.

Don would continue to draw on his influences throughout his career. His 1972 single 'Vincent', inspired by the painter Vincent van Gogh, went to number one in the UK, and he covered the Buddy Holly songs 'Everyday' and 'It Doesn't Matter Anymore'. His version of Roy Orbison's 'Crying' was praised by the Big O himself.

Nearly all of the Foundation guitars based on Buddy Holly's original Gibson J-45 bear the titles of songs written, recorded or performed by Buddy. Don McLean's is one of the very rare exceptions. At the special request of Maria Elena Holly, Don's guitar is called 'American Pie'. – *Mike Read*

Buddy Holly was my first dream musician. I used to day dream to his music and, later, mourn his death. I'm so glad I was able to be part of his story.

Don McLean

AMERICAN PIE

Recorded and released in 1971, Don McLean's 'American Pie' refers to 3 February 1959, the date of the plane crash that killed Buddy Holly, Ritchie Valens and the Big Bopper, as 'the day the music died'. The single was number one in the US for four weeks in 1972, and also topped the charts in Australia, Canada and New Zealand. At nearly nine minutes long, the song had to be split across the two sides of the single.

DON McLEAN My love of Buddy Holly was there from the beginning and it never wavered. I guess most folks today can't believe that after his death there was little interest in him or his music. In England they always remembered him, but in America not as much.

The years went by and major music changes took place like The Beatles, the Stones, Bob Dylan, the Beach Boys and much more, but Buddy's music was underneath a lot of it. You just can't beat 'Peggy Sue' or 'Rave On' for musicality and rock power.

My song 'American Pie' was released in 1971, then the John Goldrosen biography of Buddy was published in 1975, then the movie *The Buddy Holly Story* came out in 1978 and suddenly he was back because, like me, millions never wanted to give him up.

The Buddy Holly Educational Foundation has put so much love and attention into their presentation guitars and every recipient has Buddy deep inside the music they make. The Foundation is always finding new ways to keep the Holly memory all about his wonderful music.

'My love of Buddy Holly was there from the beginning and it never wavered.'

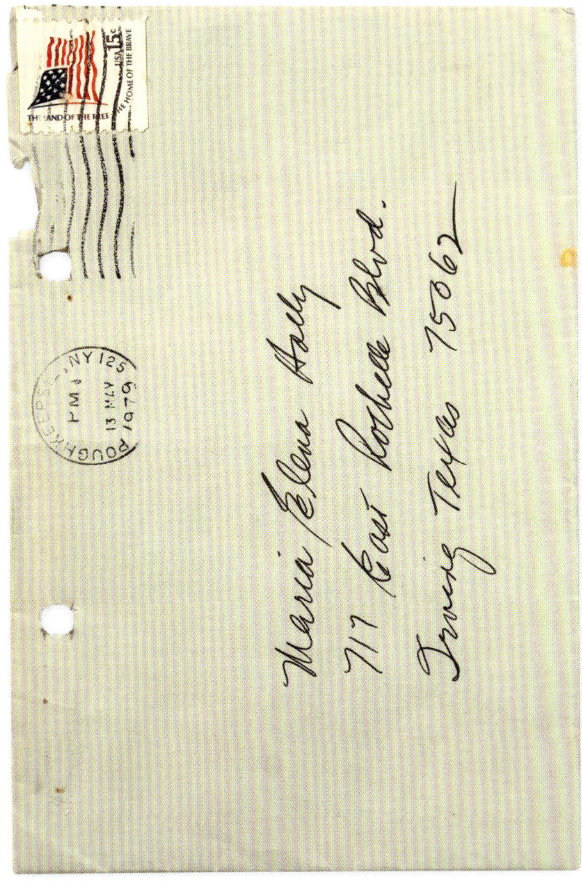
Maria Elena Holly
717 East Rochelle Blvd.
Irving Texas 75062

THE SAVOY LONDON
SAVOY HOTEL P.O. BOX 189 STRAND LONDON WC2R 0EU
Cables SAVOTEL LONDON WC2 Telex RESERVATIONS 24234 MESSAGES 24235
Telephone 01-836 4343

May 11, 1979

Dear Maria Elena –

Thanks for the lovely note and the kind words.

Buddy meant much more to me than nostalgia, or success.

Hold on to your memories – they are the real Holly story.

See you soon – Don

DON McLEAN Buddy Holly died at only 22 years of age in a horrific plane crash. The flight was taken to get some extra time to do his laundry. The music he recorded in his short life continues to amaze me. It never gets old or dated. It's always thrilling. The variety of musical styles and the playing. The Crickets were the first perfect rock group, and the template for most others to follow. Elvis was very different with the Jordanaires and a trio.

As a 12-year-old, I communed with Buddy's music. Buddy was really my friend and he and I had something special. I loved him as only a 12-year-old can love. His music brought out a yearning in my heart that I was unfamiliar with. It still does. An album cost $3 and I could only afford one at a time but, with just one, I could have a year of dreams.

The first one, *Buddy Holly*, with the cover portrait without glasses and the beautiful look on his face, mesmerised me. As a paperboy in 1959 when I read that he had died I never got over it. Then, *The Buddy Holly Story* album came out with the black glasses in a close-up film noir head shot as if from the beyond. Buddy was speaking to me from the other side now and he was taking me with him. He became a ghost that haunted me. I don't think Buddy ever recorded a bad song, every one was a hit. I don't think any artist can match his output in such a short time, maybe because it flowed from him so naturally.

He was a really great singer with a very expressive and completely unique quality. You could hear the Texan in the vibrato. Buddy was a proud Texan. When we did the documentary *The Day the Music Died*, they kept trying to get me to go to the crash site and I refused. I will never visit such a place. Buddy will always be young and Buddy will live forever.

CHAPTER SIX
Legacy

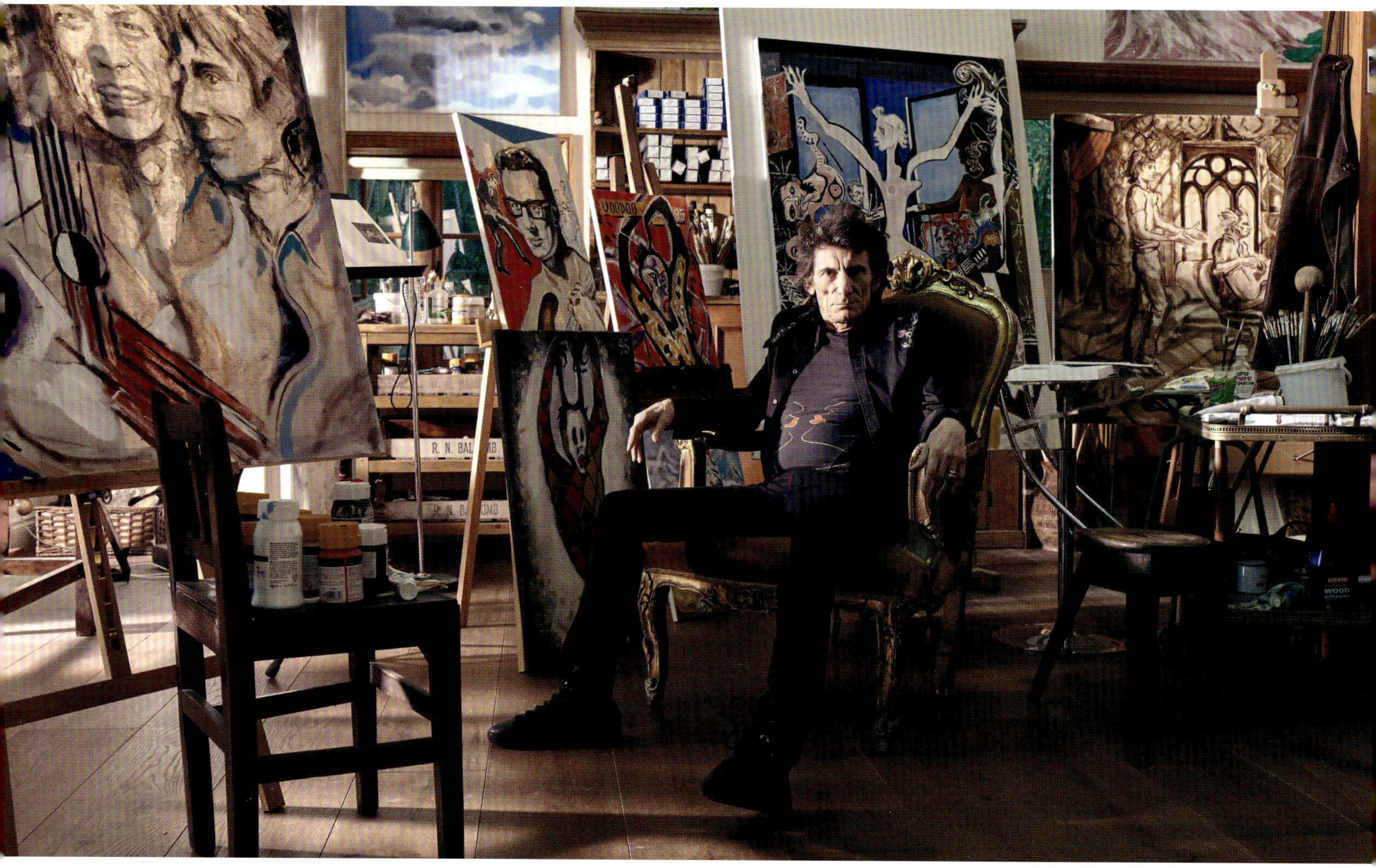

DAY 3
SEPTEMBER 22 '16
LOS ANGELES
MISS YOU ~ A
Tumblin Dice ~ B
Respectable
SHATTERED ~ E
RUBY TUESDAY ~ A
LOVIN' CUP
HONKY TONK ~ G
SHINE A LIGHT ~ G
OUT OF CONTROL ~ C
JUST YOUR FOOL ~ A
Ride 'em on down ~ B
BLUE & LONESOME
SHE'S A RAINBOW

Buddy Holly and the Rolling Stones BY PHILIP NORMAN

The Rolling Stones appeared on The Mike Douglas Show *to promote their very first US single, a cover of Buddy Holly's 'Not Fade Away,' in June 1964*

Opposite: Ronnie Wood in his studio. Ronnie's painting of Buddy features on the front cover of this book

In 1964, the Rolling Stones were causing mayhem in Britain as the scowling, sneering antithesis of the sweet, smiley Beatles – yet they were still a hardcore R&B band, performing cover versions of Chuck Berry or Muddy Waters. Their teenage manager/record producer Andrew Loog Oldham, kept on at Mick Jagger and Keith Richards to write original songs like John Lennon and Paul McCartney – where the real money was – but so far hadn't persuaded them to try.

However, for the Stones' third single on the Decca label they agreed a compromise. The A-side wouldn't be another R&B cover but Buddy Holly's 'Not Fade Away', which Jagger and fellow original Stone Dick Taylor had seen him perform live at Woolwich's Granada cinema during his one and only British tour in 1958.

Buddy's original was as plain as a Texas prairie: just himself on guitar and the Crickets' drummer, Jerry Allison, beating on a cardboard box-top.This was now transformed into a Stone-wall of sound with Keith playing a Holly-style 'rhythm lead' in the stop-start tempo invented by Bo Diddley but at double the speed, punctuated by Brian Jones' whinnying harmonica.

The recording session would have scandalised his producer, Norman Petty. It was the culminaton of a late-night party at Regent Sound Studios where Andrew Oldham and the Stones were joined by the American producer (and Oldham's role model) Phil Spector and, coincidentally, Allan Clarke and Graham Nash from the Hollies to do backup vocals. Later on, the American balladeer Gene Pitney also dropped by, bringing an outsize bottle of brandy. The taping frequently degenerated into tomfoolery with Jagger rudely mimicking Decca's chairman, Sir Edward Lewis, and Phil Spector ad-libbing an obscene recitative he named 'Andrew's Blues'.

The Stones' 'Not Fade Away' reached number three in the British charts, most listeners not even recognising it as a Buddy Holly song. Soon afterwards, Oldham locked Mick and Keith in the kitchen of the flat the three shared, refusing to let them out until they'd written an original song, and a writing partnership second only to Lennon and McCartney's was born.

Throughout the monumental career that was to come, the Stones would always keep 'Not Fade Away' in their stage show. But whereas Buddy had recorded it using a single 20-watt Fender Pro amplifier, their amps and sound system and lighting together totalled a million watts.

Buddy Holly and The Beatles BY PHILIP NORMAN

By 1958, one adult condemnation of rock and roll at least – that its stars were con-artists just using their guitars as props – could be thoroughly refuted. The charge was most ludicrous in the case of Buddy Holly, a 21-year-old Texan who played virtuoso electric lead as well as singing in an intriguing, hiccuppy voice in a trio called the Crickets. Their September 1957 hit 'That'll Be the Day' featured a dazzling Holly intro, reprised in the solo: a backward tumble of treble notes that set the blood of Britain's L-plate pickers practically alight. In Britain, Holly was a 'buddy' indeed to skiffle groups in the throes of trying to rock and roll-ise themselves (who were not only future Beatles but future Rolling Stones, future Who, future everyone-who-would-be-anyone in the 1960s beat boom). For his songs, while wholly original and more exciting every time, were constructed from the simple chords they already knew.

Nowhere was his influence more galvanic than on an obscure Liverpool group named the Quarrymen formed by art student John Lennon which schoolfriends Paul McCartney and George Harrison had recently joined. Holly handed them a ready-made repertoire to which, every few months, he added a further title that was just a touch more complicated as if to bring them on another step. And, like 'That'll Be the Day', many were written or part-written by him. He showed John and Paul that songwriters need not be remote sophisticates with names like Cole Porter but that the two of them were just as entitled to have a go.

Even the few pictures of Holly to appear in the British press brought his young British disciples comfort and encouragement, for here was no pouting deity like Elvis but an amiable-looking beanpole in glasses, hitherto the stigmata of school swots and nerds. The short-sighted John had so hated his glasses that, rather than suffer the shame of being a 'foureyes', he'd gone around half-blind. Now he could look like his hiccupping hero and see the world.

The youngest Quarryman, 14-year-old George, studied Buddy Holly and the Crickets as he never had any subject at Liverpool Institute High School. To pay his parents back for the Höfner President they'd bought him, George had a Saturday job delivering meat for local butchers E.R. Hughes. His round included the home of his childhood friend, Tony Bramwell, who owned a copy of the Crickets' first album, *The 'Chirping' Crickets*. Hughes's big iron delivery bike would be parked outside for long periods with people's weekend steaks and chops spoiling in its front pannier as Bramwell played him the 12 magic tracks, not only original rock and roll but country and R&B covers, over and over.

Holly came to Britain with the Crickets on what would be his only visit early in March 1958, performing in theatres and cinemas throughout the country – dedicated rock and roll venues then being limited to coffee bars – and reaching Liverpool's Philharmonic Hall on 20 March. George couldn't get a ticket and was consumed with envy that his friend Tony Bramwell had won a newspaper competition to see the show and met Holly afterwards.

He himself had to be content with the Crickets' fleeting appearance, dinner-jacketed, on the television variety show *Sunday Night at the London Palladium*. The flickery black and white screen showed Holly playing a two-horned shape, flat against his side, that looked less like a guitar than a spaceship fitted with a strap. It was the first Fender Stratocaster ever to cross the Atlantic.

One improvement for the Quarrymen that Paul particularly urged on John was to make recordings of their performances to let them hear how they sounded and also circulate among prospective bookers rather than have to do a live audition every time. Other groups possessed reel-to-reel tape recorders but in 1958 these were horribly expensive and far beyond their means.

Then a fellow skiffler named Johnny Byrne told George about a studio in Liverpool where people could simply walk in and record their voices just as Elvis Presley had walked into Sun Records that day in 1954. It even had the same surname as the man lucky enough to have discovered Elvis: the Phillips Recording Service. An appointment for the Quarrymen was booked with its owner, Percy Phillips, for a fee of 17 shillings and sixpence (75p) between them.

By now, their personnel had shrunk to John, Paul, George, drummer Colin Hanton and an occasional pianist named John Lowe. They were to record two songs, of which only one had so far been decided, the Crickets' 'That'll Be the Day'. Many other groups covered it but few could aspire to Buddy Holly's wondrous lead riff. 'George told me he was going to learn it,' his schoolfriend Arthur Kelly recalls. 'A couple of days later, he had.' The experience of making a record proved sadly lacking in Presley-esque romance. The Phillips Recording Service was located at its owner's home, 38 Kensington, one of Liverpool's many thoroughfares with London names. A shabby terrace house, its bay window contained a selection of electrical goods for sale, above the front door was an enormous sign, BATTERY CHARGING DEPOT EST. 25 YEARS, and a sign in an adjacent window offered 'loans £5 to £500 without security'.

Opposite and pages 368–370: Intimate images of The Beatles backstage. These are believed to be previously unpublished.

Percy Phillips – who, Colin Hanton says, 'looked like anyone's dad' – was not expected to have any affinity with rock and roll but treated the Quarrymen politely enough, even if his most pressing concern was that they had the money to pay for his time. Like his usual clientele of amateur opera singers and children reciting party pieces, they recorded at a single microphone in the middle of what must once have been the Phillips family's dining room.

The session, preserved for posterity on YouTube, seems to come from the same remote past as some Victorian music-hall turn captured on wax cylinders. First, 'That'll Be the Day' with John's rather acid lead voice and George note-perfect throughout the Holly solo, sharing the handful of watts from Paul's undersized Elpico amp.

Then a pastiche country song, 'In Spite of All the Danger', written by Paul before he met John. George is well to the fore, not only in framing riffs but ah-ah-ing a counterpoint to their harmony that just manages to stay on-key. Editing was not included in Percy Phillips's fee and after a few minutes' wait he handed over a single small shellac disc with the song titles handwritten on its yellow 'Kensington' label. Thanks to George's riffs, 'In Spite of All the Danger' was credited to 'McCartney-Harrison', his first and last experience of being Paul's musical equal in the band. The plaque that eventually replaced BATTERY CHARGING DEPOT outside 38 Kensington gives the date of the recording as 14 July 1958, but Colin Hanton is certain it took place two days earlier. This would mean that only three days after John casually sang 'that'll be the day when I die' and harmonised about 'all the danger', his mother, Julia, was knocked down and killed by a speeding motorist, a loss from which he would never recover.

The five Quarrymen had agreed to share the Percy Phillips disc on a rota of a week each. But after the pianist, John Lowe, had his week, he failed to pass it on; no one else claimed their turn and Lowe drifted away from the group soon afterwards with it still in his possession. It would lie forgotten in his attic for 23 years, then resurfaced as the most valuable record in the world.

When the Quarrymen became The Beatles (with the Crickets half in mind) they were at first as much a 'covers band' as a test-bed for Lennon/McCartney songs, and Buddy along with Chuck Berry and Carl Perkins kept them going through their long, sweltering nights of apprenticeship, first in Hamburg's red light district, then at Liverpool's Cavern Club. Even when they were 'bigger than Elvis', as their manager Brian Epstein had promised, they still didn't forget him: their 1964 *Beatles for Sale* album included a note-perfect version of his double-tracked masterpiece 'Words of Love'.

Buddy Holly Week. Sept. 7 to 14. 1980.

The fifth anniversary of "Buddy Holly Week" in 1980 was celebrated by a Buddy Holly Fan Fair at the Clarendon Hotel in Hammersmith, with memorabilia, rare records and photos on display. On Friday September 12th, an hour long dramatization of Buddy's life, "The Day The Music Died", was broadcast by Capital Radio. In Lubbock, a 7½ foot bronze statue of Buddy was unveiled, and the Buddy Holly Memorial Foundation organised a special concert with Roy Orbison, Bobby Vee and Bo Diddley.

By now it had become apparent just how permanent Buddy's influence had become. David Putnam's 1973 film "That'll Be The Day" took its title from a Buddy Holly song; New Wave stars like Blondie and Wreckless Eric covered his songs and Elvis Costello modelled his appearance on Buddy.

Remembering Buddy

Buddy Holly ... or Bluddy Holly as my Kids called him when they were very young, was an INNOVATIVE musician, who was born CHARLES HARDIN Holly in LUBBOCK, Texas. He was one of those singers who stood out on our Liverpool radio in the 50's and when the song finished, you asked "WHO was that!?" because he was different, original, unusual... in fact UNIQUE! with a distinctive voice.. not only that... he wore specs!

His backing group were The Crickets and I sometimes think, was that 'insect' name instrumental in my brother's group name?

One of my favourite Buddy songs is 'Raining in my Heart' in which he used a STRING section.. ..at that time, an outrageous accompaniment on a POP record!

Buddy sadly died at the age of 22 in a plane crash with the BIG BOPPER and Richie Valens, but he Lives ON in his Wonderful music of That'll be the DAY, Peggy Sue, True Love Ways, RAVE ON, Everyday and OH BOY... to name but two!

RAVE ON Buddy

GEORGE HARRISON ***I think one of the greatest people for me was Buddy Holly because, first of all, he sang, wrote his own tunes, was a guitar player, and he was very good – exceptionally good. Buddy Holly was the first time I ever heard A to F-sharp minor. A to F-sharp minor, fantastic!***

He's opening up new worlds there. And then 'Pretty, pretty, Peggy Sue'. A to F. Buddy Holly was sensational, so I mean a little bit of that rubbed off in as much as I no longer have a fear of changing from A to F.

Top left: A page from Buddy: Buddy Holly Memorial Issue 1981 (see page 373)

Top right: Handwritten tribute to Buddy by Mike McCartney

YUSUF / CAT STEVENS ***Way before I ever dreamed of buying a guitar, I heard Buddy Holly and fell in love with 'Peggy Sue'.***

It was the beginning of the beat generation, rock and roll had already arrived in the hot form of Elvis Presley, and we all caught fire. Buddy's influence cannot be underestimated, he did after all ignite a group of four lads from Liverpool, which then span the world round even faster towards musical utopia. That's when I rushed out to get my first guitar and join in the great show.

By the time I got my own six-string, I'd heard a whole lot of music and was deeply into R&B. Bo Diddley happened to be a real favourite of mine. I could see how Buddy Holly had lifted a few ideas from him too – spectacles included ... I mean, he even sang the song 'Bo Diddley'. Holly became the first archetypal pop writing genius. Three chords was all he needed, which is just about all I could manage in the beginning. You can clearly hear his influence in my early songwriting. If you listen to 'Here Comes My Baby', it's almost a tailor fit, Buddy Holly song. I wished he'd sung it. May he rest in peace.

BUDDY HOLLY WEEK

SEPTEMBER 7TH-14TH 1978

BUDDY HOLLY WEEK 1982
PSA
52 Carter Lane
London EC4.

WELCOME TO AMERICA'S FIRST 'BUDDY HOLLY WEEK'.

IN ENGLAND 'BUDDY HOLLY WEEK' HAS BEEN A REGULAR FEATURE ON THE ROCK CALENDAR SINCE 1976. IT ALL BEGAN WHEN I ORGANISED A PARTY TO CELEBRATE WHAT WOULD HAVE BEEN BUDDY'S 40TH BIRTHDAY ON SEPTEMBER 7TH, 1976.

ACTUALLY, IT REALLY BEGAN IN LIVERPOOL IN 1957 WHEN I FIRST HEARD BUDDY HOLLY'S 'PEGGY SUE'. I WAS 15 YEARS OLD AND LIKE MILLIONS OF OTHERS A GREAT FAN OF BUDDY'S RECORDS. OVER THE YEARS IT SEEMS IRONIC THAT BUDDY HAS BEEN MORE POPULAR IN ENGLAND THAN IN HIS HOME COUNTRY WHICH IS WHY THIS YEAR WE HAVE DECIDED TO INAUGURATE AMERICA'S FIRST 'BUDDY HOLLY WEEK'.

SINCE THE BEGINNING IT HAS BEEN GREAT TO SEE SO MANY YOUNG FANS ENJOYING THE SAME SORT OF MUSIC THEIR PARENTS DID.

IT IS HARD TO BELIEVE THAT IT IS NEARLY A QUARTER OF A CENTURY OLD, BUT THE GREAT THING ABOUT BUDDY HOLLY - THE GREAT THING ABOUT ROCK 'N' ROLL - IS THAT IT IS TIMELESS.

SOME PEOPLE SAY THAT ROCK 'N' ROLL DIED WITH BUDDY HOLLY. ROCK 'N' ROLL DEAD? THAT'LL BE THE DAY.

ENJOY YOURSELVES.

PAUL MCCARTNEY, 1983

Group shot at the Buddy Holly Luncheon, The Orangery, Holland Park, London, 7 September 1976

Buddy Holly Week September 7th – 14th 1976

You are cordially invited to lunch at The Orangery, (off Kensington High Street) Holland Park, London, W.8. on Tuesday, September 7th, 12.30 p.m. for 1.00 p.m.

We look forward to seeing you there to celebrate the start of Buddy Holly week.

This invitation is not transferable and admits one person only.

R.S.V.P.
Ann Gillham,
MPL Communications Ltd.,
12-13 Greek Street,
London, W.1.
Telephone: 01-439 0386

BUDDY HOLLY WEEK LUNCH

At the Buddy Holly Luncheon, the Orangery, Holland Park - September 7, 1976

Left to right:
Brian Brolly, MPL; Douglas Maxwell, G. Whizzard; Roy Featherstone, MCA; Brian Mulligan, Music Week; Peter Robinson, MCA; Howie Casey, Wings; Nick Nickola, UPI; Paul Winn, MPL; Alan Crowder, MPL; Tony Bramwell; Mrs. Tony Prince; Ray Coleman, M.M.; Roy Carr, N.M.E.; Tony Prince, Radio Luxembourg D.J.; John Gould, EMI; Tony Brainsby; Patti Harrison; "Unidentified Object"; "Unidentified Object"; Mrs. Vi Petty; Trevor Jones, MPL; Roger Taylor, Queen; Brian May, Queen; Elton John; Joe English, Wings; David Munns, EMI; Kevin Godley, 10c.c.; John Deacon, Queen; Eric Stewart, 10c.c.; Steve Harley; Michael Appleton; Yvonne Keeley; Paul Gambaccini, B.B.C. D.J.; Phil Manzanera, Roxy Music; Graham Gouldman, 10c.c. Shirley Natanson, EMI; Paul Watts, EMI; Eric Hall, EMI; J. J. Jackson, U.S. D.J.; "Unidentified Object"; Bob Mercer, EMI; John Beecher, Buddy Holly Fan Club.
Seated, left to right:
Christine Mackie, MPL; Eric Clapton; John Reid; Denny Laine, Wings; Joanne Laine; Norman Petty; Paul McCartney; Linda McCartney; Lol Creme, 10c.c.; Stephen Bishop; Jane McKay; Andy McKay, Roxy Music; Sharon Manzanera; Adrienne Hunter, E. G. Management; Sue Thompson; Pauline MacLeod, Daily Mirror; Paul Thompson, Roxy Music; Ann Gillham, MPL; Ian Meldrum, Australian D.J.

Missing was Alan 'Fluff' Freeman who was busy tickling the photographer.

IN 1975 PAUL McCARTNEY BOUGHT THE NOR VA JAK BUDDY HOLLY SONG CATALOGUE FROM NORMAN PETTY through his company, MPL Communications. To promote and celebrate Buddy Holly's legacy, on the 40th anniversary of his birth, McCartney launched Buddy Holly Week in 1976. For the first Buddy Holly Week, McCartney invited Petty to a luncheon he hosted at the Orangery in Holland Park, London with Petty as the guest of honour. It was attended by notable rock stars including Denny Laine, Elton John, Eric Clapton, Roger Daltrey, Queen, 10cc and more. Later in the week a rock and roll dance concert at a London theatre was attended by thousands of fans. The Buddy Holly Week would become a yearly event around Buddy's birthday, featuring memorial concerts, fan fests and competitions as an appreciation of one of rock and roll's greatest talents.

ELTON JOHN ***I was an impressionable 11 year old when Buddy Holly died – he was one of my earliest heroes.***

(Quote from Elton John at the inaugural Buddy Holly Week in 1976)

Top left (l–r): Paul McCartney, Denny Laine, Steve Holley, Maria Elena Holly and Laurence Juber at the fourth Buddy Holly Week concert, Hammersmith Odeon, London, 14 September 1979

Above right: Maria Elena meeting fans and signing autographs at the fourth Buddy Holly Week Fan Fair, Clarendon Hotel, Hammersmith, London, 13 September 1979

Right: An invitation and reply card to attend the fourth Buddy Holly Week concert held by Paul McCartney who attended and performed at the event.

Buddy Holly Week 1979

During the fourth annual Buddy Holly Week from 7 to 14 September 1979, fans gathered to celebrate at a Buddy Holly Fan Fair, which included a special exhibition giving a scrapbook tour of Buddy's life and music through photos, press clippings, original sheet music and recordings. Material was displayed from fan clubs all over the world. Those who attended the fair were invited to bring along their own memorabilia to share and some came with suitcases full of material. The fair ended with a raffle of Holly records, books, songbooks and T-shirts and in the evening guest speakers the Crickets (Jerry Allison, Joe Mauldin and Sonny Curtis), Maria Elena, and Bob Montgomery said a few words before signing autographs and speaking to fans.

On 14 September a concert was held at the Hammersmith Odeon headlined by the Crickets plus a line-up of surprise guest artists, including Mike Berry and the Outlaws, Albert Lee, Bob Montgomery, Don Everly, and Denny Laine, Paul and Linda McCartney, Steve Holley and Laurence Juber, the five members of Wings at the time. Admission was free and tickets were given away through fan clubs, and competitions in the media.

Paul and Linda hosted a pre-concert party for a select group of friends and celebrities. The Odeon stage set displayed a silver tour bus with neon signs pointing the way to Nashville, Clovis and New York.

For the grand finale – everyone on stage performed an extended version of 'Bo Diddley' with each artist featured in a solo spot. There was just one encore, by the Crickets alone, ending Buddy Holly Week 1979 with 'Rave On'.

AT'LL BE THE DAY AND WELL INTO THE NIGHT, TOO

Ford and Pippa Harris, from Stoke Picture: ALASDAIR LOOS

Jive on . . . high-kicking Pippa shows how it's done

McCartney, complete with Buddy Holly specs, arrives with wife Linda

It's rock 'n' roll time again at Buddy Holly hop

By RICK SKY

THE fever of the Fifties raved again at London's Lyceum Ballroom last night.

Over 2,000 Teddy Boys and Girls gathered in their drapes and crepes for the world's biggest ever rock n' roll party to celebrate Buddy Holly Week.

Holly, who would have been 46 yesterday, died in a plane crash in February 1959 at the height of his fame. But his music lives on for millions of fans around the world.

Among the famous names who turned up at the Lyceum—dressed in fifties gear—were Billy Connolly, Pamela Stephenson, Ringo Starr, Mel Smith, Griff Rhys Jones and Billy Fury.

And, of course, there was Paul McCartney, who launched the annual Buddy Holly Week seven years ago after buying up the rights to Holly's classic songs, including That'll Be The Day, Peggy Sue and Rave On.

Highlight of the evening was the Buddy Holly rock 'n roll championship, in which eleven couples jived against each other for the title of Britain's best Ted dancers.

Holly . . . his music lives on

he night Paul and Linda rolled back the years

ur yesterday's . . . Paul and Linda in their 50s gear Picture: ALASDAIR LOOS

SUPERSTAR Paul McCartney saluted another pop legend with an amazing look-alike act.

He slicked back his hair and donned owlish horn-rimmed glasses. And, for one night at least, Buddy Holly lived again.

Paul and wife Linda rolled back the years and kitted themselves out in authentic 50's clobber for a rock 'n' roll party to celebrate Holly Week.

Paul's outfit included a Teddy Boy jacket, drapes, crepe soles, jazzy waistcoat and a bootlace tie. And Linda completed the picture with bobby sox and dirndl skirt.

But it was Paul's faithful re-creation of the Holly look that surprised the 2,000 rockers who gathered at London's Lyceum ballroom.

Paul's agent, Tony Brainsby, refuted suggestions that there was anything ghoulish about the impersonation.

Tribute

"Paul's done it before," he said. "It's a mark of respect."

The party was the highlight of Buddy Holly Week, the annual tribute to the star who died in a plane crash in February 1959.

And the highlight of the party was the finals of the Buddy Holly rock 'n' roll dance championships.

The contest was won by a jobless couple from Merseyside, Leslie Prendergast and Tanneh Freeman.

By DICK DURHAM

Paul presented them with a cup and gold medallions and they also won a holiday trip to Texas, Holly's home state.

Leslie, 23, of Elton Avenue, Netherton, Liverpool, said: "I can't believe it. Now I want to go on to stardom."

And Tanneh, 26, of King James Square, Runcorn, added: "I didn't recognise Paul — the glasses fooled me."

One of the youngest rockers at the party was 14-year-old Dean Hall, of Olinda Road, Hackney, London.

He said: "My Mum and Dad always jived round the record player on Sundays and I've just grown up with it.

Paul's Holly look-alike

Early 60s Paul

Buddy Holly Week 1982

In 1982, on the 25th anniversary of Buddy Holly and the Crickets, first number one single, 'That'll Be the Day', it was decided that Buddy Holly Week would have a British theme. A contest was held across dance halls all over England to find the best rock and roll couple in the country, a couple who would be true 1950s music fans, at the Buddy Holly Rock and Roll Championships.

Eleven couples qualified for the grand final, held at the Lyceum in London on 7 September. The event was attended by more than 2,000 people in rock and roll regalia and also featured a 1950s disco, live music from Mike Berry and the Outlaws and the Stargazers, as well as other staged events and competitions.

Three couples, including the couple who took first place, won a trip to Texas, to spend a week visiting Buddy's home town and seeing the sights with special guest Maria Elena Holly.

The contest winners were welcomed to Lubbock by Bill Griggs, president of the US Buddy Holly Memorial Society, to see Buddy's home, his high school, the city's memorial statue of Buddy, and to make a moving pilgrimage to Buddy's simple grave.

Top right: Paul and Linda McCartney at the seventh Buddy Holly Week Rock and Roll Party, Lyceum Ballroom, London, 7 September 1982

Right: Seventh Buddy Holly Week programme, 7-13 September 1982

'That'll Be the Day' Atkin Guitar, signed by Sir Paul McCartney

For six decades, Maria Elena Holly and Paul McCartney have been the two most important and consistent advocates in promoting the musical legacy of Buddy Holly. Paul, John and George recorded the Crickets' 'That'll Be the Day' in 1958 and ever since that legendary performance they always acknowledged the influence of Buddy's music on their amazingly successful careers.

The annual 'Buddy Holly Week' celebrations that Paul sponsored and hosted for many years were another wonderful endorsement of the admiration and love he had for Buddy's short but prolific career.

Maria Elena and The Buddy Holly Educational Foundation are proud and honoured that Paul accepted a special 'That'll Be the Day' guitar, which they had custom built for him. The presentation of this unique instrument by Maria Elena to Paul took place on 2 October 2014 in Buddy's home town of Lubbock, Texas. Paul also graciously signed another 'That'll Be the Day' guitar to go on permanent display in the Buddy Holly Center, Lubbock. Accompanying the guitar was a certificate signed by Maria Elena and Paul documenting the presentation.

Maria Elena said Buddy would have been proud and thrilled that Paul, John, George and Ringo, members of the most successful band in music history, The Beatles, all acknowledged a great admiration of, and affinity with, Buddy and his magical music legacy. That legacy which encompassed the very same attributes that made The Beatles so exceptional: brilliant song-writing, innovative arrangements and production, virtuoso musical abilities, classic recordings and a catalogue of songs that will go down forever in the annals of music history.

Sadly, John and George, like Buddy, are no longer with us, but Paul and Ringo continue to make great music and perform to sell-out audiences around the world.

A thank you to Paul McCartney, a true giant of music, for sharing your extraordinary talent with us all for so many years and bringing so much pleasure, joy and happiness to the world. Long may you continue to do so. Our love and best wishes go to Paul and Ringo, our memory and love of Buddy, John and George will 'Not Fade Away'.

'That'll Be the Day': Two Quarrymen Recall Recording the World's Rarest Record

COLIN HALL On Saturday morning, 12 July 1958, five young musicians calling themselves the Quarrymen entered the doors of 38 Kensington, Liverpool, the home of 'Phillips Sound Recording Services'. They were there to cut a 78 rpm ten-inch two-sided shellac record. The five boys were: John Lennon, age 17 (vocals, rhythm guitar), Paul McCartney, age 16 (vocals, rhythm guitar), George Harrison, age 15 (lead guitar), Colin Hanton, 19 (drums) and John Duff Lowe, 16 (keyboards).

Number 38 was a very ordinary Victorian terraced house that had been converted into a very small electrical goods and battery-charging shop. It was in 1955, at the back of the shop, in what would once have been a dining room, that the owner, Mr Percy Phillips, had invested £400 to create a recording studio.

Drummer Colin Hanton recalls, 'Without hesitation, the first tune we'd chosen to record was a particular favourite of ours, Buddy Holly's "That'll Be the Day". A highlight of our live set. We loved that song and in our heads it immediately became the "A-side". Buddy's music was really popular with us and we believed we performed "That'll Be the Day" very well. On stage we also played "Peggy Sue". Looking back, I now recognise that choosing a Buddy Holly song had greater significance than any of us consciously realised at the time. His influence on us all, especially John and Paul, was immense. Buddy was the one who'd drawn the blueprint, his records set the example for John and Paul to follow, he was already inspiring them to write their own songs. To record that number was almost a tribute to Buddy, while "In Spite of All the Danger" signified a kind of passing of the baton.'

'The song "In Spite of All the Danger" was something really different,' says pianist John Duff Lowe, 'a self-penned Paul song with some special guitar playing from George for which Paul gave him a writing credit, the only McCartney-Harrison writing credit on record. John Lennon sang lead on both songs with Paul harmonising.'

Remembering the actual recording session itself, Colin Hanton says, 'First we ran through the songs to ensure there was enough space on each side of the disc for our chosen numbers. We rattled through "That'll Be the Day" in fine style, Percy timing us as we did so. Confidence was high, one run-through, no hiccups. "In Spite of All the Danger" was not so smooth, despite all the extra practising we'd done at Paul's house. We tried again. It went better but I could see that towards the end Percy was becoming agitated, telling us the song was too long for the space on the disc. He urged us to cut out a verse but John Lennon was adamant we weren't going to. Percy just shrugged. No doubt thinking we would find out the hard way, he simply told us to, "Get on with it": one take only for each song, straight onto vinyl, no taping, no editing, no second attempts.'

The recording of 'That'll Be the Day' went without a hitch. As for 'In Spite of All the Danger' it was not quite the same story. According to Colin and Duff, Percy began to get very agitated as the group continued performing, oblivious to the clock ticking closer and closer to the limit of three and a half minutes when the recording would automatically stop. Fortunately as disaster loomed George's 7th chord chimed and the recording ended leaving only half a second run off.

There was no playback. Percy Phillips carefully took the newly minted 78 rpm disc from the deck, gently wiped it with his cloth and put it into one of several paper sleeves he had to hand. Prophetically it was one for Parlophone Records. Before they knew it the Quarrymen were back on the street clutching their oh-so-precious double-sided shellac single of themselves singing and playing their instruments. Mr Phillips's words of warning rang in their ears: 'The more you play it, the less good it will sound.'

Colin recalls, 'The idea was for us to take turns playing it to our families, John first, then Paul, then George and so on … but that never happened … In fact I was unaware of what happened to it after that first day. You see just three days later John Lennon's mother, Julia, was tragically knocked down and killed in a road accident. We were all devastated. I don't know how but it ended up with a friend of the group called Charlie Roberts who eventually passed it on to Duff Lowe.'

John Duff Lowe says, 'I was the last one to borrow the record and still had it when I left the band. No one rang me up to ask me to pass it on. Eventually I put it in a drawer out of harm's way, playing it once in a while to friends who asked to hear it. It wasn't treated as the priceless artifact it became! My wife Linda used to put it somewhere safe when we went on holiday without telling me, so she was obviously more aware of its value than I was.'

In 1981 Paul McCartney discovered Duff still had the record, largely unplayed, definitely unbroken or chipped and in relatively good condition. A deal was struck, Paul regained the disc, had it 'restored' and in 1995 both sides appeared on *The Beatles Anthology Volume 1* ('In Spite of All the Danger' seamlessly edited down by some 40 seconds from the original version). Finally, the Quarrymen were in the charts.

The Buddy Holly Hall of Performing Arts & Sciences

In the 1950s, a teenager from Lubbock sparked a cultural revolution with his music, big-framed glasses, and big dreams. Today, the Lubbock Entertainment and Performing Arts Association (LEPAA) continue his legacy by revolutionising performing arts, entertainment and education through the Buddy Holly Hall of Performing Arts and Sciences.

From decades of careful preparation, LEPAA was formed in 2013 as a not-for-profit organisation with the purpose of privately raising funds to develop, construct and operate a state-of-the-art performing arts centre in downtown Lubbock.

The Buddy Holly Hall of Performing Arts and Sciences gives the city two new theatres, one seating 2,200 people and another seating 425, and permanent homes for Ballet Lubbock, Lubbock Independent School District Fine Arts, and Lubbock Symphony Orchestra. We're proud that both theatres at the hall feature an acoustic value of NC 15, the highest acoustic value possible, offering both renowned artists and young aspiring artists the opportunity to perform on stage in a world-class venue.

The Buddy Holly Hall offers the three Es to Lubbock: entertainment, education and economic impact. Buddy inspired the world's best music and musicians, so it is our dream to honour Buddy through the Buddy Holly Hall of Performing Arts and Sciences, inspiring future generations of artists, musicians and entertainers while elevating downtown Lubbock and bringing the very best entertainment to the South Plains of Texas.

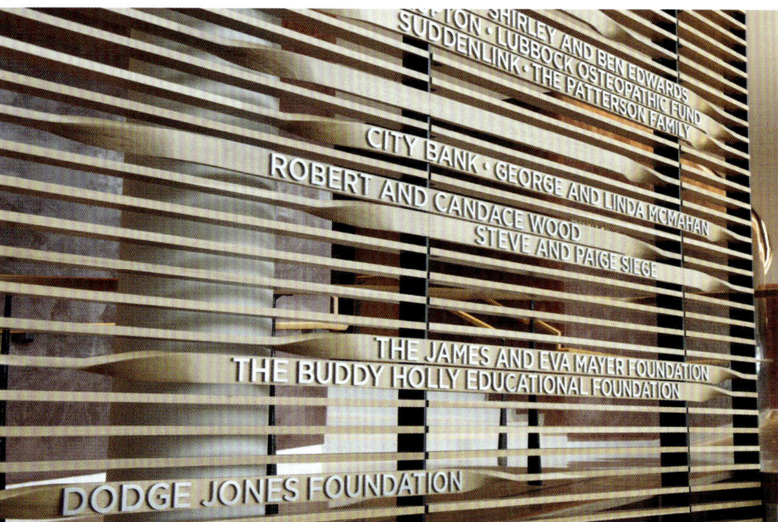

One of the best things about the Buddy Holly Hall is that it's built for the community by the community. Remarkably the entire $154 million funding to build and run it was raised privately, providing the cornerstone of our downtown revitalisation.

The hall would never have been more than just a dream without the incredible support of the CH Foundation and the Helen Jones Foundation, who each pledged $20 million to the project. Our third donation was tremendous, a $100 gift from a local barber who believed in our vision for the Lubbock community from the first day the project was announced.

The City of Lubbock graciously donated land at 1300 Mac Davis Lane across from the Lubbock Memorial Civic Center and, in 2014, an anonymous donor pledged a further $20 million to the performing arts centre, with the beautiful idea that the hall should bear the name of Buddy Holly. Through Lubbock resident Paul Beane, the LEPAA team reached out to Maria Elena Holly, who agreed without hesitation, being the guest of honour at the ground-breaking ceremony in 2017.

Every gift we've received speaks of the Lubbock community's support and desire for a new performing arts centre bearing Lubbock's most famous son's name, and the past few years since its opening have seen world class entertainers visit Lubbock, to perform there and be inspired by him.

Together we express our tremendous gratitude to the Buddy Holly Educational Foundation for their support and encouragement and we now enjoy hosting the closing concert of the annual Buddy Holly Songwriting Retreats, realising the dream he had over 60 years ago for music education and performance for the people in his home town.

KATHRYN GILBREATH
Fundraising Consultant

TIM COLLINS
Lubbock Entertainment & Performing Arts Association Board Chair

This is the Best Place to Play. 2022 Bob Dylan

Above: Bob Dylan performed at the Buddy Holly Hall and wrote this in the visitors book on 8 March 2022

The Buddy Holly Center

THE BUDDY HOLLY CENTER PRESERVES AND PROMOTES the legacy of Buddy Holly and the music of West Texas. Opening in September 1999, it is located at Fort Worth and Denver Railway Depot at 19th Street and Crickets Avenue – a nod to Buddy's band – and contributes to the Depot Entertainment District in downtown Lubbock.

The Center hosts exhibitions, tours, concerts, classes, gallery talks and workshops, and includes a permanent exhibit that showcases the life and music of Buddy Holly, displaying artifacts such as his Fender Stratocaster guitar, his signature horn-rimmed glasses, and items from his youth, alongside autographed certificates from Buddy Holly Educational Foundation ambassadors. Alongside this, the Center's gallery serves as the successor to Lubbock's original Fine Arts Center, presenting visual art exhibitions that change throughout the year. In 2011, the Center moved the boyhood home of J.I. Allison to the grounds, where songs like 'That'll Be the Day' and 'Peggy Sue' were written and practised. The house opened for public tours in 2012.

JACQUELINE BOBER oversees operations at the Center, working with a team of dedicated colleagues who work to preserve and promote the musical legacy of Lubbock's own Buddy Holly for fans and visitors from all over the world. She helps in the Center's mission to celebrate Buddy by introducing younger generations to the rock and roll pioneer.

Texas Country Music Hall of Fame

IN THE EARLY 1990S, THE TEX RITTER MUSEUM OPENED IN CARTHAGE, TEXAS, to honour the city's beloved native son and country star. The museum was the brainchild of Tommie Ritter Smith, the Director of the Panola County Chamber of Commerce and Tex's cousin. With the help of Tex's sons John and Tommy Ritter, the museum opened in the Hawthorn-Clabaugh-Patterson House on 18 October 1992.

In 1996, the Tex Ritter Museum developed into the Texas Country Music Hall of Fame with the goal to honour the contributions of other Texas-born country artists. At that time, Rusty Summerville, then Director of Design at Nashville's Gaylord Entertainment Company, joined the team to create the museum exhibits.

The first artists inducted into the Texas Country Music Hall of Fame at its grand opening in 1998 were Tex Ritter, Willie Nelson, Jim Reeves, Gene Autry, Joe Allison and Cindy Walker. Since then, the Texas Country Music Hall of Fame continues to grow with the yearly induction of other talented Texans.

Annual induction ceremonies held each August have honoured 65 entertainers who have contributed to the legacy of country music, including Kris Kristofferson, Ray Price, George Jones, Duane Allen and the Oak Ridge Boys, Waylon Jennings, Tanya Tucker, the Mandrell Sisters and Buddy Holly, just to mention a few.

Buddy Holly was selected by the Board of Directors at the Texas Country Music Hall of Fame and was inducted in 2022. The West Texas native's multi-dimensional talents were rooted in country/western and gospel music. Strains of these early musical influences can be heard in many of Holly's rock and roll hits.

His induction into the Texas Country Music Hall of Fame was held in Carthage, Texas, on 13 August 2022. Peter Bradley Jnr, a board member of The Buddy Holly Educational Foundation, graciously accepted the award on behalf of Holly's widow, Maria Elena Holly.

Jerry Handzen, Chairman of the Texas Country Music Hall of Fame Board, and museum founder and President, Tommie Ritter Smith, presented the award.

– Tommy Ritter Smith (Founder and President, Texas Country Music Hall of Fame)

The Liverpool Institute for Performing Arts

STEVE LEWIS I've spent more than 40 years in the music industry and continue to work as a music publisher and advisor to music, media and music tech companies. I met Peter Bradley Jnr in the 1990s when I was running the Music Division of Chrysalis Group Plc and he was a young singer forging his career in music, and we made two albums together. Several years later, in 2014, Peter was in touch again and asked me to become an advisor to the Board of The Buddy Holly Educational Foundation. He explained that the Foundation's mission was to burnish the legacy of Buddy Holly, bring it to the attention of a new generation of musicians, songwriters and audiences and promote the careers of aspiring songwriters. At a TBHEF event at Abbey Road Studios I introduced Peter to Chris Difford of Squeeze, and they went on to develop the Songwriting Retreats through which the Foundation has benefited so many young musicians and songwriters.

The Liverpool Institute for Performing Arts (LIPA) is another organisation close to my heart. LIPA educates creators across the entire spectrum of the arts, including music performers, songwriters, actors, film-makers and more, as well as the executives and support staff necessary to create and operate the infrastructure in which they can do their best work. I was therefore delighted to be able to bring together the two organisations in 2023 when TBHEF sponsored the 2023 LIPA Singer/Songwriter Award. Going forward, it will be presented to the student who submits three original songs and one cover recording of a Buddy Holly song which in the opinion of the judges shows both outstanding compositional and performing ability.

It was a pleasure to join Sir Paul McCartney and Peter in presenting the inaugural LIPA Singer/Songwriter Award to Ruby Walvin in 2023. Ruby and future winners will attend Chris Difford's Songwriting Retreat in Glastonbury and the Buddy Holly Songwriting Retreat in Lubbock, Texas, Buddy Holly's birthplace, all through the generosity of the Bradley family. They will write with and be mentored by accomplished writers and performers of countless hits and the Foundation will continue to support them as they embark on their careers in music.

Master of Arts in Costume Making
Toni Bate presents these graduands for their awards:
ELIZABETH JANE ASHBY
DAVID ANDREW BATES
EMMA SARAH FRANCES CROSSLAND
MICHELA MANDUCA
JASMINE ROBERTS
CONNOR PATRICK SULLIVAN

Master of Arts in Music Industry Professional Management
Keith Mullin presents these graduands for their awards:
TEVHID NAZMI BASTURK
MATTHEW MICHAEL HUBERT DACOMBE
JOSHUA ROBERT FRANCIS MURPHY
AIDAN GRIFFITH PETERSEN
DYLAN SENIOR

Foundation Certificate in Popular Music & Music Technology
Tim Pike presents these certificatees for their awards:
PHOEBE REBECCA BLACKWELL
GREGORY PATRICK SELWAY MORRISON
JULIE BAGLO SOLHAUG

Foundation Certificate in Acting
Rosemary Berkon presents these certificatees for their awards:
SCOTT MACE BARNES
LOTUS LILY HYMAN CUMMINS
CONSTANCE RHIANNON EVANS
THOMAS EDWARD FOLEY
LUCY RHIANNON HANDLEY
MOLLY PATRICIA ELIZABETH HINTON-JONES
BETHAN KELSI HOWELLS
LUCY HELEN JOHNSON
MAISIE GRACE LOUISE MUNRO

ALUMNI
Chris Meehan BA (Hons) Arts, Music & Entertainment Management (2006) describes his time with us, what he went on to do and lessons learnt.

16

PRIZES
Mike Mercer announces the prizes.
Fanfare and ***applause*** as
Richard Jupp confers **The Avedis Zildjian Prize for Percussion** on Alex Howley.
Mary Chadwick and Diane Glover confer **The Beatles Story Prizes for Music** on Liam Shields, Karman Browne, Ross Buckley, Laura Griffiths.
Amber Steadman confers the **Ede & Ravenscroft Prize for Creative and Technical Excellence** on Katerina Petmezas.
Steve Levine and Tony Platt confer **The Future Producer Prize** (supported by The Church Studios, NOVA Distribution & PPL) for music production and recording on Aneirin Wee.
Peter Bradley confers the **Buddy Holly Educational Foundation Prize for Singer Songwriter of the Year** (to be announced on the day).
Tim Sherratt confers **The Sennheiser Student Achievement Award for Performing Arts Sound Technology** on Katerina Petmezas.
Tim Sherratt confers **The Sennheiser Studio Excellence Award For Studio Recording and Production** on Marco Viscito.
David Walton confers **The AMS Neve Prize for Audio Post-production** on Ananya Nath.
David Stark confers **The Songlink Prize for Best Song Musically & Lyrically** on Ria Hanley for "Bite Back".
David Stark confers **The Songlink Prize for Best Contemporary Song** on Danelia Calles Monsivais for "Miss Reality".
Arthur Bernstein confers **The EA Bernstein III Prize** on George Mulville.
Steven Davies confers the **LIPA Prize for Filmmaking** sponsored by Blackmagic Design on Alex Quinn.
Mark Featherstone-Witty confers **The Joan Plowright (Lady Olivier) Acting Prize for Performance** on Allie Aylott.
Mark Featherstone-Witty confers **The Joan Plowright (Lady Olivier) Acting Prize for Ensemble** on Kim Beecroft.
Eleanor Chapman confers the **LIPA Prize for Dance** on Christina Vasileiadi and Nethra Menon.
Gethin Mullock confers **The Anthony Field Producer Prize** on Rhianna Swyer.
Gethin Mullock confers **The LIPA Prize for Management** on Molly Rees and Charlotte Marchant.
Lizzie Husskison confers **The LIPA Community Drama Prize for Facilitation** on Alice Gregory.
Lizzie Husskison confers **The LIPA Community Drama Prize for Directing** on Ylenia Mahnic.

17

The Surf Ballroom, Clear Lake, Iowa

BUDDY'S LEGACY IS INTIMATELY CONNECTED TO THE SURF BALLROOM and is celebrated in many ways at the historic venue. Throughout its colourful history, there is no association with the Surf that is stronger than the fateful last performance of Buddy Holly, J.P. 'The Big Bopper' Richardson and Ritchie Valens on 2 February 1959 at the Winter Dance Party. Three talented individuals were lost that night, but their legacies live on in the countless musicians who follow their lead.

The Surf Ballroom's annual Winter Dance Party tributes bring fans and artists from around the world to celebrate the impact and influence that Buddy Holly, Ritchie Valens and the Big Bopper have had on music and American culture.

Thousands of rock and roll fans from across the globe have made the pilgrimage to Clear Lake during Iowa's wintry February weather to be part of this. – *Laurie Lietz, Executive Director, and Jeff Nicholas, President, Surf Ballroom & Museum*

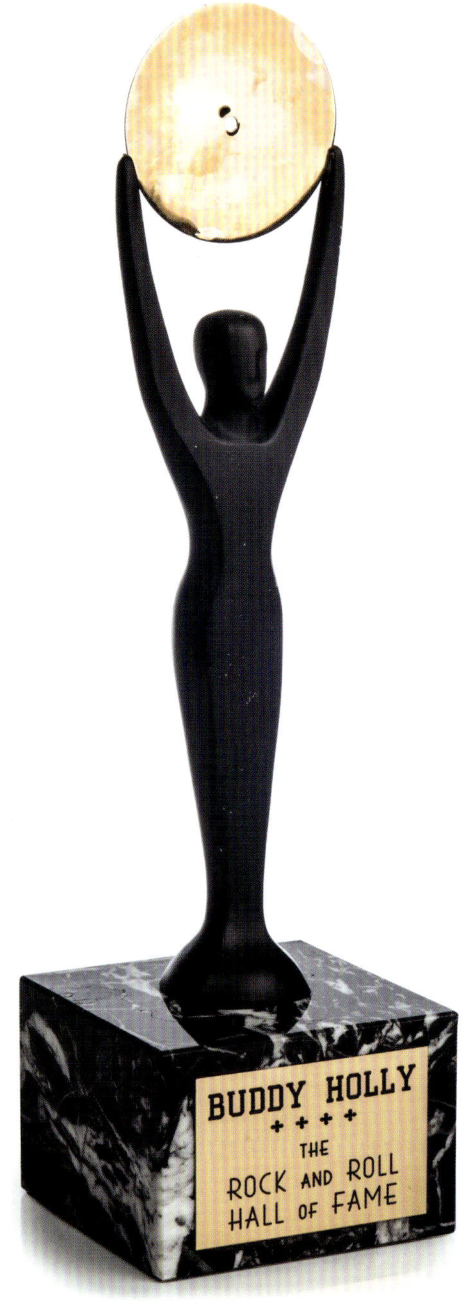

THE ROCK AND ROLL HALL OF FAME FOUNDATION

FIRST ANNUAL INDUCTION DINNER

TABLE

©1985 THE ROCK AND ROLL HALL OF FAME FOUNDATION, INC.

GREG HARRIS I've heard life-changing artists – in damp clubs, pubs, bars and arenas, and on vinyl, tapes, CDs and streams – and none has sounded better than Buddy Holly blasting from the lone dashboard speaker in my first car, a 1957 Chevrolet Bel Air. That car was the whole deal – black paint, stick shift, chrome wheels, massive seats, and a giant metal dashboard that, when slapped, thumped like a bass drum. And the song that sounded the very best through its crackling speaker, echoing through the dashboard as we raced down the highway, was 'Rave On'. That car and that sound launched a lifetime of love for Buddy Holly and his 1950s contemporaries – and the many garage and punk rock acts and singer-songwriters he influenced – and that love led me to be part of the greatest museum in the world.

Rock and roll has always pushed boundaries and questioned the status quo, while connecting people of all backgrounds and beliefs – across continents, eras and cultures, bringing us together in a way that nothing else can. It's the soundtrack of our lives, the songs that carry us through our brightest and darkest moments. Our world would be a very different place without rock and roll, and rock and roll would be very different without Buddy Holly.

In 1986, Buddy Holly was elected to the Rock and Roll Hall of Fame in our very first class along with James Brown, Elvis Presley, Ray Charles, Sam Cooke, Little Richard, Chuck Berry, Fats Domino, Jerry Lee Lewis, and the Everly Brothers. Almost four decades later, Buddy's legacy is celebrated each day at the Rock and Roll Hall of Fame, and he continues to impact and inspire young songwriters through The Buddy Holly Educational Foundation's extraordinary songwriting retreats and workshops in the UK and USA. Rave on Buddy!

Buddy –
Thank you for the music!
It changed the world &
changed my life!
At the Rock & Roll Hall of Fame
you will never Fade Away!

Cheers,
Greg

Thank you. First I just want to say what an honour it is to be part of the first gathering at the Rock and Roll Hall of Fame. And I just want to tell you what Buddy Holly meant to me. I was working at a beach resort, a 12-year-old kid's type of job. That voice and guitar came over the PA – we had a radio. I went out and bought 'That'll Be the Day' and started learning the words. A few months later I bought the album, and that album set in force a musical history and some strange events, I think. There was a group pictured on the cover. There was a guy with a Strat – wasn't that bad! – and three other guys, it was a group. The first time you saw a group in rock and roll. I thought, 'I'm going to have a group'. Over in Liverpool, the same thing was going on with four other guys. They named their group The Beatles because Buddy Holly's group was called the Crickets. 1964 these four – or 1963 actually – these four guys chose to end their great song 'I Want to Hold Your Hand' with a little syncopation Buddy Holly used in the chorus after the solo. All you guys who play rock know what I'm talking about. Well, about 20 years later a kid was writing a song about how it feels to be back in centrefield. He ended his song with the same riff. It came from the same place.

I think my point is that we all, each of us, are people who are made up of the people that we love and the people we admire. We take those reflections and hopefully grow from those. I think that's why we're here, in all ten cases tonight. And it's my great honour to induct Buddy. Anyway, at this point I would like to call his wife Maria Elena Holly to the stage. Maria, it is my great honour to induct Buddy Holly into the Rock and Roll Hall of Fame. (Transcript of John Fogerty's speech inducting Buddy Holly into the Rock and Roll Hall of Fame, 23 January 1986)

The Grammy Foundation and Buddy Holly's Lifetime Achievement

In 1997, 38 years after Buddy Holly's tragic death near Clear Lake, Iowa, the National Academy of Recording Arts and Sciences honoured his musical legacy with a Lifetime Achievement Award at the 39th Annual Grammy Awards in New York City. Had he not chartered a private plane during the Winter Dance Party tour in 1959, Holly would have been 61 years old. It was his only Grammy Award, the annual event having begun four months after his death. His fellow Lifetime Achievement honourees in 1997 included the Everly Brothers, who had befriended him on two barnstorming bus tours.

The following year, Bob Dylan, at age 57, won his first Grammy for Album of the Year as a solo artist for *Time Out of Mind*, his dark, brooding return to form. Notoriously allergic to speeches, Dylan thanked several people, then veered off to cite the spirit that had infused the album. 'I just wanted to say that one time when I was about 16 or 17 years old, I went to see Buddy Holly at the Duluth National Guard Armory, and I was three feet away from him, and he looked at me. And I just had some kind of feeling that he was … I don't know how or why, but he was with us all the time we were making this record in some kind of way.'

For Buddy Holly, the achievement of his lifetime is not only his enduring music, but all the musicians, unknown and well-known – Bob Dylan, John Lennon, Paul McCartney, Mick Jagger, Keith Richards and Graham Nash, among so many others – who saw and heard something in Holly's songs and brief, vital life that made them believe it was not only possible but critical to pursue the life of a musician. An 18-year-old Buddy Holly must have felt the same way when he witnessed 'the hillbilly cat', Elvis Presley, perform at the Fair Park Coliseum in his home town of Lubbock, Texas.

Six and a half decades after his death, Buddy Holly's spirit is still with us all the time.

JASEN EMMONS
Chief Curator & Vice President
of Curatorial Affairs
GRAMMY Museum

BOB SANTELLI I'm the Executive Director of the Bruce Springsteen Archives and Center for American Music, located on the campus of Monmouth University at the New Jersey Shore. The story of American music in the years after the Second World War would not be complete without a chapter detailing the music, life and legacy of Buddy Holly. A pioneer of rock and roll for sure, Buddy was also one of the music's first truly innovative artists, one who led a band, sang lead in it, played guitar in it, wrote the songs, and made them come alive in the recording studio and on the concert stage. An influence on The Beatles and virtually every other major rock and roll artist who came along in the 1960s, Buddy Holly was an American music original.

City of Los Angeles
State of California
Resolution
Buddy Holly Day
September 7, 2011

KEVIN MAGOWAN I noticed that Buddy Holly was the only member in the first class of the Rock and Roll Hall of Fame that did not have a star on the Hollywood Walk of Fame. With Maria Elena's permission I set out to correct this. After much deliberation, the Hollywood Chamber Of Commerce approved in June 2010. I wanted the ceremony to take place on Buddy's 75th birthday, which was the following year on 7 September. I picked the location of the star to be on Vine Street in front of Capitol Records and right in line with the stars of John Lennon, Ringo Starr and George Harrison. Paul McCartney would receive his star next to Buddy's six months later. The Beatles grew out of a shared love of Buddy Holly, so the location was perfect.

I arranged for Phil Everly, Peter Asher and Gary Busey to be the guest speakers at the ceremony. I also arranged to have Buddy's 75th birthday to be officially proclaimed 'Buddy Holly Day' in Hollywood.

Three tribute albums were released in honour of Buddy's 75th birthday and a PBS Special was taped that night.

THE BUDDY HOLLY EDUCATIONAL FOUNDATION

Honoured Friends & Acknowledgements

As well as ambassadors, the Foundation also has many Honoured Friends. Mostly, these are people who, while not always musicians, have played a part in Buddy's story.

'Buddy Holly opened up my pathway to a radio career. How fortunate I have been.'

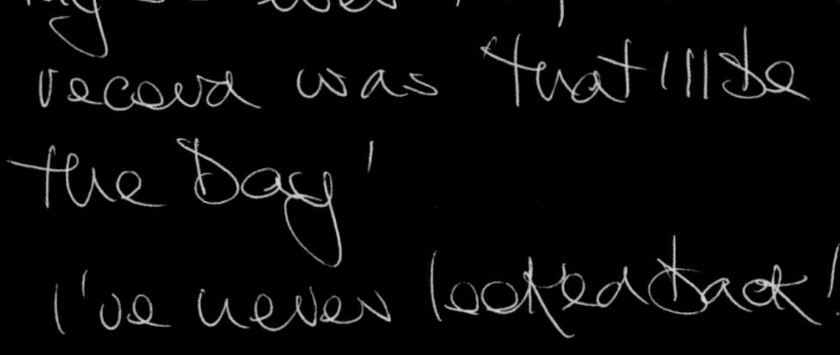

BOB HARRIS I started collecting records in 1957 at the beginning of a social revolution that was to change the world. A new generation of pioneering post-war kids were breaking free from the conventions of their parents and creating a new teenage culture of rebellion and self-expression, built around a ferociously exciting new music we called our own – rock and roll.

I began a paper round to earn the pocket money to feed my new record-buying obsession and every Thursday evening I'd wait at John Lever's record shop in Northampton for the Decca delivery van to arrive with all the brand-new singles from that fantastic stable of labels – London American, RCA, Brunswick and especially Coral, which was the label of Buddy Holly and the Crickets.

My friends would come over for 'record hops' and listen to all my new 45s. There was something about that match-up of rock and roll and vinyl. Those records absolutely pulverised the tiny Dansette speakers, and nothing had more power than 'Peggy Sue', 'That'll Be the Day' and 'Maybe Baby', still my favourite Crickets song. A few months later, Coral released 'Heartbeat' (45-Q 72346) and we loved it, of course. We played it over and over until finally I put on the B-side … and discovered one of the most beautiful records I've ever heard.

That B-side was 'Well … All Right' and as the acoustic guitar intro began to play, I looked up to see the joy on the faces of all my friends, gathered around the Dansette. I knew then that what I wanted to do was somehow try to translate this beautiful feeling onto the airwaves and play the music that enriches my life for anyone who would listen! It worked. My lifetime love really has been all right.

Buddy Holly opened up my pathway to the microphone and to a radio career inspired by the music of those wonderful, pioneering days. And how fortunate I have been.

'What a song catalogue written and recorded in such a short space of time – but which influenced so many artists and songwriters and continues to do so!'

What a song catalogue written & recorded in such a short space of time – but which influenced so many artists & songwriters & continues to do so!

Mike Read.

MIKE READ HAS FRONTED TOP-RATED national BBC TV and radio shows for more than 30 years, winning many TV and radio awards. A best-selling author, with some 36 books to his name, he has also written many songs that have been covered by major artists and also created stage musicals. Along with fellow DJ Paul Gambaccini, Jonathan Rice and Sir Tim Rice, he co-founded the hugely successful *Guinness Book of British Hit Singles*.

In 2013, Read, along with three friends, formed the British Plaque Trust, a charity established to commemorate deceased achievers in show business, sport and the general arts by unveiling blue plaques, alongside the work of English Heritage, on the buildings with which they were associated. Mike's many charitable commitments include the Prince's Trust, the Red Cross, the Variety Club of Great Britain, Nordoff and Robbins Children's Hospices, Teenage Cancer Trust and Cliff Richard's Tennis Foundation.

As an Honoured Friend of The Buddy Holly Educational Foundation, Mike has given a huge amount of time, experience and knowledge to those budding artists attending the annual Chris Difford Songwriting Retreat, held at Pennard House near Glastonbury, England.

TIM RICE

TIM RICE is best known for his work as a lyricist with some of the most popular and influential musicians and composers of his time. These include Andrew Lloyd Webber, Elton John, Bjorn Ulvaeus and Benny Andersson, Alan Menken, Rick Wakeman, Burt Bacharach and Freddie Mercury.

Tim's ventures into book publishing included being a co-founder of the hugely successful *Guinness Book of Hit Singles* (and related volumes) with his brother Jonathan, Paul Gambaccini and Mike Read. Until the arrival of the internet their Guinness works were the bibles of the British music industry. Tim also founded Pavilion Books in 1981 with Michael Parkinson and Colin Webb, which held its own in the literary marketplace for over a decade. He is also well known for his passion for cricket, having been president of MCC and the Lord's Taverners (and also of the splendid 180-plus years old London Library).

His passion for rock and roll and popular music began in 1957. The first record he bought was Tommy Steele's version of 'Singing the Blues'. Elvis was riding high in the charts with every single he released. That year also saw the debut hits of Buddy Holly and the Everly Brothers. To Tim, a 13-year-old English schoolboy, American music stars such as Buddy Holly and the Everlys seemed to come from another planet – inaccessible, irresistible and mysterious.

In 2009, Tim participated in the two days of music and tribute to the three rock musicians who died in the plane crash near Mason City, Iowa, exactly half a century before, on 3 February 1959. Exactly 50 years later the legacy and works of Buddy Holly, Ritchie Valens and the Big Bopper were remembered by a host of leading musicians including the Crickets, Bobby Vee, Bill Haley's Comets, Graham Nash, Peter and Gordon, Brian Hyland, Johnny Tillotson and many others.

I first heard a Buddy Holly record in 1957. Even at the age of 12 (me, not Buddy) I could see that he was an extraordinary talent, not like any of the other stars of the early rock n roll era but as good as any of them.

In 2019 I still listen to his timeless music....

Tim Rice

JULIAN LLOYD WEBBER

JULIAN LLOYD WEBBER Rarely – if ever – can one person have left behind such an extraordinary and lasting musical legacy by the age of 22 as Buddy Holly. His untimely death was a tragedy not only for all those that loved him but also for music itself. I have a feeling Buddy could have achieved whatever he wanted to in music – for he was a terrific musician. Even on all the many 'out-takes' that have been released since his death, you will hardly ever hear him sing a note out of tune! He would experiment and succeed, and his thinking was way ahead of his time. Shortly before his death he was talking to Maria Elena about writing a piece for classical guitar and maybe 'trying his hand' at writing a film score. I have no doubt that he could have done both. The fact that a group of hardened New York string players gave Buddy a standing ovation by the end of his final recording session says it all. Buddy Holly had that rarest of gifts, being able to instinctively communicate raw emotion to his audience through a microphone, and we miss him enormously. But most of all we miss what might have been.

Honoured to be in a book related to such a great musician – Buddy Holly was a wonderful talent – I always think he could have done anything in music which he turned his mind to..

Julian Lloyd Webber

Despite being a classical virtuoso and 'doyen of British cellists', **_JULIAN LLOYD WEBBER_** also loves popular music, being a huge fan of Bobby Vee and Buddy Holly. In 2001 Julian, an Honoured Friend, was granted the first busker's licence on the London Underground, as he launched the scheme to award licences to approved buskers. He has campaigned tirelessly against cuts in music education and has represented the music sector on many TV and radio programmes. He became the public spokesperson for the charity Live Music Now in 2014 and received the Incorporated Society of Musicians Distinguished Musician Award. A former principal of the Royal Birmingham Conservatoire, Julian Lloyd Webber has won many awards including the Crystal Award and the Classic FM Award for Outstanding Services to Music, and was the only classical musician chosen to play at the 2012 Summer Olympics closing ceremony. He was made an OBE in the 2021 Queen's Birthday Honours list. – *Mike Read*

JOHN MARASCALCO

We all know Buddy Holly as one of the great rock and roll performers, a giant of the genre and one of the greatest songwriters of his time. But what we sometimes forget is that before his own career began, Buddy was a rock and roll fan. His idols were Elvis Presley, Hank Williams and Little Richard.

The energy of their fresh, raw music was sweeping across the Southern States in the early 1950s and Buddy was inspired. He was eager to be involved himself, but this was a new kind of music and, for all of Buddy's own natural creativity, it was a music that had to be learned and one of his teachers – albeit unwittingly – was ***JOHN MARASCALCO***.

The man was a genius. He wrote some of the cornerstone tablets of rock and roll itself – 'Be My Guest' for Fats Domino, 'If You Want My Lovin'' for Gene Vincent, the glorious 'Goodnight My Love' for Jesse Belvin and 'Rock 'n' Roll Dance' for Lloyd Price. But it was the songs he wrote with Robert 'Bumps' Blackwell to be recorded by Little Richard that made the most impression on the young Buddy Holly – 'Good Golly Miss Molly', 'Rip It Up' and 'Heebie Jeebies'. Buddy loved these records and could not resist covering two Marascalco co-writes himself – 'Ready Teddy' and 'Send Me Some Lovin''. The latter was a song subsequently recorded by Sam Cooke and John Lennon – illustrious company indeed!

Little Richard and Buddy eventually established a huge mutual respect and Buddy always acknowledged how much he'd learned from those incredible Little Richard records at a point in his artistic development when his own writing was still at a formative point. And so, when it came time for the Crickets to record their debut album, *The 'Chirping' Crickets*, in 1957, it was natural that Buddy would reach out to the work of John Marascalco for inspiration. 'Send Me Some Lovin'' was on that album, while 'Ready Teddy' made it onto Buddy's eponymously titled follow-up in 1958. It was a perfect match.

Without knowing it, John Marascalco helped a young, impressionable Buddy Holly find his own beautifully crafted musical pathway. And for that, we are extremely grateful. – *Bob Harris*

The First Time I Heard Buddy's "That'll Be Day" I said to Myself, I Hope This Record Makes It, I think He Can Help Keep this Rollin, this thing Called Rock an Roll.

And He Did And It Is, thanks Buddy.

Love You Man!

John Marascalco

GLEN D. HARDIN

To many people ***GLEN D. HARDIN*** is known for his role as Elvis's piano player and musical arranger, but of course his career has included many years as a member of the Crickets, both on stage and on record.

Born near Wellington, a small town in the Texas panhandle, Glen D.'s interest in music began when a friend came to the house and played gospel music on the piano. He went on to join other musicians on stage, including occasional gigs with Sonny and Dean Curtis, and an early session in 1956 saw Glen D. playing on Sonny West's original recording of 'Oh Boy!' Buddy met Glen D. at school, and after spending three years in the US Navy as a radio operator, Glen moved out to California and joined his old friends Jerry Allison and Sonny Curtis to become a member of the Crickets in 1962.

In 1968, Glen D. briefly stepped in as the Crickets' lead singer for their single 'Million Dollar Movie' / 'A Million Miles Apart'. A year later, he was recruited to join Elvis Presley's Vegas band, soon becoming his musical arranger – an ideal job for a lifelong Elvis fan. Though deeply involved with Elvis, Glen D. occasionally rejoined the Crickets for tours and recordings, including standout UK tours in 1998 and 2001. The Crickets' final show in 2016, a tribute to Joe B. Mauldin, fittingly took place at Iowa's Surf Ballroom, where Buddy Holly had his last performance. Led by J.I. Allison, Glen D. returned to the stage, once again part of the iconic band. – *Mike Read*

The Crickets,
Dearest friends I ever had
I hope We'll Rock on forever
Glen D Hardin

BUDDY'S FAMILY WAS A LOVING, hard-working, close-knit unit. They all enjoyed playing and listening to music, at home and with friends. Being around a decade older than their little brother, Larry and Travis Holley were both wise mentors throughout Buddy's childhood, adolescence and the years up until his untimely, tragic passing, especially in supporting his early music ambitions.

Larry was the eldest of the siblings and lived nearly his whole life in Lubbock, save for the time he enlisted in the US Marine Corps, serving as a corporal. He was stationed in the Pacific and then in Nagasaki, before returning home in 1946. He was a successful businessman, a talented musician, a keen outdoorsman, a proud Baptist, an intrepid aviator and a devoted husband to Maxine, and father to Randy and Sherry.

Buddy's wonderfully supportive parents L.O. and Ella, brothers Larry and Travis, and sister Patricia were humble and well-respected members of their community.

Each one will be remembered with affection and appreciation by Buddy Holly and Crickets fans for the influence and inspiration they afforded Buddy, but most of all for the genuine deep love Buddy enjoyed from a family with worthy traditional values and compassion for others.

Larry was the last surviving member of the family Buddy knew when TBHEF was founded, and it was a pleasure to know him and involve him in our work.

"THE BUDDY I KNEW"
by
Larry Holley

I cried a little the day he came,
It so caught me by surprise.
But a score and two years later,
I could hardly dry my eyes.

All the happy, carefree moments,
We shared those years between
Are the things that really mattered
Just our simple joys and dreams.

He was just a little brother
Who would follow just behind,
Why has he gone before me
And I am left behind.

Cause the Lord who knows the answers
Of the questions about time,
Chose to take him on to glory
And he picked him in his prime.

I know he was an idol,
Like this world seeks to find.
But there's few, who really knew him,
And this is part of mine.

A Big Brother
Larry Holley

Top: Larry Holley
Left: L.O. and Ella Holley

I've always been so proud of ***DES O'CONNOR*** and everything he's achieved in his illustrious career, but his experience touring with Buddy Holly and the Crickets on what was Buddy's only UK tour would undoubtedly be among the highlights.

Buddy Holly created a revolutionary new sound in music, influencing countless artists – many of them British like The Beatles, Elton John, and the Rolling Stones. Hearing Des talk about his time with Buddy was always so fascinating, as Buddy was such an incredible inspiration to so many.

It all began in March 1958 when Des was honoured to be invited to host and compere Buddy's UK tour. Des said, 'Touring with Buddy Holly is something I'll never forget, with 31 gigs in 33 days'; They formed a very lovely friendship, and Des would say in his best country and western drawl, 'He's 6 foot 2 and he talks like that. I thought only people in the cowboy pictures talked like that.'

One of Des's favourite memories was in Harrogate when he had to wake Buddy up as he would never get on the coach. Des pulled Buddy by his feet, and Buddy said, 'Don't do that, Des. I'm tall enough!'

Buddy wanted to buy a new guitar while waiting for his own instruments to arrive from the US. Des took him to Maurice Plaquet's music shop in London, where they acquired a Höfner President guitar. Their friendship was so strong that before returning to the US, Buddy gave the guitar to Des. The guitar is now on display at the Buddy Holly Center in Lubbock, Texas.

DES O'CONNOR

One of my favourite stories about Des and Buddy was of the late, great British theatre and film producer Bill Kenwright. When Bill went to see Buddy in Liverpool as a child in long socks and shorts, Des was on stage before the show checking the mic position. Bill walked through the stalls to the bottom of the stage with his programme in his hand and looked up at Des and said, 'Excuse me, would you please be able to get me an autograph of Buddy Holly?' Des replied, 'Do you really love Buddy?' And of course Bill said yes. Without hesitation Des took him from the stalls to Buddy's dressing room and introduced him, and Buddy personally signed his programme. Bill has always said that meeting Des and Buddy literally changed his life and he would be forever grateful for Des's special kindness.

When Des first heard the tragic news about Buddy he called Maria Elena to express his deepest condolences. Maria Elena said on 3 February in 1959 she received two phone calls from Europe – one was from Elvis Presley, who was on military service in Germany, and the other was from Des calling from London.

In August 2022, our son Adam and I had the most wonderful pleasure of attending the Buddy Holly Songwriting Retreat in Lubbock, Texas … we like to think that both Des and Buddy played a big part in making that very special experience happen and that Des and Buddy are now reunited, putting on their own concert tours in heaven.
– Jodie Brooke-Wilson (widow of Des O'Connor)

SAM COOKE

Music is a part of my history and my soul. It's deeply embedded in who I am as a person and entertainer. This is rightfully so because I am the daughter of the legendary ***SAM COOKE***.

My father's musical attributes span from his time as the lead singer of the gospel group the Soul Stirrers to his legendary status as a solo artist deemed 'The King of Soul'.

Buddy Holly and my father had a deep respect for one another, especially when it came to their distinctive craft, music. They both were ahead of their time. One thing they truly have in common is they both wrote inspiring hit songs that touched people in profound ways. Performing my tribute concerts of my father's music allows me to bring back sweet memories to some and shed light on his timeless music for others. I truly believe that Sam Cooke and Buddy Holly's musical legacy will live on for generations to come. – *Carla Cooke*

CAROL CONNORS

CAROL CONNORS Buddy didn't have the movie star looks like Elvis. Some people said he looked like a school teacher because he wore these big horn-rimmed spectacles. But it gave a lot of artists and musicians and songwriters and producers who followed him confidence to be able to go on stage.

When I was in the Teddy Bears, Phil Spector wrote 'To Know Him Is to Love Him' for my voice. It was the first song he ever produced. The record became this monster hit, and it was considered one of the most important rock and roll songs. The song title was taken from Phil Spector's father's epitaph, and he turned it into a teenage lament and cast my voice. I would think that Buddy Holly loved that song because he had a sensitivity.

Once when we were on a plane, I remember singing with Phil and Marshall Leib because we had nothing to do with ourselves, and we sang 'That'll Be the Day' and 'Peggy Sue'. We all loved those songs. If you listen to 'To Know Him Is to Love Him', Phil came up with the 'Oh, no, no, no'. It was that sort of countermelody that he created. This is just my interpretation, but I think maybe 'Peggy Sue', a song he loved so much, put it in his brain to do the countermelodies on 'To Know Him Is to Love Him'.

Dear Buddy
Just a ♥ ♪ 2 say.....
Phil Spector wrote "2 Know Him
is 2 Love Him 4 my Voice —
when we were traveling we
all sang "Peggy Sue" Boy,
do we Love that song
Phil was inspired
By Buddy Holly's Music —
& I think he was a regular
guy & I
loved Love 2 think
that Buddy Loved
our song 2 Know Him
is 2 Love Him because
he felt he had a
Big HEART — I only
wish that Buddy would
have been my Buddy 2...
Love Carol Connors
The Teddy Bears (Annette)

BOB PEEPLES Buddy and I were casual acquaintances in high school; he was a senior and I was a junior. In high school everyone knew Buddy. He was a popular performer at high school assemblies and of course on his Buddy and Bob show on KDAV radio. We'd spoken a few times, but we didn't share any classes. I did share classes with his girlfriend at that time, Echo McGuire. When high school was over Buddy and I became closer. He played at the roller rink weekly and I went down with my girlfriend – we danced, I talked to Buddy and we became good friends over that period of time. Jerry Allison was at Hutchinson Junior High School in the marching band. That was when Buddy started to put the Crickets together. At that time, he didn't have a drummer.

I was interested in recording, and I had a small, semi-professional recorder called a Magnecord PT6 and a couple of microphones. I had known of the Norman Petty Studio because there had been two big hits that came out of there, 'Party Doll' by Buddy Knox, and Jimmy Boyne's 'I'm Sticking with You'. Buddy knew that I had some semi-professional recording equipment and suggested we record some songs at his home. They became known as the 'Garage Tapes'.

I asked him one time if he knew about Norman Petty, and he said he did. I asked if he'd thought about going over there, and he said he'd think about it and make contact. A month or two went past and he told me, 'We're going to Clovis to record. Do you want to come along?' I had a new Dodge, so Larry Welborn loaded his stand-up bass in the back and Niki Sullivan put his guitars in, and we went to Clovis. Buddy and Jerry were already there and had set up when we arrived. That was 25 February 1957, the day that music began, and the day that they recorded 'That'll Be the Day'. I was there most of the night but I had to be back in Lubbock to be at my job, so I left about five in the morning. They worked all night. I just watched what was going on. I was getting an education because Norman was a professional at that time, and I hadn't been around a real studio prior to that.

When Buddy passed, Niki called me. He was working for a floral delivery service at the time and had heard it on the radio. It was hard to believe what happened.

BOB PEEPLES

ART GREENHAW Among the many blessings of being part of Texas's own Light Crust Doughboys were being able to compose and arrange as we chose and play guitar and bass guitar as we caught the vision. All of the guitarists in our band have been influenced and inspired by Buddy Holly. Actually, my family in Mesquite, Texas was the 'Holley' family – Buddy's true family name spelling – so I felt a particular kinship to him. Two principal Doughboy guitarists since the 1950s – Ronnie Dawson and yours truly – have picked up many guitar styles of Buddy's: bent notes, stops, at times heavy and flashy-flanging-drumming-style guitar playing, high-up-the-neck lead guitar playing. We have used all these techniques in even our gospel music that we so love – and on our Grammy-winning and eight Grammy-nominated albums of our gospel and country roots music.

One of Buddy Holly's early musical associates, and an important, well-respected figure in Lubbock's 1950s music scene, ***LARRY WELBORN*** was playing stand-up bass in the Buddy, Bob & Larry trio as early as 1954. As an acoustic outfit they performed on radio station KDAV's *Sunday Party* as well as at various occasional local events like store and car lot openings.

A couple of years younger than Buddy, Larry helped Buddy make the transition from country to rock and roll in 1955 with a session at the Nesman studio, Wichita Falls, Texas. The tracks recorded were 'Baby, Let's Play House' and 'Down the Line'.

Larry's next session with Buddy was in January 1957 at Norman Petty's Clovis studio, when they recorded 'Brown Eyed Handsome Man' and 'Bo Diddley'.

It was in February 1957 that Larry Welborn carved his place in rock and roll history when he played bass on the classic hit version of 'That'll Be the Day' and its flipside, 'I'm Looking for Someone to Love'.

Larry went on to be guitarist with another of Lubbock's emerging rock and rollers, Terry Noland, whose band the Four Teens also included teenage bass player Joe B. Mauldin prior to him becoming a member of the Crickets. In the mid-1960s Larry teamed up with Jerry Allison again in Texas and, playing lead guitar, formed another, albeit short-lived band with singer Larry Trider and bass player Doug Walding.

Considering himself the least successful of all the musicians who played with Buddy Holly, a modest Larry continued to pursue a musical career. In later years he moved to Oklahoma where he maintained his musical status teaching guitar and banjo. There he also worked for a number of years as a solo entertainer, performing in various local venues. Playing guitar and singing songs old and new, Larry continued to highlight his association with Buddy Holly and the Crickets and his place in the Holly legacy. – *John Firminger*

GARY BUSEY'S CONNECTION TO BUDDY HOLLY began long before his portrayal of the rock legend in *The Buddy Holly Story* (1978). Born in Goose Creek, Texas, Gary had a background not too different from Buddy's own, growing up in Oklahoma and Texas, regions steeped in the same musical influences that shaped Buddy Holly. Like Buddy, his first venture was in music, as a drummer in the Rubber Band, and later as a member of Carp. He also appeared on several Leon Russell recordings. His natural connection to Buddy's world made him a fitting choice. Busey lost 32 pounds for the role and fully immersed himself in Holly's life, even staying with Buddy's parents in Lubbock to absorb the singer's personality. Gary said that while he was there he felt 'like the most total stranger who ever lived. But [Buddy's parents] accepted me so completely that in a while I thought I belonged in their home. It was as if I was as close to Buddy as they were.'

At the time of shooting, the 1975 biography that the film was based on, *Buddy Holly: His Life and Music*, written by John Goldrosen, was out of print. But the film was a great success, and played a significant role in reigniting interest in Holly's music for a new generation. Gary's dedication paid off, as he performed all the music live and played guitar himself, a rare feat in biopics of the era, and his performance earned him critical acclaim and an Academy Award nomination for Best Actor. His portrayal remains one of his best-known roles, and his work in the film is credited with bringing Buddy Holly's story to a wider audience. Today, Gary still considers Buddy Holly his 'spirit animal', and in 2018 he released a cover of 'Not Fade Away'.

The music you'll love forever.
The man you'll never forget.
The movie you must not miss.

(Tagline from *The Buddy Holly Story*)

Opposite: Behind-the-scenes photos and film stills of the making of The Buddy Holly Story *with Gary Busey as Buddy Holly, Don Stroud as Jesse Charles (Jerry Allison), Charles Martin Smith as Ray Bob Simmons (Joe B. Mauldin), Amy Johnston as Cindy Lou (Echo McGuire) and Maria Richwine as Maria Elena Holly*

WP
59

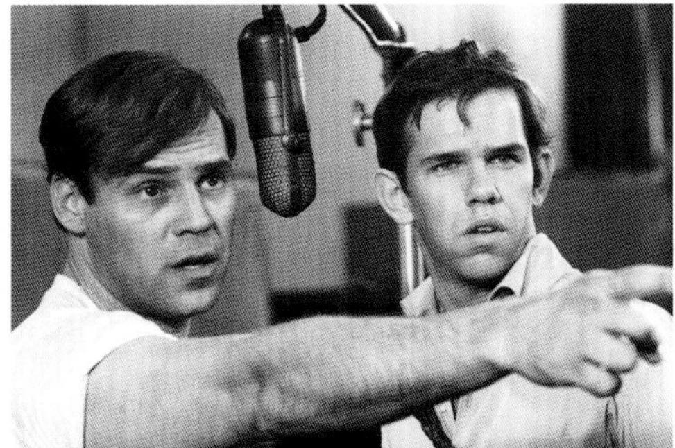

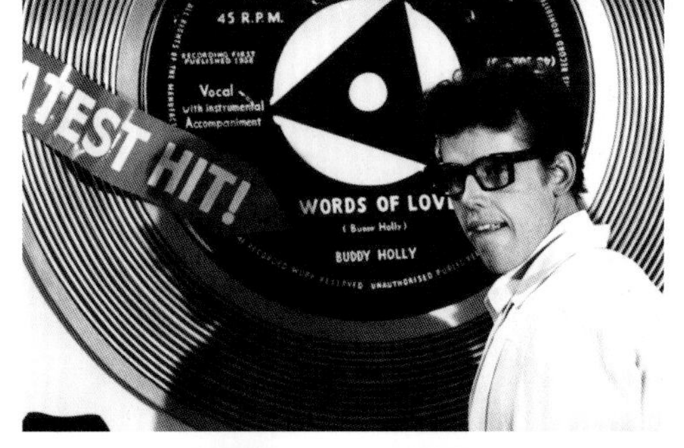
45 R.P.M.
Vocal
with instrumental
Accompaniment
HIT!
BUDDY HOLLY

KDAV
The
BUDDY
HOLLY
BAND

JOHN MUELLER Buddy Holly means a great deal to me. Learning his great songs was instrumental in my growth as a musician and singer. His character and approach to life impressed me greatly. He was a gentleman, kind, soft spoken, yet straightforward and highly focused, all qualities I admire and aspire to. Buddy was for me a hero for the working class everyday type of person. He wore glasses, he wrote his own music and performed it. He practised in a garage with Jerry Allison. He was the antidote to the glitzy Elvis personage. He pioneered the idea of a true rock and roll band, writing and creating songs as a group with each member adding their own input, something that The Beatles of course took note of and emulated. His personal sincerity and honesty of character comes through his music. I am forever grateful for his beautiful, feel-good music legacy and the true character of Charles Hardin Holley.

The songs I love.
The songs I write.
The songs I play.
They all go back to
Charles Hardin Holley.
Thanks, Buddy!

MARSHALL CRENSHAW

I was born in 1953, became a Buddy Holly fan "in real time" when my cousin Carol bought "That'll Be the Day", when it was just climbing the charts..

I saw him on TV numerous times – the last time was on the Dick Clark Saturday Night Show (sponsored by Beech-Nut gum). Buddy mimed along to "Heartbeat" on a set with a fake babbling brook and a little foot-bridge; I think he might've walked across it – I'll never know for sure because this clip is lost, isn't on YouTube.. I was disappointed that he didn't have his guitar, just stood alone and sang, but I loved the record, and still do...

Marshall Crenshaw

CHARLES ESTEN In the spring of 1991, in what would be my first true acting role, I portrayed Buddy Holly in the hit West End musical that bore his name and told his story. From the moment I got that audition until my final performance more than two years later, I was blessed to live and breathe the great young Texan and his amazing music. Night after beautiful night, my hair permed and dyed black, I got to don those iconic black horn-rimmed glasses and that equally iconic Sunburst Stratocaster and, alongside my fellow performers, play and sing one of the greatest and most influential catalogues that any songwriting artist has ever compiled. Let alone one who was sadly given such an impossibly short window of time in which to make his mark.

From London to an extensive tour of the US and Canada, and then back to London, for well over 500 performances, I got to play 18 classic Buddy Holly originals every night. And every single night, decades after they were written, as they were being sung and played by a singer with the tiniest fraction of Buddy's talent (yours truly) before a normally reserved theatre audience, Buddy's music didn't just connect – which it always did – it absolutely electrified. From the parents that remembered the songs with the greatest affection, to the kids that had never heard them before, no one was left unmoved. Audiences clapped, and sang along, and often, by the end of the night, literally danced in the aisles. And those songs were the reason why.

Again and again I was struck, and still am, by the unbelievable spark that runs through them all: their brash and attitudinal joyfulness, their brilliant simplicity, their wildly infectious hooks and solos, their heartfelt but never cloying earnestness, and perhaps most of all, their unusual timelessness. So much music from that great handful of years, even the best, sounds very much like what it was – 1950s music. To me, Buddy's songs – with and without the wonderful Crickets – have a unique freshness and thematic universality that can't be confined to that or any decade. They don't have an expiration date.

I even mean that in a personal way, as a guy that ultimately performed all of Buddy's great songs longer than he ever had the chance to. You see, after all those performances of all that music, when it finally came time for me to take off the glasses and end my run, I was honestly able to say that never – not once – had I ever been bored for a single second of a single song. Every night was an honour. Every note was a joy.

I think I'll go play some now!

FRANK ALLEN

For any aspiring guitarist/rock and roll afficionado in the mid to late fifties Buddy was the ultimate inspiration. Sure, all of them played their parts but it was Buddy who showed us what we could with some simple chords and our cheap inferior instruments that could not approach either the look or the technical superiority of a real Fender Stratocaster which we could not afford even if we could have got within touching distance of one.

By carefully adjusting the treble tones on the amplifier and using the bridge pickup (assuming the guitar had one) we could possibly replicate the stunningly effective yet fairly basic solo in Peggy Sue. Apart from which he proved that you did not require the looks of Elvis to achieve your success. Just talent and originality.

I never met Buddy or saw him on stage although I did catch his appearance on our major television show Sunday Night at The London Palladium back in '58. He, along with J. I. and Joe B. were everything I Expected and more.

In more recent times I made the acquaintance of Sonny Curtis and his lovely wife Louise who were the most hospitable people you could wish to meet. Goodness knows, Sonny must have been very tired of the interminable questions about Buddy, The Crickets and those early days of rock an roll but he never once showed anything other than a welcome friendship.

Thank you to Buddy, The Crickets and rock and roll. They were and still are a very important part of my life.

Frank Allen
The Searchers

Opposite: John Mueller is a Buddy Holly tribute artist and actor, who began impersonating Buddy in 1992 in Los Angeles, when he was cast in an avant-garde rock opera called Be Bop A Lula. *He also starred as Buddy in the US touring musical* Buddy: The Buddy Holly Story *for four years. Since 1999 he has toured as part of a show called Winter Dance Party, in which he performs alongside Ritchie Valens and Big Bopper tribute artists in casinos, performing arts centres and theatres across the US.*

Charles Esten is a singer-songwriter and actor who made his theatrical debut starring as Buddy in the UK tour of the musical Buddy: The Buddy Holly Story *in the early 1990s. From 2012 to 2018 he starred as Deacon Claybourne in the musical drama TV series* Nashville *and contributed to the show's soundtrack both as a singer and songwriter. He is a frequent performer at the Grand Ole Opry and in January 2024 he released his debut studio album,* Love Ain't Pretty.

Marshall Crenshaw is a Grammy and Golden Globe nominated singer-songwriter and a Buddy Holly fan through and through. His love of Buddy's sound has been laced into the music of his entire career, from the pop rock brilliance of his debut album in 1982, to the Buddy songs he still performs at his live gigs to this day. In 1987 he played Buddy in the Ritchie Valens biopic La Bamba*, delivering a powerful and truly authentic cover of 'Crying, Waiting, Hoping'. The previous year he had a small role in the Francis Ford Coppola film* Peggy Sue Got Married*, so the Buddy connection is strong.*

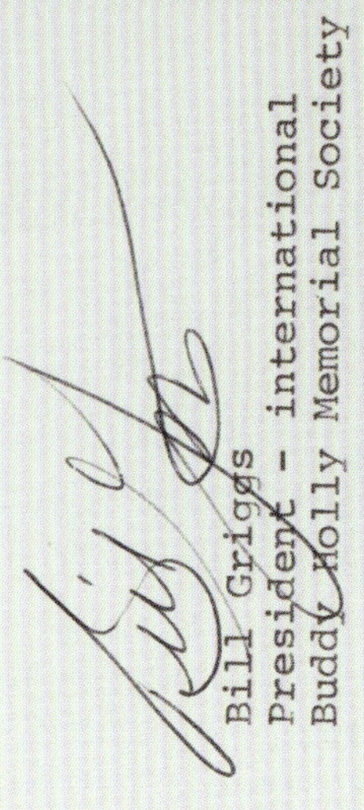

THE Buddy Holly MEMORIAL SOCIETY
3022 56TH STREET
LUBBOCK, TEXAS 79413
June 28, 1988

The Buddy Holly Memorial Society
75 Belcher Road
Wethersfield, CT 06109

Bill Griggs BY RANDY STEELE

It's been almost 70 years since a group of teenage boys from Lubbock, Texas made their way to the local 'picture show' to see actor John Wayne starring in a new Western called *The Searchers*. In the film, Ethan, the character played by John Wayne, utters the phrase 'that'll be the day' multiple times. That simple phrase would later inspire a couple of aspiring musicians named Buddy Holly and Jerry Allison to write a song called 'That'll Be the Day'. It was a song that would propel their band the Crickets to superstardom and change the course of rock and roll music, influencing countless musicians who would soon follow. The life of Buddy Holly ended tragically less than two years after the song's release. However, his legacy continues to burn brightly with no sign of dimming, in part because the fans of Buddy Holly and the Crickets remain deeply passionate. It is the late, great William (Bill) Griggs who is responsible for a large part of that passion.

Bill Griggs was born in Connecticut in 1941 to musician parents. The Griggs household was always filled with music. Rock and roll was born in the 1950s and for Bill, it was love at first listen. During his teen years, he frequented the State Theater in Hartford, Connecticut, where various rock and roll concerts took place, providing him with the opportunity to have a close-up view of the hitmakers of the era. As a result, Bill became a self-taught music historian and a superfan of Buddy Holly and the Crickets. After graduating high school in 1959, he began a career as an auto mechanic. In his spare time, he participated in drag racing, becoming a champion driver in the process and winning over 200 trophies. As his interest in drag racing was winding down, Bill began researching the history of early rock and roll, particularly Buddy Holly and the Crickets. In 1968, he visited Buddy Holly's home town of Lubbock, Texas for the first time and instantly fell in love with the people and the area. In 1975, Bill founded the Buddy Holly Memorial Society (BHMS) and began publishing the *Reminiscing* newsletter, which eventually evolved into the *Rockin' 50s* magazine and organisation.

Bill visited Lubbock multiple times through the years, and eventually moved there in 1981 to become a full-time music historian and researcher. He began publishing newsletters, each of them filled with information. Every issue contained comments and questions from the readers. The issues also contained book reviews, music charts, newly discovered photos, any news regarding music releases, and a featured interview with an artist or event related to music and events of the era. Bill quickly established himself as a 'go-to guy' when it came to 1950s rock and roll, especially if it pertained to Buddy Holly and the Crickets. Decades before music fans had the convenience of the internet, Bill dedicated himself to music history and research. He researched the lives and careers of Buddy Holly and the Crickets the old-fashioned way, by travelling thousands and thousands of miles, visiting cities and towns, libraries and newspaper archives, attending and venues, and seeking interviews with relevant people, all in the hope of discovering new information or a new photo of Buddy Holly and the Crickets.

Bill not only documented the facts of various musical events, he captured the emotions of the people who were 'there' when music history was being made. He then shared his research in his publications for the paid members of BHMS or sold copies of it to individuals. When Bill made the difficult decision in 1991 to end the BHMS, the organisation had grown to almost 6,000 members from 50 states and 34 countries. Along the way, Bill cemented his reputation as a trusted source, and he became known worldwide as *the* authority on Buddy Holly and the Crickets. Bill's attention to detail was unmatched. For example, Bill Griggs and Bill Kerns, a former writer for the Lubbock *Evening Journal* newspaper, enjoyed a fun-loving debate over Bill's ongoing request that the newspaper print a correction in the paper admitting their mistake in their 8 September 1936 edition, which had stated incorrectly that Mrs Ella Holley had given birth to a daughter, when in reality, it was a boy named Charles Hardin Holley. Bill's efforts to educate fans, collectors and others didn't stop with his publications. He hosted fans in his home on a near-weekly basis. He served as a guide during special events at the Buddy Holly Center and on bus tours around the Lubbock area. Bill spent hours on the telephone with fans from around the world on a nightly basis. If someone was producing a movie, a book, or a television special that contained anything related to Buddy Holly and the Crickets, Bill was the person who verified or validated the information it contained. In all, Bill made over 50 television appearances and had over 30 book credits to his name.

In 1978, Bill hosted the inaugural BHMS convention. The highlight of the event was Bill persuading all the remaining members of the Crickets to reunite and perform together on stage for the first time since 1957. Bill also emceed several rock and roll shows across the country. In 1986, he co-founded Lubbock's 'Budfest' concert and the Clovis Music Festival in 1987. Years before *The Buddy Holly Story* movie was released in 1978, Bill dedicated himself to researching, preserving and promoting Buddy Holly and the Crickets so that fans all over the world, including those not even born during Buddy's lifetime, could come to know the real Buddy Holly story.

In recognition of his body of work, MCA Records presented Bill with multiple gold records for his efforts to 'promote and preserve the legacy of Buddy Holly and the Crickets'. He became a trusted friend of the Holley family, serving as a pall-bearer at the funeral of Buddy Holly's father, Mr L.O. Holley. The city of Lubbock rewarded Bill with induction into the Buddy Holly/West Texas Walk of Fame on 31 July 2010.

Bill Griggs passed away on 29 March 2011. The funeral was held in Lubbock and attended by family, friends, fans, musicians and local politicians. One fan and friend travelled from England just for the opportunity to show his love and respect for Bill. The funeral culminated with a long procession to the Lubbock Cemetery, highlighted by a police escort and Lubbock's Nifty 1950s Car Club. Fittingly, Bill's final resting place is near the gravesites of Buddy Holly and the Holley family.

While there are millions of Buddy Holly and the Crickets fans around the world, there is a small group that belong on the Mount Rushmore of fans, a list that includes the likes of John Beecher and Chris Rees from England, Roddy Jordan from Australia, and Americans John Goldrosen and Bill Griggs, each of whom made a profound impact on the legacy of Buddy Holly and the Crickets. Because of recording technology, the world will always know how Buddy Holly and the Crickets sounded when they sang. Thanks to the efforts of people like Bill Griggs and those mentioned above, the world will always know how Buddy Holly and the Crickets lived, and 'Oh Boy' did they live! Rave On.

Buddy Holly & Norman Petty

BY BOB HARRIS (WITH MARK SAHA AND GREG WALKER)

TO A YOUNG ROCK AND ROLL FAN GROWING UP IN THE 1950s IN NORTHAMPTON – a boot and shoe town in the East Midlands of England – Clovis, New Mexico sounded like maybe the most mysterious and evocative place on earth. I imagined Clovis, situated nine miles west of the Texas border, to be like the Wild West towns we were seeing on our 10-inch black and white TV sets on cowboy series like *Cheyenne*, *The Cisco Kid*, *Laramie* and a hundred more shows that were popular at that time. Dirty, hot, dusty, lawless places – the sound of gunfire echoing from distant canyons.

The reality, of course, was very different. In fact, as I discovered, Clovis was an agricultural town, officially only 50 years old when it became the unlikely ground-zero location for some of the greatest rock and roll ever recorded.

The wellspring of this amazing moment was a small studio located in a former grocery store on West Seventh Street, run by a local record producer and musician who was to have a profound impact on the sound of American music. His name was Norman Petty. Petty bought the property in 1954, insulated it with mattresses hung over the studio windows, filled it with state-of-the-art equipment and fed the sound direct from the studio floor into a beautiful Ampex reel-to-reel tape recorder, among the very first to be used in any studio anywhere in the world.

Word of this unique facility quickly spread. Soon aspiring musicians were flocking to it, drawn by Petty's production skills and the superb acoustics, to record their fledgling rockabilly and country and western-inspired songs. It was a stunning combination of original music and new technology. Bright, sharp, rebellious and distinctive, the vibe they created forever became known as 'The Clovis Sound'. Roy Orbison, the Fireballs, Waylon Jennings and the guitar-led instrumental group the String-A-Longs all recorded at Clovis, as did Buddy Knox when he cut his huge number one hit 'Party Doll' – a major motivator for Holly to seek out Petty. Holly told Petty, 'If you can get a hit for Buddy Knox, you can get a hit for me.'

Buddy Holly was just 20 years old when he entered the Norman Petty Studio with his best friend and drummer, Jerry 'J.I.' Allison, to record 'That'll Be the Day' in January 1957. (Petty himself was only 29.) The record was a revelation to Petty and he offered to shop it in New York. Despite its amazing sound, 'That'll Be the Day' was a hard sell. Some of the most successful New York labels rejected it. Mitch Miller at Columbia advised Petty not to shop the demo as it might damage his reputation, but Norman persevered and finally placed it with A&R man Bob Thiele at Coral/Brunswick Records. Thiele pressed a thousand copies on the Brunswick label for a test run.

Buddy and Norman returned to Clovis and spent the magical spring/summer of 1957 recording a series of highly original classics – 'Peggy Sue', 'Everyday', 'Not Fade Away', 'Oh Boy!', 'Maybe Baby' and 'Words of Love'. When 'That'll Be the Day' took off for the stratosphere that fall, these singles quickly followed. In the fall of 1957, Buddy Holly and the Crickets dazzled the world!

Norman did not charge Buddy for studio time or his engineering services for these recordings. Instead, they came to an agreement regarding the royalties from the songs and a management deal. Buddy also took a role as session man for other artists who recorded with Petty during that halcyon summer, adding his distinctive Stratocaster guitar playing to, among others, the country single 'Sugartime' by Charlie Phillips and the rockabilly record 'Starlight' by Jack Huddle.

For some inexplicable reason Holly's star cooled in 1958, and classic releases like 'It's So Easy', 'Heartbeat' and 'Rave On' underperformed in the US charts. This despite his continued success in the UK where he had eight Top 20 hits in less than 18 months. Buddy was sure he was going to be a big star and his floundering in the American charts was very frustrating for him. Despite his friendship with Petty, Buddy felt he needed a new approach to management that Norman Petty was unable to provide. Norman felt betrayed. He'd invested so much of himself into Buddy's career. And there was more. When Buddy left to further his career in New York, his group the Crickets did not follow him. Instead, they opted to stay in New Mexico with Norman and the bond was broken.

It was a devastating moment for all of them and it was at the height of this painful dispute between friends that Buddy's light aircraft plunged into an Iowa cornfield. Time had run out on the uniquely creative collaborative of Holly, Petty and Allison.

These days, the memory of these burning hot years is kept alive. The studio, unique in musical history, still stands in Clovis, New Mexico. It is a vividly evocative time capsule, fully restored to the way it was in 1957, welcoming fans from locations even further afield than Northampton in the East Midlands of England. These visitors, like all of us, have been touched by the romance and magic of the incredible music recorded there.

They walk in the footsteps of giants.

friendsofnormanpetty.com

Above: A Norman Petty signed page from an autograph book which belonged to Jean Hartford

Left: A publicity photo of the Norman Petty trio, the reverse is signed by all three members

Below: A Buddy Holly custom built replica guitar, presented to Kenneth Broad and Norman Petty Studios by The Buddy Holly Educational Foundation

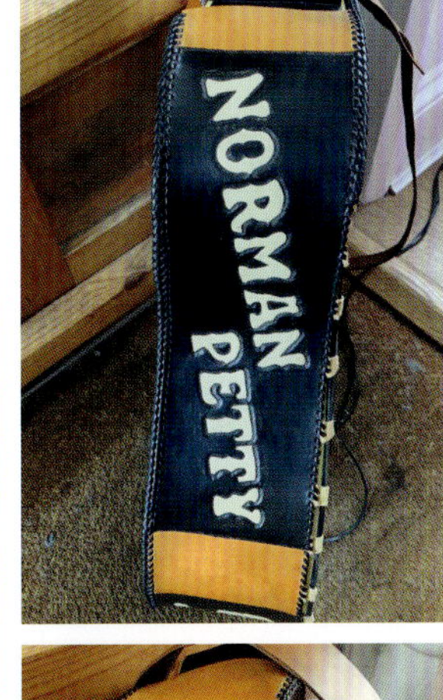

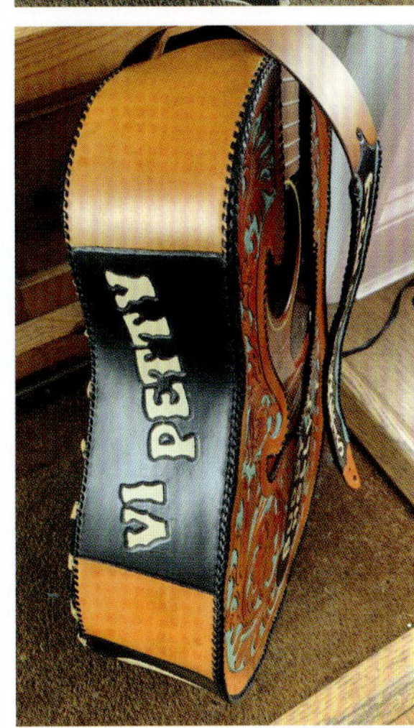

Contributors

PAUL JONES has various claims to fame. He was lead singer and harmonica player with Manfred Mann on hits like 'Do Wah Diddy Diddy' and 'If You Gotta Go, Go Now'. Going solo there were more hits, and tours with bands like the Who and the Small Faces. Then came acting: films like *Privilege*, theatre in London's West End and on Broadway, at the National Theatre and the Royal Shakespeare Company, and much television.

Founder and frontman of Britain's the Blues Band since 1979, Paul presented BBC Radio 2's *Blues Show* for 32 years. He's played on records by Van Morrison, Eric Clapton, Tina Turner … and his own songs have been recorded by artists such as Ten Years After, Helen Shapiro and Al Kooper with Carlos Santana.

Paul was 15, with a serious crush on a girl called Sue, when Buddy Holly's 'Peggy Sue' came out; but it was a line from the other side of that record, 'Everyday', ('Everyone says "Go up and ask her"'), which meant more to him. 'So I did ask her, but it didn't get me anywhere. But the way that Buddy made something out of the "turnaround" on that song impressed me permanently: "a-hey, a-hey-hey". He influenced countless singers with that.'

EDNA GUNDERSEN I grew up in the remote, dusty desert border town of El Paso, Texas, five hours southwest via Highway 62 from the equally isolated, flat, windswept outpost of Lubbock. Both produced rock sensations who died tragically young – El Paso's Bobby Fuller at 23 and Lubbock's Buddy Holly at 22. They lit the fuse of my career in music journalism. As the senior critic at *USA Today* for 28 years, I profiled most major figures in rock and pop music, from pioneers like Chuck Berry and John Lee Hooker to techno sensation Deadmau5 and pop star Ariana Grande. I interviewed three Beatles, Bob Dylan, the Rolling Stones, David Bowie, Bruce Springsteen, Prince, Madonna, U2, the Who, Eric Clapton, the Beach Boys, Tina Turner, Stevie Wonder, Aretha Franklin, Neil Young, Elton John and scores more. So many artists credited Holly as a wellspring. His imprint was obvious on artists as varied as the Bee Gees, the Ramones and Elvis Costello. Holly arguably eclipsed Elvis Presley and Chuck Berry as an influencer and revolutionary by writing his own songs, experimenting with studio techniques, fusing genres, establishing creative autonomy. In the lonely nowhere of the Texas panhandle, a myopic visionary rose to become the world's first cool nerdy teen idol. A rock star, unlike so many since, who will not fade away.

JOHNNIE WALKER started broadcasting in 1966 on the pirate radio station Swinging Radio England and, later, Radio Caroline, where he loved playing Buddy Holly songs, especially 'That'll Be the Day', 'True Love Ways' and 'Everyday'.

He was one of only two pirate DJs who decided to carry on broadcasting after the Marine Offences Act in August 1967, thus making him a radio legend and a potential criminal in one move.

He joined BBC Radio 1 in 1968 where he championed many artists. He left Radio 1 after seven years to work in the USA, which included time at KSAN in San Francisco. He joined BBC Radio 2 in 1999 taking over the *Drivetime* show. Still on Radio 2, today he presents *Sounds of the 70s* and *The Rock Show*.

'There was never anyone like Buddy Holly, before or after. It's incredible that in such a short time he recorded so many wonderful tracks that not only stand the test of time but get even better with time. His ability to go from a great rock and roll song to the most tender and emotional love song was another thing that made him so special.'

TONY BLACKBURN One of the greatest singer-songwriters of all time has got to be Buddy Holly. I became aware of him by listening to Radio Luxembourg in the mid-1950s when I was at Bournemouth College. I remember hearing 'That'll Be the Day' by the Crickets and was totally hooked on their unique sound. Buddy was one of the original pioneers of rock and roll music, and for someone in their teens, this was something very exciting, as we had been brought up on crooners until the likes of Elvis and Bill Haley came along. For me, Buddy Holly was my favourite at that time. His voice and sound were so different to anything I had heard before, the songs were so catchy, and the lyrics said what we teenagers related to; and, unlike a lot of the overproduced music we get today, you could hear all the lyrics.

I loved 'Peggy Sue', but for me 'True Love Ways', 'Raining in My Heart', and the song written for him by Paul Anka, 'It Doesn't Matter Anymore', were masterpieces. He also had a unique look about him with his large glasses; he didn't look like your average singer of those days. His early death was such a tragedy as I'm sure he would have continued to give us many more great recordings, but I thank him for providing the soundtrack to my early life as a teenager who was totally in love with the new sound people like Buddy Holly gave us.

Like so many of his generation, music journalist, broadcaster and author ***PAUL SEXTON*** learned about the indelible legacy of a young man from Lubbock, Texas from the lyrics of Don McLean's 'American Pie'. True to the song, something touched him deep inside, and it opened the door to Buddy Holly's musical shrine, in which an all-too-compact collection of perfectly crafted rock and roll classics is preserved for the ages. Sexton, a London-based contributor to all of the UK's national press as well as to BBC Radio 2, *Billboard* and countless other outlets, had his official biography of the Rolling Stones' Charlie Watts, *Charlie's Good Tonight*, published by HarperCollins in 2022. Paul's appreciation of Buddy's peerless songs grew not just via their glorious originals but in the hands of celebrated disciples from The Beatles to Blondie and Mark Knopfler to the Mavericks. If pressed, he names 'Learning the Game' and 'Well … All Right' as particular favourites from a magical catalogue.

GEORGE SCOTT In 2017, I was approached about making a film about Buddy Holly by my long-time collaborator Nick de Grunwald. I jumped at it. The idea of making a film about an artist who made such an impact on the world in such a short period of time was irresistible.

Aesthetically, Buddy Holly may have been the most unlikely-looking rock and roll star ever. But he was, after Elvis Presley, unquestionably the most influential. His short career lasted barely 18 months from 'That'll Be the Day' topping the *Billboard* charts to the plane crash that killed him in February 1959 in Iowa. Something that emphasises his impact is how the day of his death was immortalised in Don McLean's 1971 song 'American Pie', and has become known as 'the day the music died'.

The film I made with my producer, Celia Moore, tells the story of Buddy Holly's life and career through interviews with those who knew him and worked with him. Combined with contributions from music fans we paint a picture of an artist who changed music. If rock and roll started with Elvis, then pop music started with Buddy Holly and the Crickets.

As a songwriter, he revolutionised music by introducing dynamic new rhythms and unpredictable melodies beyond traditional blues roots. In the songs of Buddy Holly, written and recorded in the late 1950s, we can already hear the beat group sound of the 1960s, and beyond.

Buddy Holly's story remains one of the most dramatic tales in music, one which nearly 60 years after his breakthrough hit, 'That'll Be the Day', deserved to be told again for a new generation. His life was tragically short. His legacy is triumphantly infinite.

I am honoured to have told the story of his life and work, and preserved it in film for a whole new generation.

CHRIS REES is an engineer by trade and a proud father and grandfather who lives in the UK. He discovered the music of Buddy Holly and the Crickets during the heady glam rock period of the 1970s and became a fast fan of the singer with a voice and talent that seemed totally at odds with what was considered to be the norm in the 1950s rock and roll era. Chris sought out Buddy's music wherever he could and swallowed up every book and magazine article he could find about his hero.

Finally Chris was able to visit Buddy's home town of Lubbock and have a few days getting to know his family. Chris has pursued his love of photography and Buddy for many years and worked with the late Bill Griggs on a photo catalogue listing all of the known pictures of Buddy throughout his life.

'Was Buddy really that good? Yes, he was. That good and more.'

KEVIN TERRY is a fan from Oklahoma who discovered Buddy Holly while listening to WKY radio in Oklahoma City. They were advertising the Biggest Show of Stars in 1957 and were playing 'Peggy Sue' by Buddy Holly. Kevin became an avid fan of Buddy's and upon hearing of his death in 1959, he wanted to know more about his life. Then in 1978 while talking to Larry Holley, who invited him down to Lubbock to the premiere of *The Buddy Holly Story*, Kevin met the rest of the Holley family. They became great friends and Kevin made many trips to Lubbock to visit the family.

Eventually his interest centred on the plane crash and Buddy's death. Through the years Kevin and his wife Alice would make many trips to Clear Lake, Iowa and meet many of the remaining people related to the crash. He began researching and co-writing books on the last tour and the plane crash with fellow researcher Ryan Vandergriff. Kevin still lives in Oklahoma and enjoys listening to and researching Buddy Holly.

RANDY STEELE is a sales and marketing executive from Texas with 40 years of experience. With a passion for storytelling, Randy excels in creating content and experiences that engage and inspire companies and customers alike.

A graduate of Texas Tech University in Buddy Holly's home town of Lubbock, Randy is an enthusiastic fan, collector and historian of Buddy Holly and the Crickets. He has spent decades tirelessly researching the 1959 Winter Dance Party tour, along with the careers and personal lives of Buddy Holly and the Crickets, Ritchie Valens and J.P. 'The Big Bopper' Richardson. He has authored articles published in America and in England.

On the journey to celebrate the contributions of these wonderful artists, Randy has earned friendships around the world, a consideration as a leading expert in the field, and the respect and trust of the Holley, Valens and Richardson families. For Randy the goal has always been the same: to share their stories in an authentic manner so that their music and their lives will never fade away.

DICK COLE is a renowned photographer from Waterloo, Iowa, who for over 70 years has captured musicians, comedians and other celebrities on film. His passion for photography ignited at age 11 when he first saw a friend's darkroom print. By 12, he was selling his own black-and-white photographs door-to-door to businesses in Waterloo.

At just 17, Dick became a staff photographer for the *Waterloo Daily Courier*, where he documented notable acts, including Buddy Holly. He first photographed Holly on 28 April 1958, during the Alan Freed Big Beat tour, then months later had the opportunity to meet Holly at the Electric Park Ballroom where he took the photo that Maria Elena Holly calls her favourite.

Dick and his wife Pat had five children, four grandchildren and one great grandson. They ran Cole Photography, a portrait studio in Cedar Falls and Waterloo, Iowa, for over 40 years.

Dick was honoured at Holly's Hollywood Walk of Fame ceremony in 2011, ensuring that the legacy of Buddy Holly endures. Dick was inducted into the Iowa Rock and Roll Hall of Fame in 2012.

KENNETH BROAD was pastor of Central Christian Church in Portales, New Mexico, 20 miles from Clovis. When his growing church needed a better sound system, he heard that Norman Petty designed and installed them. He called Petty and that's where their friendship began.

Years later Norman was diagnosed with leukaemia. With Ken right by his side, Norman didn't hesitate to lean on his capable friend. Realising he was terminal, he asked Kenneth to look after Vi. Ken promised he would – probably not fully anticipating what he was getting into. Norman passed away in 1984. In 1985, Ken retired as a pastor and became enveloped in caring for Vi and the business that supported her. In 1986, Vi went into hospital for surgery and shockingly fell into a coma, never waking up. Ken, faced with unfinished Petty work, stayed the course.

Besides dealing with music publishing, Ken oversaw re-releases of Petty recordings by London's ACE Records. He began educating people about Norman, becoming the official tour guide of Petty's original recording studio. Year after year, Kenneth made himself available to give tours. In 2009, as curator of Norman Petty Studios, he was named Clovis Citizen of the Year. In 2014, the Tourism Association of New Mexico inducted Ken and Norman Petty Studios into its Hall of Fame. Word of these great studio-museum tours has continued to spread across the globe. Ken has given thousands of them – always free, always unique and personal, and always filled with passion. And 40 years after Norman's passing, he is still at it!

Ken loves telling visitors stories of how his friend pioneered recording techniques right where they are standing. He loves to sit them down in Norman's chair, behind the original control board, and play them a crisp, clear Buddy Holly track. Though everyone has heard the songs many times, when Ken plays you one in that control room, it is a magical experience. It's like a real time machine – transporting you straight to 1957. And like Norman used to do, Ken turns the volume up, letting you become part of the legend!

JUDE VIDAL is a photojournalist based in Harrogate in the UK. Together with Peter Bradley Jnr, they conceived the idea of producing a coffee table book celebrating Buddy Holly's legacy, by photographing some of the biggest iconic musicians who have been inspired by his legacy. The idea originally started by shooting the songwriting retreats run by The Buddy Holly Educational Foundation, in a journalistic style that Jude felt would resonate with an audience well. This then expanded into a wider project with photoshoots across the world photographing artists on location. The visual storytelling was paramount to Jude as this reflects her own style of photography.

The project grew in scope and it was decided that the book would be produced to support the Teenage Cancer Trust and Teen Cancer America charities.

'Some of these shoots will live with me forever, and it is a privilege to be able to use my art to extend the legacy of Buddy Holly and raise much needed funds for the charities.'

The Buddy Holly Educational Foundation Songwriter Retreats

BETH NIELSEN CHAPMAN Long before I strummed my first guitar at the age of 11, the strains of Buddy Holly hit songs had built the foundation of my musical life, instilling in me an unquenchable appreciation of what makes a song great.

So, it was a huge thrill for me to be invited to come to a gorgeous estate called Pennard House nestled in Somerset, England in 2015 to attend the Chris Difford Songwriting Retreat, sponsored by The Buddy Holly Educational Foundation. I told my songwriting friends back in Nashville that I had been to songwriting heaven. Kind of like going to Downton Abbey, having a full English breakfast, and then getting to write a song with legends like Graham Gouldman every day for a week!

Little did I know that I would come back every year and that each magical week would be so life changing and deeply nourishing for me as a songwriter. I have now attended eight Buddy Holly retreats at the CDSR in Somerset, as well as several others in Lubbock, Texas, Whitby, Yorkshire, and Lafayette, Louisiana.

The bringing together of legendary world-class songwriters with up-and-coming talented songwriters has been a recipe for brilliance, mentorship and connections between creators that extend far past the time of each retreat. It is the highest honouring of the art and craft of songwriting that I could imagine, and a tribute to the memory of Buddy Holly.

At the beginning of the week of each retreat, songwriters pour in, wide-eyed with wonder, from many corners of the earth, bringing diverse musical styles. Every day the vortex of creative flow gets more and more amped up as we are put into groups of three and sent off to the many spots tucked away in the vast house and gardens to write a new song (or two) in a few hours.

At lunch we are all under the same songwriting spell, humming our snippets and comparing notes with the other groups, pinching ourselves to be in this dream. Then we are launched back into the remainder of the afternoon to wrap up our tunes for the day.

After dinner there is a song swap and the sheer energy and power of what just got created since breakfast is jaw dropping and further infuses and inspires us all, so that by day three, songs are literally popping through us non-stop.

Some years the after-party around the campfire stretched into the early morning and sometimes the raucous singalong in the sitting room required an intervention so those on the upper floors could get to sleep.

But the songs kept coming and on the last night we would walk down the luxurious lawns to the bottom of the garden and pile into a beautiful, ancient church. We'd perform a concert of the songs we wrote all week for the locals, having spent the day scrambling back into our groups trying to relearn and prepare to play the songs live, raising the roof while raising money to fix the roof of the church.

I have left every retreat with new songs insanely overlapping in my head and my full heart bouncing with enormous waves of gratitude to The Buddy Holly Educational Foundation for creating this opportunity for songwriters. What a divine geyser of pure song genius was Buddy Holly and how amazing it is to give this gift in the honouring of his legacy.

With thanks

The late, great Jeff Beck's words encompass the sentiments of every wonderful contributor to this amazing book. I thank everyone for endorsing our project.

Without the love and support of Maria Elena, my vision of creating such an historic account of what Buddy and the Crickets' music meant to so many could never have been achieved. Thank you, my dear friend. x

Grateful thanks, also, to my beloved wife Janet and our son Peter Jnr. Your encouragement, patience and belief in my mission never wavered. xx

The Buddy Holly Educational Foundation is proud to sponsor and partner the two Teen Cancer charities in the USA and UK, inspired by the passionate dedication and commitment from Roger and Pete in their incredible fundraising efforts.

The Buddy Holly Educational Foundation is also proud to sponsor and partner with Teenage Cancer Trust and Teen Cancer America, working with our Ambassador network of music icons inspired by Buddy and the Crickets to raise life-changing sums for two incredible charities. Buddy would be honoured at the many millions of dollars raised for these causes in his name.

'Time goes by, I'll still remember you'
('That Makes It Tough', Apartment Tapes, December 1958 – January 1959)

PETER BRADLEY SNR
Co-founder TBHEF

The Buddy Holly Educational Foundation

Thank you to the legions of fans worldwide for taking the time to peruse this extraordinary compilation of Buddy Holly's life and musical legacy.

In the years following that fateful day of 3 February 1959, The Buddy Holly Educational Foundation was created by Maria Elena Holly and Peter Bradley Snr to honour Buddy's legacy and his dream of extending musical education to new generations of aspiring songwriters, composers, orchestrators, producers and arrangers.

The Buddy Holly Educational Foundation moves to a beat we call L.E.A.R.N.

LEGACY
Buddy Holly's remarkable music and prolific songwriting is as fresh and influential today as it was when he was alive.

EDUCATION
Buddy and Maria Elena Holly shared a dream of providing musical education to young people, regardless of means or ethnicity. The Foundation raises funds and provides educational materials to schools to encourage young people to learn how music can change their lives.

AMBASSADORS
Our Foundation counts more than 80 internationally renowned artists as ambassadors, many of whom have contributed to *Words of Love* and have received, or are in line to receive, exact replicas of one of Buddy Holly's original Gibson J-45 guitars. Those in possession of one of these rare guitars receive them on loan, and they are later passed along to another ambassador as inspiration for their future songwriting.

RECORDING
To build on Buddy's Texas roots, our foundation has partnered with the Texas Heritage Songwriters Association, SXSW, the Lubbock Entertainment & Performing Arts Association and the Buddy Holly Center to provide aspiring artists scholarships to attend one of our songwriting retreats, where they work side by side with our ambassadors to write, record and perform new music together.

NEXT GENERATION
Today's music is built on the backs of yesterday's giants.

'Rock and roll as we know it wouldn't exist without Buddy Holly. The bespectacled '50s teen idol roughed up familiar musical influences – rhythm & blues, rockabilly, country and western – with upbeat tempos, a jittery vocal approach, and youthful lyrics filled with edgy declarations of love, lust and heartbreak.' – Rock and Roll Hall of Fame

To learn more about the work of The Buddy Holly Educational Foundation, please visit us at www.tbhef.org.

RICK FRENCH
Chairman TBHEF

Photography Credits & Acknowledgements

All reasonable effort has been made to identify and contact the copyright holders of the images and artwork in this publication. Any omissions are inadvertent.

Unless otherwise stated, all photographs and ephemera © Simon Godsave and The Bradley Family

Copyright © Arsene/J.I. Allison | Courtesy of Rollercoaster Records
Pages 121, 130 (bottom), 131

Copyright © Art Greenhaw/Light Crust Doughboys Collection, Hill College Library, Hillsboro, Texas
Page 393

Copyright © ATV Television
Page 207

Copyright © Barbara FG
Pages 40-41

Copyright © Barry Ollman
Page 113 (top right)

Copyright © Beth Nielsen Chapman
Page 47

Copyright © Bill Francis | Courtesy of Flair Photography
Pages 200 (x9), 201 (top right x1 and bottom x2), 204

Copyright © Bob Lee | Courtesy of the Bradley Family
Pages 126 (top x4), 127, 174 (top left and centre left), 179 (top left and bottom left), 180, 181 (x2), 220 (bottom x3), 226 (x3), 227 (top), 228, 250 (top left and bottom left), 343 (bottom right), 391 (bottom right)

Copyright © Brian Beaver
Pages 286-287

Copyright © Bruno of Hollywood | Courtesy of BMG
Pages 248 (top right and bottom left), 250 (top right)

Copyright © Buddy Holly Center
Pages 17 (top), 22 (top), 51 (top left)

Copyright © Caroline Pietrowski | Courtesy of Chris Rees Collection
Page 321

Copyright © Catherine Sebastian
Page 46 (top)

Copyright © CBS Photo Archives | Getty Images
Page 188

Courtesy of Chris Rees Collection
Pages 174 (bottom left), 194, 222 (bottom left), 327, 343 (top left and bottom left)

Copyright © Columbia Pictures
Page 395

Copyright © Dave J. Hogan | Getty Images
Page 153

Copyright © Dave Stone | Courtesy of Rollercoaster Records
Page 21 (left)

Copyright © Debbie Harry
Page 282 (top)

Copyright © Dick Cole and BMG
Pages 223 (top and bottom right), 232, 233 (bottom left) 234-235, 236

Copyright © Dolly Parton
Pages 170-171

Copyright © Eagle Rock Films
Pages 69 (bottom left), 342 (bottom)

Copyright © Ed Rode
Page 175

Copyright © Eddie Randall
Page 233 (bottom left)

Copyright © Emmylou Harris
Page 259

Copyright © Eric Clapton
Pages 136-137

Copyright © Expired Film Club
Pages 27, 233 (x6), 249 (x4), 312-313

Copyright © Freeman Hover
Page 128 (top)

Copyright © Gary Gershoff
Page 396 (bottom)

Copyright © Gary Tollett | Courtesy of Rollercoaster Records
Page 108 (top)

Copyright © Georgiana Hagen | Courtesy of Rollercoaster Records
Page 113 (bottom and centre left)

Copyright © Getty Images
Pages 122 (centre right), 189 (top right and bottom)

Copyright © Gordon Payne
Page 267

Copyright © Hank Marvin
Pages 308-309

Copyright © Harry Hammond | Courtesy of the V&A Collection
Page 206 (x2)

Copyright © Henry Diltz
Pages 166-167

Copyright © Heritage Auctions
Pages 109 (bottom), 311

Copyright © Holley Family | Courtesy of the Bradley Family
Pages 22 (bottom left), 51 (bottom left), 58 (top right), 59, 100, 101 (top right and centre right), 318, 390

Copyright © Holley Family | Courtesy Chris Rees
Pages 32 (top), 33 (x2)

Copyright © Holley Family | Courtesy of Rollercoaster Records
Pages 11 (bottom x3), 12, 13, 16 (bottom right), 31 (bottom), 50, 52 (bottom), 57 (top)

Copyright © IG Holmes/Steve Bonner | Courtesy of Rollercoaster Records
Page 28

Copyright © James Allison | Courtesy of Rollercoaster Records
Pages 57 (top), 112 (bottom), 241 (x2), 242 (x3)

Copyright © Jane Ellefson | Courtesy of the Bradley Family
Pages 322-323

Copyright © Jane Rose
Pages 150-151

Copyright © Jerry Ivan Allison | Courtesy of Rollercoaster Records
Pages 32 (bottom) 122 (bottom left), 186 (top right)

Copyright © Jimmy Velvet
Page 197 (bottom right)

Copyright © JME Lacombe
Pages 288-289

Copyright © John Chown | Courtesy of Rollercoaster Records
Page 219 (bottom left)

Copyright © John Fogerty
Page 158

Copyright © John Goldrosen
Page 15

Copyright © John Goldrosen | Courtesy of Rollercoaster Records
Pages 11 (top), 22 (bottom left), 21 (right), 102 (top right)

Copyright © Jude Vidal and The Buddy Holly Educational Foundation
Pages 38, 39 (bottom), 44, 46 (bottom), 61, 67, 68, 69 (top and bottom right), 70-71, 75, 77 (top), 78-79, 86-87, 90, 133, 134-135, 138-139, 147, 155, 159, 168, 172, 260-261, 264, 266, 269, 270-271 (bottom), 273, 274 (right), 277 (top and bottom left), 297, 298-299, 302-303, 304, 305, 306, 310, 335 (bottom), 344-345, 353, 360-361, 364 (bottom x2), 378 (left x3, bottom right x2), 388 (bottom), 389 (top), Endpapers (x8)

Copyright © Kevin Terry
Page 335 (top left)

Copyright © Larry Matti | courtesy of the Bradley Family
Pages 328-329 (x2), 330-331 (x3), 332-333 (x5)

Copyright © LEPAA
Page 379 (bottom left)

Copyright © Lew Allen
Pages 29 (top right), 182-183, 184-185

Copyright © Lorenzo
Pages 141, 143, 169, 279, 295, 300, 301, 348, 349, 359, 360-361

Copyright © Lubbock High School | Courtesy of Chris Rees
Page 18 (top right)

Copyright © Maria Elena Holly | Courtesy of the Bradley Family
Pages 8 (left), 230, 243 (top left and bottom right), 382 (top right)

Copyright © Matt Lee
Page 365 (top left and bottom right x2)

Courtesy of the Museum of Pop Culture, gift of Michael and Barbara Malone
Pages 29 (left), 30-31 (top)

Copyright © Niki Sullivan | Courtesy of Rollercoaster Records
Page 112 (top left)

Copyright © Estate of Nokie Edwards
Page 142

Copyright © Norman Petty Studios, LLC
Pages 105 (top left), 110, 111, 115 (top x2), 116 (centre right), 118 (bottom x2), 119, 123 (x2), 124 (bottom left), 125 (top right), 128 (bottom), 177 (bottom left), 186 (centre right), 187 (top right), 190, 191 (bottom), 192 (top x5), 193 (top), 194 (top), 195 (x4), 199 (bottom right), 201 (top left), 208 (x2), 209 (top), 212 (bottom), 213 (top), 214, 227 (bottom), 231 (x5), 245 (x3), 391 (top)

Copyright © Pat Loduha | Courtesy of the Bradley Family
Pages 237 (bottom), 238, 239 (top left)

Copyright © Peter Blake
Page 407

Copyright © Peter Bradley Jnr
Pages 88-89, 140-141, 149, 274 (left) 275, 360-361, 342 (top), 395

Copyright © Phil Fisk
Page 364 (top)

Copyright © Philip Gotlop | Courtesy of Rollercoaster Records
Pages 202 (top x3), 203 (top)

Copyright © Polly Samson
Page 341

Copyright © Randall Michelson
Page 149, 283

Copyright © Randy Steele
243 (centre left), 326

Copyright © Randy Steele | Courtesy of the Buddy Holly Center
Page 17 (bottom)

Copyright © Reeves Photography | Chris Rees Collection
Pages 14, 16 (top right)

Copyright © Robert Ellis
Page 65 (top)

Copyright © Robert Illingworth | Courtesy of Chris Rees
Page 222 (bottom right)

Copyright © Sam Rich
Pages 278, 290-291

Copyright © Sharon Kay Lassiter / Photos by Johnny Rodgers | Courtesy of the Bradley Family
Page 325 (x4)

Copyright © Shawn Nagy
Page 53 (bottom)

Copyright © Simon Godsave
Pages 36-37, 39 (top), 42, 43, 45, 46 (bottom), 62-63, 64, 65 (bottom), 72-73, 74, 76 (top), 77 (bottom), 80-81, 82, 84-85, 91, 92, 93, 144-145, 146, 156-157, 158 (bottom), 161, 163, 164-165, 173, 262-263, 265, 268, 271, (top), 272, 280-281, 282 (bottom), 285, 292-293, 294, 339, 351, 346, 347, 351, 352, 354-355, 386, 387, 388 (top), 392, 393, 401 (top right), 402, 406, 408

Copyright © Stephen Johnson
Page 307

Copyright © Steve Bonner | Courtesy of Rollercoaster Records
Pages 229 (top, centre right, bottom), 247 (top left)

Copyright © Stuart Westwood
Pages 276, 277 (bottom right)

Copyright © Supersize Art
Page 105 (bottom left)

Copyright © Thomas Kriegsman
Page 186 (top left and bottom x2)

Copyright © Timothy Kehr | Courtesy of Rollercoaster Records
Page 324

Copyright © Tom Pallant
Page 76 (bottom)

Copyright © Tony Czikil | Courtesy of the Bradley Family
Pages 314 (top), 315 (x2), 316-317 (x13)

Copyright © Val Warren
Page 248 (centre right)

Copyright © William Claxton
Back endpaper, opp. page 408

Publisher's Note

Genesis would like to give a huge thank you to Maria Elena Holly, Peter Bradley Snr, Peter Bradley Jnr and The Buddy Holly Educational Foundation for allowing Genesis the opportunity to publish this unique document of Buddy Holly's life and work. We are honoured to be a part of making this book a reality after the idea was first brought to Brian Roylance at Genesis by Maria Elena Holly in 1990.

This would not have been possible without the incredible passion and dedication of Peter Bradley Jnr and Trudie Myerscough-Harris.

We are very grateful to everyone at the Teenage Cancer Trust Music and Entertainment team, particularly for the time and support given by Pete Townshend, Roger Daltrey and Micky England, and our thanks go to Nicola Joss, Jools Broom and Robert Rosenberg at Trinifold Management.

Many thanks to Simon Godsave for helping us to navigate the Bradley Family's extraordinary archive of Buddy Holly artifacts and for his wonderful photography.

A special thanks to Chris Rees for taking the time to guide us with his extensive knowledge of Buddy Holly and for sharing his collection with us.

To all the photographers, writers, contributors, ambassadors and honoured friends of TBHEF for their 'words of love' and for sharing your memories and insights of Buddy Holly and his music with our readers.

And to our editors Alexandra Rigby-Wild and Megan Lily Large, and to everyone at Genesis for all your hard work.

The Buddy Holly Educational Foundation

MARIA ELENA HOLLY was working in the Latin America division of Peer Music Publishing Company in 1958 when she met and married a young rocker named Buddy Holly. Already a music business veteran, Maria Elena helped Buddy manage his career when he split from Norman Petty in late 1958. After Buddy's passing, Maria Elena protected and promoted Buddy's legacy by managing his estate and business affairs, trademarking his name and other marks, and assisting with the extraordinarily successful *Buddy* stage musical and Oscar-winning *Buddy Holly Story*.

In the early 2000s she met ***PETER BRADLEY SNR***, a successful entrepreneur and lifelong Buddy Holly and the Crickets fan from humble origins in the North of England. They discussed their love for Buddy, and when he asked how he might help, Maria Elena asked him to fulfil a dream they had shared. Buddy, she said, wanted to educate young musicians so they would avoid the mistakes he had made in his career. With the help of Maria Elena's attorney, Stephen Easley, they founded The Buddy Holly Educational Foundation, to honour Buddy's legacy as well as to realise Buddy and Maria Elena Holly's dream of extending musical education, including songwriting, production, arranging, orchestration and performance, to new generations regardless of income or ethnicity or learning levels. Both Maria Elena and Mr Bradley Snr have served on the Foundation Board since its founding in 2010, with Mr Bradley serving as its first Chairman, and now as Chairman Emeritus.

RICK FRENCH was elected chairman of The Buddy Holly Educational Foundation in 2022. He is a national trustee of the Rock and Roll Hall of Fame; a board director of Teen Cancer America, founded by Roger Daltrey and Pete Townshend; and a board advisor to the Texas Heritage Songwriters Association, of which Buddy Holly is an inductee. Rick is Chairman & CEO of French/West/Vaughan, one of North America's largest public relations agencies, and managing partner of film and television production company Prix Productions, which is producing the upcoming Buddy Holly biopic *That'll Be the Day*. Rick is also executive producer of music documentaries *Satisfied*, which tells the behind-the-scenes story of the making of the hit Broadway musical *Hamilton*, and *Don't Forget Me*, which chronicles the life and untimely death of Eddie Cochran. Rick is the proud recipient of the 2023 Ambassador of Rock Award from Broadway's The Path Fund.

Originally a professional musician signed by Lucien Grange to Polydor at just 16, ***PETER BRADLEY JNR*** has led the Foundation's most significant projects since 2012, when he joined the Board of TBHEF. In 2014 he began our Songwriting Retreats, which forged our reputation in the music industry and realised one of Buddy's greatest ambitions, first with Chris Difford at Glastonbury, and then from 2019 in Lubbock, and then founded the LIPA Buddy Holly Songwriting Award. He was Executive Producer on two BBC television documentaries, *Rave On* and *Classic Albums: The 'Chirping' Crickets*, and the Royal Philharmonic Orchestra album *True Love Ways*. Under Peter's leadership, TBHEF has grown to include over 100 of music's biggest stars as ambassadors, many appearing on Mark Knopfler's Guitar Heroes, raising over $2 million for TCT and TCA, and all now included in this book, definitively detailing Buddy Holly's influence on the generations of successful musicians who followed him. Peter is also the only international trustee of the Rock and Roll Hall of Fame, a Director of Teen Cancer America, Executive Producer of the forthcoming biopic, the 2024 recipient of The Path Fund's Ambassador of Rock Award, and balances all of this with managing his family's successful fine jewellery business.

DAVID HIRSHLAND is an entertainment attorney and music business executive who has worked with legendary artists like Iggy Pop, the Guess Who and Los Lobos and contemporary alt rock stars such as Ryan Adams, Kings of Leon and Wilco, and the estates of Johnny Cash, Willie Dixon, Muddy Waters, Woody Guthrie and Stevie Ray Vaughan. David moved from law practice to Bug Music Publishing, rising to President, before Bug merged with BMG Music Rights, where he was Executive Vice President. Prior to his legal career, David was an agent at the Rosebud Agency and later formed his own management company. In 2015, Mr Hirshland spearheaded the purchase of Buddy Holly's copyrights, master rights, film and NIL rights to protect and promote Buddy's legacy, joining the Board of The Buddy Holly Educational Foundation, where he has served since. David is an Executive Producer for the new Buddy biopic *That'll Be the Day*.

As CEO of Kobalt, one of the world's largest music publishers, ***LAURENT HUBERT*** oversees all facets of the business and along with the senior management drives the strategic direction of the business. Laurent has over 20 years of experience in a top executive capacity and was instrumental in the development of BMG's business growth and sale to UMPG. Laurent led the US division of the reincarnated BMG-KKR venture, coming in as the first employee, and subsequently built a $250 million yearly top line revenue business with $60 million in EBITDA and staff of 150. In 2015, as CEO of BMG Mr Hubert worked with David Hirshland to arrange for the purchase of Buddy Holly's copyrights, master rights, film and NIL rights along with David Hirshland to protect and promote Buddy's legacy, thereafter joining the Board of The Buddy Holly Educational Foundation where he has served since.

PHIL SANDHAUS has served for over 35 years as a music artist and estate manager, and record label executive, working with artists such as Buddy Holly, The Beatles, the Beach Boys, David Bowie, Frank Sinatra, Miles Davis, the Rolling Stones, and the B.B. King and Whitney Houston estates. Sandhaus Entertainment is currently working with the Andy Kaufman, Eartha Kitt, Peter Tosh, Waylon Jennings and Ram Dass estates and the CBGB brand. Phil ran WME Legends, an artist estates management group at William Morris Endeavor, and is currently producing *The Misty Copeland Story* for New Line/Warner Bros. He was a manager for both David Bowie and the Rolling Stones, and served as Executive Producer of *M. Butterfly*, the movie version of the Tony Award-winning Broadway play. Phil was a Business Development Consultant for Frank Sinatra Enterprises, and his prior record label management positions include Columbia, Capitol Records and BMG.

Before enjoying a career in music, ***CHRIS STEWART*** was CEO of Gelber Group, a financial futures and trading firm at the Chicago Board of Trade (CBOT). He now serves on the Rock and Roll Hall of Fame Board (2006–present), where he works on the Development and Induction committees. He serves as a board member for the Country Music Hall of Fame (2016–present), where he works on the Development committee. Through all his musical associations and friendships with other artists, Chris has found that one of the most impactful and influential artists for most is Buddy Holly. Chris believes strongly in music preservation and education. He splits his time between his Nashville and Chicago homes, enjoying free time with his wife and three sons.

SIMON GODSAVE is a commercial photographer from England who grew up surrounded by the music of Buddy Holly and his peers, always played by his dad at home. Acquiring Peter Bradley Jnr as a commercial client initially, he and Peter soon identified their mutual love of the pioneers of rock and roll, and Buddy Holly and the Crickets in particular, and it became a natural evolution to begin photographing songwriting retreats and Buddy Holly memorabilia for TBHEF, and then to photograph Foundation ambassadors. Simon now manages Foundation projects with Peter and *Words of Love* has been a labour of love for him since 2019, with over half of the pages carrying his photography and much of the book influenced by him editorially. It perfectly completes the circle started when he grew to love Buddy's music at home. Still listening to Buddy, Simon's dad Alan diligently restored many of the photographs in this book.

TRUDIE MYERSCOUGH-HARRIS has been at the heart of the music industry for more than 30 years. She is an artist manager, looking after a roster of world-class talent on both sides of the Atlantic, including the glorious work of Duane Eddy, Beth Nielsen Chapman and Donna Taggart. She and Bob Harris run the beautiful, boutique Under the Apple Tree publishing company in partnership with peermusic, the biggest independent music publishing company in the world. Trudie has produced award-winning television and radio documentaries for BBC TV, BBC Radio 2 and Sky Arts, all of which were ratings triumphs. She was the organisational force behind the staging of the annual UK Americana Music Awards, establishing the evening as one of the most important events in the British music calendar. On behalf of The Buddy Holly Educational Foundation, she has staged stunningly successful songwriting retreats in Britain and America and pulled together all the threads of this beautiful project, *Words of Love*. She works from her office set deep in the Oxfordshire countryside where, on her desk, is a notice given to her with the deepest affection by her children Miles, Dylan and Flo. It reads simply 'The Queen of Everything'. And she really is.

It takes a huge number of people to selflessly give their time to work with us on the many projects we run to honour Buddy's legacy. The Buddy Holly Educational Foundation would like to take this historic opportunity to thank the following …

Our founders, Maria Elena Holly and Peter Bradley Snr
The Holley Family, Randy and Sherry, and the late Ella, L.O., Larry, Travis and Patricia – may they rest in peace
The Crickets, the late J.I. Allison, Joe B. Mauldin and Niki Sullivan, and other wonderful artists associated with the band over the years: Sonny Curtis, Albert Lee, Gordon Payne,
Glen D. Hardin and the late Keith Allison, Larry Welborn and Buzz Cason
Our esteemed ambassadors and honoured friends featured within this book, who celebrate Buddy's legacy and help us achieve our goals
The late Lyle Walker and David Bigham, and Kenneth Broad and Greg Walker of Norman Petty Studios in Clovis, NM, Ron Skinner and Randy Petty from the 'Friends of Norman Petty'
The late Bill Griggs
John Beecher, Chris Rees, Randy Steele, John Firminger, George Scott, Kevin Terry and Ian Higham
Stephen and Becky Easley
Our advisers Mike Read and Steve Lewis
John Wayland at Tuggle, Burton & Co
Rebecca Rothstein, Jordan Kaplan, Simon Davies, Michelle Aland, Becky Mancuso-Winding, Jennifer Van Kleeck and all at Teen Cancer America
Kate Collins, Jane Ashton, Des Murphy, Angie Jenkison, Micky England, Jamie Johnson, Katie Yates, Katie Crossey and all at Teenage Cancer Trust
The team at the University Hospital of San Antonio who run the Buddy and Maria Elena Holly Adolescent and Young Adult Cancer Programme
Scott Bomar and the team at BMG US
Alistair Norbury, Joanna Horton and the team at BMG UK
Mark Knopfler, Guy Fletcher, Paul Crockford, Sherry Elbe and the team at British Grove Studios
Sir Peter Blake and Chrissie Blake
Flora Turnbull and Eugenio Donadoni at Christie's
T Bone Burnett, Larry Jenkins and Jay Hass at Neofidelity

Roger Daltrey and Pete Townshend, Robert Rosenberg, Bill Curbishley, Jools Broom and all at Trinifold, and Nicola Joss

Jeff Rosen, Irving Azoff, Jon Landau, Alison Oscar, Merck Mercuriadis, John Silva, Martin Kierszenbaum, Ralph Baker, Michael Eaton, Cecil Offley, Colin Newman, Paul Loasby, Jane Rose, Joyce Smyth, Dave Trafford, Jenny Taylor, Pia Squillino, Jono Hart, Sheryl Louis, Kenny Laguna, Carianne Brinkman, Karla Moheno, Sara Bricusse, Sally Avery-Frost, Jeff Varner, Rachael Paley, Sharon Corbitt, Adam Fells, Owain Davies, Sarah Mitchell, Tania Hogan, Ken Leventhal, Rachael Iverson, Amber Owens, Bruce Sugar, Bruce Grakal, Scott Ritchie, Sharon Ely, Larry Jenkins, Tommas Arnby, Adam Wood, Jeff Pollack, Elizabeth Devlin, Kelly McNamara, Nicola Powell, Tom Hambridge, Max Maxson, Dave Mann, David Salidor, Bill Francis, Eddy Gore, Tania Hogan, Stuart Camp, Kendal Marcy, Tommy Manzi, Gary Borman, Elisabeth Ashley, Brian Goode, Kat Killingley and Michael Winder, Mark Spector, Tracy Bufferd, Laurie Mansfield, Donna Jean Kisshauer, Adam Woods, Rona Elliot, Nathan Clarke, Kerry Adamson, Rachel Iverson, Kelly Ridgway, Michelle Fisher, Darrell Gilmour, Jean Shivers, Steve Ithell, Louise Morris and Bill Kenwright CBE

Greg Harris, and the team at the Rock and Roll Hall of Fame,
Bob Santelli at the Springsteen Foundation and all the team at the Grammy Foundation
George Scott, Phil McDonald, Celia Moore and the late Nick de Grunwald at 1515 Productions
Sheena Barnett at Graceland and the Elvis Presley Estate
Jeremy Huffleman and the team at Abbey Road
Ronnie Wood and Sally Humphreys Wood
The Gibson Foundation and Juliette Avery at Gibson UK
Ben Blanc-Dumont, Stephen Taylor, Mike Taft and David Mulqueen at Fender
Garry Shrum, Pete Howard and all at Heritage Auctions
Kevin McManus, Olly Taylor and Harvey Goldsmith at the British Music Experience in Liverpool, UK
Laurie Lietz, Jeff Nicholas and the team at the Surf Ballroom
Chris and Louise Difford, and the Dearden Family at Pennard House
Brooke Witcher at the City of Lubbock, and Jacqueline Bober and her team at the Buddy Holly Center
Jeff Humsinger, Melissa Key, Charlton Northington, Holly Fields, Cliff McElhaney, Tim Collins and the late Kathy Gilbreath at LEPAA
Mark Falgout and family in Lafayette
Our dear late friends Sonny West and Bob Peeples and their families
The late Des O'Connor and his widow Jodie Brooke-Wilson and their son Adam
David and Jo Frizzell
Allan and Jeni Clarke
Beth Nielsen Chapman
Kimmie Rhodes
Don McLean
John Thomas
Kevin Magowan
Victor Valdez and Nereida Melendez
Gaby Gear, Maria Elena's granddaughter
Sherry and Sheryl Davis
Dan Roberts at Stringworks, Alister Atkin and Mick Johnson, our craftsman luthiers
Judy Edwards and Pete Allen the Leatherman
Barbara Lee and the late John Lee, who have produced our ambassador and honoured friend certificates
Phil Critchley and Mick Spencer, who worked tirelessly on the early drafts of this book
Morgan Howell at Supersize Art and Dominic Mohan
Kirsty Bell, Ben Charles Edwards and the team at Goldfinch Productions
Craig Leach and the team at Raymond Weil
Tom Fuller and his team at Image Design Custom
Dan Biggane and the team at Vintage Rock

And lastly, a huge thank you to our editorial team who worked so tirelessly to make this book possible. From Genesis Publications we're eternally grateful to Catherine Roylance, Nick Roylance, Alexandra Rigby-Wild and Megan Lily Large. From TBHEF, Trudie Myerscough-Harris, Simon Godsave, Alan Godsave, Ben Harvey, Peter Bradley Snr, Peter Bradley Jnr and Stephen Easley. Mike Read, Bob Harris, Paul Sexton, Andrew Trendell, Paul Jones, Johnnie Walker, Neil McCormick and Iain Lee.

Words of Love took over six years to create, and in that time we lost some dear friends. Our condolences to the families of the late Larry Holley, Jerry 'J.I.' Allison, Keith Allison, Duane Eddy, Don Everly, Jeff Beck, Nokie Edwards, Charlie Gracie, Buzz Cason, Larry Welborn, Des O'Connor, Sonny West, Bob Peeples, John Marascalco, Kathy Gilbreath, Nick de Grunwald and John Lee. We mourn the loss of them all and are grateful for their part in Buddy's legacy.

Mark Knopfler's Guitar Heroes

GUY FLETCHER has appeared on stage or in the studio with many world-renowned artists as a keyboard player, arranger and musical director (Cockney Rebel, Roxy Music, Dire Straits) but he is best known for his long-term collaboration as a musician, producer and engineer with Mark Knopfler. His deep connection with Knopfler made him the ideal choice to helm a significant music project supporting the Teenage Cancer Trust and Teen Cancer America.

The Guitar Heroes project aimed to gather influential guitarists and musicians to create an iconic version of the instrumental track 'Going Home', originally composed by Mark Knopfler as the theme for the 1983 film *Local Hero*. It was a monumental task, taking over two years to complete and Fletcher not only produced the track but also crafted, edited and mixed it, coordinating the participation of over 60 guitarists and musicians who have been significantly influenced by Buddy Holly.

Guitar Heroes features an impressive line-up, including many TBHEF ambassadors, who have come together to honour Knopfler's musical legacy while supporting the Teenage Cancer Trust and Teen Cancer America. The project stands as one of TBHEF's greatest achievements and highlights Guy Fletcher as a pivotal figure in the music industry. The project's success is a testament to the enduring influence of Mark Knopfler and the collective spirit of the musical community in supporting important causes.

Top: Mark Knopfler and Peter Blake with Peter's artworks for the Guitar Heroes project. The UK version is on the left and the US version is on the right.

Above right: Mark Knopfler and Sting pictured at Mark's British Grove Studios with eight guitars donated by Fender, Gibson, Gretsch and Atkin. They were signed by the performers and sold for the project. A Les Paul Gold Top (pictured right) raised £403,200 at Christie's, London in January 2024 as part of Mark Knopfler's own guitar auction.

THIS IS THE RECORD THAT PLAYS LIKE A VISITING BOOK signed in music by dozens of the most distinguished artists in the world. Each entry in the register carries a unique and distinctive signature that documents their stellar contributions to a remarkable sonic adventure.

The epic new version of 'Going Home (Theme from Local Hero)' by Mark Knopfler's Guitar Heroes is so chock-full of hallowed participants, each one a true master of their trade, that the phrase 'all-star' somehow doesn't cut it. It's a project realised in pure selflessness for the greater good, originally from an idea by broadcaster and writer Mike Read, to raise essential funds for the exemplary work of Teenage Cancer Trust and Teen Cancer America. At the same time, it's a joyful recreation of Mark's much-loved movie theme, with a cast and on a scale never attempted before.

From the dazzling recreation of his *Sgt. Pepper* artwork by the sanctified Peter Blake, to the sequence of incredible performances by the finest guitarists on the planet – never mind A-list keyboard players, drummers et al. – you have a piece of history in your hands.

For Teenage Cancer Trust and Teen Cancer America to be the beneficiaries of the release is beautifully apposite, especially with the participation of the two charities' tireless figureheads, Roger Daltrey and Pete Townshend. – *Paul Sexton*

Mark Knopfler's Guitar Heroes – Going Home (Theme from Local Hero)

The biggest project The Buddy Holly Educational Foundation has ever undertaken, 'Going Home (Theme from Local Hero)' by Mark Knopfler's Guitar Heroes raised over $2 million. It featured 34 ambassadors and honoured friends all performing together on one song in aid of Teenage Cancer Trust and Teen Cancer America. In the artwork by Sir Peter Blake, inspired by his seminal Sgt. Pepper *album cover, can be seen: Albert Lee, Pete Townshend, Hank Marvin, Roger Daltrey, Waddy Wachtel, James Burton, Vince Gill, Joe Bonamassa, Steve Cropper, Guy Fletcher, Paul Carrack, Tony Iommi, Peter Frampton, Sting, Joe Louis Walker, John Sebastian, Brian May, Ringo Starr, Nile Rodgers, Keith Urban, Sam Fender, John Jorgenson, Joe Brown, Joe Walsh, Buddy Guy, David Gilmour, Ronnie Wood, Joan Jett, Mark Knopfler, Jeff Beck, Duane Eddy, Bruce Springsteen and Eric Clapton.*

Additionally, on the record and artwork were Orianthi, Jonathan Cain, Ry Cooder, Joe Satriani, Zak Starkey, Tom Morello, Connor Selby, Sonny Landreth, Zucchero, John McLaughlin, Andy Taylor, Joan Armatrading, Mike Rutherford, Steve Vai, Sheryl Crow, Derek Trucks and Susan Tedeschi. Sadly, the artwork was completed by Sir Peter before the guitarists Brad Paisley, Alex Lifeson, Phil Manzanera, Keiji Haino, Rick Nielsen and Steve Lukather had recorded their contributions.

The artwork also features references to the film Local Hero*, the two charities and Mark Knopfler's home town of Newcastle. To mark TBHEF's involvement, the UK version of the artwork features Buddy's Höfner President, purchased on the 1958 UK tour, and the US version shows Buddy's Gibson Les Paul and matching amplifier.*

The Buddy Holly Educational Foundation, Teenage Cancer Trust and Teen Cancer America

MANY BUDDY HOLLY EDUCATIONAL FOUNDATION AMBASSADORS are also ambassadors and supporters for Teenage Cancer Trust (TCT) and Teen Cancer America (TCA). Roger Daltrey and Pete Townshend are Patrons of TCT and Founders of TCA. So it was very natural for the Foundation to begin raising funds for these two wonderful causes.

Young people are often caught between two worlds when they find themselves battling these terrible diseases, too old to be among small children on paediatric wards and too young to be surrounded by more senior adults. TCT and TCA provide facilities and programmes for their treatment. This allows them to face their struggle with the support of their peers, maintaining their dignity and positivity, while receiving age-appropriate, focused care.

In 2019, with the support of The Buddy Holly Educational Foundation, TCA opened the first Buddy and Maria Elena Holly Cancer Treatment Area for teens and young adults at the University Hospital of San Antonio, in Buddy's home state of Texas. More are planned as TBHEF and its Buddy-influenced ambassadors raise substantial sums of money through charitable music projects.

NILE RODGERS ***I'm a two-time cancer survivor, and fortunately I was an adult and I didn't necessarily need comfort from others around me, but I could understand how teenagers could be very perplexed. Believe me, the first time I got involved with TCT, I was brought to tears, and a little choir came and sang with us, which was completely amazing. I've been involved with TCT ever since I was turned on to it, and I'm always there for it.***

ROGER DALTREY ***It's not my charity, it's one I've been a patron of and been determined to get the music business to really support. That age group we serve, adolescents and young adults, is the age group that is the life blood of the music industry. And I've got to say the music business, and indeed the comedy industry, have been incredibly supportive of this charity, it's really amazing.***

Afterword BY ROGER DALTREY AND PETE TOWNSHEND

Words of Love is a perfect title for this stunning definitive history of Buddy Holly. As well as being one of the great rock and roll pioneers, Buddy wrote and sang some of the most beautiful and enduring ballads about love. Songs such as 'True Love Ways', 'Everyday', 'Wishing', 'Learning the Game' and 'It's So Easy', as well as 'Words of Love' itself, are full of Buddy's warmth, tenderness and understanding. When his lyrics are combined with his wonderful voice, the sincerity shines through and the songs still speak to listeners today because they seem to embody love itself.

How appropriate, then, that The Buddy Holly Educational Foundation should do more than simply whisper words of love, but truly perform real acts of love, by raising millions of dollars for charities. Pete and I are proud supporters of the Foundation's work and we were particularly thrilled and grateful that all the Foundation's profits from the limited edition of this book went to two charities that are very dear to our hearts: Teen Cancer America and the Teenage Cancer Trust in the UK.

Buddy's words 'Crying, Waiting, Hoping' describe the plight of many people in this world. The compassion and love that shines through this project is the answer to those needs.

So, to Maria Elena Holly, Peter Bradley Snr and his son Peter Bradley Jnr, who orchestrated the whole of this particular mission, to all the people who have contributed their time and talent to bring it to fruition, and to all the generous supporters in the Foundation's network of ambassadors, we would like to offer our sincere and heartfelt gratitude.

Thanks and love, **ROGER DALTREY AND PETE TOWNSHEND**

When I first received this Nobel Prize for Literature, I got to wondering exactly how my songs related to literature. I wanted to reflect on it and see where the connection was. I'm going to try to articulate that to you. And most likely it will go in a roundabout way, but I hope what I say will be worthwhile and purposeful.

If I was to go back to the dawning of it all, I guess I'd have to start with Buddy Holly. Buddy died when I was about 18 and he was 22. From the moment I first heard him, I felt akin. I felt related, like he was an older brother. I even thought I resembled him. Buddy played the music that I loved – the music I grew up on: country and western, rock and roll, and rhythm and blues. Three separate strands of music that he intertwined and infused into one genre.

One brand. And Buddy wrote songs – songs that had beautiful melodies and imaginative verses. And he sang great – sang in more than a few voices. He was the archetype. Everything I wasn't and wanted to be. I saw him only but once, and that was a few days before he was gone. I had to travel a hundred miles to get to see him play, and I wasn't disappointed.

He was powerful and electrifying and had a commanding presence. I was only six feet away. He was mesmerising. I watched his face, his hands, the way he tapped his foot, his big black glasses, the eyes behind the glasses, the way he held his guitar, the way he stood, his neat suit. Everything about him. He looked older than 22. Something about him seemed permanent, and he filled me with conviction. Then, out of the blue, the most uncanny thing happened. He looked me right straight dead in the eye, and he transmitted something. Something I didn't know what. And it gave me the chills.

(Extract from Bob Dylan's Nobel Prize for Literature acceptance speech, 5 June 2017. Official use of this quote and photograph approved by Bob Dylan. Bob is an ambassador of TBHEF and has the 'Think It Over' guitar.)

The
Midnight
Shift

BUDDY HOLLY
CENTER

Ave L
Texas Ave
Buddy Holly Ave
EXIT ONLY
14'-3"
RAMP

LUBBOCK I.S.D.
SCHOOL BUS

J.T. HUTCHINSON

Crickets Ave

Depot
District

Buddy Holly